Reforming Severance Pay

AN INTERNATIONAL PERSPECTIVE

Reforming Severance Pay

AN INTERNATIONAL PERSPECTIVE

Robert Holzmann and Milan Vodopivec
Editors

THE WORLD BANK
Washington, D.C.

ISBN: 978-0-8213-8849-5
eISBN: 978-0-8213-8851-8
DOI: 10.1596/978-0-8213-8849-5

Library of Congress Cataloging-in-Publication data have been requested.

Cover photos: Eric Miller (left), Jim Pickerell (upper), Thomas Sennett (right)/World Bank Photo Library. DuxX/istockphoto.com (lower).
Cover design: Naylor Design, Inc.

Contents

Tables

Preface

Throughout the developed and developing world there is growing demand for policies that would facilitate access to jobs by the most vulnerable, improve their earnings, and reduce their dependency on public support. As a result, governments are increasingly focused on removing obstacles faced by employers to create jobs and on instilling incentives for individuals to (re-)enter the labor market or to move toward more productive employment possibilities.

Severance pay—a program compensating formal workers for dismissal by employers or with an end-of-service benefit—is often blamed for distorting employer hiring and firing decisions. Together with restrictive labor market regulations and other formal labor market features, this program is held responsible for excessive job protection with a negative impact on labor market outcomes, in particular affecting the most vulnerable.

Despite this strong negative assessment among many labor market economists, surprisingly little is known about this program that exists in most countries around the world as a legally mandated benefit. This lack of knowledge may derive from the special "positioning" of the program between labor code and social insurance; its origins were in the first policy domain, but its objectives for key programs were replicated in the second domain—in particular unemployment and retirement benefits.

To our knowledge, this is the first-ever book to shed light on this program in a comprehensive manner—its historical origins, its rationale, and its characteristics across the world. It reviews the soundness of the empirical accusation, assesses recent country reforms, and offers policy reform alternatives and policy guidance.

The proposed policy directions include folding severance pay into existing social insurance programs, where they exist, and to make severance pay contractual between market partners as a way to enhance efficiency in a knowledge-based economy. Folding severance pay into employment benefits may also be an opportunity to move away from unemployment insurance, which is fraught by moral hazard, toward a promising "hybrid" system of unemployment insurance savings accounts supplemented by social pooling. And for countries that do not yet have unemployment and retirement benefit systems, this may be an opportunity to establish one in exchange for lifting the mandate of severance pay altogether. There is no better time than now for reforming severance pay to realistic benefit levels, strengthening compliance of benefit payments by employers, and safeguarding minimum benefits by governments.

Please read and enjoy!

Tamar Atinc   Arup Banerji
Vice President   Sector Director
Human Development Network   Social Protection and Labor

Acknowledgments

This book has had a long history and gestation, and as a result, we owe many thanks to many people. Most of the papers were initially produced for a conference on severance payments held at the International Institute for Applied System Analysis (IIASA) in Laxenburg near Vienna, Austria, November 7–8, 2003. The event was jointly organized by the World Bank, IIASA, and the Ludwig Boltzmann Institute for Economic Policy Analysis, Vienna. Special thanks for managerial help and intellectual support for this successful event go to Landis MacKellar (IIASA) and the late Rainer Ernst Schuetz (Ludwig Boltzmann Institute); the cofinancing of the event by the Austrian Federal Ministry of Finance is gratefully acknowledged.

Professional diversions and the assessment that the time was not yet ripe to put the papers into a published volume led to long delays in next steps. In the meantime, a number of conference paper authors were invited to submit their contributions to the Austrian economic journal *Empirica*. Four of the papers in this book were previously published in *Empirica*'s volume 32 in 2005. The intensifying international discussion about the effects of severance pay, the emerging alternatives such as unemployment saving accounts, and the many queries to the World Bank publishing unit by interested external clients regarding the publication of the long-announced book motivated us to rekindle and finalize our collective efforts. Special thanks for the encouragement on this long road go to Paola Scalabrin from the World Bank Office of the Publisher and to former colleagues at the World Bank's Social Protection and Labor Department; in particular Gordon Betcherman (University of Ottawa), Carmen Pages (Inter-American Development Bank), and Stefano Scarpetta (Organisation for Economic Co-operation and Development).

The management of the Human Development Network (HDN) encouraged and supported our efforts. Despite the financial belt tightening at the World Bank, the new HDN Vice President, Tamar Manuelyan Atinc, the new Sector Director for Social Protection and Labor, Arup Banerji, and his Sector Manager, Bassam Ramadan, made the publication financially possible.

Last, but not least, we would like to extend to the contributors of the volume our thanks for their patience and great collaboration. They have shared our belief in the importance of the topic from the beginning, engaged with us substantively throughout the different versions, and kept the faith that the volume would finally be published. Special gratitude goes to Donald Parsons, who not only contributed two important chapters but also provided steady, unwavering moral support to the project. We would also like to thank peer reviewers for their constructive comments, which significantly improved the volume.

Abbreviations

AFC	Administradora de Fondos de Cesantia de Chile
CARA	constant absolute risk aversion
CTS	Compensación por Tiempo de Servicio
EBS	Employee Benefit Survey
EDAPs	Entidades Depositarias del Ahorro Previsional
EFW	Economic Freedom of the World
EPL	employment protection legislation
EPZ	export processing zone
ERISA	Employee Retirement Income Security Act of 1974
EU	European Union
FC	firing cost
FGTS	Fundo de Garantia de Tempo do Servicio (severance indemnity fund for employees)
GDP	gross domestic product
IA	individual account
IESS	Instituto Ecuatoriano de Seguridad Social
IIASA	International Institute for Applied System Analysis
ILO	International Labour Organization
INE	Instituto Nacional de Estadística (National Statistical Institute)
IRA	individual retirement account
LAC	Latin America and the Caribbean
MENA	Middle East and North Africa
MPO	Ministerio do Planejamiento e Orcamento (Ministry of Planning and Budget)
MVK	*Mitarbeiter vorsorgekassen* (employee benefit funds)
NICB	National Industrial Conference Board
OECD	Organisation for Economic Co-operation and Development
OMIL	Oficinas Municipales de Inserción Laboral (municipal employment agency)
OUI	optimal unemployment insurance
PAYG	pay as you go
PROTRAC	Protección al Trabajador Cesante
R&D	research and development

SAFC	Sociedaded Administradoras de los Fondos de Cesantia (Society of Fund Administrators)
SENCE	Servicio Nacional de Capacitación y Empleo (national training and employment service)
SF	solidarity fund
SGO	Seguro General Obligatorio (social insurance program)
SP	severance pay
TEWA	Termination of Employment of Workmen Act
TFR	*trattamento di fine rapporto* (termination pay)
UF	Unidades de Fomento
UI	unemployment insurance
UISA	unemployment insurance savings account
VRS	voluntary retirement scheme
WWI	World War I
WWII	World War II

CHAPTER 1

Severance Pay under Review: Key Issues, Policy Conclusions, and Research Agenda

Robert Holzmann and Milan Vodopivec

Introduction

Severance pay is quite likely the most widely applied compensation or income support program in the world—it exists in almost all countries across income levels in either mandated or voluntary form. At the same time, it is perhaps the least understood program with regard to its origins, rationale, and economic effects. The many investigations of its labor market impacts have been largely inconclusive. A few high-income countries initiated structural reforms with results well below expectations. Severance pay is a frequent component in reform considerations around the world, as it is considered to be responsible for undesirable labor market outcomes and a high level of informality. Yet, little guidance exists regarding how severance pay could best be reformed. Some researchers and policy makers are enthusiastic about unemployment savings accounts into which existing severance pay could be folded, but evidence of their performance is thin.

Against this background, a stock-taking conference was organized in Laxenburg near Vienna in 2003—a joint event by the World Bank; IIASA (International Institute for Applied System Analysis) in Laxenburg, Austria; and the Ludwig Boltzmann Institute for Economic Policy Analysis in Vienna. The purpose of the conference was to learn from regional overviews and country reform proposals and experiences and to present and discuss empirical evidence as well as conceptualizations of the topic, with the ultimate goal of offering better policy guidance for countries around the world. However, the topic proved to be much more complex than envisaged, the empirical work much more time-consuming than expected, and the participants' other commitments much more overwhelming than hoped. This put the revision of the papers and publication of this volume in the slow lane. Some papers were published in 2005 in *Empirica*: Addison and Teixeira; Cardinale and Orszag; Holzmann; Jaramillo and Saavedra; and Koman, Schuh, and Weber. Other papers were dropped, a few were added, and all papers in this volume were completely revised. This distance from the topic, fresh insights, and more comprehensive country lessons have helped improve the papers and the policy conclusions.

The purpose of this opening chapter is to introduce the topic, summarize the chapters, and present policy conclusions and suggested next steps. First, the chapter briefly reviews the key issues regarding severance pay that give rise to reform considerations, analysis, and proposals. The next section summarizes the content of the following chapters, providing an overview and brief chapter conclusions. Next, the overall content of the chapters is transformed into broad policy conclusions based on a conceptualization that moves from issues, objectives, and evidence to reform options and proposals. The last section suggests a number of priority research areas to address key knowledge gaps at the analytical, empirical, and policy levels.

Issues with Severance Pay

Severance pay is one of the most common but also most controversial social programs. Introduced by legislation or collective agreement, it requires that employers pay lump-sum compensation to qualifying laid-off workers, with the amount usually depending on years of service and the person's recent earnings. These programs can have several, sometimes quite sophisticated, objectives, ranging from providing compensation for job loss to stabilizing employment and preventing unemployment by discouraging layoffs to encouraging long-term relationships that retain valuable workers and reduce transaction costs resulting from labor turnover. But while mandated severance pay is the most prevalent income support system in developing (but not developed) countries (Vodopivec 2004, 2009), these programs are often considered to be one of the least appropriate options for income protection: They not only provide deficient and incomplete protection but are often responsible for distorting the behavior of firms and workers, and thus imposing other efficiency costs.

INCOME PROTECTION EFFECTS

On the income protection front, severance pay is believed to suffer from three main weaknesses. One is the crudeness of the mechanism—that is, the absence of a link between the benefit and contingency needs—as the same amount is paid regardless of the duration of unemployment. This is in contrast to other income support mechanisms, such as unemployment insurance. Furthermore, in contrast to severance pay, other programs typically link the receipt of benefits to employment services and other active labor market programs. Corroborating the crudeness, MacIsaac and Rama (2000) find that severance pay was overly generous in Peru, where per capita consumption of unemployed workers who received severance pay was higher than the consumption of otherwise similar employed workers.

The second weakness of severance pay, viewed from the income protection perspective, is "nonperformance"—the fact that, despite legal entitlement, many workers fail to obtain benefits. Nonperformance is related to the limited risk-pooling ability of the program, coupled with its mostly unfunded nature and the fact that the liabilities often arise when a firm is least capable of paying them. For example, in 1998, Malaysia's employers disbursed only 83 percent of the severance pay claims of laid-off workers (Mansor et al. 2001). MacIsaac and Rama (2000) estimate that in Peru only about half of all workers legally entitled to severance pay are likely to receive the benefit if they are dismissed. (The payment is more likely if workers have a written contract and if they work in a large, unionized firm that pays social security contributions.) And recent surveys for Indonesia in 2007 and 2008 suggest that workers receive only 10–14 percent of the severance payment due (Alatas et al. 2011; World Bank 2010). Such nonperformance due to lack of compliance by the employer is reportedly widespread among formal migrant workers

(Holzmann and Pouget 2010). To avoid the reputational fallout and promote funded savings, some countries of the Gulf Cooperation Council are thinking of moving toward prefunded provisions.

One of the best documented cases is the nonperformance of Slovenia's severance pay program. Combining information from the Firm Survey of Labor Costs with information about claims filed with the Guarantee Fund by workers whose employers defaulted on their severance pay obligations, Vodopivec, Madzar, and Dolenc (2009) show that in 2000, one-third of total severance pay obligations incurred by Slovenian firms were not honored, and only a small portion of defaulted severance pay claims were reimbursed by the Guarantee Fund. They also found that nonperformance affected both sexes equally but that workers older than 40 were disproportionally represented. Among firms that incurred severance pay liabilities, larger and more productive firms were more likely to meet their fiduciary obligations by making the payments.

The third weakness is that severance pay contributes to labor market duality, often increasing noncoverage of the most vulnerable groups. Namely, the generosity of severance payments militates against the access of particular groups of workers to jobs and thus prevents them from being covered by formal income support programs. Blanchard (2000) shows that an increase in firing costs leads to higher unemployment of marginal groups of workers because of their inferior access to jobs. The productivity of these workers before hiring is not easily ascertained, so their probability of being hired in the presence of increased firing costs is lower. Indeed, the Organisation for Economic Co-operation and Development (OECD) (1999) finds that stricter employment protection legislation reduces employment among youths and prime-age women, thus rendering them more susceptible to unemployment risk. Similarly, Kugler and Saint-Paul (2000) show that higher firing costs increase discrimination against unemployed workers, because they increase the costs associated with hiring a bad worker. Moreover, in the presence of higher severance costs for older workers, separation decisions may be biased against young workers. In other words, it seems that large firing costs contribute to the emergence of dual labor markets, with well-protected formal sector workers (predominantly prime-age males) and much less protected informal sector workers and the unemployed. In line with these findings, Besley and Burgess (2004) and Ahsan and Pagés (2009) show that pro-worker legislation may work against the poor in developing countries.

EFFICIENCY EFFECTS

In theory, severance pay is associated with both potential efficiency gains and potential efficiency losses. Among the gains, severance pay may promote longer-lasting employment relationships and thus improve employers' incentives to provide training, thereby increasing the productivity of workers as well as their future employability. Moreover, longer-lasting employment instills trust, cooperation, and loyalty between the employer and workers, and encourages team spirit among workers, which may increase productivity and reduce the resistance of workers to the introduction of new technologies (OECD 1999). Such effects may be particularly strong under severance pay programs that are introduced voluntarily.

Among the costs, severance pay is recognized as a source of labor market "sclerosis," reducing the intensity of labor market flows, particularly to and from unemployment.

As Blanchard (2000) shows, severance pay increases firing costs and thus reduces the probability of exit from employment to unemployment, but at the same time it imposes additional costs on employers and thus hinders job creation. (The predicted effects of severance pay on unemployment are therefore ambiguous.) As noted above, Blanchard's model also shows that severance pay contributes to labor market dualism. Calmfors and Holmlund (2000) show that high firing costs slow the pace of structural change by reducing employers' incentives to introduce new technologies and thus likely reduce productivity growth and overall economic growth.

There does not appear to be direct empirical evidence regarding the positive effects of severance pay on firm productivity (based on firm-level data). Nickell and Layard (1999) find a positive effect of employment protection on aggregate growth, but the effect disappears once differences in the level of productivity among countries are controlled for. Moreover, it is not clear which circumstances and interactions may be instrumental for such effects.[1] Likewise, Soskice (1997) and Belot, Boone, and van Ours (2007) show that strict dismissal regulations could increase productivity because of additional job security for workers, increasing job tenure and work effort and making workers more likely to invest in firm- or job-specific human capital and to cooperate in the implementation of productivity-enhancing work practices or new technologies. Koeniger (2005) reports a weak positive relationship between employment protection legislation (EPL) strictness and research and development (R&D) intensity in OECD countries.

In contrast, considerable evidence suggests negative efficiency effects of mandatory severance pay, as summarized in chapter 2 and discussed in chapter 3. A number of studies show that strict employment protection, including hiring and firing rules as well as severance pay, reduces employment. In his seminal and highly controversial study, Lazear (1990) used cross-country analysis to find that severance pay increases unemployment and reduces both employment and labor force participation. Several similar studies followed, many of them contradicting Lazear's findings (see chapters 2 and 3).

Evidence that employment protection, including severance pay, reduces inflows to and outflows from unemployment has proved more consistent and thus more compelling. Employment protection contributes to longer unemployment spells (stagnant unemployment pool), thus compounding the difficulty of leaving unemployment. For example, several recent, credible studies—among them Micco and Pagés (2006); Haltiwanger, Scarpetta, and Schweiger (2010); Bassanini et al. (2010); and Cingano et al. (2010) that use the difference-in-differences approach at the industry level—find that strict dismissal regulations reduce job turnover (see detailed review in chapter 2). There is also mounting evidence that broader labor regulations, particularly those involving collective bargaining and dispute resolution, can be the most damaging (see, among others, Autor, Kerr, and Kugler 2007); chapter 3 discusses this issue further.

A word of caution: Labor market effects of the employment protection legislation described above need to be separated from the effects of severance pay, at least for the richer countries where most of these studies have been carried out. In a critical review of the empirical literature, Parsons (chapter 3) concludes that "severance pay, unaccompanied by other labor regulations, has little impact on worker separation (and accession) or average employment level." He adds that the impact of EPL reforms may depend on the regulatory environment in the economy as a whole, and there may be important interactions between severance pay mandates and collective bargaining rules.

Evidence also exists that job protection reduces productivity, possibly by hindering technological change because of reduced mobility of workers. Among recent studies that use a difference-in-differences approach are Autor, Kerr and Kugler (2007), which shows that the adoption of stricter job security provisions in the United States had a positive effect on capital investment and a negative effect on total factor productivity. Bassanini and others (2010) showed that mandatory dismissal regulations in OECD countries have a negative effect on productivity growth in industries where dismissal restrictions are more likely to be binding. The effects of severance pay per se, as opposed to the effects of EPL in general, need further study.

It is worth mentioning that severance pay does not create a moral hazard problem by lowering job search effort, but it does affect incentives to enter unemployment and hence creates a different moral hazard problem. De Ferranti and others (2000) report that large litigation costs arise from disputes over the cause of separation in Latin America. Similar results on the importance and distortions of dispute settlements are reported for India (Ahsan and Pagés 2009).

Chapter Overview

The chapters in the book are organized as follows: chapters 2–4 review and evaluate severance pay programs around the world to better understand their rationale, their performance, and reform trends, while chapters 5–10 investigate specific severance pay reform avenues that have been implemented in some countries and are increasingly being proposed as a way forward for severance pay, unemployment insurance benefit, and individual retirement schemes: individual savings accounts in their diverse incarnations.

Chapter 2—"Severance Pay Programs around the World: History, Rationale, Status, and Reforms" by Robert Holzmann, Yann Pouget, Milan Vodopivec, and Michael Weber—offers an overview of existing programs, examines their historic development, assesses their economic rationale, and describes some recent major reform attempts. While a significant part of the chapter is devoted to a comprehensive cross-country review of existing severance arrangements and their characteristics, the authors go beyond mere description. They develop and empirically test three hypotheses about the economic rationale of the program: (1) that severance pay is a primitive income protection program; (2) that it is an efficiency-enhancing human resource instrument; and (3) that it is a job protection instrument. They also review recent reforms in Austria, Chile, Italy, and the Republic of Korea.

Their inventory of mandated severance pay programs and related social policy and country indicators in 183 countries offers a rich information base to better understand the programs, including initial hypothesis testing.

Chapter 3—"Mandated Severance Pay and Firing Cost Distortions: A Critical Review of the Evidence" by Donald Parsons—provides a critical review of the empirical evidence of mandated severance pay programs on labor markets and of some broader economic outcomes. Severance pay mandates are an appealing job displacement insurance strategy in developing countries that have only modest government administrative capacities, but they carry the threat of adverse indirect effects. Parsons' critical review of the empirical literature reveals that severance benefit mandates, unaccompanied by other labor regulations, have no apparent impact on labor market behaviors. Indeed, many severance mandates in the industrialized world do not greatly exceed those provided voluntarily by larger firms in the United States. Benefit mandates in the developing world are sometimes more extravagant, and the absence of substantial effects may result from limited enforcement. More aggressive economic regulations do appear to have substantial adverse effects on the labor market, but it is important not to equate these with simple severance insurance plans.

Chapter 4—"The Firing Cost Implications of Alternative Severance Pay Designs," also by Donald Parsons—suggests an important conceptualization that has a strong bearing on analysis and benefit design. Economists have concerns about the firing cost implications of mandated severance plans. Analysis reveals that the firing cost consequences of such plans depend critically on the precise structure of the plan. Severance savings plans, after all, have no firing cost implications. Severance insurance plans, which pay benefits only for involuntary separation, and severance savings plans, which pay benefits across the full range of separation types, are opposite poles on a policy continuum. Generally the firing cost implications of separation benefit plans are sensitive to the types of job separations that qualify a worker for benefits and the underlying incidence of job separation risks. Severance insurance plans, which cover an increasing percentage of separations, approach severance savings plans in performance. Parsons illustrates the variety of plan types using U.S. and international examples.

Chapter 5—"Effects of the Austrian Severance Pay Reform" by Helmut Hofer, Ulrich Schuh, and Dominik Walch—explores two key aspects of the 2003 reform: reduction in labor market distortions and furthering of a funded pension pillar. The comprehensive reform has received substantial international attention; it extended the coverage of the system considerably, allowing every employee to collect entitlements irrespective of the duration of employment. The new scheme was expected to remove perceived obstacles to job mobility and was intended to form the nucleus of a second (mandated and funded) pillar for the Austrian pension system.

Using the quasi-experimental design of the reform situation, the authors apply a difference-in-differences strategy to test the hypothesis that the new severance payment scheme improves the efficiency of labor reallocation by removing the incentives for workers not to move to better jobs. The results, however, reveal that the quantitative medium-term impact of the former severance pay system on job mobility was rather limited. Other factors, such as economic conditions, seem to play a much bigger role in affecting job changes in Austria. The results indicate that the adverse financial incentives of the old severance pay scheme have been (at least for jobs lasting no longer than five years) too small to have sizable effects on labor mobility in Austria. Experience since the reform also suggests that frequent withdrawals of funds after job termination substantially reduce potential funds for retirement income and hence contribute little toward a funded pillar. This phenomenon has been accentuated (or perhaps motivated) by the low level of remuneration achieved by the funds, which is thought to be linked to the capital guarantees the funds need to provide.

Chapter 6—"Severance Pay Reform in the Republic of Korea" by Jungyoll Yun and Jai-Joon Hur—addresses one of the problems with the existing severance pay system in Korea: the inefficient intertemporal allocation of consumption on the part of unemployed workers. It makes a strong case for the introduction of an alternative corporate pension system. This discussion takes place in light of the 2005 reform that initiated the voluntary conversion of an end-of-service pay scheme into an occupational pension system, with the objective of replacing an unfunded scheme that pays lump-sum benefits with a funded system that provides an annuity after retirement. As of November 2010, about 2.0 million of 7.7 million eligible workers (26 percent) had joined the corporate pension scheme. Against this background, the authors demonstrate that a corporate pension system can effectively play the two critical roles of a severance pay scheme: insurance against unemployment shock and intertemporal consumption smoothing. In contrast, this chapter points out some practical problems embedded in the current severance system in Korea that keep it from being converted into a corporate pension. The authors suggest that more aggressive tax incentives or subsidies need to be provided to ensure more effective conversion of the current retirement allowance system into a corporate pension system. They also suggest the introduction of a loan provision feature to supplement the corporate pension and facilitate the conversion.

Chapter 7—"Unemployment Insurance Savings Accounts in Latin America: Overview and Assessment" by Ana Ferrer and Craig Riddell—provides an overview and assessment of accounts that have been created over recent decades in a number of Latin American countries in response to concerns about the labor market effects of traditional unemployment insurance programs. Pooling resources across time for one person compared with pooling across all insured persons at one point in time was expected to avoid the moral hazard problems of traditionally designed programs. The authors review the experience in Argentina, Brazil, Chile, Colombia, Ecuador, Panama, Peru, and República Bolivariana de Venezuela. While the design objectives of the accounts still seem to hold, this approach presents problems of its own. First, it is questionable that these systems can provide adequate protection against unemployment risk. Second, their effects on the promotion of informal labor markets and their administrative costs are yet to be determined. Third, their effectiveness as a form of unemployment insurance depends critically on the performance and credibility of the financial institutions that manage the funds. Last but not least, the way the system is implemented, existing labor regulations, the extent of the informal economy, and the scope for collusive behavior all greatly influence the success of these programs.

Chapter 8—"The Welfare Consequences of Alternative Designs of Unemployment Insurance Savings Accounts" by Hugo Hopenhayn and Juan Carlos Hatchondo—evaluates the performance of alternative design options for unemployment insurance savings accounts (UISAs). The authors develop a life-cycle model (an extension of Hopenhayn and Nicolini 1997) that captures key trade-offs faced by workers in their actual lives and explicitly allows for a moral hazard; that is, the possibility that a worker will decide to quit his or her job or not to accept a job offer. The model includes savings for both precautionary motives and life-cycle considerations, to complement retirement benefits. Applying the model to the context of Estonia in the late 1990s, the authors find that good incentives can go a long way to replace monitoring and enforcement in combating the moral hazard and that, under UISAs, a moderate amount of insurance, low replacement rates, and high tax rates are most cost-effective.

Chapter 9—"The New Chilean Unemployment Insurance System: Combining Individual Accounts and Redistribution in an Emerging Economy" by Solange Berstein, Eduardo Fajnzylber, and Pamela Gana—assesses the October 2002 reform and outlines the key elements of the 2009 reform extensions. Under this scheme, workers contribute to two funds: a fund formed by individual accounts and a solidarity fund. For temporary workers, the employer pays the full 3.0 percent; for nontemporary workers, the employee pays 0.6 percent and the employer 2.4 percent, of which 1.6 percent goes to the individual account and 0.8 percent to the solidarity fund. In case of unemployment, workers have access to their own savings and, under some circumstances, can supplement them with resources from the solidarity fund (benefits are typically paid in five monthly payments, defined as a percentage of their previous wage).

The experience during the first eight years has been positive in terms of coverage and sustainability. In May 2009, the government introduced a set of reforms designed to improve the adequacy of benefits by facilitating access to the pooled component. Welfare evaluations suggest that, in general, most workers value the program, although their valuation may depend on their level of risk aversion and personal labor history. This unique and innovative system seems to be producing the expected efficiency effects. Overall, it seems to be a success and has largely avoided the distortions that plague unemployment insurance systems while offering income support for those at the low end of the income distribution. However, in parallel with this scheme, Chile retains both mandated and quasi-mandated severance pay schemes for dismissal and redundancy, with no firm plans for integrating the former into the savings accounts.

Chapter 10—"Reemployment Incentives under the Chilean Hybrid Unemployment Benefit Program" by Gonzalo Reyes, Jan C. van Ours, and Milan Vodopivec—complements chapter 9 by providing an analysis, including econometric estimation of duration models, of job-finding rates of unemployment benefit recipients under the Chilean program. The authors are the first to provide rigorous empirical evidence about whether individual accounts internalize the cost of unemployment and thus mitigate the moral hazard present in standard unemployment insurance programs. They show that beneficiaries who use solidarity funding are less likely to exit unemployment in early months than those who rely on UISAs only. They also find job-finding rates to be positively correlated with preseparation UISA balances for beneficiaries who use solidarity funding but uncorrelated with balances for those who rely on UISAs only. While the findings are consistent with the effects expected under the internalization of unemployment costs via UISAs, they do not clearly pinpoint the causal link. Alternative mechanisms, particularly selection into the use of UISAs, might be responsible for the observed correlations.

Conclusions and Proposed Reform Directions

The following nine chapters provide information, analysis, and ideas about possible reform directions. In the concluding section, we offer a framework for how to think about severance pay reform across different development levels. The framework moves from the perceived issues with severance pay to objectives, review of evidence, reform options, and proposed directions.

ISSUES

The introduction to this chapter highlighted three main concerns with traditional, mandated, service-length-linked, and defined benefit severance pay in case of redundancy or dismissal:

- The implied financial firing costs are distorting labor market outcomes, as they affect employers' hiring and firing decisions and employees' mobility decisions. The typical assumption is that labor mobility is reduced, with a negative impact on efficiency of labor market allocation. A vesting period and a nonlinear benefit schedule linked to service length is believed to trigger time-specific firing and mobility decisions by employers and employees that are not aligned with their long-term interests.

- Given the current funding of severance pay in most countries, smaller firms are exposed to liquidity or even solvency risk as a result of concurrent multiple termination of work contracts that give rise to severance pay. And such redundancies (that is, dismissals for economic reasons) typically dovetail with demand or supply shocks that limit the credit financing of additional (wage) expenditures.

- Lack of liquidity and, worse, bankruptcy can hit intended beneficiaries just when they need cash to smooth consumption or finance job search expenditures. But workers in countries with a weak legal framework and enforcement risk losing their severance pay rights simply through lack of compliance on the part of the employer, or by agreeing to give up their rights in return for promised future hiring and vice versa.

OBJECTIVES

These concerns must be assessed against the three main objectives underlying the historic development of severance pay over the past 130 years:

- Severance pay as a primitive form of social benefit that predates the introduction of unemployment and pension benefits, and offers some income support in their absence;

- Severance pay as an efficiency-enhancing human resource instrument that, together with other remuneration components, offers a balance between the employer and employee in knowledge-intensive productions; and

- Severance pay as an employment protection device as the result of unintended and at times inherited benefit design or of intended and expanded benefit design owing to political economy decisions that cannot be reversed.

REVIEW OF EVIDENCE

The policy discussion, analysis, and empirical investigations have been largely focused on the employment protection device, less on the efficiency-enhancing objective, and virtually not at all on the social policy objective.

- Most empirical investigations on the labor market and broader economic effects of severance pay have folded the impact assessment into a broader analysis of employment protection legislation (EPL), with conflicting results that became more stable once microdata could be used. These later investigations often reflect a negative impact of EPL and procedures on labor market outcomes. However, this result does not hold in the few studies that isolate the severance pay impact. Chapter 5 on the 2003 Austrian reform shows that, in contrast to expectations, the reform triggered little change in labor market mobility. This finding is in line with chapter 4, in which the author suggests that the fewer firing costs and labor market distortions emerge, the more contingencies are covered under a severance pay program. However, most of this evidence is from high-income countries, with few rigorous evaluations in low-income countries.

- Very few studies address the human resource aspect of severance pay alone or in conjunction with other remuneration devices, and even fewer can demonstrate a convincing impact. Such an effect may, in any case, not be expected to emerge from a mandated scheme that applies severance pay rules indiscriminately across enterprises in all sectors and of all sizes. Even fewer and more dated studies investigate the efficiency effects of contractual severance pay arrangements at the sector or firm level, although the continued application of such schemes in high-income countries suggests that they deliver some net benefits, even if they cannot be assessed.

- The link between severance pay and some social benefits (unemployment, old age) has been part of policy discourse in a number of countries but has not been investigated empirically to any extent, either before or after a reform. Moving toward individual (unemployment cum retirement) accounts as in the Austrian reform has contributed little long-term saving; people prefer the cash option to finance current consumption. Similarly, voluntary transitions from severance pay toward corporate pensions have attracted only about 25 percent of eligible workers—much less than hoped. And not a single reform effort has folded the traditional severance pay and traditional unemployment insurance program into, say, a combination of unemployment insurance savings accounts and social pooling. Chile is an exception—it has successfully established a hybrid unemployment-savings-cum-social-pooling program—but the severance pay program has remained in place.

- A number of countries in Latin America have reformed their unemployment insurance schemes toward individual unemployment savings accounts. The available investigations do not permit strong statements about the success or failure of these reforms. The only exception seems to be (again) Chile, where diverse investigations provide a positive assessment, including a few rigorous econometric investigations that conform to the priors of reduced distortions and investigations that look at the redistributive effects of the social pooling device.

REFORM OPTIONS AND BROAD DIRECTIONS

Against this background, a limited number of reform options exist that address the objectives as well as the efficiency and redistributive concerns. The options are country-specific and must be seen against the enabling environment, which is broadly linked to development status and income level.

- High-income countries that have a developed (and mandated) unemployment benefit scheme and old-age pension scheme have little need for a mandated severance pay program from a social policy perspective. Severance pay can be folded into any one of the other programs as an enhancement or supplement (possibly at the same time strengthening the savings components of these programs, to enhance work incentives). If severance pay seems to be needed because the unemployment or pension scheme is inadequate or not well designed, this should be directly addressed. For example, severance pay may offer access to liquidity that traditional unemployment and retirement insurance schemes do not.

- Inasmuch as severance pay is considered to be an efficiency-enhancing human resource device, it should not be mandated but should be left to contractual agreements with social partners at the national or sector level, or to individual contracts at the firm level. Mandated schemes are unlikely to provide the needed differentiation and flexibility. Such options are probably better suited for middle- to high-income countries that have the required institutional environment.

- Two key options are possible for low- and middle-income counties that do not yet offer unemployment or pension benefits. The first is to provide such benefits for formal sector workers and reduce or even eliminate the often very high severance pay benefit mandate. For unemployment benefits, this will require a specific design to mitigate moral hazard problems while addressing redistributive concerns, and an administrative capacity to implement promising approaches, such as individual saving accounts.[2] In the absence of such an enabling environment, the other option is to streamline the existing severance pay program by making it less distorting and more realistic in benefit design and level, and more operational in implementation and delivery. Unfortunately, no successful country examples exist to substantiate this proposal.

Research Agenda: Next Steps

The ability to reallocate productive inputs (including labor) to their most efficient uses and the incentives to acquire and upgrade human capital depend vitally on the performance of labor market institutions, including employment protection legislation and severance pay. As the theoretical insights in this book suggest, the implied trade-offs among job security, efficiency, fairness, and growth are very complex. Thus, views about the effects of labor market institutions—including employment protection legislation and severance pay in particular—differ, despite a large and quickly growing volume of research in this area. With increased pressures from globalization, balancing job security and enhancing productivity has a clear appeal to policy makers in both the developed and developing world, and there is a clear interest in providing answers to key questions and dilemmas. From the policy perspective, the following aspects are of particular importance:

- *Disentangling the effects of individual components of employment protection legislation (EPL) on labor market outcomes.* As the literature reviews in this book suggest, the financial costs imposed by severance pay programs may not be the key factor contributing to deleterious effects of EPL. So, what are the culprits? Separation regulations—especially dispute settlement arrangements—are strong candidates, but more research is needed. Moreover, if other components of EPL are relaxed, would severance pay become a binding constraint; that is, a factor responsible for nondesirable labor market outcomes? Another important question relates to the possible nonlinearity of the severance pay effect, as extremely high financial obligations in place in some low-income countries may prove to be the decisive factor in shaping labor market outcomes.

• *Shedding more light on the productivity effects of severance pay (and pension benefits).* This question arises in the context of fostering "flexicurity" (see, for example, European Commission 2007). While proponents argue that flexicurity increases productivity and employment without sacrificing employment security or hurting vulnerable groups, the evidence relating to productivity effects is tenuous. After all, greater labor mobility and associated worker dislocations surely cannot be viewed as a goal per se but rather as a means to promote productivity. More research into the effects and particular channels of productivity effects is needed regarding both positive effects (increasing job tenure and work commitment, and larger investment in job-specific human capital) and negative effects (reducing the ability of firms to react quickly to changes in technology or product demand, discouraging experimentation with new technologies, and reducing effort of workers). Specific areas for research are the effects of possible interactions with other benefits, such as corporate pensions, and the role of severance pay as a human-resource-enhancing instrument in light of the emergence of other benefit options, such as share options.

• *The effects of severance pay on labor market duality and other distribution effects of severance pay.* The implications of increased flexibility for inequality, equity, and inclusion also need to be better understood; that is, more research is needed about the extent and conditions under which increased flexibility helps the least able persons. More information is needed about the nonperformance problem of severance pay—how often do workers in low- and middle-income countries actually receive severance pay? What are the key mechanisms of avoidance? The interaction between high benefit levels and enforcement of regulations also needs further investigation.

• *Liquid severance pay versus illiquid individual savings accounts, and the liquidity demand across income levels.* Liquidity-constrained or myopic individuals may prefer severance pay as a lump-sum payment over individual savings accounts that are less liquid, such as unemployment savings accounts that release resources on a restricted monthly basis or accounts that are fully illiquid until retirement (and beyond), such as national or corporate pensions. The latter may be preferred by risk-averse persons or those who are aware of their weakness in following through with a savings plan as a self-binding mechanism. And the distribution of liquidity preference may change across income levels—low-income groups are typically subject to more risks and have fewer risk instruments, including liquid assets, available. But little is known about the liquidity preferences of individuals in terms of the impact of the enabling environment, the level of individual financial literacy, or the possible explanations related to behavioral economics or finance.

Closing these and other knowledge gaps is crucial to identifying appropriate design of the reforms and building political support to implement them.

Notes

1. A stream of literature on the effects of worker-management, cooperation, and participatory approaches in management finds mildly positive effects of these features on productivity of firms but does not pinpoint the exact ingredients and interactions that contribute to the success. Tyson and Levine (1990) single out measures to enhance substantive participation as instrumental for higher productivity, but the extent to which employment protection boosts such measures is unclear.

2. See Vodopivec (2009) for adjustments needed to traditional unemployment insurance programs to transfer them successfully to developing countries, and Robalino, Vodopivec, and Bodor (2009) for possibilities to address incentive and redistributive concerns under savings accounts schemes.

References and Other Resources

Addison, J., and P. Teixeira. 2005. "What Have We Learned About the Employment Effects of Severance Pay? Further Iterations of Lazear et al." *Empirica* 32: 345–68.

Ahsan, A., and C. Pagés. 2009. "Are All Labor Regulations Equal? Evidence from Indian Manufacturing." *Journal of Comparative Economics*, 37 (1): 62–75.

Alatas, V., V. Brusentsev, D. Newhouse, A. Perdana, and W. Vroman. 2011. "Severance Pay in Indonesia: A Descriptive Assessment." Draft, World Bank, Washington, DC.

Autor, D. H., W. R. Kerr, and A. D. Kugler. 2007. "Do Employment Protections Reduce Productivity? Evidence from US States." IZA Discussion Paper 2571, Institute for the Study of Labor, Bonn.

Bartelsman, E., S. Scarpetta, and F. Schivardi. 2005. "Comparative Analysis of Firm Demographics and Survival: Evidence from Micro-level Sources in OECD Countries." *Industrial and Corporate Change* 14 (3): 365–91.

Bassanini, A. 2010. "Inside the Perpetual-motion Machine: Cross-country Comparable Evidence on Job and Worker Flows at the Industry and Firm Level." *Industrial and Corporate Change* 19 (6): 2097–134.

Bassanini, A., A. Garnero, P. Marianna, and S. Martin. 2010. "Institutional Determinants of Worker Flows. A Cross-country/Cross-industry Approach." OECD Social, Employment and Migration Working Paper 107, Organisation for Economic Co-operation and Development, Paris.

Belot, M., J. Boone, and J. van Ours. 2007. "Welfare-Improving Employment Protection." *Economica* 74 (295): 381–96.

Besley, T., and R. Burgess. 2004. "Can Labor Regulation Hinder Economic Performance? Evidence from India." *Quarterly Journal of Economics* 119 (1): 91–134.

Blanchard, O. 2000. "The Economics of Unemployment. Shocks, Institutions, and Interactions." Lionel Robbins Lectures, London School of Economics. http://econ-www.mit.edu/faculty/download_pdf.php?id=800.

Calmfors, L., and B. Holmlund. 2000. "Unemployment and Economic Growth: A Partial Survey." *Swedish Economic Policy Review* 7 (1): 109–53.

Cardinale, M., and M. Orszag. 2005. "Severance Pay and Corporate Finance: Empirical Evidence from a Panel of Austrian and Italian Firms." *Empirica* 32: 309–43.

Cingano, F., M. Leonardi, J. Messina, and G. Pica. 2010. The Effects of Employment Protection Legislation and Financial Market Imperfections on Investment: Evidence from a Firm-Level Panel of EU Countries." *Economic Policy*, 25 (01), 117–63.

De Ferranti, D., G. E. Perry, I. S. Gill, and L. Serven. 2000. *Securing Our Future in a Global Economy.* World Bank, Latin and Caribbean Studies. Washington, DC: World Bank.

European Commission. 2007. *Towards Common Principles of Flexicurity: More and Better Jobs through Flexibility and Security.* Luxembourg: Office for Official Publications of the European Communities.

Haltiwanger, J., S. Scarpetta, and H. Schweiger. 2010. "Cross Country Differences in Job Realloca-tion: The Role of Industry, Firm Size and Regulations." EBRD Working Paper 116, European Bank for Reconstruction and Development, London.

Holzmann, R. 2005. "Reforming Severance Pay: Toward an Understanding of Program Rationale, Economic Impact and Reform Options." *Empirica* 32: 251–53.

Holzmann, R., and Y. Pouget. 2010. "Social Protection for Temporary Migrant Workers: Con-ceptual Framework, Country Inventory, Assessment and Guidance." Study prepared for the Global Forum of Migration and Development, Puerto Vallarta, November 8–11. World Bank and Marseille Center for Mediterranean Integration.

Hopenhayn, H., and J. P. Nicolini. 1997. "Optimal Unemployment Insurance and Employment History." *Journal of Political Economy* 105 (2): 412–38.

Hopenhayn, H., and R. Rogerson. 1993. "Job Turnover and Policy Evaluation: A General Equilib-rium Analysis." *Journal of Political Economy* 101 (5): 915–38.

Ichino, A., and R. T. Riphahn. 2005. "The Effect of Employment Protection on Worker Effort: A Comparison of Absenteeism During and After Probation." *Journal of the European Economic Association* 3 (1): 120–43.

Jaramillo, M., and J. Saavedra. 2005. "Severance Payments in Latin America." *Empirica* 32: 275–307.

Koeniger, W. 2005. "Dismissal Costs and Innovation." *Economics Letters* 88 (1): 79–85.

Koman, R., U. Schuh, and A. Weber. 2005. "The Austrian Severance Payments Reform: Toward a Funded Pillar." *Empirica* 32: 255–74.

Kugler, A. D., and G. Pica. 2008. "Effects of Employment Protection on Worker and Job Flows: Evidence from the 1990 Italian Reform." *Labour Economics* 15 (1): 78–95.

Kugler, A., and G. Saint-Paul. 2000. "Hiring and Firing Costs, Adverse Selection and the Per-sistence of Unemployment." Discussion Paper 2410, Centre for Economic Policy Research, London.

Lazear, E. P. 1990. "Job Security Provisions and Employment." *Quarterly Journal of Economics* 105 (August): 699–726.

Levine, D. I., and L. A. Tyson. 1990. "Participation, Productivity, and the Firm's Environment." In *Paying for Productivity: A Look at the Evidence*, ed. A. S. Blinder, 183–237. Washington, DC: Brookings Institution.

MacIsaac, D., and M. Rama. 2000. "Mandatory Severance Pay in Peru: An Assessment of Its Coverage and Effects Using Panel Data." World Bank, Development Research Group, Public Service Delivery, Washington, DC.

Mansor, N., T. E. Chye, A. Boehanoeddin, F. Said, and S. M. Said. 2001. "Malaysia: Protecting Workers and Fostering Growth." In *East Asian Labor Market and the Economic Crisis: Impacts, Responses, and Lessons*, ed. G. Betcherman and R. Islam, 141–94. Washington, DC: World Bank.

Micco, A., and C. Pagés. 2006. "The Economic Effects of Employment Protection: Evidence from International Industry-Level Data." IZA Discussion Paper 2433, Institute for the Study of Labor, Bonn.

Nickell, S., and Layard. R. 1999. "Labor Market Institutions and Economic Performance." In *Handbook of Labor Economics*. Edition 1. ed. O. Ashenfelter and D. Card. Amsterdam: Elsevier.

OECD (Organisation for Economic Cooperation and Development). 1999. *OECD Employment Outlook 1999*. Paris: OECD.

———. 2010. *OECD Employment Outlook 2010*. Paris: OECD.

Poschke, M. 2009. "Employment Protection, Firm Selection, and Growth." *Journal of Monetary Economics* 56 (8): 1074–85.

Robalino A. D, M. Vodopivec and A. Bodor. 2009. Discussion Paper "Savings for Unemployment In Good or Bad Times: Options for Developing Countries." IZA Discussion Paper 4516, Institute for the Study of Labor, Bonn.

Saint-Paul, G. 1997. "Is Labour Rigidity Harming Europe's Competitiveness? The Effect of Job Protection on the Pattern of Trade and Welfare." *European Economic Review* 41 (3–5): 499–506.

Saint-Paul, G. 2002. "Employment Protection, International Specialization, and Innovation." *European Economic Review* 46 (2): 375–95.

Soskice, D. 1997. "German Technology Policy, Innovation and National Institutional Frameworks." Tyson and Levine 1990, *Industry and Innovation* 4 (1): 75–96.

Vodopivec, M. 2004. *Income Support for the Unemployed: Issues and Options*. Regional and Sectoral Studies Series. Washington, DC: The World Bank.

———. 2009. "Introducing Unemployment Insurance to Developing Countries. " IZA Policy Paper 6, Institute for the Study of Labour, Bonn.

Vodopivec, M, L. Madzar, and P. Dolenc. 2009. "Non-performance of the Severance Pay Program in Slovenia." Social Protection Discussion Paper 0901, World Bank, Washington, DC.

World Bank. 2010. *Indonesia Job Reports: Toward Better Jobs and Security for All*. Washington, DC: The World Bank.

CHAPTER 2

Severance Pay Programs around the World: History, Rationale, Status, and Reforms[1]

Robert Holzmann, Yann Pouget, Milan Vodopivec, and Michael Weber

Introduction: Objectives, Methods, and Structure

Severance pay programs exist in most countries around the world. They typically provide lump-sum cash payments to workers who involuntarily or voluntarily separate from their employers. The size of the payment is usually related to the number of years worked with the last employer, and it is linked to the last salary in the job. Such payments were provided by employers in many countries before they were required by law. Firm-based severance pay schemes often exist in parallel with legislated provisions. Moreover, firms may use voluntary severance pay programs as an important management tool for retaining skilled workers. In most cases, precedent for these programs existed before the introduction of formal social insurance schemes around the world, so severance payment systems may be considered a primitive form of unemployment compensation or pension allowance. Despite their widespread use, many aspects of severance pay programs—including their origin, coverage, and interaction with other income support programs—have not been well researched, particularly for developing countries. Even the most basic descriptive information about severance payment schemes around the world apparently has not been compiled.

One of the difficulties of examining the topic of severance pay is that different types of cash payments can be considered as forms of severance payments, and many different terms exist in English and other languages. Terms include dismissal compensation, redundancy compensation, termination benefits, seniority pay, indemnities, and leaving allowances. While one can, in principle, assign special objectives to each benefit type (for example, dismissal compensation to involuntary job separation and termination benefits to any kind of separation, including retirement), reality proves more complex, as severance payments seem to serve multiple concurrent functions.

The objective of this chapter is to review severance pay programs around the world by providing an overview of existing programs, examining their historic development, assessing their economic rationale, and describing current reform attempts. While the thrust of the chapter is devoted to a comprehensive cross-country presentation of existing severance arrangements and their characteristics, it goes beyond a mere description to develop and empirically test three hypotheses about the economic rationale for the programs: (1) severance pay is a primitive income protection instrument; (2) it is an efficiency-enhancing human resource instrument; and (3) it is a job protection instrument. The chapter also reviews the recent reforms in Austria, Chile, Italy, and the Republic of Korea.

The chapter is structured as follows. The first section examines the historic origins of severance pay and identifies competing economic justifications for its existence (with additional details in annex A). The following section explains how the severance pay programs work by summarizing their stylized features, then describes the compiled inventory of existing severance pay programs around the world, explaining key features of the programs, their broad characteristics, and commonalities and differences between countries and regions. (Annex B offers details of programs in individual countries in a comprehensive matrix.) The next section discusses the economic rationale of severance pay, develops the three hypotheses noted above, and tests them with simple but robust econometric specifications. The concluding section offers a brief summary, policy implications, and suggestions for future research.

The Origins of Severance Pay

While mandated pension, health, and unemployment benefits and their historical origins are well known and documented, the same cannot be said for severance benefits.[2] This section aims to provide a better understanding of severance pay by examining why these programs were created in the first place. It focuses on three key events that influenced the introduction of severance pay programs around the world—the introduction of national labor codes, early industrial restructuring, and the expansion of the welfare state after World War II (WWII)—and alludes to key hypotheses proposed to explain the economic rationale of severance pay. The section ends with a summary of the historic lessons.

SEVERANCE MANDATES: THREE EXPLANATIONS

The literature on this topic[3] suggests three main historical determinants of severance mandates around the world: (1) the creation of broader labor codes, (2) early industrial restructuring and spells of high-level unemployment in the interwar period, and (3) the expansion of the welfare state after WWII. These determinants are at times intermingled with two main reasons why firms choose to voluntarily provide severance pay: one-off payments during industrial restructuring to allow for quick action and avoid political fallout, and seniority-related payments (corporate pensions and severance) that balance the interest of firms and workers in knowledge-intensive firms.

In developing countries, these historic events may not have had the same significance. Legislation in these countries seems to have arisen by copying the colonial powers' labor codes and social security systems. But despite these common origins, actual system designs in developing countries are quite diverse, as discussed later in this chapter.

Labor Code

The primary origin of severance payments was the creation of and link to the labor codes in the industrializing countries of the North in the nineteenth century. The birth of modern labor standards can be traced back to 1802, when Sir Robert Peel introduced the English Factory Act. It was a symbolic act that placed restrictions on the working hours of apprentices. By 1875, both Great Britain and the United States had achieved complete legal equivalence in the relationship between employer and worker. The same is true for countries of continental Europe around the same period. Each party was free to accept or reject offers, terminate contracts, and expect to pay damages if the termination amounted to breach of contract.

Building on the limited nineteenth century civil codes, twentieth century legislatures took up the question of the regulation of employment contracts and intervened to secure protection for workers in case of dismissal. This was done by means of amendments to civil, commercial, or industrial codes; legislation on contracts of employment; the promulgation of labor codes; or even by special legislation (Herz 1954, 299–230).

It appears that severance payment at this time was granted if the notice period for dismissal was not respected by the employer. That is, dismissal payment was a compensation for breach of labor contract by the employer. As the notice period at this time was short, the codified severance payments are assumed to have been small.

Early Industrial Restructuring

The second main elements for the emergence and persistence of severance payments were the technological changes of the late 1800s and the large-scale unemployment of the Great Depression in the 1930s. Although fully developed dismissal compensation is almost entirely a post–World War I (WWI) development, laws providing short periods of dismissal notice date back to the nineteenth century in several European countries.

It appears that issues of job security first emerged in the railroad industry. For example, in the 1870s and 1880s in France, a great number of railroad dismissal cases came to court and led to judgments that can be seen as important starting points for the establishment of severance pay (see box 2.1).

BOX 2.1 Railroad Workers and Severance Pay

The case of railroad workers demanded particular attention, because they worked in a new industry. Established industries had specific dismissal procedures, which were often tied to localities, but such norms did not exist in the railroad industry. Moreover, railroad workers had highly specialized skills that tied them to working on railroads and thus had weaker bargaining power vis-à-vis their employers. By training to work in the railroad industry, they limited their future to working in this specific area.

Cases of railroad workers also came to court because of pension problems, as workers could lose their pensions upon being fired. Severance pay may have served as an instrument to compensate for these losses. By 1890, laws had evolved to confirm the previous court rulings controlling for abuses of pension funds. Subsequently, legislation began to favor the granting of special job protection to railroad workers.

Throughout France, the practice of severance pay evolved through the lower courts, which recognized increasingly longer notice periods and greater indemnities for dismissed workers. Severance pay also covered a growing number of sectors. By the 1950s, severance pay allowances already figured into white collar and supervisory employment. It also expanded to manual workers, as evidenced in national and regional plant agreements.

SOURCE: Herz 1954.

Following the end of WWI and the creation of the International Labour Organization (ILO) in 1919, legislation began to recognize labor rights, and various types of workers councils sprang up in Europe that protected workers at the time of dismissal. In South and Central America, specific provisions for dismissal compensation were introduced. In 1936, Japan adopted a contributory funded system for dismissal payments.

Greece established special regulations for workers displaced by cigarette machinery and those dismissed because of new methods of handling ship cargoes. In Germany before the Nazi regime, collective agreements had been widely adopted. In 1927, more than 12 million people were covered by such agreements. Some employers adopted particularly innovative approaches to severance pay (see box 2.2). At that time, the French system focused on voluntary provisions secured through collective bargaining.

In April 1932, the governing body of the ILO approved a report of the unemployment committee favoring dismissal compensation for salaried employees. The Advisory Committee on Salaried Employees stated in 1936, "[I]n countries where formal rules are not in existence they should be introduced by legislation or collective agreements" (Herz 1954, 301). By 1940, about 40 countries had passed laws providing notice or compensation for dismissed industrial workers or salaried employees. Until 1940, severance payments were generally only for salaried employees, but in countries with no unemployment insurance programs, the trend was to include all workers. Many companies' plans were initially adopted to meet particular situations, such as technological displacement. Legislation later became broader in its coverage.

Introduction and Expansion of the Welfare State

The economic, social, and political events of the interwar period and WWII were the third critical component of the introduction and expansion of the welfare state. These events led to the legal establishment of social security programs to address key contingencies of formal sector workers in the postwar period. These employee benefits in cash or kind were now typically legislated outside the labor code or similar legislation, and coverage expanded to a greater share of the labor force with improved eligibility conditions and increased generosity.

This expansion affected formal sector workers around the world and had a bearing on the coverage and generosity of severance pay. The scope of coverage of severance pay was often increased in parallel with the expansion of social security benefits. Expanding social insurance coverage proved difficult, and unemployment insurance not advisable in low- and middle-income countries with a large informal economy. This gave rise to the expansion of severance pay programs to a larger group of workers, to improved generosity, or to provisions that were similar to those of severance pay but were typically legislated outside the labor code, such as the unemployment insurance savings accounts introduced in Latin America (see Ferrer and Riddell 2011).

Developing countries of the decolonizing South often inherited or copied the laws and regulations of the former colonial powers. In many instances it has been suggested that the provision of severance pay in developing countries was deemed a transient legislative measure, the need for which would decline with the development of fuller employment policy and an extensive social security system, emulating the development in the North. For example, the provision of severance pay was "subject to this obligation coming to an

---

BOX 2.2 Severance Pay as Commitment Technology? An Early Example of the Human Resource Management of Severance Pay

While there is little evidence about how and why severance pay evolved, the case of the Carl Zeiss Foundation in Germany stands out for its unique approach and enduring implications. It also provides one of the first documented cases of the use of severance pay (1889). Its social welfare approach responded to particular competitive circumstances and exemplifies how severance pay might serve as a human resource management and efficiency-enhancing instrument.

The Carl Zeiss Foundation (owner of the later world-renowned producer of specialized glasses) offered paid vacation, sickness benefits, a nine-hour working day, pension fund, and compensation in case of dismissal. These seemingly overgenerous provisions actually held strategic value for both the firm and its workers. Firms and workers both faced the challenge of establishing the trust required for a long-term employment relationship. The employer was required to invest heavily in workers' training, which made them more attractive to be poached by other employers who might offer higher wages. If that happened, the first firm would suffer productivity losses and incur additional costs for recruiting and hiring new workers. To keep employees, firms had to pay a high wage premium, but pay exceeding the workers' actual productivity would render this approach unsustainable. Employers could also benefit from flexibility in dismissals given uncertain market conditions.

The experience of the Carl Zeiss Foundation reflects these conditions. The firm's success depended on the implementation of highly technical and continuous training, which in turn required a long-term relationship with employees. As Zeiss workers were sought after by competitor firms and labor was becoming more mobile, the stability of a long-term employment relationship was threatened. But uncertainties in this new market also meant that Zeiss workers faced the possibility of layoffs. In response to this situation, the articles of agreement of the foundation (as the sole owner of the firm) guaranteed social obligations such as severance pay and pensions. The pension fund helped commit Zeiss workers to the long-term employment relationship, especially as their pensions grew the longer they remained employed with the firm (the Zeiss pension fund grew almost tenfold between 1895 and 1905). With severance pay equal to half a year's salary, it also served as a significant deterrent to firing workers, since the costs incurred would be especially high for skilled workers with more experience. Evidence suggests that both mechanisms helped maintain stable, long-term employment relationships. A telling sign is that during Germany's economic downturns of the 1930s, an unusually low proportion of workers depended on social welfare in Jena, home base of Carl Zeiss.

SOURCE: Based on Abraham and Prosch 2000.

---

end on the promulgation of legislation concerning social insurance (Costa Rica) or to the replacement of compensation by benefits from a welfare fund (Dominican Republic, Egypt, Lebanon, Syria)" (Herz 1954, 319).

Among what were to become the Soviet countries, only for Estonia did the authors uncover evidence of early severance pay legislation (1934 and 1936). Severance pay and dismissals were essentially meaningless during the Soviet period, and unemployment insurance did not exist. Employees could be dismissed only for extremely limited reasons, which required complex dismissal procedures. With the transition to a market economy, all the former Soviet countries adopted severance pay legislation and unemployment benefits.

HISTORIC LESSONS

Historic accounts are useful to understand the reason for the complexity of severance pay arrangements. They shed light on the development of these arrangements over time in and across countries, and they helped guide the development of the cross-country inventory in this chapter and inspired the analysis.

A historic overview of severance pay suggests the following:

- Many severance pay disbursements occurred during large-scale industrial restructuring, with provisions directly negotiated between firms and workers (trade unions) in an ad hoc manner and adjusted to the specific restructuring process. They often happened outside legislated rules or collective agreements.

- In various firms, severance pay provisions were used together with occupational pensions in knowledge-intensive sectors to establish a commitment technology for both employer and employee. The loss of an occupational (defined benefit) pension by early leavers was balanced against severance pay commitments and firing costs for the employer.

- Firm- or industry-specific agreements still play a role in most countries above and beyond legislated rules or collective agreements, with little information about the terms of reference. In some countries—most prominently Germany, Japan, and the United States—these agreements are the basis of severance pay, as a mandated scheme does not exist.

- Mandated severance pay provisions are a primitive form of social protection. They were introduced in most, but not all, countries before other social protection mechanisms, in particular, unemployment and retirement benefits.

- In developed economies, severance pay was not abolished once related social security benefits had been established. In most developing countries, severance pay is still the key provision for the formal labor force, as access to and eligibility for unemployment and retirement benefits remain limited.

- In countries with limited formal sector employment, severance pay is often seen as a key instrument for job protection. Severance pay, together with long notice periods and firing restrictions, protects workers in formal jobs from income loss in case of a dismissal.

- The difference in coverage for unemployment and pension benefits between developed and developing economies suggests that the rationale for severance pay, its design features, and its interactions with related social benefits are different. This, in turn, suggests a need to differentiate conceptual frameworks between high- and low-income countries. Some groups of workers in middle-income countries have characteristics in common with the former and some with the latter.

Mandated Severance Pay Programs: Modalities, Overview, Reforms

Building on the historical background in the previous section, a cross-country matrix of mandated severance pay and related variables was compiled (annex B). It attempts to present comparable information on the highly complex severance pay provisions that address key features for analysis and policy reform. The matrix contains detailed information from 2010 or latest about mandated severance pay itself and about a variety of other country characteristics, including related social benefits, labor regulation, and the economic environment. This section starts with a review of key features of the severance pay system, then continues with review of existing severance pay programs throughout the world.

HOW DOES MANDATED SEVERANCE PAY WORK?

Severance pay mandates require that firms make payments to workers upon separation from the firm. As with other cash benefit programs, many issues arise in the design of severance pay. Most fundamentally, under what conditions should the government pre-empt voluntary and collectively bargained severance plans and mandate its own? Which workers should be eligible for the benefit, under what contingencies, and with what level of benefits? How are the benefits to be paid? Which types of firms are obliged to pay for these compulsory systems? What happens if a firm is unable to make such payments owing to insolvency? Are there any financing arrangements that facilitate such payments?

Legal source and coverage. Severance pay can be mandatory (required by law), usually established by the labor code; based on collective agreements established at the industry or national level; or voluntary, if firms themselves decide whether to make such payments. One can obtain, with some efforts, good information about mandated schemes, only very incomplete information about collective agreements, and virtually none about voluntary schemes. As a result, the benefit features presented here apply to mandated schemes only. Mandatory programs may apply to all employees, to the private sector only, or to specific industrial sectors or occupations. Some countries limit mandatory programs to firms above a certain size threshold, as larger firms are deemed better able to incur such expenses. The information in the matrix highlights sectors (all or private only) and excluded categories if the information is available.

Eligible contingencies. In some countries, mandatory severance pay is required for all types of separations; in other countries, some types of separation may disqualify workers. For example, workers dismissed as a result of misconduct (separated by their own fault) and those who voluntarily quit typically do not qualify for the entitlement. Other countries provide mandatory severance pay only to workers who are discharged for redundancy (economic) reasons but not for other valid reasons (dismissal); yet others mandate severance pay only for cases of collective dismissals or for certain groups of workers (such as white collar workers). The inventory differentiates among six main contingencies giving rise to eligibility: dismissal, redundancy, bankruptcy, disability, retirement, and end of service. The first four are involuntary separations; the last two can be voluntary or involuntary. In cases of severance savings provisions based on individual accounts, all separating workers—regardless of the reason for separation—typically may make some withdrawals from their accounts.

Parsons (2011b) makes an important distinction between severance insurance pay and severance insurance savings, arguing that these are polar opposites on a continuum, with actual provisions spread across the spectrum. On one side is the indemnity for dismissal—compensation for losing a job as a result of the employer's decision to sever the contract. On the other side is a payment that is due when a person leaves the firm (end-of-service pay). The more contingencies give rise to eligibility, the more the severance pay moves from indemnity insurance to a savings provision, with implications for hiring and firing costs for the employer (Parsons 2011a).

Benefit type and benefit level. Severance pay has traditionally been of the defined benefit type, and most designs still take this form. Increasingly, however, defined contribution benefits are being introduced. Under defined benefit plans, severance pay usually depends on years of service and last wage, and usually has a vesting period (that is, a minimum number of months of employment are required for eligibility). Typically, each year of service is rewarded in proportion to the person's wage; for example, half of the monthly wage for each year of service. More complex formulas exist in which compensation is adjusted according to years of service or age tiers. Under such structures, older workers or those with long service records are usually entitled to more generous severance pay. In some countries, the generosity of severance benefits may differ by the type of separation (for example, dismissal, redundancy, collective redundancy, end of service); between white and blue collar workers; between permanent and fixed-term workers; or between those covered by collective agreements and those not covered. In some countries, workers receive a seniority premium depending on the reason for separation (usually in cases of nonfault dismissal). Some countries do not have explicit benefit formulas and leave determination of the severance pay, as well as the authorization to lay off workers, to special government bodies or court decisions.

For defined contribution arrangements, the benefit level depends on the contribution rate, the contribution base (wage), and the interest rate earned. Eligibility typically does not depend on cause of separation, although that factor may affect immediate access to the benefit and size of the available resources.

As a rule, severance pay is paid in a lump-sum fashion, but it can also be paid in regular monthly payments (see the description of the Austrian severance pay system below). In countries where employers contribute to individual unemployment accounts, payments might be deferred until retirement and could conceivably be converted to annuities.

Funding and taxation. In general, severance pay is financed by employers. In countries with individual accounts, workers may also contribute. In some countries, the government provides financial assistance, particularly for large-scale restructuring operations that involve worker retrenchment in mass layoffs.

The type of funding of severance pay has a bearing on incentives for employers and employees, including their trust in the arrangement. There are four broad types of funding:

- Internal and current funding—full payment out of current revenues at the time of separation, treating severance pay as a current wage expenditure

- Internal funding with book reserves within the firm, with the provisioning partially or fully tax-exempt, at times dependent on assets bought as collateral (say, government bonds)
- External provisioning via individual accounts held by a financial market institution (insurance company, commercial bank, or specialized institution)
- External provisioning through centralized, typically government, institutions

Various considerations apply in deciding which type of funding to use. Financing severance pay out of current cash flow creates a challenge for smaller employers even in good times and a nonpayment threat for the worker in case of insolvency of firms of any size. In countries with weak legal foundations, noncompliance by employers—even those that are solvent and liquid—is reportedly not uncommon, and risks making any notionally generous benefits largely irrelevant. To address the solvency and liquidity risks, some countries have established special guarantee funds. Reserving internally may provide some limited protection but it may also offer benefits for both the firm and the employee, especially in countries with underdeveloped financial markets. Firms have access to additional self-financing, and workers may profit from a higher rate of return (wage growth) than they could achieve in the financial market. External provisioning with financial market institutions reduces the compliance, liquidity, and solvency risks for the firm but exposes the worker to other risks; in particular, financial institution's solvency and financial market risks, including low rates of return. External provisioning with centralized government institutions may better insure against liquidity and solvency risks, but government funds, in general, have a bad track record on financial performance (Iglesias and Palacios 2001).

Severance benefits may be subject to different types of taxation. Three broad types can be differentiated: (1) tax exempt; (2) partially taxed through tax allowances, ceilings, or special rates; or (3) fully taxed as normal wages or income. Severance payments made by employers are typically, but not always, fully deductible as business expenditures, as wages are. Any difference in tax treatment—full deductibility by the employer or partial taxation of severance pay by the employee compared with wages—invites tax arbitrage and collusion.

Our matrix of mandated severance pay programs around the world presents several variables on country environment, as they may help explain both design features and the labor market effects of severance pay. Many country features could be identified, but the following are especially important:

- The level of informality, which is closely, but not fully, linked to per capita income
- The level of labor market regulation; in particular, the dismissal process and the length of the dismissal notice
- The scope of coverage and level of social benefits (or their absence); in particular, for unemployment and old-age benefits
- The development of the financial market as an enabling condition for some funding options
- The strength of trade unions across the country and in specific sectors

The level of formality has a bearing on both coverage for retirement and related benefits, as well as the type of unemployment benefits. In an economy with high informality, a typical unemployment insurance scheme is unlikely to work, as the status of the unemployed cannot be easily observed and the scheme would create major moral hazards. It is rare to find such schemes in highly informal economies, which increases the importance of severance unemployment income protection and tighter dismissal regulation as an employment protection. In case of no or limited access to retirement benefits, severance pay may also be used as a retirement income mechanism, often with no limitations on the number of years used for its calculation.

In the analysis of the effect of labor market programs on labor market outcomes, the generosity of severance, along with other social benefits (measured through the level of social payroll taxes), advance notice, and other components are often lumped together into an index to measure the strength of employment protection legislation (see, for example, Haltiwanger, Scarpetta, and Schweiger 2008; Heckmann and Pagés 2004; OECD 1999). To allow for testing of some hypotheses and to encourage further analysis by the academic community on the scope and design of severance pay, the matrix includes data on some of these variables.

OVERVIEW OF MANDATED SEVERANCE PAY PROGRAMS AROUND THE WORLD

In describing the salient features of mandated severance pay programs around the world, the authors have tried to be as comprehensive as possible. The database is based on the broadest collection of mandated severance pay schedules currently available (World Bank Doing Business Indicators 2011), which covers 183 countries and allows the assessment of key features of severance pay in relation to broad country characteristics (such as GDP per capita), although some features, such as taxation of benefits and level of informality, are not well covered in a number of countries. In these cases, up-to-date information was collected but judgment calls were required at times between comprehensiveness and full comparability. These instances are noted in the main text and in annex B.

Scope of the coverage. Except in some low-income, predominantly African and Pacific Island countries, most countries have either mandatory or quasi-mandatory severance pay systems. The information on the latter is incomplete—it is confined to countries with comprehensive collective agreements and those that have essentially no agreements. Of the 183 countries in the matrix, 152 have mandated schemes (83 percent), 18 (10 percent) have quasi-mandated schemes through comprehensive collective agreements, and only 13 (7 percent) have neither. At least 22 countries have both mandated severance pay and coverage under comprehensive collective agreements. For another 44 countries, available information suggests no or little coverage under such agreements. This leaves 98 countries for which no information is available on the scope of collective bargaining provision of severance benefits.

The presence of mandatory severance pay systems varies broadly with the income level of the country (figure 2.1, panel a).[4] The lowest share of mandated severance pay (70 percent) and the highest share of collective agreements when mandated provisions do not exist (almost 100 percent) are found in high-income countries. In contrast, low-income countries have the highest mandated share (almost 95 percent) and no known

FIGURE 2.1 **Incidence of Mandated and Quasi-Mandated Severance Pay Programs**

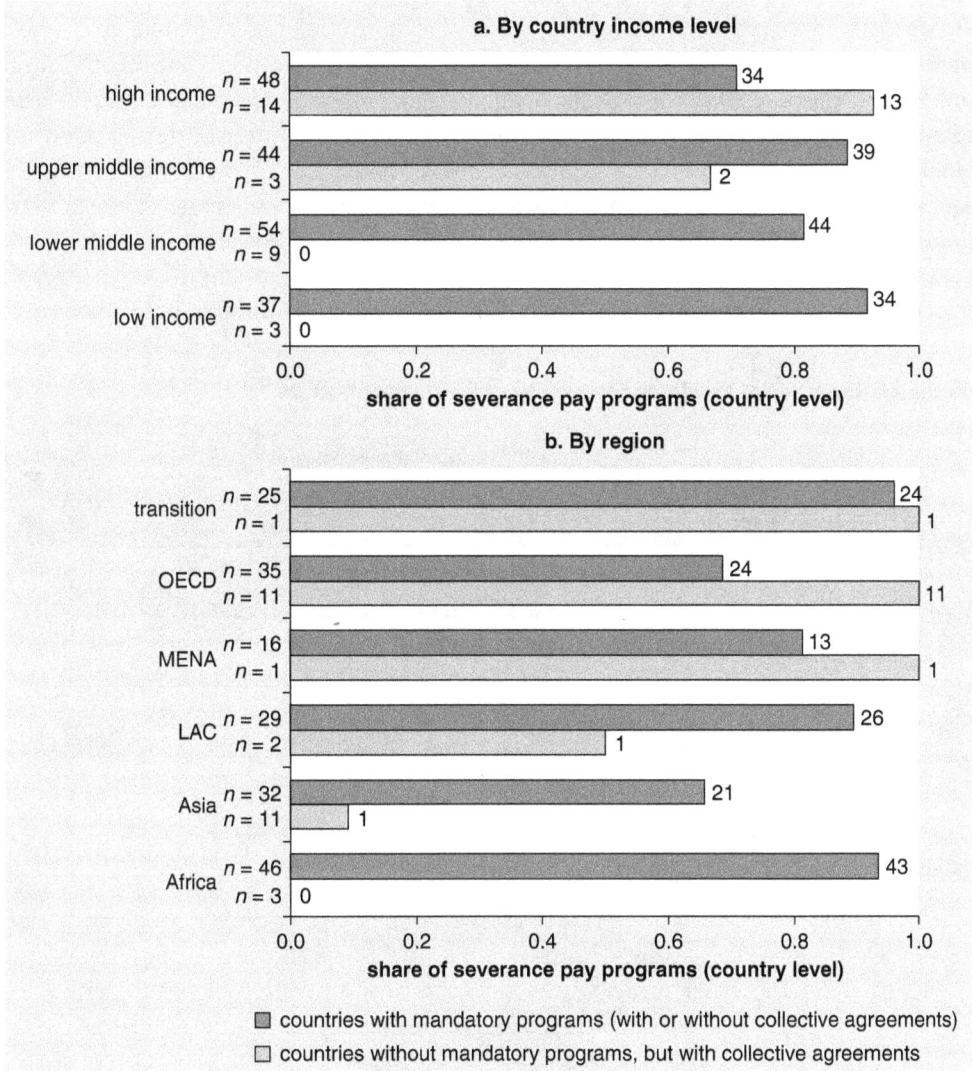

a. By country income level

high income	n = 48 → 34
	n = 14 → 13
upper middle income	n = 44 → 39
	n = 3 → 2
lower middle income	n = 54 → 44
	n = 9 → 0
low income	n = 37 → 34
	n = 3 → 0

share of severance pay programs (country level)

0.0   0.2   0.4   0.6   0.8   1.0

b. By region

transition	n = 25 → 24
	n = 1 → 1
OECD	n = 35 → 24
	n = 11 → 11
MENA	n = 16 → 13
	n = 1 → 1
LAC	n = 29 → 26
	n = 2 → 1
Asia	n = 32 → 21
	n = 11 → 1
Africa	n = 46 → 43
	n = 3 → 0

share of severance pay programs (country level)

0.0   0.2   0.4   0.6   0.8   1.0

☐ countries with mandatory programs (with or without collective agreements)
☐ countries without mandatory programs, but with collective agreements

SOURCE: Annex B.

NOTE: LAC = Latin America and the Caribbean, MENA = Middle East and North Africa, OECD = Organisation for Economic Co-operation and Development.

comprehensive collective agreements. Upper-middle-income countries have high shares of mandated provisions. With respect to regions, severance pay is mandated in nearly all transition countries and about 90 percent of African, Middle East, and Latin American countries.[5] Only two-thirds of Organisation for Economic Co-operation and Development (OECD) and Asian countries have them; those that do not are concentrated in the Pacific Island countries (figure 2.1, panel b). In contrast, quasi-mandatory systems are well represented only among high-income/OECD countries, where about 40 percent of countries have them. All OECD countries have either a mandatory or quasi-mandatory system, although overall coverage may be low, as in the United States, which has no mandatory severance and low collective bargaining density.

In most countries, severance pay programs cover primarily the private sector; the share is particularly high among OECD countries, where it reaches almost 80 percent (figure 2.2). This may be explained by the special status enjoyed by public employees, whose positions are highly protected. In contrast, in the transition economies of Central and Eastern Europe, 70 percent of the severance pay programs cover all sectors. In these countries, a special employment position for civil servants did not exist during the communist era and was not introduced with the move toward a market economy. In Africa and Asia, some 50 percent of countries mandate severance pay in all sectors. While in most countries firms of all sizes are covered, some countries limit coverage to firms with more than 5 workers (Colombia, Korea until 2011); more than 10 (Germany, Morocco, Nepal, Slovenia, República Bolivariana de Venezuela); more than 15 (Australia, Italy, the Kyrgyz

FIGURE 2.2 **Incidence of Mandated Severance Pay Programs in Sectors**

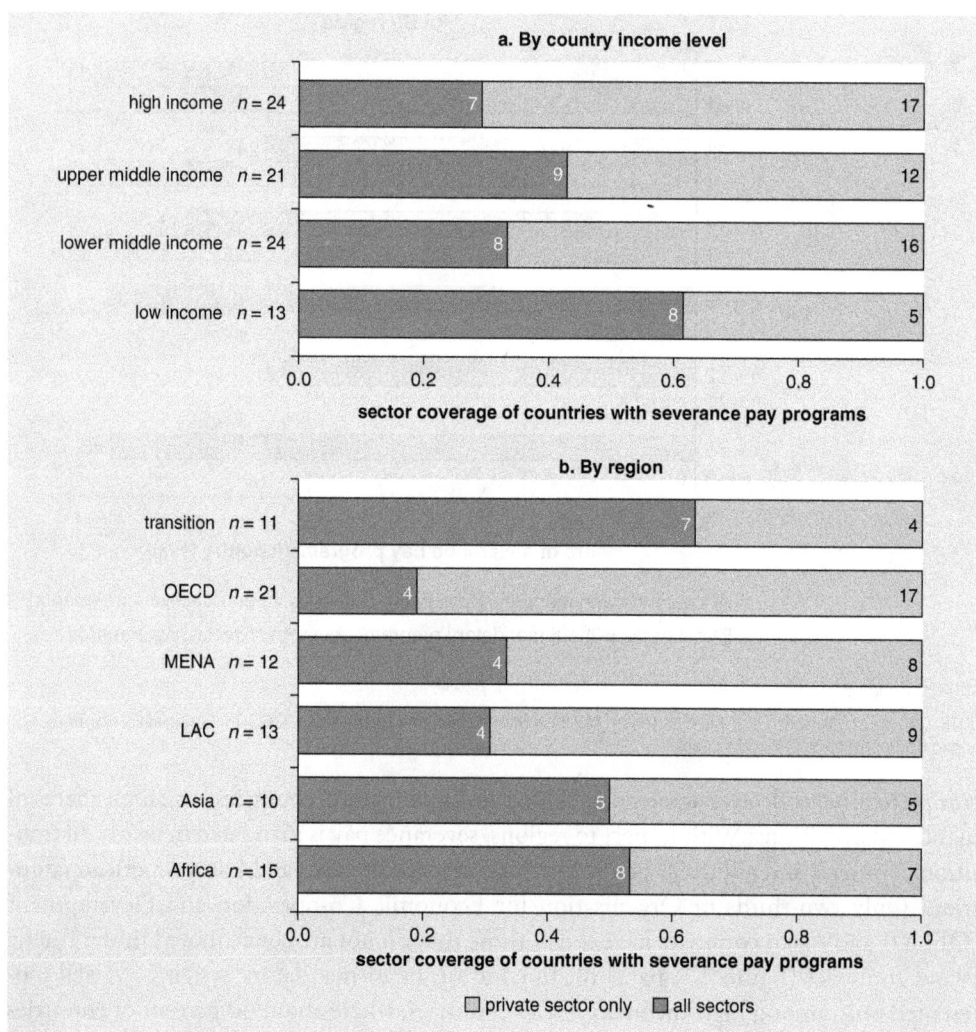

SOURCE: Annex B.

NOTE: LAC = Latin America and the Caribbean, MENA = Middle East and North Africa.

Republic, Sri Lanka); more than 20 (Bulgaria, Denmark, Finland, Hungary, Pakistan, Poland, Switzerland); more than 30 (Turkey); or more than 50 (India) (see annex B).

Eligible contingencies. The vast majority of countries with mandated schemes base benefit eligibility on the traditional contingencies—dismissal and redundancy—with only modest differences across income levels and regions. By level of income, redundancy reasons are more prevalent than dismissal reasons; by region, the picture is less clear (figure 2.3). For many of the 152 countries that mandate severance pay, redundancy and other eligibility conditions can be separated. For 46 countries, the redundancy criteria are known but not the others, hence they are put into their own category (redundancy and unknown). Explicit reference to bankruptcy and incapacity is made in some 10 percent of the countries overall but in 20 percent of the transition economies. Old age (retirement) as an explicit contingency exists in only a few countries clustered around the upper-middle-income level and in Latin America. The prevalence of end-of-service pay increases with the income level of countries, from nil in low-income countries to almost 30 percent in high-income countries. At the regional level, end-of-service pay is most prevalent in countries in the Middle East and North Africa (MENA), where it reaches above 50 percent, followed by OECD countries with 30 percent.

Another critical eligibility condition for severance pay is the vesting period: the minimum number of months of employment required before the benefit formula becomes operative. While these minimum service requirements differ little in median values across income levels, means increase sharply with income level, from 10 months in low-income countries to 33 months in high-income countries (figure 2.4). This is also reflected across regions, with OECD countries showing the highest mean level. What is striking in the regional comparison is the low median for Latin America (3 months) and the high values for Switzerland (240 months) and Denmark (144 months). The high numbers for Switzerland and Denmark strongly influence the average for the OECD group and suggest a different role for severance pay that may be linked to the importance of corporate pensions in these countries. Without these two countries, the OECD average would be 17 months.[6]

Benefit level. This section focuses on mandated benefit levels for redundancy; that is, employer-initiated separation for economic reasons. This benefit has the most comprehensive information base; it is the most important contingency; and it is also the most relevant benefit from a policy perspective. In most countries, the benefit formula is uniform across contingencies; in a few countries, benefits differ across contingencies in a complex manner. Annex B provides detailed information for redundancy benefits at different points of service length (1, 5, 10, and 20 years) as well as on the benefit formula (defined benefit and defined contribution) for end-of-service benefits for those few countries where they are reported to exist.

The generosity of severance pay varies strongly among countries, in a manner that is closely linked to income level. Almost universally and for all presented lengths of service, low-income countries offer the highest benefit and high-income countries the lowest. Generosity and mean benefit levels are monotonically decreasing for median-income countries. Measured at 1 year of service, the median benefit is 2.2 weeks for high-income countries and almost double that (4.3 weeks) for low-income countries. For 20 years of service, the mean benefit level increases from 37.58 weeks to 68.95 weeks (figure 2.5, panel a).

FIGURE 2.3 **Eligibility Contingencies for Severance Pay (in percent)**

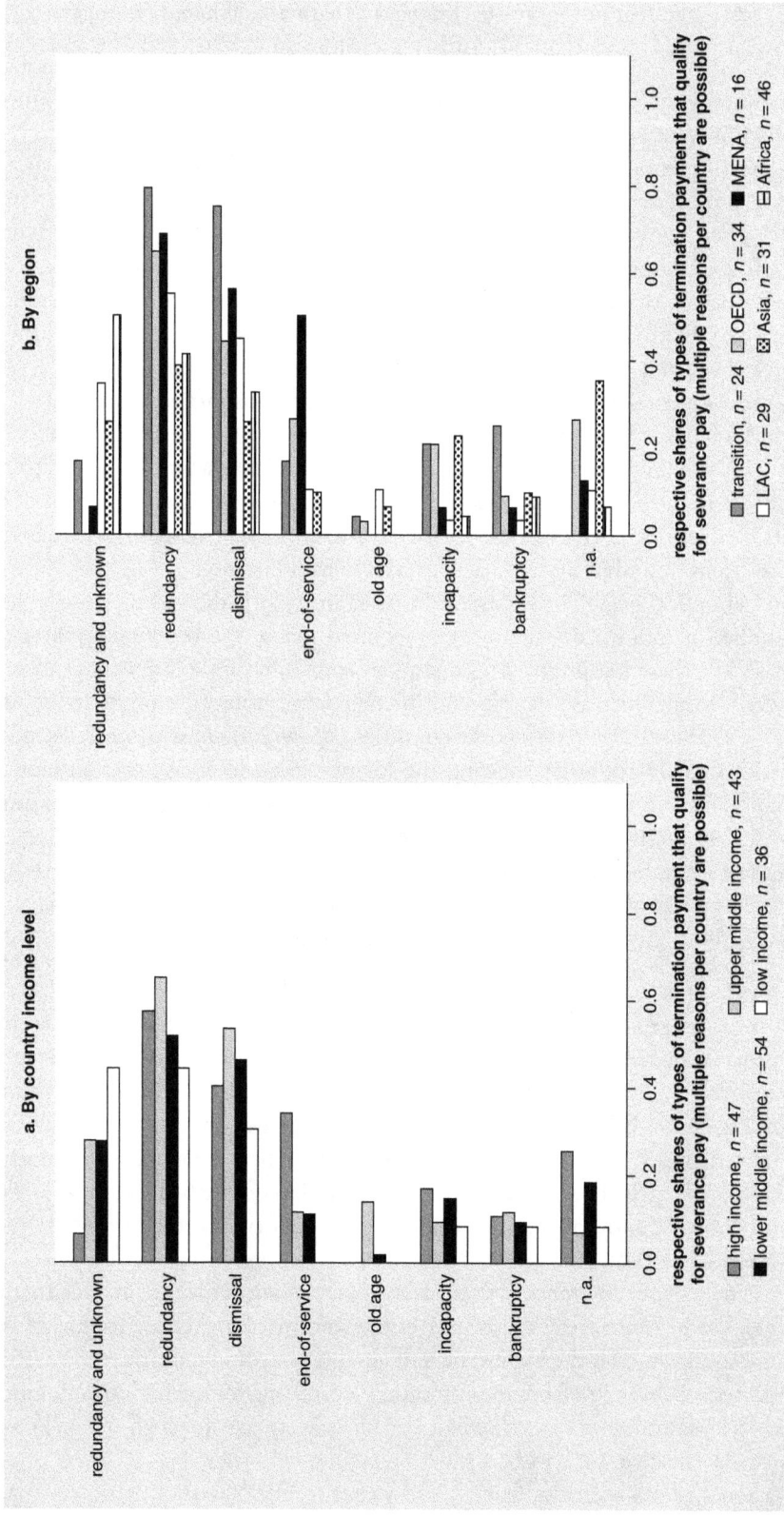

a. By country income level

b. By region

respective shares of types of termination payment that qualify
for severance pay (multiple reasons per country are possible)

■ high income, *n* = 47   ▨ upper middle income, *n* = 43
■ lower middle income, *n* = 54   □ low income, *n* = 36

respective shares of types of termination payment that qualify
for severance pay (multiple reasons per country are possible)

▨ transition, *n* = 24   □ OECD, *n* = 34   ■ MENA, *n* = 16
□ LAC, *n* = 29   ▨ Asia, *n* = 31   ⊞ Africa, *n* = 46

SOURCE: Annex B.

NOTE: LAC = Latin America and the Caribbean, MENA = Middle East and North Africa; OECD = Organisation for Economic Co-operation and Development. n.a. = not available.

FIGURE 2.4 **Vesting Periods for Benefit Eligibility (in months)**

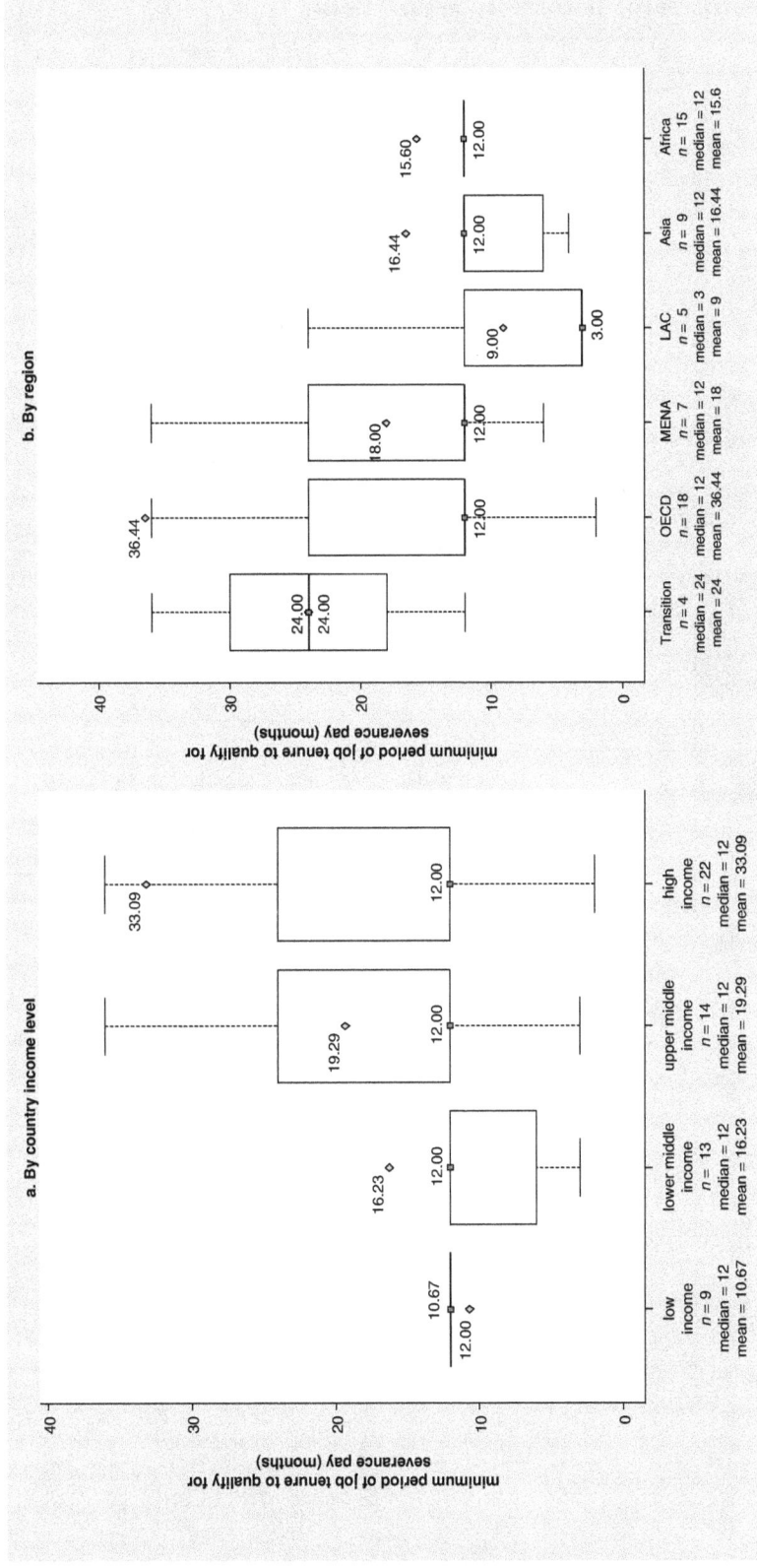

a. By country income level

b. By region

SOURCE: Annex B.

NOTE: LAC = Latin America and the Caribbean.

FIGURE 2.5 **Severance Pay Generosity by Length of Service**

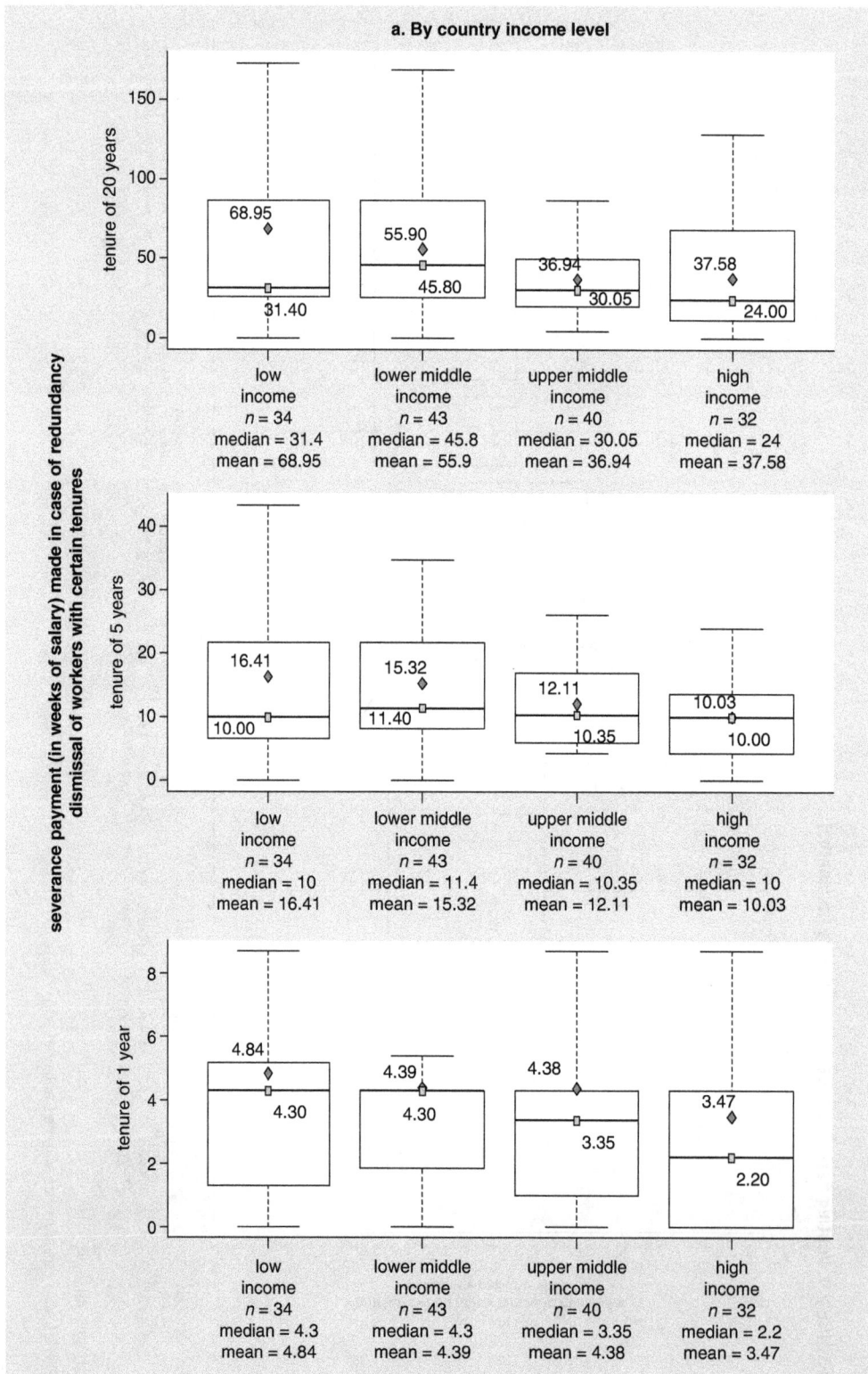

a. By country income level

severance payment (in weeks of salary) made in case of redundancy dismissal of workers with certain tenures

tenure of 20 years

low income	n = 34, median = 31.4, mean = 68.95 (68.95 / 31.40)
lower middle income	n = 43, median = 45.8, mean = 55.9 (55.90 / 45.80)
upper middle income	n = 40, median = 30.05, mean = 36.94 (36.94 / 30.05)
high income	n = 32, median = 24, mean = 37.58 (37.58 / 24.00)

tenure of 5 years

low income	n = 34, median = 10, mean = 16.41 (16.41 / 10.00)
lower middle income	n = 43, median = 11.4, mean = 15.32 (15.32 / 11.40)
upper middle income	n = 40, median = 10.35, mean = 12.11 (12.11 / 10.35)
high income	n = 32, median = 10, mean = 10.03 (10.03 / 10.00)

tenure of 1 year

low income	n = 34, median = 4.3, mean = 4.84 (4.84 / 4.30)
lower middle income	n = 43, median = 4.3, mean = 4.39 (4.39 / 4.30)
upper middle income	n = 40, median = 3.35, mean = 4.38 (4.38 / 3.35)
high income	n = 32, median = 2.2, mean = 3.47 (3.47 / 2.20)

(continued)

FIGURE 2.5 **(continued)**

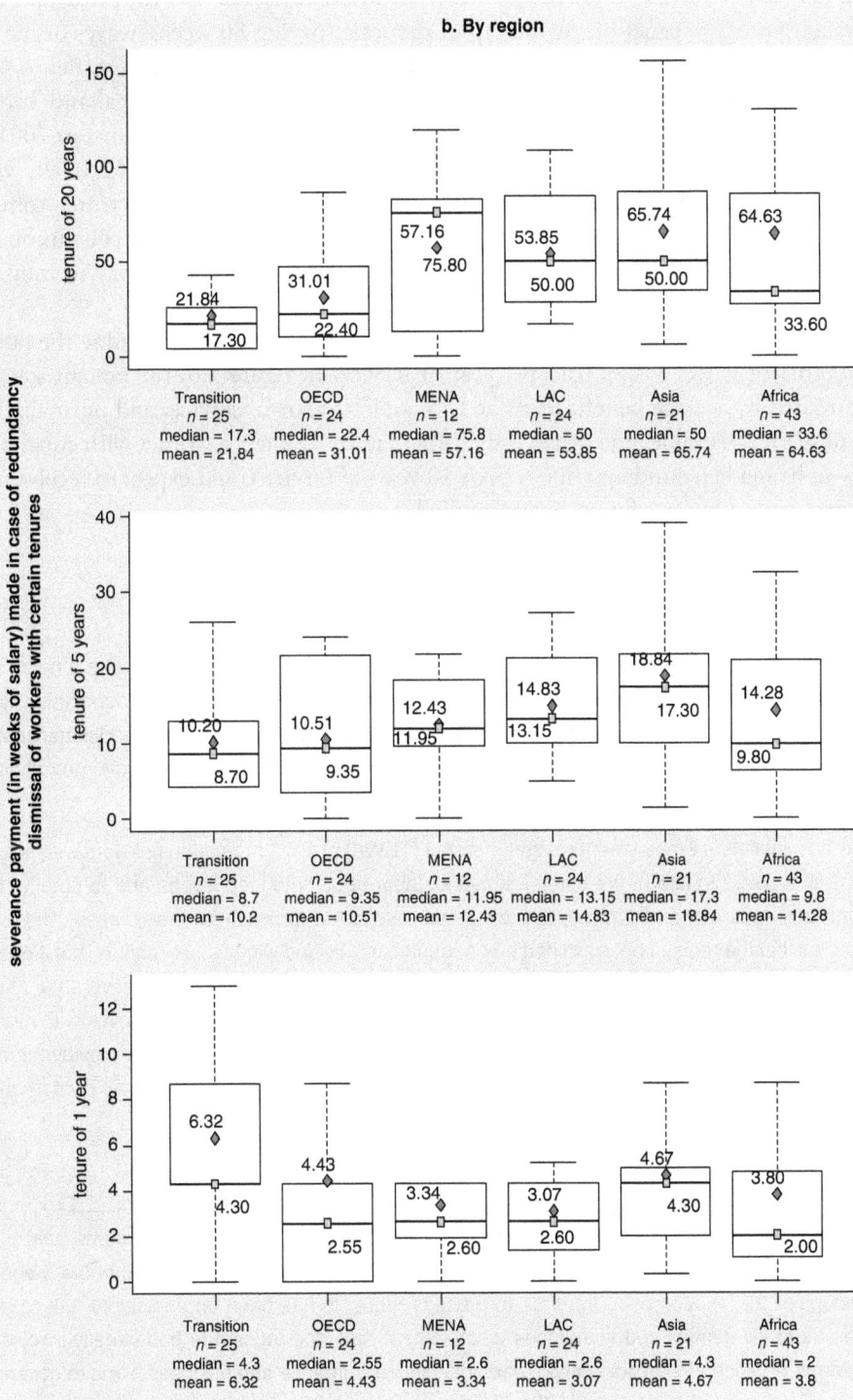

b. By region

SOURCE: Annex B.

NOTE: LAC = Latin America and the Caribbean.

The benefit also varies by region: The highest level (except for low-tenured workers) is found in Asian countries, followed by Africa, the Middle East and North Africa, and Latin America (figure 2.5, panel b). At the top of the scale (paying 80 weeks' wages or more to a worker with 20 years of service) are 14 African countries, 11 Asian countries, 8 Latin American countries, 4 MENA countries, and 2 OECD countries (Portugal and Turkey). One of the most costly systems is in Sri Lanka, with the maximum amounts in 2001–02 reaching 36–50 months' wages (see box 2.3) and currently standing at 169 weeks' wages (more than 40 months) for redundancy pay. On the other end of the spectrum—offering the least generous severance pay—are transition countries. (Although this conclusion does not hold for low-tenured workers, who are entitled to higher severance pay in transition economies than in other economies due to the flat-rate structure.)

Another way of looking at the generosity of severance pay is to examine the ratio of the number of weeks' wages paid per year of service. In figure 2.6, the benefit schedule is aggregated by average benefit levels at 1, 5, and 10 years of service, and normalized by years of service.[7] A value larger than 2 signifies that, on average, a worker with equal probability to be made redundant after 1, 5, or 10 years of service could expect to receive more than two weeks of wages for each year worked.

BOX 2.3 Sri Lanka's Severance Pay System

Sri Lanka's severance pay system imposes one of the highest costs internationally. It not only provides extremely high compensation to laid-off workers and inflicts correspondingly high costs on employers, but its discretionary nature and nontransparency impose additional costs by generating uncertainty about the ability of a company to lay off workers (the government has the authority to reject an employer's plans) and by lengthy procedures.

The Termination of Employment of Workmen Act (TEWA) of 1971 requires employers with more than 15 workers to inform the commissioner of labor about intended layoffs and to obtain the commissioner's authorization not just for group layoffs but for each individual case. The act requires that the request be examined and a response provided within three months, but it does not specify the compensation to be provided for the laid-off workers. Another severance payment, a gratuity (Gratuity Act No. 12 of 1983), is also paid by employers. Companies with more than 15 employees must pay the gratuity to all workers upon termination of their employment if they have more than five years of service with the employer. Gratuity payments amount to one month's salary for each two years of service.

In practice, the level of compensation approved by the commissioner under TEWA has been up to a maximum of 6.0 months' wages per year of service; the average in 2002 was 2.1 months' wages per year of service (Abidoye, Orazem, and Vodopivec 2009). The total sums paid out to laid-off workers have been large, with the maximum amounting to 36–50 months' wages (Vodopivec 2004). Moreover, the time to process requests has been unpredictable, taking an average of six months and sometimes much longer. Also, the procedure has usually involved hearings at which employers explain their financial performance and business plans to government bureaucrats to justify the layoffs.

SOURCE: Vodopivec 2004.

FIGURE 2.6 **Severance Pay Generosity Index**

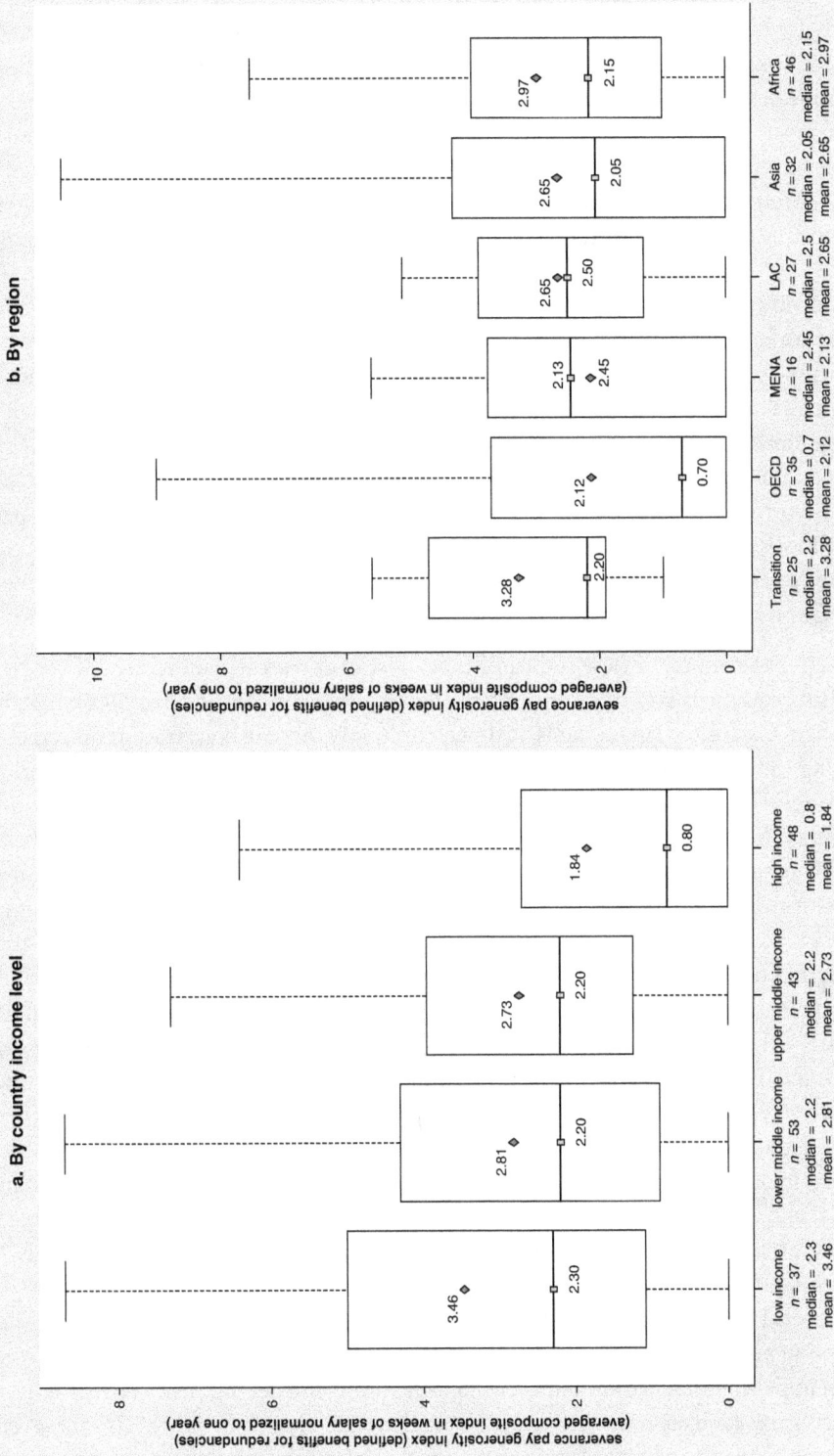

a. By country income level

severance pay generosity index (defined benefits for redundancies)
(averaged composite index in weeks of salary normalized to one year)

low income	lower middle income	upper middle income	high income
n = 37	n = 53	n = 43	n = 48
median = 2.3	median = 2.2	median = 2.2	median = 0.8
mean = 3.46	mean = 2.81	mean = 2.73	mean = 1.84

b. By region

severance pay generosity index (defined benefits for redundancies)
(averaged composite index in weeks of salary normalized to one year)

Transition	OECD	MENA	LAC	Asia	Africa
n = 25	n = 35	n = 16	n = 27	n = 32	n = 46
median = 2.2	median = 0.7	median = 2.45	median = 2.5	median = 2.05	median = 2.15
mean = 3.28	mean = 2.12	mean = 2.13	mean = 2.65	mean = 2.65	mean = 2.97

SOURCE: Annex B.

NOTE: LAC = Latin America and the Caribbean.

Measured at mean benefit level, the generosity index is 3.46 for low-income countries. It falls gradually to 2.81 for lower-middle-income; 2.73 for higher-middle-income; and 1.84 for high-income countries. Measured at the median level, the decline with income level is less pronounced, except for high-income countries. Across regions, the highest average mean value is found among transition economies (3.27) followed by Africa (2.97), and the lowest is found in OECD countries (2.12). The highest median values are found in Latin America and the Caribbean (2.50) and MENA (2.45) countries, compared with OECD countries (0.70) (figure 2.6, panel b). Another aspect of generosity is the mandated maximum amount of the severance pay. The evidence suggests that the maximum severance pay benefit in some countries may reflect any number of years (say 40 months' salary for 40 years), but this is more the exception than the rule. The service limits in the benefit formulas are typically much lower.

The severance pay benefit levels presented above do not include seniority premiums; that is, additional payments required in some countries in cases of nonfault dismissals (dismissal without just cause, which typically includes separations for economic reasons). Such payments are quite common in Latin American countries (Brazil, Colombia, Ecuador, Panama, and Peru). Such additional compensation has a clear connotation of a penalty for a firm, which means it can be closely associated with the job protection function of the severance pay program (a discussion of the economic rationale for severance pay programs can be found later in this chapter).

Funding. The country review indicates that most countries rely on internal flow financing to fund severance pay, with only a few allowing for or requesting that book reserves be established. Cash flow financing is 100 percent in low-income countries; it decreases with increasing income level. Book reserves are currently limited to Japan and, as an option, to Korea among high-income countries, and to Poland among high-middle-income countries (see figure 2.6, panel a). In the past, firms in a few other countries and circumstances have been obliged to create book reserves for future severance pay expenses (Austria before the 2003 reform, Italy ongoing after the 2007 reform for firms with fewer than 50 employees, Korea before the 2005 reform, and Venezuela with a continued option for internal and external funding) or to reinsure their payments with insurance companies (Chile and Korea). A small number of countries have set up public guarantee funds to compensate, at least partly, the severance pay claims of workers whose employers are insolvent (typically, such funds also compensate workers for unpaid wages). According to the documentation, these funds exist in Austria (for the workers under the old severance pay regime) and Chile and a number of other middle- to high-income countries in Europe, Latin America, and Asia, including Colombia, Estonia, Finland, Hungary, Israel, Italy, Korea, Romania, Slovenia, and Thailand. These guarantee funds typically are funded by employer contributions and organized at the national level. In Italy, the end-of-service pay provisioned with firms is guaranteed by the social security fund.

External funding through individual accounts or centralized funds is limited to a small but growing number of middle- to high-income countries, with individual accounts concentrated in upper-middle-income and a few high-income countries (figure 2.7, panel a). In these countries, firms (and sometimes workers themselves) are obliged by law to deposit severance pay contributions in individual savings accounts. These deposits then earn interest and are paid out either as a lump sum or in monthly payments, subject to continuing eligibility. This is

FIGURE 2.7 **Funding Methods**

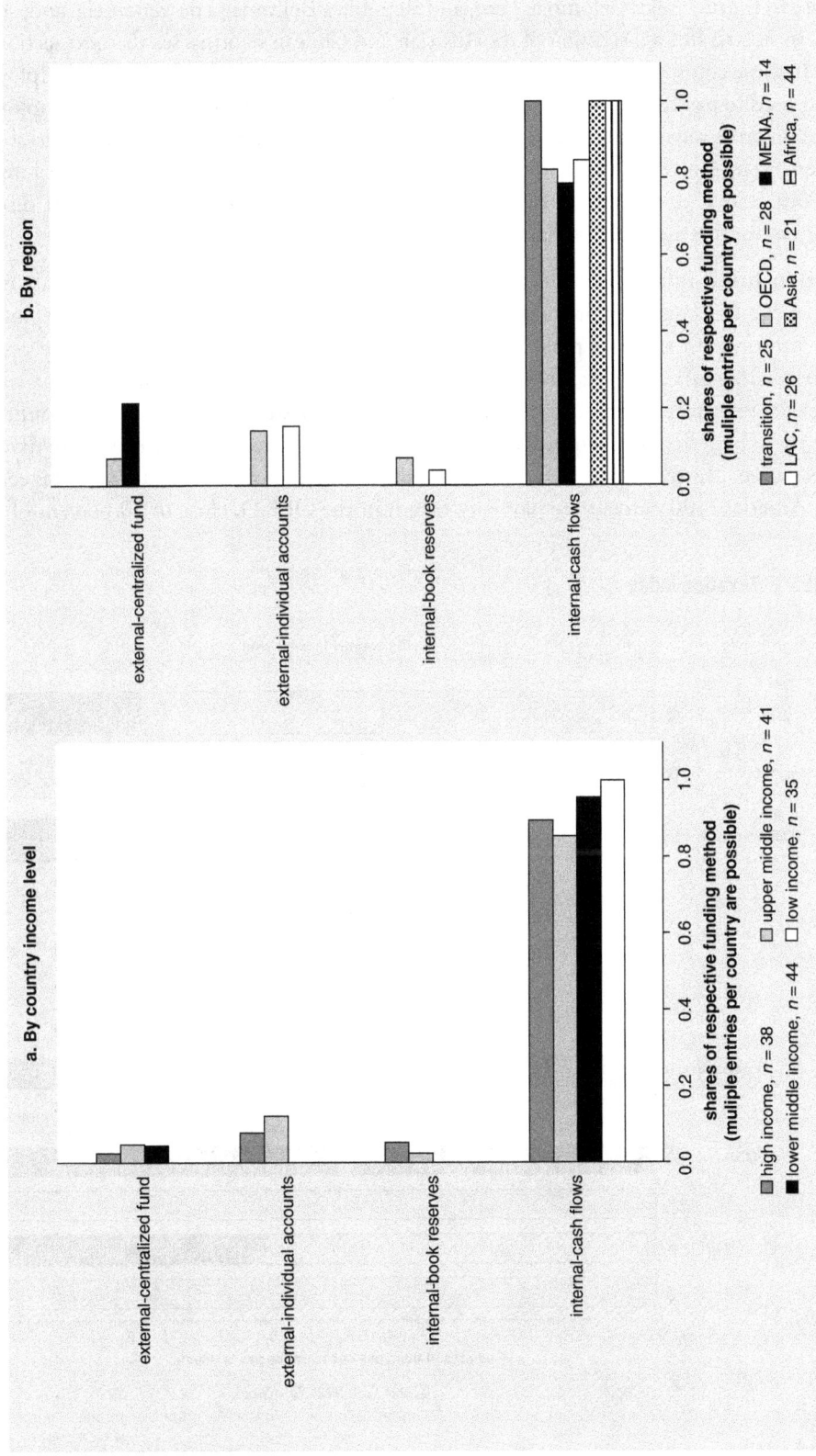

a. By country income level

b. By region

shares of respective funding method
(muliple entries per country are possible)

shares of respective funding method
(muliple entries per country are possible)

external-centralized fund
external-individual accounts
internal-book reserves
internal-cash flows

high income, *n* = 38
lower middle income, *n* = 44
upper middle income, *n* = 41
low income, *n* = 35

transition, *n* = 25
LAC, *n* = 26
OECD, *n* = 28
Asia, *n* = 21
MENA, *n* = 14
Africa, *n* = 44

SOURCE: Annex B.

NOTE: LAC = Latin America and the Caribbean.

the case in Brazil, Chile, Colombia, Peru, and República Bolivariana de Venezuela, and, since 2003, in Austria (for a discussion of the Austrian and Chilean reforms, see the next section).

In some countries (in Northern Africa and Latin America and in Barbados), employers are required to pay contributions to a centralized fund. The contribution rates of employers (levied on gross wages) range from a low of 0.5 percent in Barbados and Morocco; to about 2.5 percent in Algeria, Chile, and the Arab Republic of Egypt; to 8.0 percent in Colombia and Peru; and 17.0 percent in República Bolivariana de Venezuela. Government discretionary support is available in many OECD and transition countries.

Taxation rules. Information on taxation is difficult to collect. In this study, only one-third of the 152 countries provided information. The available and perhaps unrepresentative information suggests major differences across income levels and especially across regions. Across income levels, about 50 percent of countries fully tax severance pay, while almost 40 percent of lower-middle-income and a small share of high-income countries make these benefits tax exempt (figure 2.8, panel a). The tax treatment is quite diverse across regions. In transition economies, almost 90 percent of benefits are fully taxed; in Latin America, 100 percent are partially taxed; in the OECD, close to 50 percent of the

FIGURE 2.8 **Taxation Rules**

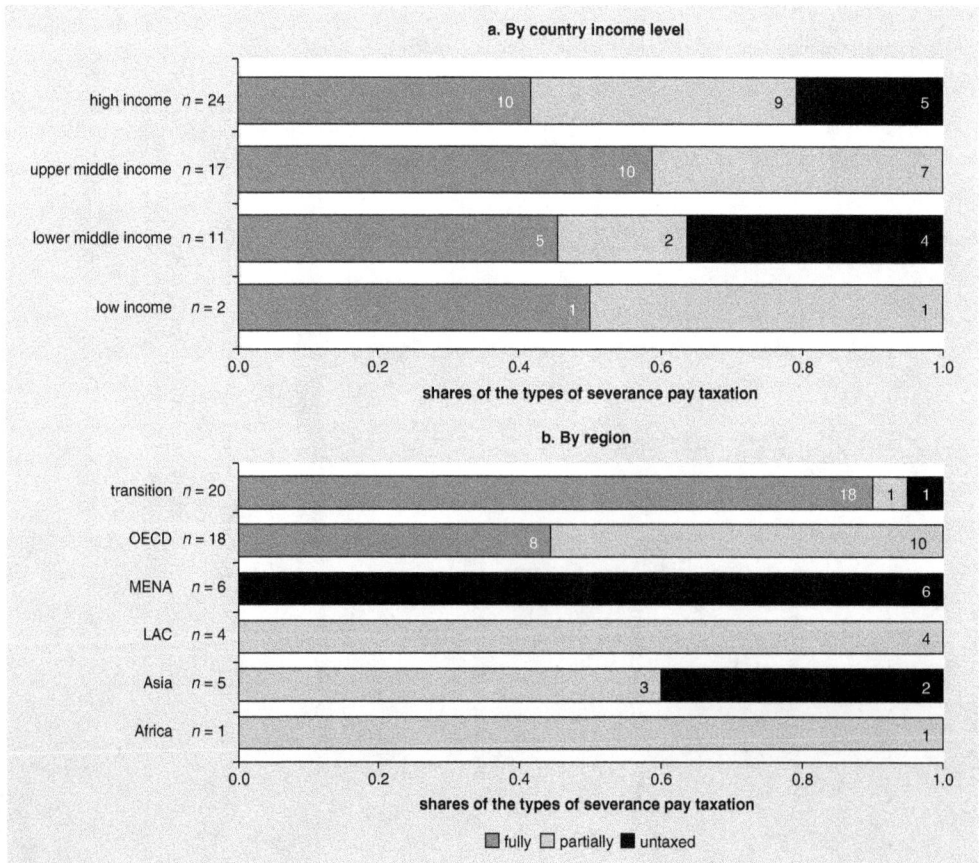

SOURCE: Annex B.

NOTE: LAC = Latin America and the Caribbean.

countries tax fully, and the rest tax partially. In Asia and Africa, full taxation never takes place; in fact, in 50 percent of the African countries and 40 percent of the Asian countries, benefits are tax exempt (as are, often, old-age income benefits).

Overall, the review showed that countries take widely different approaches to providing severance pay, but the vast majority use current revenues to finance it. High-income/OECD countries tend to have less generous systems, require more demanding prior employment eligibility conditions, often allow any reason for separation, and rely much more on collective-agreement-based systems. The inverse relationship between the income level of a country and severance pay generosity is very pronounced and valid at different lengths of service. In the vast majority of countries, severance pay is financed from the firm's cash flow. A few countries require firms to create book reserves or reinsure their payments with insurance companies, and very few have set up public guarantee funds.

The review of legal provisions as well as the analysis of incidence and generosity of severance pay fall short of a comprehensive investigation of the impact of severance pay in developing countries. To what extent is the mandate evaded, thus encouraging informal employment rather than income and job protection? To what extent is the mandate reneged on by partial or full noncompliance by employers? What is the impact of severance pay on poverty, labor supply, and so on of the individual and the household? These and numerous other relevant topics must be left to future research.

REFORM DIRECTIONS

The severance pay inventory includes information about recent reforms. This is to supplement the latest cross-country information with a sense of recent changes and emerging reform directions. Most countries have undertaken no or only minor parametric reforms since the 1990s.[8] Since early 2000, a few upper-middle- to high-income countries have engaged in interesting and partly innovative reforms: Chile (2002 and 2008), Austria (2003), Italy (2004 and 2007), and Korea (2005).

Chilean Reform of October 2002

The Chilean reform introduced an innovative scheme that combines the effectiveness of risk pooling with the increased incentive neutrality of individual accounts. Under this scheme, dependent workers contribute into two funds: a fund formed by pure individual accounts and a solidarity fund. For temporary workers, the employer pays the full 3.0 percent; for nontemporary workers, the employee pays 0.6 percent and the employer 2.4 percent, of which 1.6 percent goes to the individual account and 0.8 percent to the solidarity fund (Acevedo, Eskenazi, and Pagés 2006; Berstein, Fajnzylber, and Gana 2011). In case of unemployment, workers can access their own savings and, under some circumstances, they can complement them with resources provided by the solidarity fund to finance five monthly payments, defined as a percentage of their previous wage. In this context, the initial use of one's own funds can be interpreted as a deductible for accessing the solidarity fund, therefore providing a self-policing mechanism.

The experience during the first eight years of the reform has been positive in terms of coverage and sustainability. The accumulated experience over this period allowed the government to introduce in May 2009 a set of reforms designed to improve the adequacy of benefits by facilitating access to the pooled component. Current welfare evaluations (Berstein, Contreras, and Benvin 2008) suggest that, in general, most workers value the program, even if their valuation depends on their level of risk aversion and type of labor history. Risk-averse, older, and more educated persons are more likely to benefit from the consumption-smoothing properties. Chilean women are less likely to benefit from the program, as their labor histories are more likely to have been interrupted than those of men. Evaluations of the system in terms of labor incentives are currently under way (see Berstein, Fajnzylber, and Gana 2011). Very significantly, efficiency effects produced by this unique and innovative system seem to conform to the expectations in the recent study by Reyes, van Ours, and Vodopivec (2010). For beneficiaries using the solidarity fund, the pattern of job-finding rates over the duration of unemployment is consistent with moral hazard effects, while for beneficiaries relying on unemployment insurance savings accounts (UISAs) only, the pattern is free of such effects. The authors also find that for benefit recipients not entitled to use the solidarity fund, the amount of accumulation on the UISA does not affect the exit rate from unemployment, suggesting that such persons internalize the costs of unemployment benefits.

Overall, the new scheme seems to have been a success and has largely avoided the distortions that plague unemployment insurance systems. The 2009 reform focused on four aspects (Berstein, Fajnzylber, and Gana 2011): (1) an increase in coverage of the solidarity fund observed since the implementation of the scheme; (2) an increase in the low level of replacement rates; (3) a change in the investment regime more in line with futures of the unemployment insurance members; and (4) improvement in coverage of nonmonetary benefits, such as job search and retraining. Yet, in parallel with this scheme, Chile retains both mandated and quasi-mandated severance pay schemes for dismissal and redundancy, with no known plans for integrating the former into the savings accounts.

Austrian Reform of 2003

For all new labor contracts and for voluntary changers, the Austrian reform of 2003 (Hofer, Schuh, and Walch 2011; Koman, Schuh, and Weber 2005) moved the traditional severance pay toward an occupational pension cum income support for those dismissed with longer tenure. The severance pay entitlements of workers who are eligible under the old program remain unchanged.

The reform of the severance pay scheme had been a controversial topic of discussion for some time. Trade unions wanted an extension of entitlement to voluntary separations and seasonal employment. The general view was that the old severance pay program hurt labor mobility. The goal of the government was to transform severance pay into an occupational pension scheme that would be the second pillar (in European and World Bank definitions) of a multipillar pension scheme.

Under the new scheme, which started on January 1, 2003, coverage and entitlement are substantially increased, as enrollment starts with the first day of employment. The scheme also applies to temporary workers and is not dependent on the form of contract termination. Employers have to contribute 1.5377 percent of payroll into a fund specified by an agreement between employer and worker council, and licensed by a financial market authority that handles the administration and asset management. The maximum charge by an administrator is 3.5 percent of the yearly contribution revenue.

If a worker with tenure exceeding three years is dismissed, he or she can choose between a lump-sum payment of the accumulated amount or continued saving toward a future pension. In the case of a voluntary quit or job tenure less than three years, no lump-sum payments are made, but the acquired claim remains and can be transferred to the fund of the new employer. This differential treatment by type of separation (dismissal or quit) and length of tenure has a social benefit objective: It provides potential income support for the dismissed with long tenure, but it keeps money for future retirement for voluntary leavers and the short-term employed.

The second-pillar pension or unemployment insurance benefit dimension is also visible in the benefit payout option. If the money is withdrawn as a lump-sum payment, the low tax rate of 6 percent for this type of employer-sponsored benefit is applied. However, if the benefit is disbursed in monthly installments (including annuities bought at retirement), no tax is levied.

Simulations based on individual administrative records for the period 1984–2001 suggest that the new rules are less generous and that the contribution rate may be too low to generate significant benefits (Koman, Schuh, and Weber 2005). Experience since reform also suggests that frequent withdrawals of funds after job termination substantially reduce potential funds for retirement income (Hofer, Schuh, and Walch 2011). This phenomenon has been accentuated (or perhaps motivated) by the low level of remuneration achieved by the funds, which some claim is linked to the capital guarantees the funds have to provide. Econometric investigations suggest that the new scheme has had little effect on job mobility or, expressed differently, the old scheme may have had little detrimental effect.

Overall, the performance of the new scheme has been modest. This may be due to design issues such as withdrawal rules, the capital guarantee, and the low contribution rate but may also reflect limited improvements in incentives over the previous scheme. Discussion about further reform has been sidetracked by the recent financial crisis.

Italian Reforms of 2004 and 2007

The Italian severance pay system has a number of particularities; in fact, some claim that severance pay as conventionally understood does not exist in Italy (for example, Garibaldi and Pacelli 2004). Italy's two schemes do not fall squarely into the severance pay category as it is known in other countries. The first scheme (*tutela obbligatoria*) provides dismissal compensation for unfair termination and distinguishes between firms with 15 or fewer employees and those with 16 or more. If a court rules that a worker has been unfairly dismissed, smaller firms have to pay 2.5 to 6.0 months' wages as compensation. Larger firms have to reinstate the employee, or the employee may elect to receive 15 months' wages instead. The economic interpretation of severance pay emerges, as courts reportedly often rule in favor of the employee.

The second scheme is end-of-service pay (*trattamento di fine rapporto*, TFR), available upon separation from the firm. However, if the worker has at least eight years of tenure or the employer agrees, this pay can be used earlier for health-related expenditures, to buy a house, or for specific periods of unpaid leave. For each year of service, the employer contributes 1/13.5 of the employee's gross yearly wage to an individual TFR account. The account is revalued annually by a factor of 1.5 percent fixed plus 75 percent of the Consumer Price Index inflation from the previous year. In effect, the employee provides a loan to the firm until separation; however, he or she can use this money for selective events before separation. Public policy changes over the past decade have been geared toward strengthening the retirement component with pension reforms that will reduce benefit levels under the public scheme in the background. To this end, in 2004 the government gave workers the option of enrolling in a supplementary pension scheme in return for giving up their TFR; both new labor market entrants and older workers were encouraged to enroll. The choice of the new system cannot be reversed, but workers who stay with the old system can reconsider at any time. To support such a choice and strengthen supplementary pensions, the 2004 law included a number of radical innovations (Cesari, Grande, and Panetta 2008): making participation the default option for severance pay; favorable taxation of benefits whether paid as a lump sum or an annuity; and changes in contributions, benefits, advances, redemption, and portability. By 2007, the Italian government had decided that companies with 50 or more employees must shift all future severance pay contributions to the government, which would pay the benefits directly, regardless of which system the employee chose (Corsini, Pacini, and Spataro 2010).

So far, fiscal and other incentives have had limited effects. By the end of 2008, only 26 percent of eligible workers had signed up for the supplementary pension scheme. The explanations for the low response range from temporary effects of the financial crisis to systemic problems, including the credibility of supplementary schemes and workers' liquidity preferences. A number of economists are worried about the liquidity and broader economic effects for small and medium-sized enterprises that are losing access to cheap internal financing (Calcagno, Kraeussl, and Monticone 2007).

Korean Reform of 2005

The Korean severance pay reform of 2005 initiated a voluntary conversion of an end-of-service pay scheme into an occupational pension system with the objective of replacing an unfunded scheme that pays lump-sum benefits with a funded system that provides an annuity after retirement (Yun and Hur 2011). The original severance pay scheme, introduced in 1953 and made mandatory in 1961, aimed to provide income support for both the unemployed and retirees at a time when neither an unemployment benefit nor a pension system existed. A mandated defined benefit pension plan was introduced in 1988 and an unemployment insurance system in 1995. The generosity of the pension scheme was reduced after the financial crisis of 1997–98, when it became clear that, despite increasing reserves, the system would not be sustainable because of incomplete system maturation. The first old-age pension benefits were paid in 2008.

With the 2005 reform, employees and employers could either continue their severance pay scheme by mutual consent or start a corporate pension system (defined contribution or defined benefit). Under the corporate pension system, employees forgo the option of withdrawing benefits before separation (as allowed under severance pay schemes) except for purchase of housing or long-term care. Furthermore, the rate of return depends on the performance of the financial institutions with which the pension scheme is established (for example, asset management companies, insurance companies, or banks); under the severance pay scheme, the implicit rate of return is individual wage growth.

The take-up rate for the new scheme has been disappointingly low. As of November 2010, only about 2.0 million out of 7.7 million eligible workers (26 percent) had joined the corporate pension scheme. To motivate the conversion to corporate pensions, the government reformed the corporate tax act at the beginning of 2011, limiting the tax deductibility of the employer's contributions to external funding. Previously, employers had enjoyed tax privileges when they reserved for severance pay commitments with book reserves.

The reforms in Chile, Austria, Italy, and Korea have a number of commonalities:

- All four have unemployment schemes that provide income support for the dismissed and comprehensive pension schemes whose generosity is scheduled to decline. This reduces the need for severance pay as a consumption-smoothing device for the unemployed while offering the opportunity to use the resources to strengthen the supplementary pension pillar. This factor was considered in the reforms.

- A person's willingness to forgo access to liquidity during his or her working life is seemingly limited, as inferred by the limited rollover in Austria and the low rate of funded scheme selection in Italy and Korea. This liquidity preference is likely to be influenced by the low rates of return offered by the funded schemes, which may reflect the recent financial crisis, the status of the country's financial market development, and the continued dominance by the banking system.

- Labor market considerations played a limited role in the reforms, and the effects on the labor market have been small (Austria) or nonexistent (Italy). Labor market considerations seem to have played no role in the Korean reform.

An important factor in severance pay reform is the political economy. Reducing job protection for formal sector workers is politically difficult, to say the least, and often meets with stiff resistance because it increases the prospects for layoffs and dismissals from previously protected jobs. However, many countries (for example, the transition countries of Central and Eastern Europe) have taken this difficult step. The introduction of well-designed, cost-effective active and passive labor market programs that provide more efficient protection to workers in the long run (in lieu of protecting jobs) and that help allay the short-term political costs of reforms has proved instrumental in achieving this policy shift.[9] But the necessary and sufficient ingredients for such change are far from well known. For example, despite the continuous efforts of employers, Sri Lanka's severance pay system (one of the most restrictive in the world) has not reduced its generosity and procedural complexity; in fact, several changes in the past decade have, if anything, increased its generosity (see box 2.4).

The Motivation behind Severance Pay: Reviewing Hypotheses and Evidence

The purpose of this section is to examine severance pay programs as part of a broader institutional framework, thereby stimulating further research. The section begins with hypotheses about the economic rationale for severance pay and reports some simple cross-country regressions using the authors' data inventory. As the data do not allow for testing the efficiency effects of severance pay, the section closes with a brief and selective review of the empirical literature.

ECONOMIC RATIONALE FOR SEVERANCE PAY

The few papers about the origins of severance pay and the limited theoretical and empirical literature on this topic suggest three main hypotheses about the economic rationale for severance payments. First, severance payments are a primitive form of social benefits that

---

BOX 2.4 **Political Economy Complexities in Reforming Severance Pay Programs**

Sri Lanka's strict severance pay regulations (embodied in the Termination of Employment of Workmen Act No. 45 of 1971) were enacted at a time when Sri Lanka was pursuing inward-looking economic policies, characterized by an import-substitution industrialization policy, stringent exchange controls, price controls on many commodities, and nationalization of a wide range of establishments. TEWA was intended to arrest the rising rate of unemployment that resulted from these policies, as many industries could not operate in the restrictive environment and had to retrench. During the second reading of the bill in the legislature, the minister of labor explained that "the intention in creating this law is not to put employers into difficulty, but solely to prevent the loss of employment of workers for unreasonable or frivolous reasons. Where employers face justifiable difficulties—for example, the shortage of raw materials—and need to terminate the services of workers, the Commissioner of Labour has an opportunity to intervene and, after discussion with other departments and ministries, take some remedial action relevant to both employer and workers to prevent the reduction in the strength of the organization or of the workforce."

The intention of TEWA was clearly to prevent or discourage mass retrenchment rather than individual terminations. However, the statute as enacted did not carry such a limitation, and terminations other than those intended have been covered under TEWA. The fact that the generosity at the introduction was increased above the intention of the government and the persistent generosity of the program despite several changes in the act demonstrates the political complexities of regulations that benefit only the minority of workers (about two-thirds of Sri Lanka's workforce labors in the informal sector) given the presence of strong, well-organized trade unions.

SOURCE: Ranaraja 2005.

---

predate or complement existing benefits for unemployment and retirement. Second, severance payments are designed to be an efficiency-enhancing human resource instrument, either as an ad hoc support to large-scale enterprise restructuring or as a more permanent device to tighten bonds between workers and firms to reduce the transaction costs and loss of firm-specific knowledge and skills owing to turnover. Third, while severance payments may have these income protection or efficiency objectives, they also function as a job protection instrument, a function that has gained importance and a life of its own.

The three hypotheses are not mutually exclusive and may apply concurrently. In some instances, the severance pay mandate is focused on one objective. In other instances, programs may cater to multiple objectives. Only in-depth case studies and more advanced empirical studies are likely to disentangle these multiple motives. It is hoped that these preliminary econometric efforts will provide a motivation for further efforts.

Severance Pay as a Social Benefit Program

As described above, severance pay came into existence in the absence of other forms of social safety nets as an employer-sponsored benefit program providing compensation for unfair dismissals. At the very beginning, employers simply paid to compensate workers for not respecting the customary advance dismissal notice. Later, and during periods of large-scale restructuring, additional cash compensation was added to provide an employer-financed safety net, as public systems were minimal or nonexistent. In some cases (for example, the United Kingdom), voluntary severance benefits have been provided to top up low, flat-rate unemployment insurance/assistance benefits. In many countries, mandated or quasi-mandated severance payments were the precursors of public old-age retirement provisions—they were paid to individuals at a certain advanced age and were independent of the employer's actions.

The obvious link between severance pay and social benefits emerges in policy discussions, theoretical models, and empirical analyses. At the policy level, the provision of severance pay was "subject to this obligation coming to an end on the promulgation of legislation concerning social insurance (Costa Rica) or to the replacement of compensation by benefits from a welfare fund (Dominican Republic, Egypt, Lebanon, Syria)" (Herz 1954, 319). Thus, severance pay can be replaced by social benefit programs that cover similar risks; that is, unemployment and old age. If no substitution takes place (severance payments are not reduced or phased out once unemployment and old-age benefits are introduced), one must look at other explanations, including political power exerted by trade unions or differences in the instruments as they correspond to different risks or needs. For example, Pissarides (2001) shows that the introduction of severance payments may provide insurance against income risk when moral hazard or other frictions prevent unemployment insurance from providing sufficient coverage. In such circumstances, severance pay could provide perfect insurance against the uncertainty of job protection.

Severance Pay as a Human Resource Instrument

A second set of explanations for the existence of severance payments sees them as instruments for managing human resources in an enterprise. In a short-term perspective, severance pay responds to the need for enterprise restructuring by providing compensation that makes mass dismissals socially and politically more palatable. According to the historic evidence, such considerations have been clearly present at the time of major technological changes from the late nineteenth century to today. Under such circumstances, severance pay programs are motivated by human resource management concerns, such as preserving the morale of remaining workers and avoiding potential damage caused by departing workers if they are not appropriately compensated.

Under the human resource rationale, severance pay becomes an efficiency-enhancing wage instrument, keeping workers in the firm and nurturing productive worker relationships; for example, by avoiding the loss of firm-specific knowledge and skills and the transaction costs associated with frequent hiring (Lazear 1990). By withholding part of the wage from the employee until he or she retires (or is fired), enterprises try to ensure that individuals with valuable firm-specific knowledge and skills are less likely to quit or sell their transferable human capital to a competing firm. In a similar vein, severance pay may provide incentives for employees to invest in firm-specific human capital or contribute more in the workplace. In particular, longer lasting employment is conducive to instilling trust, cooperation, and loyalty between the employer and the workers. It also encourages team spirit among workers, which may contribute to higher productive efficiency and reduce the resistance of workers to the introduction of new technologies (OECD 1999).

Suedekum and Ruehmann (2003) demonstrate that two opposing forces may be at work: on the one hand, the incentive effect of job protection; on the other hand, the lethargy effect, because being fired does not contain the same strong penalty (unless those dismissed for cause are ineligible for benefits). Alvarez and Veracierto (2001) show in a model with contractual and reallocation frictions that the introduction of severance payments may result in a Pareto improvement.

Severance Pay as an Employment Protection Device

While the first two rationales for severance pay suggest positive returns, they are not well researched or empirically validated. In contrast, the notion of severance pay as job protection carries a negative connotation with economists but is a worthy objective to many others. The theoretical impact of employment protection on labor market outcomes and efficiency is ambiguous, and this ambiguity is echoed in the often puzzling empirical results (see Addison and Teixeira 2003 and 2005; Boeri 1999).

Severance pay as employment protection (not income protection) arises from the additional costs of separation that mandated severance brings to job separations. Firing costs emerge from the mandated benefits, the permitted causes (say, on personal and economic grounds), and ruling by the courts on what is a fair dismissal.

Under such a rationale, mandated termination (or end-of-service) payments that are due regardless of the reason for separation and thus do not contribute to job protection should not be considered under the umbrella of severance pay. Such programs are retained earnings that belong to the employee and are thus a credit from the employee to the enterprise. However, Garibaldi and Pacelli (2004) use an Italian case and a small partial equilibrium dynamic model to show that some of the labor market effects of such termination payments are fully comparable with those of a firing tax or severance pay with wage rigidity.

How are these three postulated economic rationales for severance pay borne out by empirical research? The following sections provide econometric results based on basic, but widely accepted, specifications and review the empirical findings in the literature. The econometric investigation focuses primarily on the first hypothesis—severance pay as a social benefit—by examining factors behind the incidence and generosity of the severance pay. The human resource rationale is more likely to emerge from collective and voluntary provisions, for which information is scarce. The job protection rationale has been extensively researched; a brief summary of the findings is presented.

DETERMINANTS OF THE INCIDENCE AND GENEROSITY OF SEVERANCE PAY

The empirical strategy is as follows. The determinants of the incidence and generosity of existing severance pay programs are identified and checked to see to what extent they are consistent with the three economic rationales for severance pay. Among the explanatory variables used are logarithm of per capita income, generosity of unemployment benefits and pensions, length of the notice period, and union density. Generosity is measured according to the Severance Pay Generosity Index (figure 2.6), which shows weeks of pay per year of service for an average of 1, 5, and 10 years of tenure.

The rationale for including the per capita income variable is as follows. According to the development theory (see Botero and others 2004), rich countries impose more regulations (including the regulation of job protection) than poor countries, because in rich countries the benefits of such regulations (fulfillment of social objectives, for example) exceed the costs. In contrast, poor countries simply cannot afford the administrative costs or the distortions associated with such regulations. Hence, there should be a positive correlation between the level of development and the incidence and generosity of severance pay. An important modification of this link arises when the emergence of social and private insurance (which is itself associated with the level of development) works against the likelihood and generosity of formal severance pay programs. This reasoning suggests an inverse U-shaped relationship between per capita income and both the incidence and generosity of formal severance pay programs. The explanation also supports, or is at least consistent with, the social benefit and job protection hypotheses about severance pay.

In theory, an ideal plot with the severance pay generosity on the y-axis and the (log) per capita GDP on the x-axis would show an upward slope for countries in the lower-income group, slowly flatten for countries in the middle-income category, and turn into a downward slope for high-income countries.

The empirical evidence is broadly but not fully consistent with this assumption, with one exception. Bivariate associations between the Severance Pay Generosity Index and log (per capita GDP), shown by trend lines for each income group, suggest a positive association for both low- and upper-middle-income countries, and a negative association for lower-middle- and high-income countries. Figure 2.9 presents the data and estimations with (panel a) and without (panel b) countries that have zero generosity values (that is, nonmandated countries). The robust linear regression line for all countries has a negative slope for both data sets, with a steeper and significant descent for the full data set.[10] The negative slope is also consistent with figure 2.6. Overall, data and estimations give some support to a mild inverse U-shaped relationship that is evident for the low- and high-income countries, and equivocal for the middle-income countries. Panels c and d of figure 2.9 present an estimation based on a polynomial structure of the per capita GDP variable (including all countries, not separately by income groupings).

Before testing the relationship of severance pay to other social benefits, notice period, and union density, the relationship of these other social policy and labor market instruments to the income level of the countries is explored, again using per capita GDP (in logs). Figures 2.10–2.12 present these relationships. For the generosity index of unemployment benefits, the available replacement rates for the average income worker are used; for pension benefit generosity, the prospective replacement rate of the average income worker as calculated by the OECD APEX (Analysis of Pension Entitlements across Countries) model is used. Figures 2.10 and 2.11 have two panels each: panel a, which includes zero generosity when benefit programs do not exist, and panel b, with positive benefit levels only. The notice period (figure 2.12) is the average number of weeks for workers with 1, 5, and 10 years of service from the World Bank Doing Business 2011 database.

Figures 2.10 and 2.11 signal contrasting relationships of generosity and income level, depending on the inclusion or exclusion of zero values (that is, the absence of a mandated program). The contrasts differ between unemployment and pension benefits. Figure 2.10 plots the relationship between the generosity of unemployment benefit systems and income level with and without zero values for unemployment benefit generosity for countries that provide the information. Figure 2.10, panel a suggests a significant positive relationship

FIGURE 2.9 **Generosity of Severance Pay and per Capita GDP**

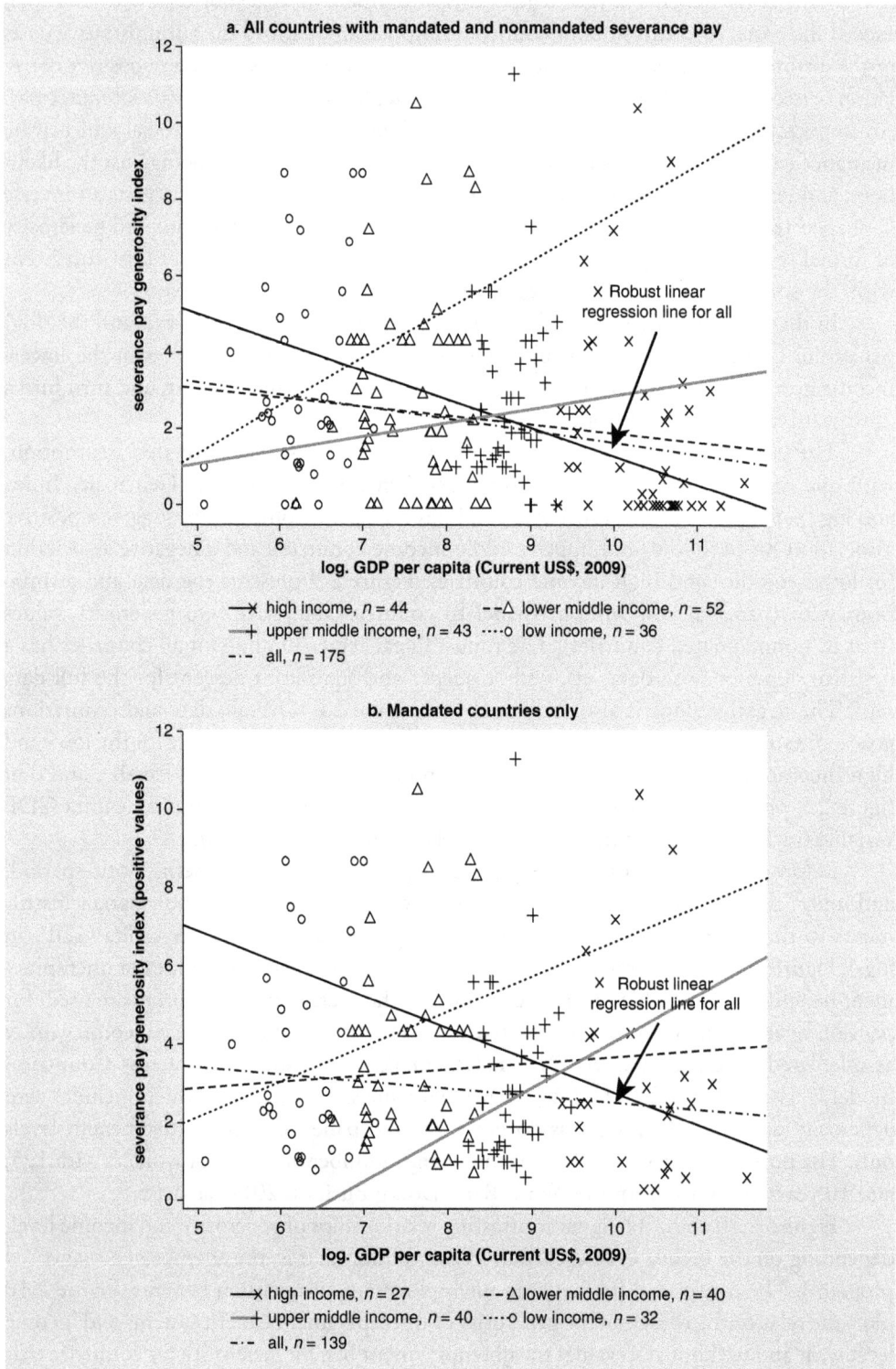

a. All countries with mandated and nonmandated severance pay

severance pay generosity index

X Robust linear regression line for all

log. GDP per capita (Current US$, 2009)

—×— high income, $n = 44$ – –△ lower middle income, $n = 52$
—+— upper middle income, $n = 43$ ····o low income, $n = 36$
–·– all, $n = 175$

b. Mandated countries only

severance pay generosity index (positive values)

X Robust linear regression line for all

log. GDP per capita (Current US$, 2009)

——× high income, $n = 27$ – –△ lower middle income, $n = 40$
——+ upper middle income, $n = 40$ ····o low income, $n = 32$
–·– all, $n = 139$

(continued)

FIGURE 2.9 **(continued)**

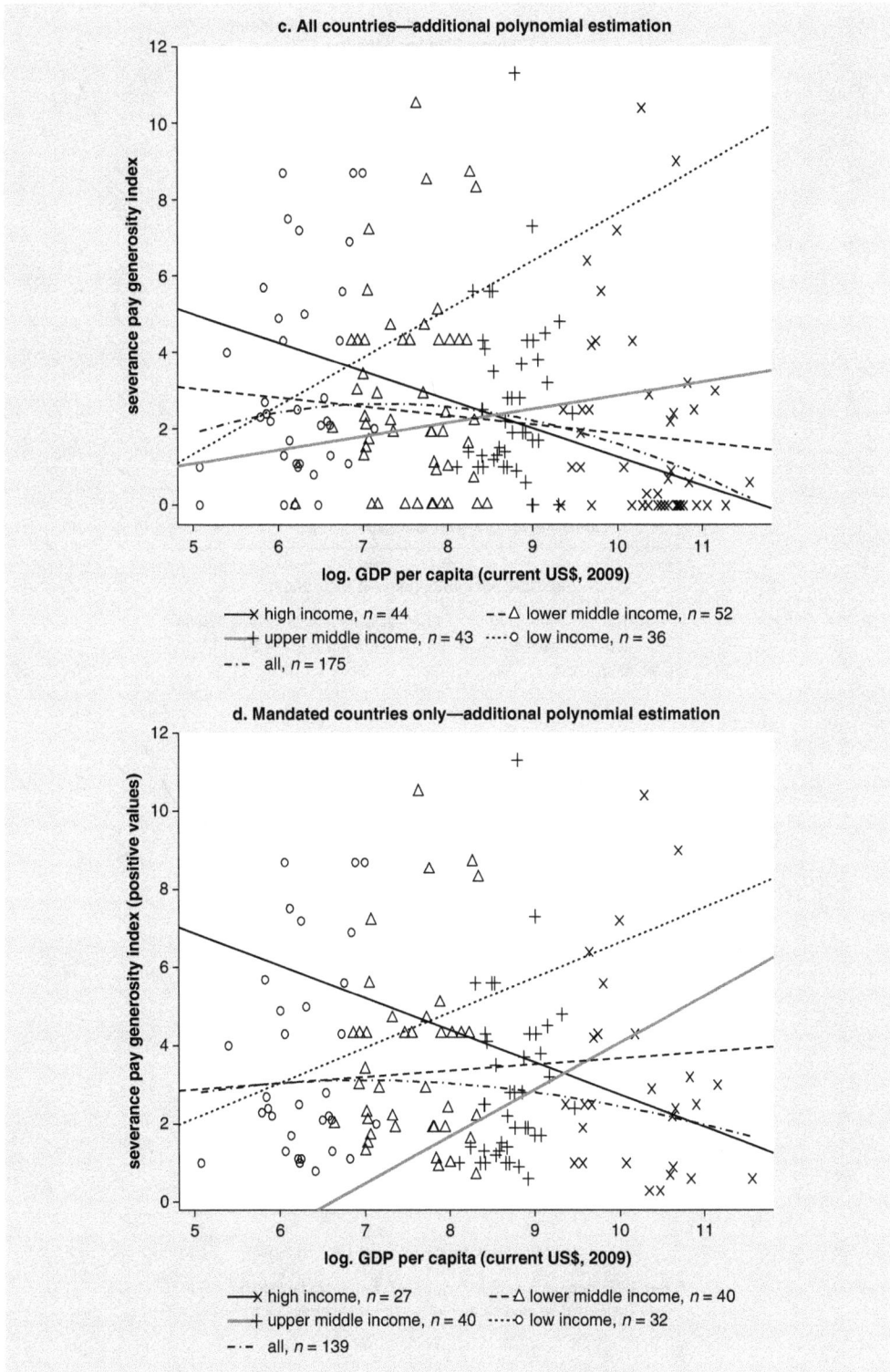

c. All countries—additional polynomial estimation

→× high income, *n* = 44   --△ lower middle income, *n* = 52
→+ upper middle income, *n* = 43   ····○ low income, *n* = 36
–·– all, *n* = 175

d. Mandated countries only—additional polynomial estimation

→× high income, *n* = 27   --△ lower middle income, *n* = 40
→+ upper middle income, *n* = 40   ····○ low income, *n* = 32
–·– all, *n* = 139

SOURCE: Authors' computations based on data presented in annex B.

FIGURE 2.10 **Unemployment Benefit Generosity and per Capita GDP**

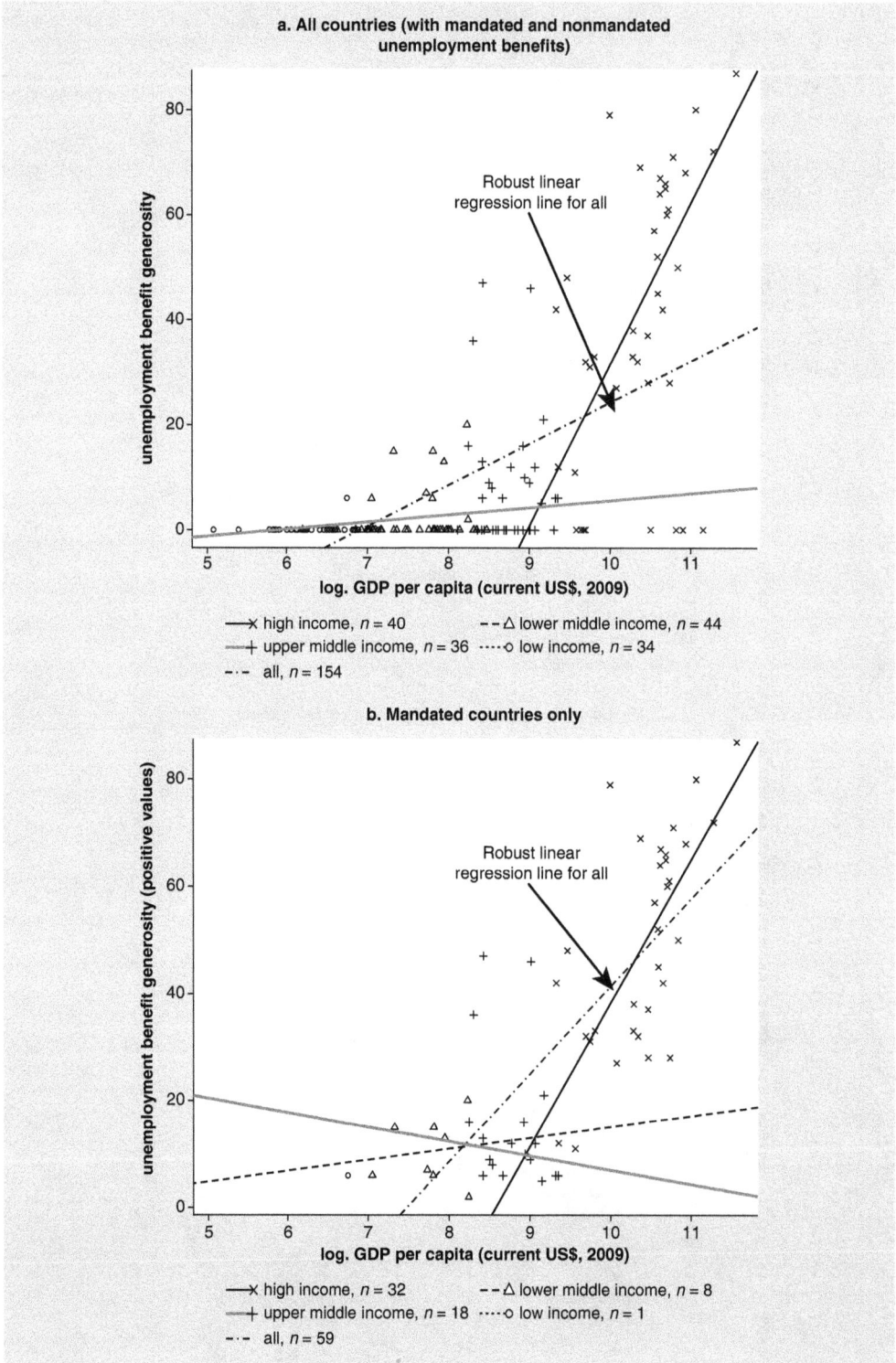

a. All countries (with mandated and nonmandated unemployment benefits)

Robust linear regression line for all

—×high income, *n* = 40   − −△ lower middle income, *n* = 44
—+upper middle income, *n* = 36   ····◇ low income, *n* = 34
−··− all, *n* = 154

b. Mandated countries only

Robust linear regression line for all

—×high income, *n* = 32   − −△ lower middle income, *n* = 8
—+upper middle income, *n* = 18   ····◇ low income, *n* = 1
−··− all, *n* = 59

SOURCE: Authors' computations based on data presented in annex B.

FIGURE 2.11 **Pension Benefit Generosity and per Capita GDP**

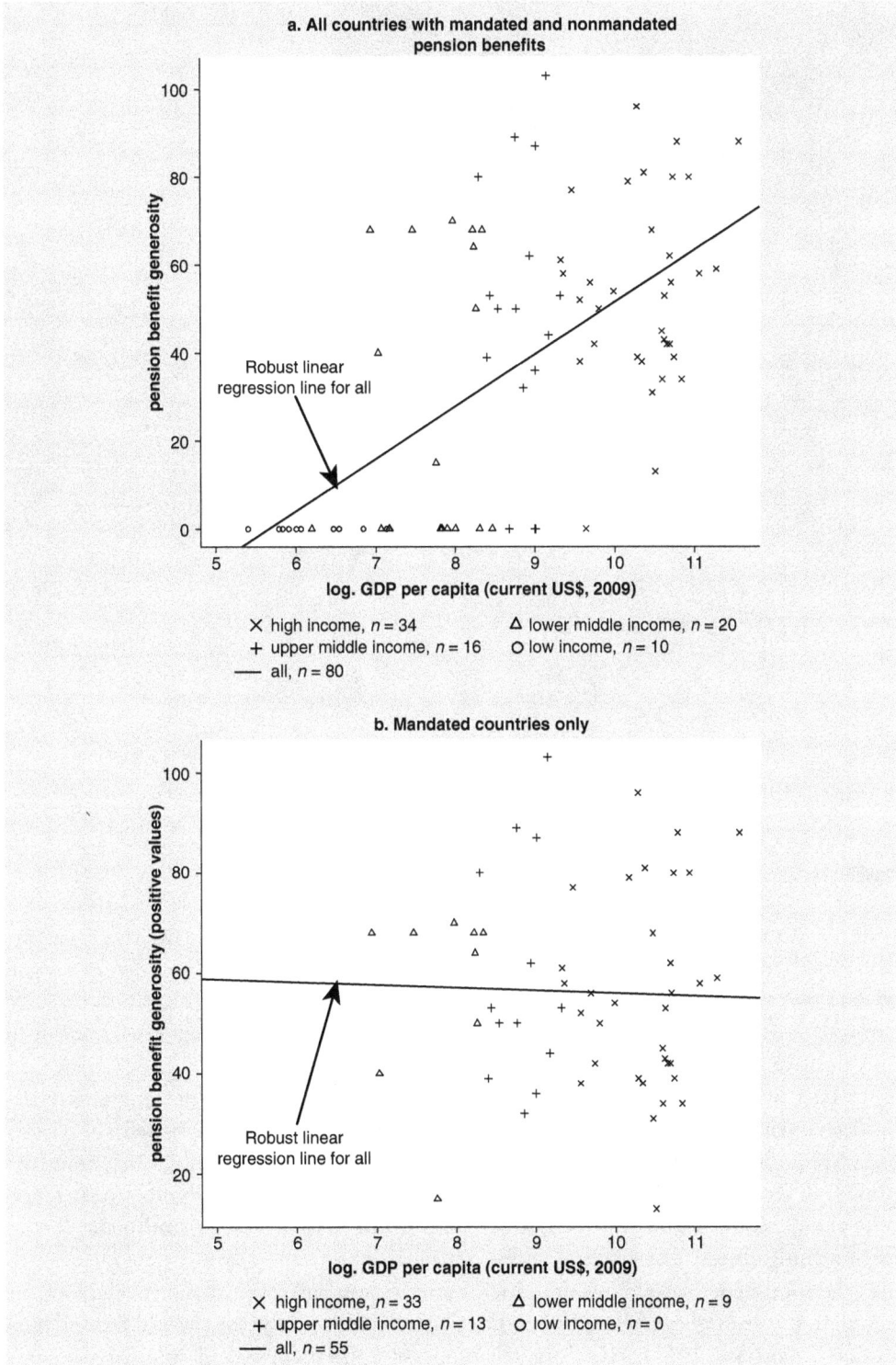

a. All countries with mandated and nonmandated pension benefits

Robust linear
regression line for all

log. GDP per capita (current US$, 2009)

pension benefit generosity

X high income, n = 34   Δ lower middle income, n = 20
+ upper middle income, n = 16   O low income, n = 10
— all, n = 80

b. Mandated countries only

Robust linear
regression line for all

pension benefit generosity (positive values)

log. GDP per capita (current US$, 2009)

X high income, n = 33   Δ lower middle income, n = 9
+ upper middle income, n = 13   O low income, n = 0
— all, n = 55

SOURCE: Authors' computations based on data presented in annex B.

FIGURE 2.12 **Notice Period (in Weeks) and per Capita GDP**

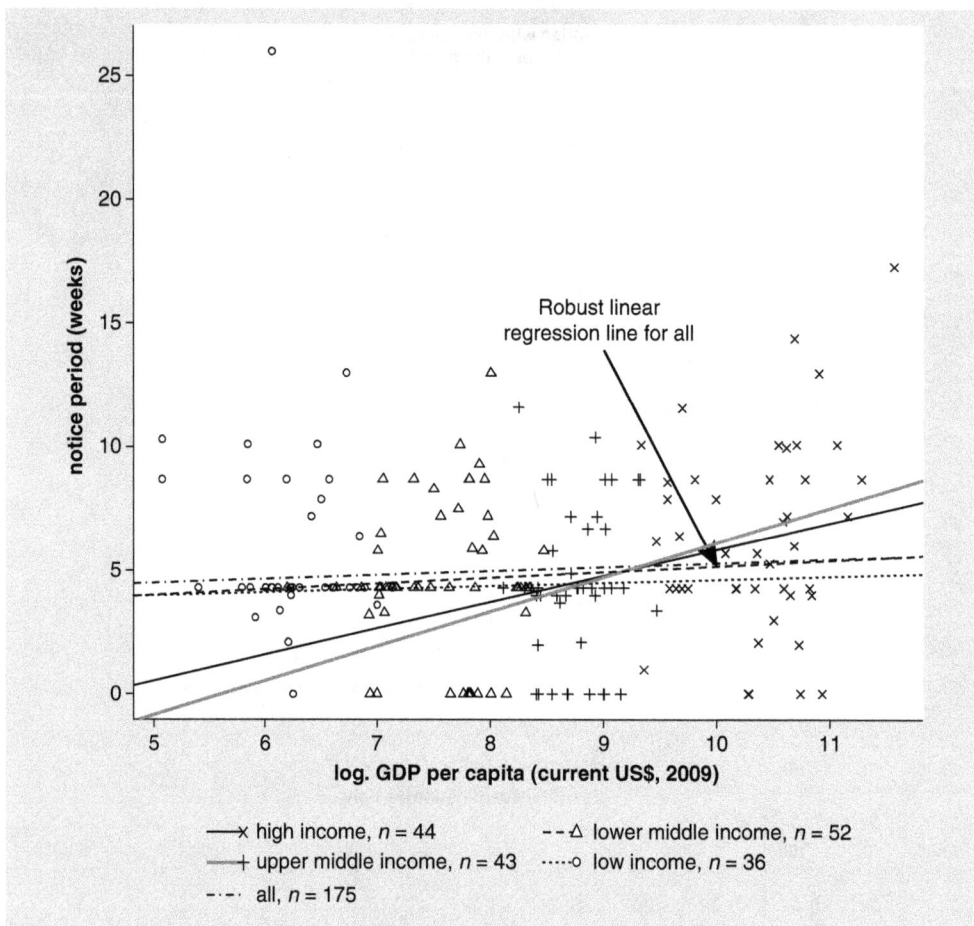

SOURCE: Authors' computations based on data presented in annex B.

with the income level of countries if the zero values are included. If only positive values are considered, this relationship becomes even stronger (figure 2.10, panel b) when looking at all data points or only the high-income group. The following applies to pension benefits: strongly positive relationship if zero values are included; mildly negative relationship if only positive generosity values are considered.

This interpretation is not straightforward, but it suggests important differences between unemployment and pension benefit generosity. Unemployment benefits are clearly less widespread, and zero generosity reaches into higher income countries. Once countries provide unemployment benefits, there is a significant positive relationship between generosity and the country's income level, which may be linked to decreasing informality, better job matching objectives, or redistributive considerations.

Pension benefit programs are much more widespread, even if the coverage of the population is strongly correlated with the country's income level (see World Bank Doing Business database 2011).[11] Only a few upper-middle-income and one high-income country (Equatorial Guinea) have no benefit scheme, giving rise to a positive slope when all countries for which information is available are considered (figure 2.11, panel a). When only positive generosity values are considered (figure 2.11, panel b), there is a mildly negative yet statistically insignificant relationship with income level, which may be related to the level of financial market development and the capacity to replace mandated (and often unfunded) pension schemes with voluntary and funded provisions as income level increases.

The notice period for dismissals exhibits a positive slope for high- and upper-middle-income groups (figure 2.12). For low- and lower-middle-income groups, as well as for the overall robust estimation, the slope is close to zero, implying no relationship between income and notice period in these groups. This is somewhat surprising, as lower-income countries are often thought to have more rigid employment protection laws. The positive relationship with the income level for higher income economies makes the notice period consistent with efficiency and redistributive considerations.

To explore the social benefit hypothesis more directly, the effect of the generosity of other cash benefit systems (in particular, unemployment benefits and pensions) on the generosity of severance pay is examined. Assuming that other cash benefit systems are substitutes for severance pay, the introduction of unemployment insurance benefits or an increase in their generosity may lead to a reduction in severance pay benefits, thus yielding a negative association between the generosity of the two benefit systems. (A similar assumption is made for pensions.) Without historic data, it is not possible to investigate how the introduction of unemployment benefit systems has affected the generosity of severance pay.

Figure 2.13 displays the interactions for the generosity index for severance pay and unemployment benefit systems. The regression lines for each income level suggest positive associations for the lower- and upper-middle-income groups and a negative association for the high-income group if all countries (including those with zero generosity) are included. The robust linear estimation across all countries exhibits a significant negative coefficient (figure 2.13, panel a). The coefficients for each income level are significant as well. If only positive values for benefit generosity are considered, the coefficient for high-income countries turns to zero while the overall relationship remains slightly negative. However, for all these models, only the intercept remains statistically significant.

The correlation between the generosity of severance pay and unemployment benefits is positive for low-income groups; with rising income level, the correlation becomes less positive. It ultimately turns significantly negative for high-income countries and for all countries when those with zero generosity are included. This result is due to zero mandated values in high-income economies, which all offer severance pay via collective agreements. Thus, if complementarity exists between the two benefits, the strength of this relationship is definitely decreasing with income level, and it is apparently turning into substitutability for higher income countries, which seems to imply a shift from mandated severance pay program to severance pay arrangements based on collective agreements.

A possible overall complementarity of severance pay and unemployment benefits is consistent with the results of Parsons (2005a, b, c). On the basis of both theoretical modeling and empirical analysis of the United States, Parsons found that severance pay and unemployment insurance are complements. Moreover, he noted that a study of private severance pay before and after the introduction of public unemployment benefits in the

FIGURE 2.13 **Generosity of Severance Pay versus Unemployment Benefit**

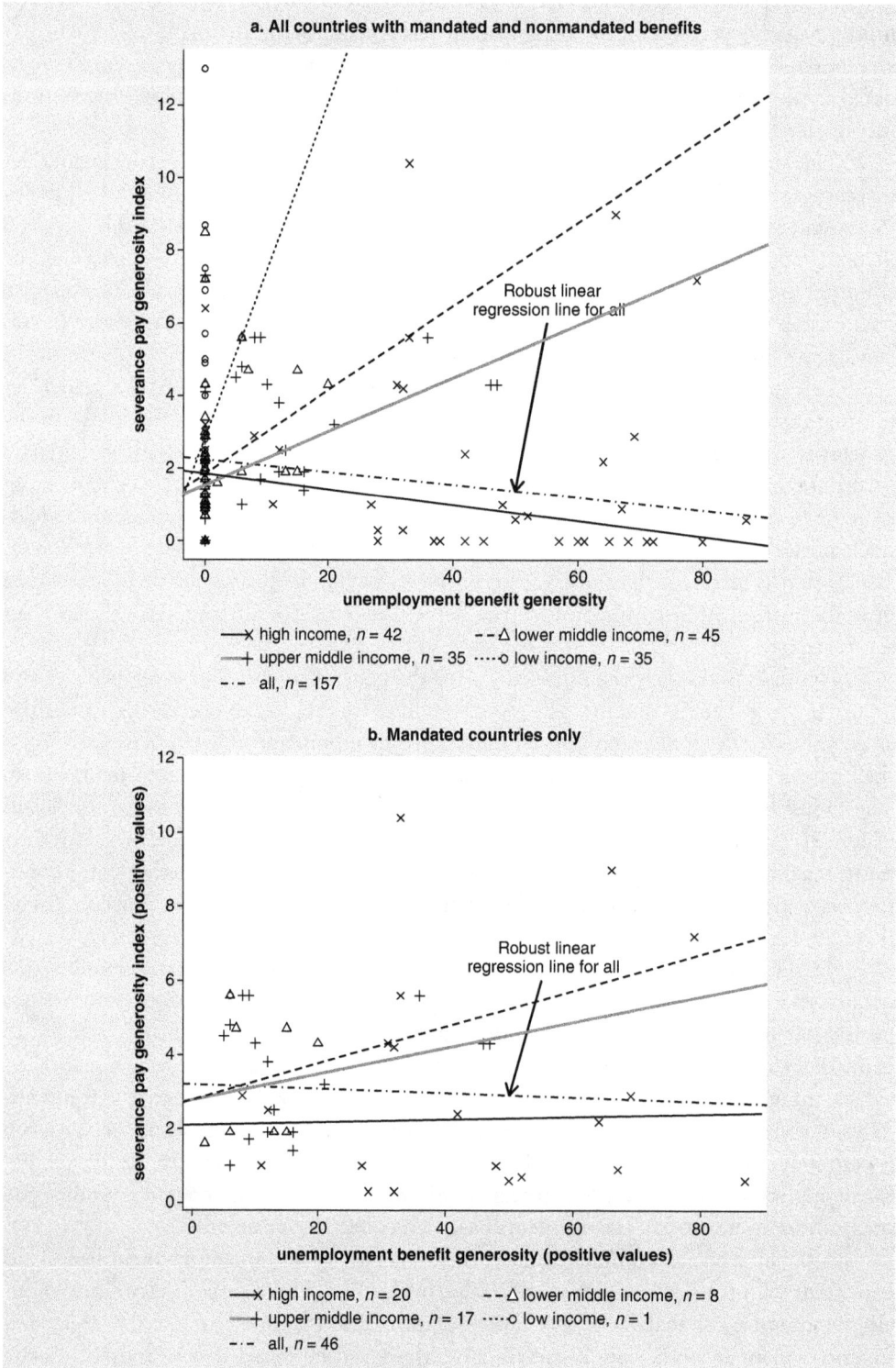

1930s found no evidence of crowding out of private severance by public unemployment insurance (Parsons 2005a).

Figure 2.14 suggests that the relationship between the generosity of severance pay and pension benefits is weakly positive for all considered country income groups except lower-middle-income countries, which have a small sample size. As with data for the generosity of unemployment benefits, replacement rates for the average income earner are used to measure the generosity of the pension benefit. The resulting broadly positive associations of severance pay and pension benefits are more in line with complementarity between social benefits and severance pay generosity across countries.

Figure 2.15 shows the association of severance pay generosity and notice period for all countries (panel a) and for those with positive values only (panel b). Again, there are differences between and within the samples. If all 181 countries are considered, the robust estimation signals a significant negative association and hence substitutability between severance pay generosity and notice period. For the subgroups, however, the graph and related estimates signal a change with income level: a high level of substitutability for low-income countries, mild complementarity for high-income countries, and mixed signals for middle-income countries. If only positive values (126 countries) are considered, the complementarity aspect dominates except for the high-income group, which shows signs of a mild substitutability. As in the previous cases of all values or positive values only, there are interesting signals of regime change in the presence and absence of benefit programs and regulations. This phenomenon requires further investigation.

The inclusion of union density among the explanatory variables allows a test of whether the influence of trade unions (proxied by union coverage) translates into more generous severance pay. A positive link between union density and severance pay would be consistent with both the social benefit and job protection hypotheses. However, bivariate associations between the Severance Pay Generosity Index and union density, shown by trend lines for each income group, suggest a negative association for low-, upper-middle-, and high-income countries, and a positive association for lower-middle-income countries if all countries are considered (figure 2.16, panel a). This would be largely in contrast to political power theory. However, if only positive generosity values are considered, a positive link emerges for all but the low-middle-income group. This may suggest that once a program is established, unions are able to exert a positive impact on generosity that is linked with union density.

The following are multivariate estimates of severance generosity, regressed on log of per capita income, generosity of unemployment and pension benefits, notice period, and union density.

$$\text{G-SP} = a + b \log (\text{pc-GDP}) + c\,\text{G-UB} + d\,\text{G-PB} + e\,\text{NP} + f\,\text{UD} + u$$

where
G-SP	generosity index of severance pay (weeks per year of service)
log (pc-GDP)	log of per capita GDP (2009, in US$)
G-UB	generosity of unemployment benefits (replacement rate for average worker)
G-PB	generosity of pension benefits (replacement rate for average worker)
NP	notice period (in weeks)
UD	union density (share of unionized labor in workforce)
u	residual

FIGURE 2.14 **Generosity of Severance Pay versus Pension Benefit Generosity**

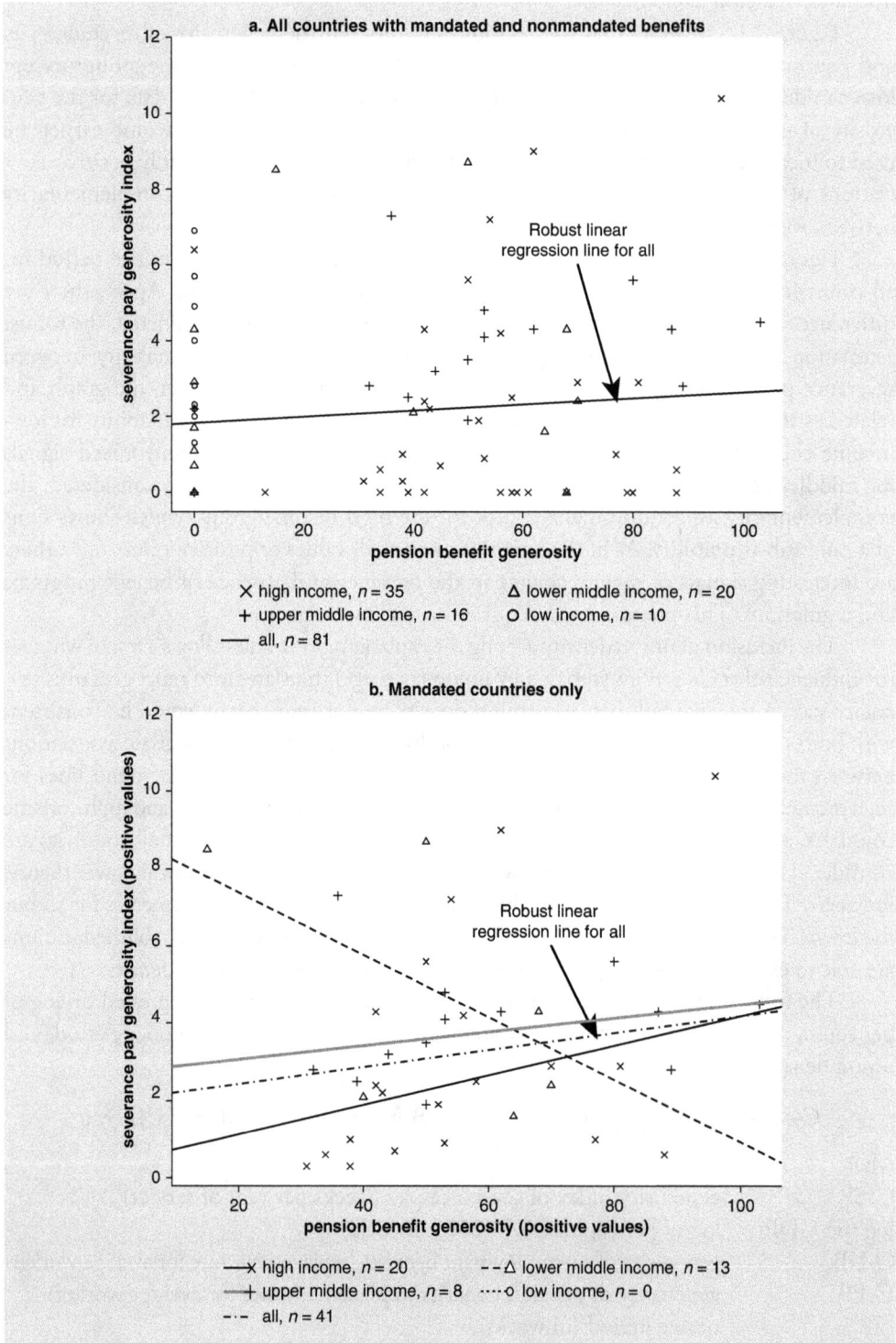

SOURCE: Authors' computations based on data presented in annex B.

FIGURE 2.15 **Severance Pay Generosity and Notice Period**

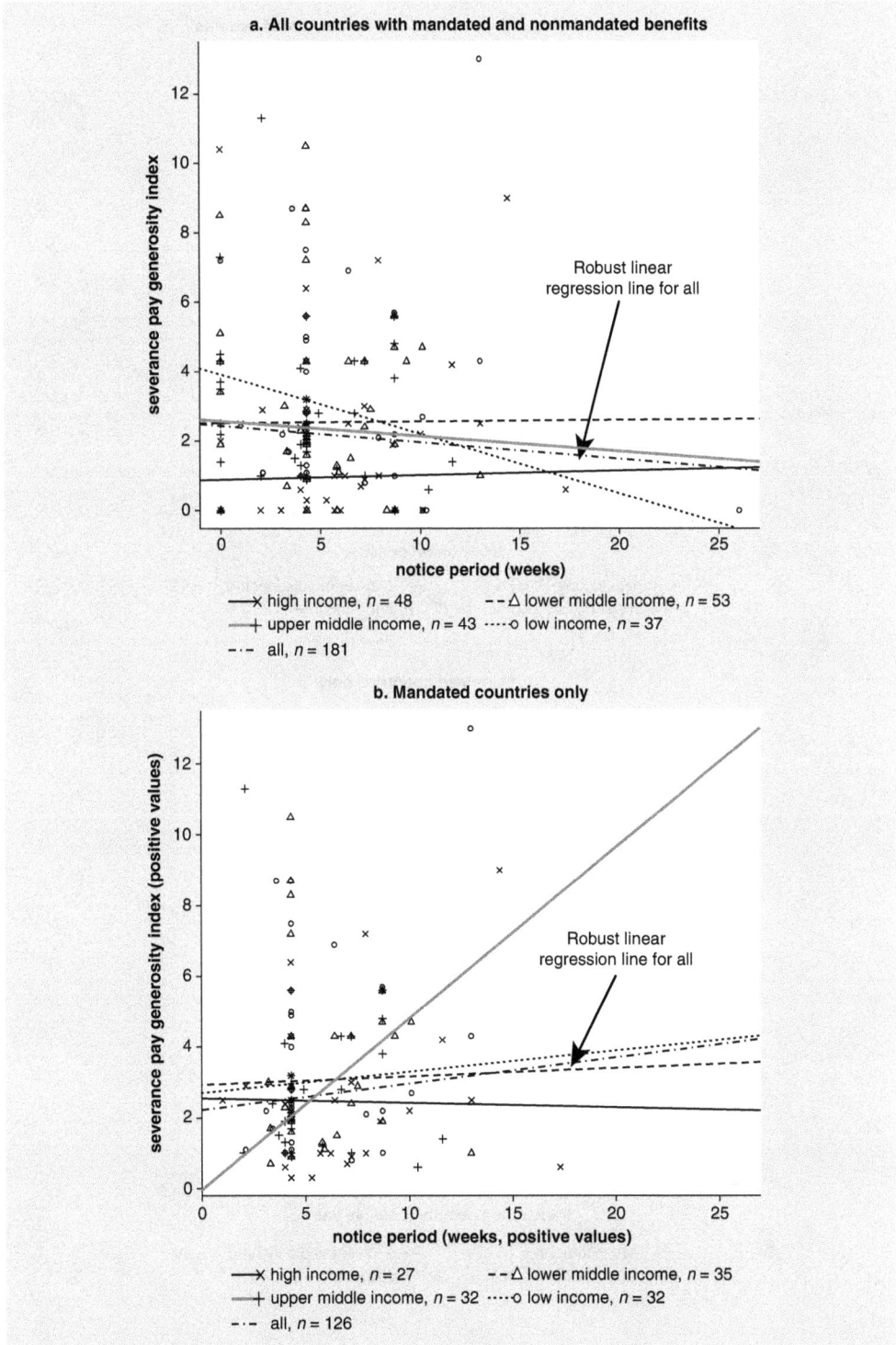

a. All countries with mandated and nonmandated benefits

y-axis: severance pay generosity index
x-axis: notice period (weeks)

Robust linear
regression line for all

—×— high income, *n* = 48   – –△ lower middle income, *n* = 53
—+— upper middle income, *n* = 43   ····o low income, *n* = 37
– ·– all, *n* = 181

b. Mandated countries only

y-axis: severance pay generosity index (positive values)
x-axis: notice period (weeks, positive values)

Robust linear
regression line for all

—×— high income, *n* = 27   – –△ lower middle income, *n* = 35
—+— upper middle income, *n* = 32   ····o low income, *n* = 32
– ·– all, *n* = 126

SOURCE: Authors' computations based on data presented in annex B.

FIGURE 2.16 **Severance Pay Generosity and Union Density**

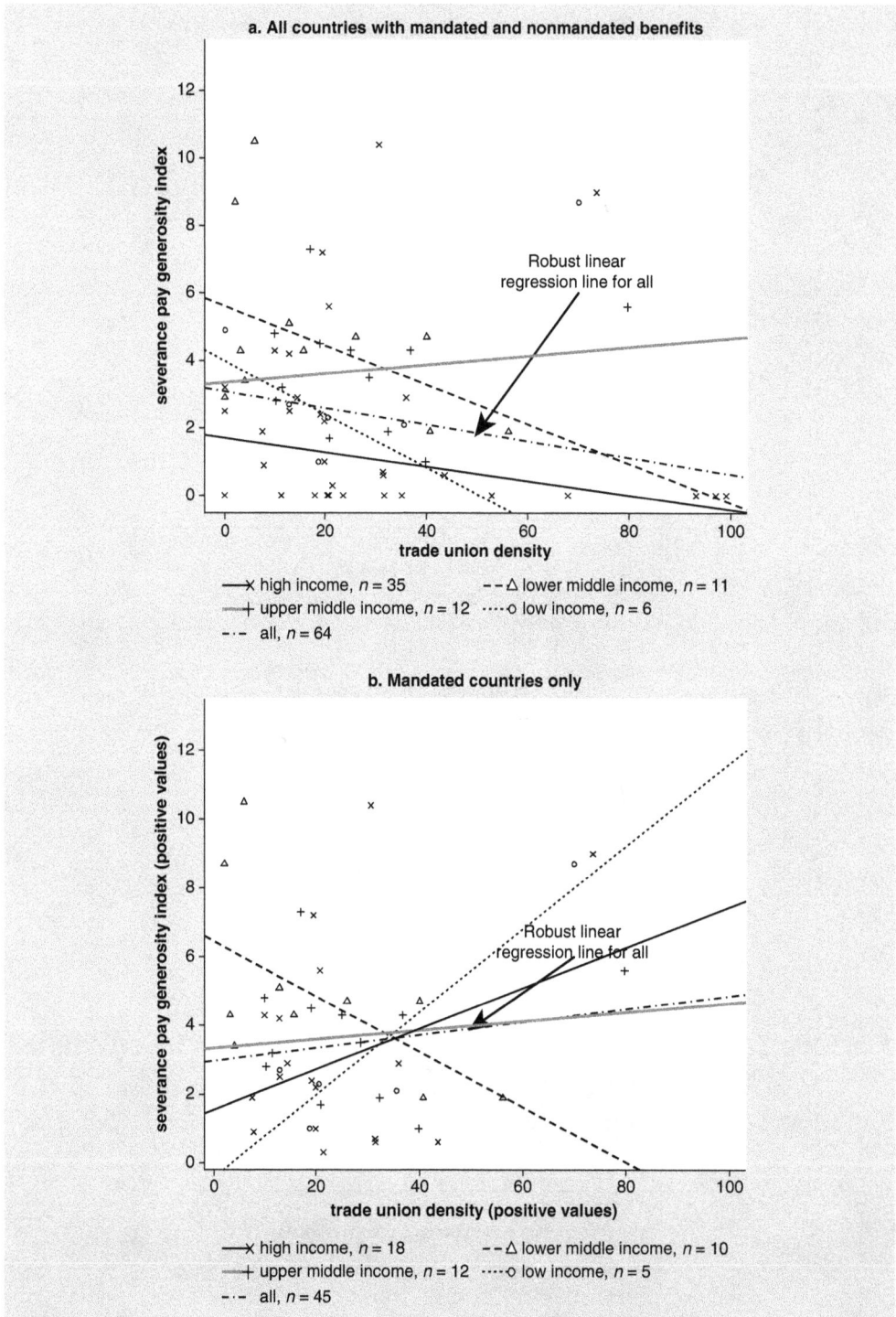

In an extended model, additional variables are added to try to assess whether benefit regimes (for example, unemployment insurance versus assistance, or pay as you go (PAYG) versus funded pensions), country income groupings, or regions exert significant influence.

Controlling for different explanatory variables at the same time should enhance confidence in the estimates. However, not all variables are available for all countries, which reduces the sample size as more variables are added.

The basic model for all values across separate and simultaneous estimations suggests the following results (see table 2.1):

- A consistently negative and significant impact of per capita GDP on severance pay generosity
- A consistently negative impact of unemployment benefit generosity that is only weakly significant in some models
- A consistently positive and mostly significant impact of pension benefit generosity
- An inconsistent and never significant impact of notice period
- A consistently negative but only sporadically significant impact of union density

Adding variables to the basic model does not typically change the sign of the coefficients but often renders them insignificant. The explanatory power is often, but not always, taken over by the income grouping as well as the regional dummies (results not shown). The significance is increased once robust estimation is undertaken. Other specifications and estimations (for example, using a probit approach or polynomial specification of the income term, with and without log) did not lead to improvements in the results. For details on the estimation, see annex C.

Applying the basic model to positive values reduces the number of observations to 19 and renders all coefficients except per capita income insignificant. The change in signs, however, is consistent with the observations in the figures above and a regime change between all generosity values and positive generosity values only. For example, an increase in union density is consistent with the conjectured increase in generosity of severance pay.

In sum, the following tentative results are suggested. They serve as an *amuse-gueule* for further and more detailed investigations and estimations:

- The figures in this chapter and the estimations across all models suggest a strongly negative and significant link between severance pay generosity and per capita income (or economic well-being of a country). A mild inverse U-shaped relation to income has limited statistical support. Furthermore, high-income countries have much less tendency to mandate severance pay, instead leaving it to contractual agreements at the sector or firm level.
- The results are broadly consistent with the social benefit view of severance pay and with substitutability with unemployment benefits. But the data suggest a changing function across the income level of countries, with stark complementarity for low-income countries that is gradually reduced until it turns toward substitutability for high-income countries.

TABLE 2.1 **Drivers of Generosity of Severance Pay: Results for Basic Model**

Model	1	2	3	4	5	6	7	8	9	10
Intercept	4.80*** (0.96)	4.36** (1.45)	2.24*** (0.25)	7.71*** (1.10)	1.83*** (0.47)	8.79*** (1.88)	3.09*** (0.42)	5.03*** (0.95)	2.43*** (0.34)	7.29** (2.13)
(Log) GDP per capita	−0.32** (0.11)	−0.28 (0.18)		−0.78*** (0.13)		−0.65** (0.20)		−0.31** (0.10)		−0.59* (0.26)
Unemployment benefit generosity		−0.003 (0.01)	−0.017* (0.01)							−0.03 (0.01)
Pension benefit generosity				0.03*** (0.01)	0.01 (0.01)					0.03*** (0.01)
Union density						−0.02 (0.01)	−0.03 (0.01)			−0.02* (0.01)
Notice period (weeks)								−0.05 (0.05)	−0.05 (0.05)	0.10 (0.06)
R-squared	0.10	0.11	0.07	0.40	0.02	0.41	0.12	0.11	0.01	0.69
Adjusted R-squared	0.09	0.09	0.06	0.38	0.01	0.39	0.11	0.10	0.01	0.64
N	175	153	157	80	81	63	64	175	181	39

SOURCE: Authors' estimates.

NOTE: N = number of observations. Values in parentheses below the coefficients depict the standard deviation.

* , ** , *** = significance at 10, 5, and 1 percent error intervals, respectively.

- In contrast, the associations with pension benefits do not confirm the social policy function of severance pay. The two benefits seem to be complementary across country income levels, and this relationship is robust and mostly significant. Hence, as in the case studies of Austria, Italy, and Korea, the transformed severance pay may complement potentially reduced future pension benefits, but such a reduction does not emerge from the cross-country estimations.

- There is no consistent and statistically significant link between severance pay generosity and notice period. The bivariate analysis hints at substitutability if zero and positive values are considered and at complementarity for positive values only, although this result may be spurious.

- The relationship between severance pay generosity and trade union density is mostly negative, with stable and, at times, significant parameters. This result is at odds with a power theory of trade unions and generosity. Again, a bivariate analysis hints at substitutability if zero and positive values are considered and at complementarity for positive values only.

- Last but not least, the use of regional dummies suggests homogeneity within regions and variation between regions, but mainly between OECD and non-OECD countries. Regional effects of reforms with innovators and followers may have been at work for severance pay programs; there are strong indications for such processes in the area of pensions (see Orenstein 2003).

BRIEF REVIEW OF THE EFFICIENCY EFFECTS OF SEVERANCE PAY

Another way to explore the economic rationale for severance pay is by examining the established empirical effects of severance pay shown by other researchers. If they show that severance pay increases efficiency, that would support the human resource management hypothesis; if not, that would support the job protection hypothesis. However, the problem is that very few investigations exist that measure the impact of severance pay on labor market outcome directly and in a convincing manner. Empirical studies are typically of the cross-country type and hence not very robust or methodologically reliable. Furthermore, most of the studies focus on broader job protection indicators and measurement, which mingles the effects.

The authors are not aware of direct empirical evidence on the positive effects of severance pay on firm productivity based on firm-level data. Nickell and Layard (1999) find a positive effect of employment protection on aggregate growth, but the effect disappears once differences in the level of productivity among countries are controlled for. Moreover, it is not clear which circumstances and interactions may be instrumental for such effects.[12] Likewise, Koeniger (2005) reports a weak positive relationship between employment protection legislation strictness and research and development intensity in OECD countries.

In contrast, considerable evidence suggests negative efficiency effects of mandatory severance pay. A number of studies show that strict employment protection, including hiring and firing rules as well as severance pay, reduces employment. Among the early studies, Lazear (1990) finds that severance pay increases unemployment and reduces both employment and labor force participation (in their update of his findings, Addison and Teixeira (2003) confirm the first finding, but cast some doubt on the others). Fallon and

Lucas (1991) show that strengthening job security regulations led to a strong decline of employment in India and Zimbabwe.

More recent studies confirming the link between job security and lower employment levels include Haffner and others (2001) for OECD countries; Heckman and Pagés (2000) for OECD and Latin American countries; Haltiwanger, Scarpetta, and Vodopivec (2003) for OECD and transition countries; Besley and Burgess (2004) and Ahsan and Pagés (2009) for India; and Saavedra and Torero (2004) for Chile. Heckman and Pagés (2000) attribute a reduction in employment of 5 percentage points to job security provisions in Latin America. Montenegro and Pagés (2004) report that job security regulations in Chile reduced employment opportunities of the young and the unskilled while promoting the employment rates of skilled and older workers. OECD (1999) finds insignificant effects on overall employment rates, but points out that negative effects are concentrated among prime-age women, youth, and older workers. To the extent severance pay increases youth unemployment, this has additional negative consequences in terms of the persistence of unemployment and reduced future earnings capacity. Kugler and Pica (2008) and Boeri and Jimeno (2005), on the contrary, find small or no effect of an increase in dismissal cost for Italian firms with fewer than 15 employees on overall employment or employment growth, whereas Schivardi and Torrini (2008) find only modest effects of stricter employment protection on firm growth near the threshold of 15 workers. Studies also show that severance pay contributes to part-time employment and self-employment. Moreover, De Ferranti and others (2000) report that severance pay systems produce large litigation costs (arising from disputes over the cause of separation) in Latin America.

There is also mounting evidence that employment protection reduces inflows to and outflows from unemployment and thus contributes to longer unemployment spells (stagnant unemployment pool). Flows through employment may not be affected that strongly (for a recent survey, see OECD 1999 and 2004; for evidence on transition economies, see Haltiwanger, Scarpetta, and Vodopevic 2003; see also Botero and others 2004, Kugler and Saint-Paul 2004, and Kugler 1999 and 2004). Reduced labor market flows may hinder labor force adjustment and the reallocation of jobs, and may thereby slow down aggregate productivity growth (see Davis and Haltiwanger 1999 for a survey of the effects of job reallocation on aggregate productivity growth).

Evidence exists that job protection reduces productivity and overall growth. The influential OECD (1999) study assessed the extent of job protection against individual dismissal for a regular employee who is given notice on personal grounds or because of economic redundancy. The study considers the strictness of employment protection based on three criteria: procedural inconveniences the employer faces when trying to dismiss employees; notice and severance pay provisions; and prevailing standards and penalties for unfair dismissals. Using a synthetic index of these three employment protection components, recent empirical results indicate that higher firing costs adversely affect workers' productivity and economic growth (Scarpetta and others 2002). Exploiting firm-level microdata, Autor, Kerr, and Kugler (2007) show that the adoption of stricter job security provisions in the United States had a positive effect on capital investment and a negative effect on total factor productivity. Cingano and others (2010) had similar findings using Italian data to examine a 1990 reform that raised dismissal costs for Italian firms with fewer than 15 employees. Micco and Pagés (2006) also find some weak evidence of a negative relationship between dismissal costs and labor productivity for 18 OECD and non-OECD countries, although their results may be affected by the fact that Nigeria is included in the sample. Scarpetta and Tressel (2004) show that strict employment protection has a significant negative impact on productivity, but only in countries with an intermediate degree of centralization/coordination in wage bargaining. OECD (2007) and the revised analysis in Bassanini, Nunziata, and Venn (2009), based on a difference-in-differences approach for 16 OECD countries, suggest that mandatory dismissal regulations have a negative impact on productivity growth in industries where dismissal restrictions are more likely to be binding.

Evidence is strong and rising that employment protection legislation and processes have negative effects on worker separation and accession, and therefore on turnover, with consequences for sector composition and economic growth. Among recent studies based on microdata, Autor, Kerr, and Kugler (2007) show that the adoption of wrongful discharge protections by state courts in the United States had a negative effect on job flows and firm entry. Similarly, Boeri and Jimeno (2005) and Kugler and Pica (2008) confirm negative effects of an increase in dismissal costs on job turnover in Italian firms. Kugler (1999, 2004) and Kugler, Jimeno, and Hernanz (2003) find that reduction in dismissal costs increased accessions as well as separations of workers in Colombia and Spain, respectively. Kahn (2007) reports that employment protection legislation (EPL) reduces the separation rates of those already employed (mostly prime-age adults) at the expense of new entrants and the more highly mobile; that is, the young and less skilled. On the contrary, no evidence that dismissal protection affected worker flows was found by microeconometric studies for Germany (Bauer, Bender, and Bonin 2007), Portugal (Martins 2009), or Sweden (von Below and Thoursie 2010). The negative impact of employment protection on turnover was confirmed by cross-country studies performed on aggregate data (see Boeri and Garibaldi 2009; Gomez-Salvador, Messina, and Vallanti 2004; Messina and Vallanti 2007). Studies using a difference-in-differences approach on OECD countries arrive at similar conclusions (see Bassanini and others 2010; Cingano and others 2010; Haltiwanger, Scarpetta, and Schweiger 2010; Micco and Pagés 2006; and OECD 2010): The negative relationship between dismissal costs and job flows is greater in industries with a greater propensity to reallocate labor.

The effects of EPL described above need to be separated from the effects of severance pay, at least for the richer countries where most of these studies have been carried out. In a critical review of the empirical literature, Parsons (2011a, 149) concludes that "severance mandates unaccompanied by other labor regulations have little impact on worker separations (and accessions) or average employment levels." He adds that the impact of EPL reforms may depend on the regulatory environment in the economy as a whole, and there may be important interactions between severance pay mandates and collective bargaining rules.

The evidence from the United States emphasizes the role of trade unions in expanding the coverage of severance pay and the use of severance pay as a human resource management tool. In his thorough review of severance pay programs for the period 1930–99, Parsons (2005a, b) reports that severance pay among clerical and sales workers is only modestly less extensive than the coverage of managers and professionals. He argues that the evolution of formal coverage of blue collar workers is intimately related to the develop-ment of the organized labor movement; that is, controlling for worker occupation, union status significantly increases the likelihood of severance pay coverage (Parsons 2005a). This means that the prevalence of severance pay for managers and professionals is likely also driven by efficiency wage considerations. Interestingly, Parsons (2005a, b) also reports that large firms in the United States are more likely than small firms to have formal sever-ance pay plans.

This summary of the findings suggests that economists have shown that employment protection legislation matters for labor market outcomes. However, severance pay systems alone seemingly have no significant impact, at least in the upper-middle- to high-income countries where most of these studies have been undertaken. Researchers have not yet investigated to what extent mandated severance pay could become the binding constraint once other employment protection legislation has become less restrictive. For low- and lower-middle-income countries where unemployment benefits are still the exception but severance pay is the rule, the impact of severance pay on labor market outcomes and its effectiveness as an unemployment support program awaits comprehensive investigation and further research.

Conclusions

Severance pay programs for formal sector work exist in most countries around the world, often providing the only formal income support to a worker who is made redundant; how-ever, little is known about how these programs work, particularly in developing countries. To help fill that gap, this chapter described the origin of these programs, summarized the salient features of severance pay programs throughout the world, formulated and exam-ined hypotheses about the economic rationale for the existence of these programs, and reviewed recent reforms.

The chapter showed that the origin of mandated severance pay can be traced to three main events: (1) the creation of labor codes; (2) the large-scale industrial restructur-ing that began at the end of the nineteenth century and high unemployment pressures in the interwar period; and (3) the expansion of the welfare state after WWII. Despite these common origins, a review of existing severance pay programs showed that countries use widely different designs and parameter values.

The inventory of mandated severance pay programs and related social policy and country indicators in 183 countries offers a rich information base to better understand the programs and allow for first hypothesis testing. For example, the data support the hypoth-esis of the widespread nature of severance pay around the world: Of the 183 countries, all except 13 (7 percent) provide mandated or quasi-mandated severance pay programs; the latter are largely concentrated in high-income countries and nonexistent in low-income countries. High-income/OECD countries tend to offer less generous programs and are less likely to mandate such systems, while many low- and middle-income countries offer the most generous systems and rely on compulsion. In most countries, employers account for severance payments as a current operating expense; few institutional arrangements exist to ensure that firms will be able to meet their severance payment obligations to separated workers.

The chapter also examined the economic rationales for severance pay and found partial support for all three hypotheses it advanced: that severance pay serves as a social benefit payment, a human resource management tool, and a job protection mechanism.

Evaluations of both income protection and efficiency properties of severance pay programs—usually conducted for developed countries and mostly as part of a broader assessment of EPL—are typically fairly negative. The direct estimation of severance pay effects for developed economies indicates few and limited effects once severance pay is separated from other restrictive employment protection measures. If other studies are able to isolate the pure severance effects on employment outcomes, better integration of severance pay with other social benefits may be a possibility, especially with unemployment and retirement where they exist. If further studies show few or no efficiency effects of mandated compared with voluntary severance pay arrangements as a human resource instrument, this may mean rethinking the mandate.

An interesting finding, especially for policy makers in developing countries, is that severance pay (and job protection in general) in developed countries poses fewer restrictions on employers than in developing and transition countries: It offers less generous payments, is simpler to administer (and thus generates fewer costs), and is often not mandated but determined by collective bargaining or firm-level decisions. This is another indication that in a globalized world, improving labor market outcomes and increasing productivity by creating a more flexible labor market (including by liberalizing overly restrictive EPL) is inescapable.

The absence of unemployment benefits in low- and middle-income countries often leads to high employment protection through mandated severance pay and dismissal rules. The challenge will be to move toward less restrictive EPL while providing effective and incentive-oriented income support schemes in a job-enabling environment; that is, the quest for a low- and middle-income country version of flexicurity. Moving along these lines would involve reducing notional generosity while improving compliance and hence effective generosity. Low- and middle-income countries should explore the introduction of individual savings accounts, which provide a broad risk management instrument; in most cases these countries will have to undertake reforms to create the enabling environment for such accounts.

Despite promising recent reforms in several countries, finding the best avenues to reform severance pay remains a task for future research. Critical contributions for such research are suggested in three areas. First, it would be useful to disentangle the individual and joint effects of employment protection legislation, with severance pay being one of its components. If severance pay programs were shown to have nonpositive effects on labor market outcomes, one could think about replacing the mandate with contractual arrangements or folding them into other social benefits. A second fruitful area for research is to investigate the efficiency effects of voluntary severance pay programs, both for themselves and compared with other, more modern remuneration schemes that attempt to improve and capture worker knowledge. The results of such research could provide information that would help with de-mandating severance pay programs. Last but not least, it is important to explore the liquidity preferences of workers, which seem to explain much of the support for the continuation of existing severance pay programs and the rejection of plans to fold them into unemployment benefit or corporate pension schemes.

Notes

1. A first version of this chapter was prepared for the joint World Bank/International Institute for Applied System Analysis/Ludwig Boltzmann Institute for Economic Policy Analysis Workshop on Severance Payments, IIASA/Laxenburg, November 7–8, 2003 (see Holzmann 2005; Holzmann, Iyer, and Vodopivec 2003). Subsequent attempts to complete the historic analysis and improve the inventory on severance pay proved more time-consuming than anticipated, and the finalization of the chapter was also delayed by other commitments and changes in positions. The authors are thankful to all who contributed to its completion and review, in particular, Zoran Anusic, Kripa Iyer, Gordon Betcherman, Annette Brown, and Don Parsons. All gaps and errors are our own.

2. Requests for information from the International Labour Organization (ILO) and the International Social Security Association (ISSA) produced limited information, as did selective requests to individual researchers. Special thanks go to Roddy McKinnon from ISSA, who helped dig up some of the historical material.

3. The following literature deals with severance-type payments in a historic perspective. For the experience of the United States, the United Kingdom, Japan, and some European countries with severance or dismissal payments up to the early 1940s, see Hawkins (1940, 1942). Historic hints and information after WWII are contained in two articles in the *International Labor Review*, in papers by Herz (1954) and Visisombat (1968). The latter paper contains information about the experience in French-speaking Africa. A book from this period (Meyers 1964) provides information about the United States. Recent writings on severance payments with historic references include Miron and Weil (1997), Basu and others (2003), and Parsons (2005a, b). An interesting and seemingly open research field concerns the role of social partners (trade unions and employers' organization) in the historic evolution of severance pay, and their current role (or lack of it) in the reform of severance pay.

4. For the country income groupings and thresholds, see http://data.worldbank.org/about/country-classifications/country-and-lending-groups.

5. The country grouping is done by expected main similarities and deviates in some aspects from the World Bank institutional classification. OECD covers old and new member countries, such as Mexico and Chile in Latin America and the Caribbean; Czech Republic, Hungary, Poland, and Slovenia in Europe; and Central Asia-Europe and Central Asia (ECA). Transition covers other ECA countries and some Asian countries (such as China and Vietnam); Asia covers both South and East Asia and the Pacific Islands; MENA covers the countries in the Middle East and North Africa; and Africa covers the countries south of the Sahara.

6. In Figures 2.4 to 2.6, the numbers in diamonds are the mean values; those in squares are the median values (Quartile 2). The box contains 50 percent of the data. The box size is therefore defined by the inter-quartile range (IQR)–the difference between Quartile 1 and Quartile 3. The whiskers (upper and lower bars out of the box) are defined as 1.5 times the IQR in both directions. See http://www.statmethods.net/graphs/boxplot.html and McGill, Tukey, and Wayne (1978).

7. Clearly, the choice of years of service is arbitrary and the equal weight biases the result compared with empirical weights reflecting actual distribution of benefit payment by service length. This information, however, is not available.

8. The inventory on policy reforms profited tremendously from input and review by a team of Tower Watson Uruguay: Maximiliano Sosa, Jessica Gerpe, and Rodrigo Baudo. All errors and missed reforms, however, are the responsibility of the authors.

9. During the early transition of Eastern European countries, reductions in job protection were accompanied by active and passive programs to ease restructuring and layoffs. While the

programs were initially generous and increased fiscal costs, their generosity was significantly reduced over time as the goals of the restructuring agenda were met, though reducing entitlements was difficult (see Vodopivec, Wörgötter, and Raju 2005).

10. The robust estimation excludes extreme values. For details on the estimation and statistical criteria, see annex C.

11. Selected data are available as retrievable spreadsheets on the World Bank's Social Protection website at http://www.worldbank.org/pensions.

12. A stream of literature on the effects of worker-management, cooperation, and participatory approaches in management finds mildly positive effects of these features on productivity of firms but cannot pinpoint the exact ingredients or interactions that contribute to the success. Tyson and Levine (1990) do single out measures to enhance substantive participation as instrumental for higher productivity, but it is unclear to what extent employment protection boosts such measures.

Annex A. Historic Perspectives across Countries and Regions

These perspectives combine regional and historical information on severance pay, focusing first on developments in the United States, the United Kingdom, and Japan, then extrapolating some ideas about how severance pay evolved in developing and transition countries, relying on the sparse evidence available on this topic.

Severance Pay in the United States

In the United States, one of the earliest examples of severance pay was in 1922, when the Delaware and Hudson Railroad adopted dismissal compensation as part of its benefit program. A large oil company paid dismissal compensation in 1925 when it was implementing a merger. The first big dismissal plan was in the Chicago clothing industry. The Amalgamated Clothing Workers and Hart, Schaffner, and Marx had built a comprehensive industrial relations program. About 236 dismissed workers received US$500 each in 1926. Severance payments ranging from US$150 to US$500 had been paid on several occasions earlier in the industry. The amounts of compensation were determined more by the financial condition of the firm than by the needs of the workers because of prevailing market conditions. The contribution was made by the firm and by the remaining workers, who temporarily gave up their unemployment insurance rights. There were plenty of such incidents in the clothing industry, where workers were dismissed as a result of increased mechanization of the industry. Until 1929, most of the dismissal plans aimed to assist those displaced by mergers, consolidations of offices and plants, or changes in working rules.

Dismissal plans including severance pay also emerged in large industries such as rubber manufacturing (1929), oil refining (1931 and 1936), banking (1934), public utilities (1938), food manufacturing (1938), and auto manufacturing (1940) (Hawkins 1940). In these cases, severance pay plans depended on the experience and age of the workers but usually were available to all employees.

In San Francisco, the building of the Golden Gate and Bay bridges implied displacement of the large workforce employed on ferryboats. A union arbitrator recalled this experience (box A.1).

The practice of paying compensation to dismissed employees was followed in the United States by many firms even before any unemployment insurance laws were passed. However, legislation on mandatory severance pay was never enacted, not even on the state level. The United States was one of the few industrialized countries not to have done so. Instead, it left the issue to the firms and collective agreements. The firms adopted severance payment plans to reward faithful employees but also as a public relations exercise and to sustain plant morale. Parsons (2005a) noted that during the 1930s, employers adopted different types of advanced notice plans. Flat-rate plans largely helped get rid of inefficient labor and served as a mechanism for protecting plant morale by quickly dispersing disgruntled workers. Graduated plans seemed to specifically reward workers for their long service to the company. Many companies also had informal or ad hoc plans they applied according to the particular situation of workers. Thus, companies seemed to target different severance plans to different types of workers.

> **BOX A.1 Golden Gate and Bay Bridges—Job Displacement and Severance Pay**
>
> "Before the bridges, everybody went by ferryboat, and the old railroad commission gave the ferryboat companies a higher return, because they'd be out of business when the bridges opened. But the workers—what about them? There were about 4,000 of them… they wanted severance pay, but in 1932 nobody had ever heard of severance pay. The average length of service was 15 years, and we wanted one month's pay for every year of service. To make a long story short, we went to the president of the Southern Pacific railroad, which ran most of the ferries, and told him we wanted severance pay…. 'Or what?' he said. 'Or we'll go on strike,' I said. Well, there was no way to get across the bay except by ferryboat. So he said, 'I have some figures here for one offer only,' and he turned them over, like cards. He said, 'I'll give you one month's pay for every year of service, and that's it.' Well,.., that was exactly what we were demanding! But we didn't take it right away. We said, 'We'll caucus.' We took it."
>
> SOURCE: Excerpt from interview with Sam Kagel, arbitrator, *San Francisco Chronicle*, "Ah, the '30s, Full of Struggle And the Joy of Life," Carl Nolte, Sunday, May 2, 1999.

In the 1940s and 1950s, severance plans did not expand nearly as much as in the 1930s. Unions became more involved in promoting these plans as part of collective agreements, but severance pay coverage grew much more slowly than pension, health, or insurance coverage. Severance pay was used when workers were unjustly dismissed or retrenched through consolidation or because of technological change. From the 1970s onward, severance pay coverage decreased. Some industries appeared to drop severance pay plans between the 1960s and 1970s. In subsequent decades, severance pay coverage actually decreased despite higher job insecurity. Parsons (2005b) suggests that severance pay was not responsive to demand, as its use did not necessarily increase during downturns. In fact, severance pay primarily reflected the employer's desire to limit the morale impact of dismissals.

Severance Pay in the United Kingdom

In the United Kingdom during the 1920s, some dismissal plans developed as supplements to unemployment insurance. In 1928, Cadbury Brothers Ltd., had to lay off about 500 workers. The chocolate industry had undergone considerable mechanization, leading to more efficient processes. In addition to unemployment benefits, the firm had a regular plan for dismissal compensation. Special provisions were made for lump-sum payments to those moving out of the district, emigrating, or going into business. In the United Kingdom, because of the national insurance law, the tendency was toward periodic payments of equal sums that did not vary with service or salary of the employee. Trade unionism was strong in the United Kingdom and had secured a number of agreements limiting the employer's absolute right to dismiss.

In subsequent decades, redundancy payments became institutionalized through the Redundancy Payment Act of 1965. This legislation essentially helped the state subsidize industrial restructuring. Redundancy payments were meant to encourage employees to leave employment in declining industries and move to growing sectors. Severance pay also became increasingly useful to address unjust dismissals, which often sparked collective action or strikes. In both the United Kingdom and New Zealand, severance pay could help decentralize and individualize dismissals, and thereby avoid strikes and better manage labor disputes.

Severance Pay in Japan

Before the Japanese "leaving" allowance act was passed in 1936, and before the "fortnight dismissal wage" law of 1926 was enacted, larger enterprises adopted many voluntary schemes of dismissal compensation as standard procedure or to meet particular emergencies requiring reductions in workforce. Compensation was also paid to those laid off because of sickness, accident, or old age, and occasionally to those who quit voluntarily and those who were discharged for strike activity. Compensation in the case of nonfault dismissals was more generous, which can be attributed to paternalism. The transition of the Japanese feudal economy to an industrial one was so quick that the human feelings of the employer and the sense of justice of the employee heavily influenced dismissal policies.

In June 1935, the Japanese Bureau of Social Affairs conducted a study of all industrial and mining concerns employing 50 or more workers and found that 1,582 firms had written regulations governing leaving allowances. Workers and employers also addressed provisioning for severance pay as early as 1936. In many firms, workers and employers adopted internal regulations for provisioning through contributions by both workers and employers (Hawkins 1942). Dismissal plans in Japan in that period were relatively generous compared with plans in the United States.

In summary, developments up to WWII suggest that the rising importance of severance payments was linked to many factors. These range from industrial restructuring to top-ups to flat unemployment benefits, and originally were concentrated in a few sectors and focused on white collar workers only. Legal arrangements ranged from those mandated in a labor code or special laws to general or selective collective bargaining arrangements to voluntary schemes.

Origins of Severance Pay in Developing and Transitional Countries

As illustrated in the cases of France, the United States, and the United Kingdom, a primary factor in making severance payments almost ubiquitous in the world was the conscious expansion of social programs after WWII, as well as a distinct trend in the translation or copying of labor market programs from the industrialized North to the decolonizing South. The development of a "social welfare state" in the North led to the gradual expansion of such programs to ever larger parts of the population, and to the introduction or expansion of related programs, in particular, unemployment benefits and old-age pensions. But while severance payments remain typically linked to the labor code and related legislation or to collective bargaining arrangements (and thus stem from an employee/employer relationship), the other related social programs are typically established by special social laws and are determined by public action.

In developing countries, the introduction or expansion of severance-type payments has received little attention, and only limited references exist. It has been suggested that the provision of severance pay in a number of developing countries was deemed a somewhat transient legislative measure, the need for which would decline with the development of fuller employment policy and an extensive social security system.

For example, the provision of severance pay was "subject to this obligation coming to an end on the promulgation of legislation concerning social insurance (Costa Rica) or to the replacement of compensation by benefits from a welfare fund (Dominican Republic, Egypt, Lebanon, Syria)" (Herz 1954, 319).

In Latin America, the origins and development of severance pay can be assessed by tracing the introduction of related legislation and how labor movements may have subsequently shaped severance pay. Indeed, legislation on severance pay appeared concurrently with the introduction of labor codes in a number of Latin American countries. The first mention of severance pay legislation occurred in Mexico (1917), Bolivia (1924 and 1925), Chile (1924), Peru (1924, 1925, 1930) Argentina (1930), Colombia (1934), El Salvador (1935), Venezuela (1936), and Uruguay (1944). In most countries, severance pay applied to salaried workers, commercial employees, or wage earners.

In considering the rationale for introducing severance pay, Mexico's practice of severance allowances has been interpreted as an "expression of accumulation of property-like equity in employment, which entitles the worker to a form of liquidated damages upon the destruction of his job" (Mayer 1964, 72; see box A.2 below).

In **Argentina**, the introduction of severance pay followed the consolidation of the early labor movement in 1930 under the General Confederation of Labor (CGT). By 1932, CGT had delivered a series of legislative demands for shorter working hours, severance pay, and other welfare measures. These demands would form part of ongoing political debate, and though many would be adopted over the coming years, they were not enforced. During the subsequent Peronist era, the creation of a labor secretariat helped formalize the relationship between unions and the state, and effectively implemented worker benefits and protections.

Several countries took active measures to ensure funding for severance pay. **Chile** addressed the funding issue by requiring employers to deposit 8.33 percent of each employee's salary (up to 3,500 pesos) with the national savings bank. The employee could collect this amount, plus the interest earned on it, upon termination of employment (Hawkins 1942). In 1928, **Ecuador** adopted legislation for provisioning as well, though employers were required only to set aside the appropriate salary, not necessarily to deposit it in a separate account.

In many **Latin American** countries, Herz (1954) noted the strong role of legislation protecting workers and the heavy involvement of courts in dismissal cases, speculating that this was the case because of weak collective bargaining. For example, in Mexico and Guatemala, employers had to justify dismissals through formal procedures, and employees usually received dismissal compensation unless they were guilty of misconduct. Job protection—specifically, punishment for unjust dismissals—still appears to be the motivation behind severance pay. Labor laws have been layered on top of each other, reflecting the notion that workers have acquired rights and their benefits should not be curtailed. The historically strong relationship between leftist political parties and unions seems to explain the promulgation of labor-protecting legislation.

BOX A.2 **Severance Pay in Mexico: Compensation for Liquidated Damages of Job Ownership**

Mexico stands out for having early legislation that justified a form of severance pay. Its 1917 constitution reflects the significant symbolic role of the working class and peasants, and specific articles introduced the concept that workers had a right to their jobs. Employers were required to prove that they had just cause for firing a worker. Otherwise, workers were entitled to three months' wages as indemnity or could choose reinstatement in their previous job. Should employers refuse reinstatement, workers received severance pay graduated by years of service in addition to the indemnity pay.

As labor laws evolved to increase protection for workers, employers attempted to limit the class of workers to which these laws applied. Simultaneously, legislation leaned toward reinstatement rather than severance pay, in recognition of specific labor market characteristics. Dismissal implied not only a loss of precious seniority but also starting at the bottom of the job and wage ladder. Severance pay was considered inadequate compensation for such damages. A further rationale for reinstatement was the lack of insurance against the risks of job loss. In reality, reinstatement was an unattractive option to workers and employers, as both considered their relationship a "broken marriage." Workers feared retribution by their employers, who could make working conditions unpleasant enough to induce them to quit. While workers could have accessed a greater settlement by demanding reinstatement, many settled out of court and for less than the statutory severance pay. Union representatives could pressure workers to settle and sanction workers by preventing their future employment in a given industry. Moreover, even when employers had legal justification for large-scale dismissal, the burden of proof and onerous legal proceedings made collective bargaining and severance pay the preferred option. Needless to say, severance pay was a luxury afforded only to workers in the formal sector; the large informal sector had no such protection.

SOURCE: Based on Frederic Meyers, "Ownership of Jobs: A Comparative Study," Institute for Industrial Studies, University of California, Los Angeles, 1964.

In **African countries**, the introduction of severance pay appears to have been influenced by late colonial relationships. Visisombat (1968) provides interesting reading regarding employment law developments in post-WWII French-speaking Africa. He reports that before 1952, employment law across French overseas territories varied. These laws were standardized with the passing of the 1952 Labor Code for Overseas Territories, which brought together "rules scattered through various decrees and orders issued by governors" in Africa. The 1952 Code marked "an important, perhaps even historic, stage in the development of African social legislation...due to the fact that it applied equally to all workers without discrimination on grounds of sex, nationality, legal status or origin and in all African countries for which the Ministry for Overseas France was responsible, but not the North African protectorates (Morocco and Tunisia) or the Algerian departments" (Visisombat 1968, 122). The 1952 Code referred to "separation grants," but only those provided for under the contract of employment or collective bargaining agreement. In other words, severance pay was not mandated under the 1952 Code.

Following independence, a large number of newly independent African governments adopted national labor codes throughout the 1960s. Although country differences have emerged, to a large extent, the 1952 Code has been influential in shaping the development of these national codes in the former overseas French territories. In the postcolonial era, many of the new labor codes made improvements to better protect the rights of employees threatened with the loss of employment; however, few countries introduced statutory severance pay. In the late 1960s, the labor codes of Côte d'Ivoire, Mali, and Tunisia were the only ones that provided "a legal and compulsory form to this type of grant" (Visisombat 1968, 138).

Severance pay legislation in **France** evolved only slowly between 1890 and 1950, largely following regional and national plant agreements and bargaining. These laws essentially solidified judge-made laws and lower court decisions, so it was unlikely that these practices would have been significant in the 1952 Code that was transferred to francophone African countries. It is also worth mentioning that some African countries had severance pay legislation in place before independence. For example, the first mention of severance pay legislation in Madagascar occurred in 1952. This legislation referred to compensation in case of work stoppages (specifically related to employees in the sugar industry).

In **Asia**, severance pay dates back to the 1950s in countries such as Sri Lanka and India, while it is more recent in countries such as Thailand and Malaysia. Asher (2003) notes that particularly in India, each amendment to labor legislation has provided greater protection to the worker. Some of the severance pay practices appeared related to retrenchment occurring during the energy crisis (1973, 1979), but they also reflected the fact that a shortage of raw materials could stop work and lead to retrenchment. In Sri Lanka and India, severance pay would appear to have been a useful measure during economic restructuring. However, the more expensive voluntary retirement schemes were far more common for curtailing the workforce during restructuring. Perhaps the benefits paid under severance pay were insufficient to cut back enough labor.

Particularly in Sri Lanka, the use of voluntary retirement schemes also reflected the highly politicized nature of labor movements. From its inception in the 1930s, the trade union movement was aligned along political parties rather than occupational categories. From a historical perspective, workers were perceived as victims of exploitation who needed state support. Moreover, employment security was still considered an instrument for guaranteeing income security. Thus, job protection (often tied to political patronage) looms large in Sri Lankan labor movements. These factors help explain why workers supported trade union representatives during the economic restructuring of the early 1990s. Their representatives could always bargain them into a better deal, leading to increasingly larger redundancy compensation packages (Kelegama and Salih 1998).

Little information exists about the origins of severance pay legislation in the **Middle East**. Herz (1954) documented early legislation that determined an advance notice period. In Lebanon, severance pay was meant to be temporary legislation, to be replaced by a welfare fund; however, it is still prevalent in Lebanon today. Severance pay appeared to evolve as part of large social protection systems in this region, reflecting the state's dual roles in regulating the labor market and as an employer. Stronger union activity in the early 1990s appeared to strengthen severance pay (Robalino and Mataoanu 2005). Today, almost all countries in the Middle East and Northern Africa have severance pay and pension provisions for their formal labor force, but very few have unemployment benefits (Angel-Urdinola and Kuddo 2010). A special feature of severance pay concerns the many migrants to the seven countries of the Gulf Cooperation Council. For them, severance pay is (besides basic health care) the only social protection benefit and is legislated by the labor code (Holzmann and Pouget 2010).

Among former Soviet countries, only Estonia has evidence of early severance pay legislation (1934 and 1936). Severance pay—or any dismissals, for that matter—were essentially meaningless during the Soviet times and did not exist. Employees could be dismissed only for extremely limited reasons, each of which required different and complex dismissal procedures. With the transition to the market system, all these countries adopted new severance pay legislation and unemployment benefits. Unemployment benefits cover very few workers; severance pay is much more comprehensive and, at times, notionally generous and innovative. In a number of countries (including the Czech Republic, Hungary, Poland, and Slovakia), severance pay is not paid if the worker continues with a new employer (Kuddo 2009).

Annex B. Inventory of Severance Pay across the World

Economy	Legal base		Coverage		Eligible contingencies	Defined benefits for redundancy							End-of-service pay		Defined contribution	
	Mandatory	Collective agreements	Sectors	Excluded categories	Dismissal/ Redundancy/ Bankruptcy/ Incapacity/ Old-age/ End-of-service	Minimum tenure required (months)	Benefits at 9 months	Benefits at 1 year	Benefits at 5 yrs	Benefits at 10 yrs	Benefits at 20 yrs	Generosity index	Minimum tenure required (months)	Generosity index	Minimum tenure required (months)	Contribution rate (% of salary)
Afghanistan	1	0	..	..	R,...	..	0.0	8.7	17.3	26.0	26.0	4.9				
Albania	1	..	..	..	D,R	36	0.0	0.0	10.7	21.4	42.9	1.4				
Algeria	0	1	a	..	D,R	36	13.0	13.0	13.0	13.0	13.0	5.6				
Angola	1	..	..	..	R,...	..	0.0	2.2	10.8	21.7	54.2	2.2				
Antigua and Barbuda	1	..	..	..	R,...	..	0.0	2.4	12.0	24.0	48.0	2.4				
Argentina	1	1	p	Agricultural workers and domestic workers	R	..	4.3	4.3	21.7	43.3	86.7	4.3				
Armenia	1	0	a	None	D,I	..	4.3	4.3	4.3	4.3	4.3	1.9				
Australia	1	1	p	Firm size less 15	R	12	0.0	4.0	10.0	12.0	0.0	2.4				
Austria	1	1	p	Agricultural workers and domestic workers	E	..	n.a.	n.a.	n.a.	n.a.	n.a.	n.a.			0	1.54
Azerbaijan	1	..	a	Army, judiciary	D,R	..	13.0	13.0	13.0	13.0	13.0	5.6				
Bahamas, The	1	..	..	..	R,...	..	1.5	2.0	10.0	20.0	24.0	2.0				
Bahrain	1	0	p	Expats (own system)	E	12	n.a.	n.a.	n.a.	n.a.	n.a.	0.0	12	1.0		

(continued)

Economy	Legal base		Coverage		Eligible contingencies	Defined benefits for redundancy							End-of-service pay		Defined contribution	
	Mandatory	Collective agreements	Sectors	Excluded categories	Dismissal/ Redundancy/ Bankruptcy/ Old-age/ Incapacity/ End-of-service	Minimum tenure required (months)	Benefits at 9 months	Benefits at 1 year	Benefits at 5 yrs	Benefits at 10 yrs	Benefits at 20 yrs	Generosity index	Minimum tenure required (months)	Generosity index	Minimum tenure required (months)	Contribution rate (% of salary)
Bangladesh	1	..	p	Firms size less 5, managerial positions	R,I	12	0.0	5.0	25.0	50.0	100.0	5.0				
Belarus	1	1	a	None	D,R,B	..	13.0	13.0	13.0	13.0	13.0	5.6				
Belgium	0	1	n.a.	n.a.	n.a.	n.a.	n.a.	n.a.	n.a.	n.a.	n.a.	0.0				
Belize	1	0	..	..	R,..	..	0.0	0.0	5.0	10.0	20.0	0.7				
Benin	1	0	..	..	D,R	..	0.0	1.3	6.5	14.1	31.4	1.3				
Bhutan	0	0	n.a.	n.a.	n.a.	n.a.	n.a.	n.a.	n.a.	n.a.	n.a.	0.0				
Bolivia	1	..	p	Agricultural workers	D,R	3	..	..	..	..	..	..				
Bosnia and Herzegovina	1	..	..		D,R	24	0.0	0.0	7.2	14.4	28.9	1.0				
Botswana	1	..	..	..	D,R	60	1.8	2.4	12.0	36.0	84.0	2.8				
Brazil	1	0	p	Agricultural and domestic workers	D–E	n.a.	1.2	1.7	8.3	16.6	33.3	1.7			..	8.00
Brunei Darussalam	0	0	n.a.	n.a.	n.a.	n.a.	n.a.	n.a.	n.a.	n.a.	n.a.	n.a.				
Bulgaria	1	1	p	Firm size less 20	R,O,I	..	4.3	4.3	4.3	4.3	4.3	1.9				
Burkina Faso	1	0	p	none	D,R	12	0.0	1.1	5.4	11.9	29.3	1.1				

(continued)

ANNEX B **(Continued)**

| Economy | Legal base | | Coverage | | Eligible contingencies | | Defined benefits for redundancy | | | | | | | End-of-service pay | | Defined contribution | |
	Mandatory	Collective agreements	Sectors	Excluded categories	Dismissal/ Redundancy/ Bankruptcy/ Old-age/ Incapacity/ End-of-service	Minimum tenure required (months)	Benefits at 9 months	Benefits at 1 year	Benefits at 5 yrs	Benefits at 10 yrs	Benefits at 20 yrs	Generosity index	Minimum tenure required (months)	Generosity index	Minimum tenure required (months)	Minimum tenure required (months)	Contribution rate (% of salary)
Burundi	1	0	:	:	R...	:	0.0	0.0	8.7	13.0	13.0	1.0				
Cambodia	1	0	:	:	R...	:	1.0	2.1	10.7	21.4	26.0	2.1				
Cameroon	1	:	p	none	D,R	24	0.0	1.5	7.6	15.2	30.3	1.5				
Canada	1	:	a	Managerial positions and nonfederally regulated workers	R	12	0.0	0.0	5.0	10.0	20.0	0.7				
Cape Verde	1	:	:	:	R...	:	3.3	4.3	21.7	43.3	86.7	4.3				
Central African Republic	1	0	:	:	R...	:	17.3	17.3	17.3	17.3	17.3	7.5				
Chad	1	0	:	:	R...	:	0.0	0.0	5.4	11.9	27.1	0.8				
Chile	1	1	p	Domestic workers and managerial positions	D,R	12	0.0	4.3	21.7	10.0	47.7	3.2				
China	1	:	p	none	D,R	:	4.3	4.3	21.7	43.3	86.7	4.3				
Colombia	1	0	p	none	D,R	:	4.3	4.3	15.7	30.0	58.6	3.5				
Comoros	1	0	:	:	R...	:	4.3	4.3	21.7	43.3	86.7	4.3				
Congo, Dem. Rep.	0	0	n.a.	n.a.	n.a.	n.a.	n.a.	n.a.	n.a.	n.a.	n.a.	n.a.				
Congo, Rep.	1	0	:	:	R...	:	0.0	0.0	6.1	13.4	29.9	0.9				

(continued)

ANNEX B (Continued)

Economy	Legal base		Coverage		Eligible contingencies		Defined benefits for redundancy						End-of-service pay		Defined contribution	
	Mandatory	Collective agreements	Sectors	Excluded categories	Dismissal/ Redundancy/ Bankruptcy/ Incapacity/ Old-age/ End-of-service	Minimum tenure required (months)	Benefits at 9 months	Benefits at 1 year	Benefits at 5 yrs	Benefits at 10 yrs	Benefits at 20 yrs	Generosity index	Minimum tenure required (months)	Generosity index	Minimum tenure required (months)	Contribution rate (% of salary)
Costa Rica	1	:	p	none	D,R	:	2.0	2.8	15.2	25.1	25.1	2.8				
Côte d'Ivoire	1	1	p	none	D,R	12	0.0	1.3	6.5	14.1	31.4	1.3				
Croatia	1	:	p	none	D,R	24	0.0	0.0	7.2	14.4	26.0	1.0				
Cyprus	0	1	n.a.	n.a.	n.a.	n.a.	n.a.	n.a.	n.a.	n.a.	n.a.	n.a.				
Czech Republic	1	1	p	Firm size less 20	R,I	:	13.0	13.0	13.0	13.0	13.0	5.6				
Denmark	1	1	p	Firm size less 20, domestic workers, seafarers, blue collar workers	D,R,E	144	0.0	0.0	0.0	0.0	0.0	0.0				
Djibouti	0	0	n.a.	n.a.	n.a.	n.a.	n.a.	n.a.	n.a.	n.a.	n.a.	n.a.				
Dominica	1	:	:	:	R...	:	0.0	0.0	9.0	19.0	49.0	1.2				
Dominican Republic	1	1	a	Freelance, tenants and sharecroppers, etc.	D,R,O	3	2.4	3.8	20.9	41.8	83.6	4.1				
Ecuador	1	:	a	none	D,R	:	13.0	14.1	27.1	54.2	108.3	8.3				
Egypt, Arab Rep.	1	:	p	Domestic wokers	R	:	4.3	4.3	21.7	54.2	119.2	4.7				
El Salvador	1	:	:	:	R...	:	3.2	4.3	21.4	42.9	85.7	4.3				
Equatorial Guinea	1	:	:	:	R...	:	4.8	6.4	32.1	64.3	128.6	6.4				

(continued)

ANNEX B **(Continued)**

Economy	Legal base		Coverage		Eligible contingencies	Defined benefits for redundancy							End-of-service pay		Defined contribution	
	Mandatory	Collective agreements	Sectors	Excluded categories	Dismissal/ Redundancy/ Bankruptcy/ Incapacity/ Old-age/ End-of-service	Minimum tenure required (months)	Benefits at 9 months	Benefits at 1 year	Benefits at 5 yrs	Benefits at 10 yrs	Benefits at 20 yrs	Generosity index	Minimum tenure required (months)	Generosity index	Minimum tenure required (months)	Contribution rate (% of salary)
Eritrea	1	..	..		R...	..	1.5	2.0	10.0	25.0	65.0	2.2				
Estonia	1	..	..	..	D,R,B	..	8.7	4.3	4.3	4.3	17.3	1.9				
Ethiopia	1	..	p	Managerial positions	D,R,B	..	3.2	4.3	10.0	17.1	31.4	2.7				
Fiji	1	..	..	..	R...	12	0.0	1.0	5.0	10.0	20.0	1.0				
Finland	0	1	n.a.	n.a.	n.a.	n.a.	n.a.	n.a.	n.a.	n.a.	n.a.	0.0				
France	1	1	p	none	D,R,E	12	0.0	0.9	4.3	8.7	23.1	0.9				
Gabon	1	0	..	..	R...	..	0.0	0.0	4.3	8.7	17.3	0.6				
Gambia, The	0	0	n.a.	n.a.	n.a.	n.a.	n.a.	n.a.	n.a.	n.a.	n.a.	n.a.				
Georgia	1	..	a	none	D,R	..	4.3	4.3	4.3	4.3	4.3	1.9				
Germany	1	1	p	Firm size less 10, managerial positions	R,E	6	0.0	2.2	10.8	21.7	43.3	2.2				
Ghana	1	1	a	Army, state security	R	..	6.5	8.7	43.3	86.7	173.3	8.7				
Greece	1	..	a	none	D,R,I	2	24.0	24.0	24.0	24.0	24.0	10.4				
Grenada	1	..	..	..	D,R	..	0.0	1.0	5.0	10.0	20.0	1.0				
Guatemala	1	..	..	..	D,R	..	3.8	5.1	25.3	50.6	101.1	5.1				
Guinea	1	..	..	..	R...	12	0.0	1.1	5.4	10.8	21.7	1.1				

(continued)

ANNEX B (Continued)

Economy	Legal base Mandatory	Collective agreements	Coverage Sectors	Excluded categories	Eligible contingencies Dismissal/Redundancy/Bankruptcy/Incapacity/Old-age/End-of-service	Defined benefits for redundancy Minimum tenure required (months)	Benefits at 9 months	Benefits at 1 year	Benefits at 5 yrs	Benefits at 10 yrs	Benefits at 20 yrs	Generosity index	End-of-service pay Minimum tenure required (months)	Generosity index	Defined contribution Minimum tenure required (months)	Contribution rate (% of salary)
Guinea-Bissau	1	:	:	:	R...	:	13.0	13.0	21.7	43.3	86.7	7.2				
Guyana	1	:	:	:	R...	12	0.0	2.0	10.0	25.0	52.0	2.2				
Haiti	0	0	n.a.	n.a.	n.a.	n.a.	n.a.	n.a.	n.a.	n.a.	n.a.	n.a.				
Honduras	1	:	:	:	D,R	:	3.3	4.3	21.7	43.3	86.7	4.3				
Hong Kong SAR, China	1	:	:	:	D,R	24	0.0	0.3	1.4	2.9	5.8	0.3				
Hungary	1	:	p	Firm size less 20	D,R,B,E	36	0.0	0.0	8.7	13.0	21.7	1.0				
Iceland	0	1	n.a.	n.a.	n.a.	n.a.	n.a.	n.a.	n.a.	n.a.	n.a.	n.a.	:		:	:
India	1	:	a	Firm size less 50	R,I	12	2.1	2.1	10.7	21.4	42.9	2.1				
Indonesia	1	1	p	Domestic workers	D,R,B,I,E	:	4.3	13.0	34.7	56.3	108.3	8.5				
Iran, Islamic Rep.	1	:	a	none	D,R,E,O,I	:	0.0	4.3	21.7	43.3	86.7	4.3				
Iraq	0	:	n.a.	n.a.	n.a.	n.a.	n.a.	n.a.	n.a.	n.a.	n.a.	n.a.				
Ireland	1	1	:	none	R	24	0.2	0.7	2.6	5.0	9.8	0.6				
Israel	1	1	:	Workers excluded if employer contributes to pension plan	D,I,E	12	0.0	4.3	21.7	43.3	86.7	4.3				
Italy	1	1	p	none	E		n.a.	n.a.	10.0	n.a.	n.a.	0.0			:	7.00
Jamaica	1	0	p	none	D,R	24	0.0	0.0	10.0	20.0	50.0	1.3				

(continued)

ANNEX B **(Continued)**

Economy	Legal base		Coverage		Eligible contingencies	Defined benefits for redundancy							End-of-service pay		Defined contribution	
	Mandatory	Collective agreements	Sectors	Excluded categories	Dismissal/ Redundancy/ Bankruptcy/ Old-age/ Incapacity/ End-of-service	Minimum tenure required (months)	Benefits at 9 months	Benefits at 1 year	Benefits at 5 yrs	Benefits at 10 yrs	Benefits at 20 yrs	Generosity index	Minimum tenure required (months)	Generosity index	Minimum tenure required (months)	Contribution rate (% of salary)
Japan	0	1	n.a.	n.a.	n.a.	n.a.	n.a.	n.a.	n.a.	n.a.	n.a.	0.0				
Jordan	1	..	p	Agricultural workers and domestic workers	D,R,E	..	0.0	0.0	0.0	0.0	0.0	0.0				
Kazakhstan	1	..	..	none	D,R,B,E	..	4.3	4.3	4.3	4.3	4.3	1.9				
Kenya	1	..	a	Army, police	R	..	1.6	2.1	10.7	21.4	42.9	2.1				
Kiribati	0	0	n.a.	n.a.	n.a.	n.a.	n.a.	n.a.	n.a.	n.a.	n.a.	n.a.				
Korea, Rep.	1	0	p	none	D,R,E	12	0.0	4.3	21.7	43.3	86.7	4.3				
Kosovo	1	..	..	..	R,...	..	0.0	0.0	8.7	13.0	17.3	1.0				
Kuwait	1	0	p	Expats (own system)	D, R, E	12	1.6	2.1	10.7	32.5	75.8	2.5	12	0.7		
Kyrgyz Republic	1	..	a	Firm size less 15, managerial positions	R	..	13.0	13.0	13.0	13.0	13.0	5.6				
Lao PDR	1	..	..	..	..	..	3.9	5.2	39.0	78.0	156.0	6.9				
Latvia	1	..	..	..	D–E	..	4.3	4.3	8.7	13.0	17.3	2.5				
Lebanon	0	..	n.a.	n.a.	n.a.	n.a.	n.a.	n.a.	n.a.	n.a.	n.a.	0.0				
Lesotho	1	..	..	..	R,...	12	0.0	2.0	10.0	20.0	40.0	2.0				
Liberia	1	..	..	..	R,...	..	3.0	4.0	20.0	40.0	80.0	4.0				

(continued)

ANNEX B **(Continued)**

| Economy | Legal base | | Coverage | | Eligible contingencies | | Defined benefits for redundancy | | | | | | End-of-service pay | | Defined contribution | |
	Mandatory	Collective agree-ments	Sectors	Excluded categories	Dismissal/ Redundancy/ Bankruptcy/ Incapacity/ Old-age/ End-of-service	Minimum tenure required (months)	Benefits at 9 months	Benefits at 1 year	Benefits at 5 yrs	Benefits at 10 yrs	Benefits at 20 yrs	Generosity index	Minimum tenure required (months)	Generosity index	Minimum tenure required (months)	Contribution rate (% of salary)
Lithuania	1	..	..	..	D,R,E	..	4.3	8.7	17.3	21.7	26.0	4.8				
Luxembourg	1	..	p	none	D,R	60	0.0	0.0	4.3	8.7	26.0	0.6				
Macedonia, FYR	1	..	..	..	D,R	..	4.3	4.3	8.7	13.0	21.7	2.5				
Madagascar	1	0	..	none	D,R,B	6	0.0	1.7	8.3	16.7	26.0	1.7				
Malawi	1	..	a	Police,army	D,R	12	0.0	2.0	10.0	30.0	80.0	2.3				
Malaysia	1	0	a	none	D,R	12	0.0	1.7	16.7	33.3	66.7	2.8				
Maldives	0	0	n.a.	n.a.	n.a.	n.a.	n.a.	n.a.	n.a.	n.a.	n.a.	0.0				
Mali	1	0	..	none	D,R	12	4.3	5.2	8.7	14.1	27.1	2.8				
Marshall Islands	0	0	n.a.	n.a.	n.a.	n.a.	n.a.	n.a.	n.a.	n.a.	n.a.	0.0				
Mauritania	1	..	..	..	R,..	..	0.8	1.1	5.4	11.9	27.1	1.1				
Mauritius	1	..	..	..	R,..	12	0.0	0.4	4.3	14.3	42.9	0.9				
Mexico	1	..	p	none	D,R	..	14.1	14.6	21.4	30.0	47.1	7.3				
Micronesia, Fed. Sts.	0	0	n.a.	n.a.	n.a.	n.a.	n.a.	n.a.	n.a.	n.a.	n.a.	0.0				
Moldova	1	..	a	none	D,R,B,I	..	9.6	9.6	13.6	18.6	28.7	4.7				
Mongolia	1	..	..	..	D,R	..	4.3	4.3	4.3	4.3	4.3	1.9				

(continued)

ANNEX B **(Continued)**

Economy	Legal base		Coverage		Eligible contingencies		Defined benefits for redundancy						End-of-service pay		Defined contribution	
	Mandatory	Collective agreements	Sectors	Excluded categories	Dismissal/ Redundancy/ Bankruptcy/ Incapacity/ Old-age/ End-of-service	Minimum tenure required (months)	Benefits at 9 months	Benefits at 1 year	Benefits at 5 yrs	Benefits at 10 yrs	Benefits at 20 yrs	Generosity index	Minimum tenure required (months)	Generosity index	Minimum tenure required (months)	Contribution rate (% of salary)
Montenegro	1	..	..	..	R...	..	26.0	26.0	26.0	26.0	26.0	11.3				
Morocco	1	1	p	Firm size less 10, domestic workers, seafarers, mine workers, etc.	D,R	6	2.2	2.2	10.9	27.3	76.4	2.4				
Mozambique	1	..	..	..	D,R	..	13.0	13.0	32.5	65.0	130.0	8.7				
Namibia	1	..	..	..	R...	12	0.0	1.0	5.0	10.0	20.0	1.0				
Nepal	1	..	a	Firm size less 10	R	6	0.0	4.3	21.4	42.9	85.7	4.3				
Netherlands	0	1	n.a.	n.a.	n.a.	n.a.	n.a.	n.a.	n.a.	n.a.	n.a.	0.0				
New Zealand	0	1	..	..	R	12	0.0	0.0	0.0	0.0	0.0	0.0				
Nicaragua	1	..	a	none	D,R,E	..	3.3	4.3	18.8	21.7	21.7	3.4				
Niger	1	1	p	none	D,R	12	4.3	5.2	8.7	3.5	30.3	2.4				
Nigeria	1	..	a	Domestic workers, air workers, seafarers, managerial positions, army, police, etc.	R	..	1.7	2.3	11.4	22.9	45.8	2.3				
Norway	0	1	..	..	..	..	0.0	0.0	0.0	0.0	0.0	0.0				
Oman	1	0	a	Expats (own system)	E	12	n.a.	n.a.	n.a.	n.a.	n.a.	0.0	12	17.3		

(continued)

ANNEX B **(Continued)**

Economy	Legal base		Coverage		Eligible contingencies	Defined benefits for redundancy							End-of-service pay		Defined contribution	
	Mandatory	Collective agreements	Sectors	Excluded categories	Dismissal/Redundancy/Bankruptcy/Old-age/Incapacity/End-of-service	Minimum tenure required (months)	Benefits at 9 months	Benefits at 1 year	Benefits at 5 yrs	Benefits at 10 yrs	Benefits at 20 yrs	Generosity index	Minimum tenure required (months)	Generosity index	Minimum tenure required (months)	Contribution rate (% of salary)
Pakistan	1	..	a	Firm size less 20	D,R,I	..	3.2	4.3	21.4	42.9	85.7	4.3				
Palau	0	0	n.a.	n.a.	n.a.	n.a.	n.a.	n.a.	n.a.	n.a.	n.a.	0.0				
Panama	1	..	p	Members of cooperatives	R	..	3.0	4.0	19.0	34.0	44.0	3.7				
Papua New Guinea	1	..	..	..	R,...	..	1.3	1.7	8.7	17.3	34.7	1.7				
Paraguay	1	..	..	..	R,...	..	2.1	2.1	10.7	42.9	85.7	2.9				
Peru	1	..	p	none	R–E	..	0.0	2.9	14.3	17.1	17.1	2.5			..	8.33
Philippines	1	..	p	none	R,I,B	6	4.3	4.3	21.7	43.3	86.7	4.3				
Poland	0	1	n.a.	n.a.	n.a.	n.a.	n.a.	n.a.	n.a.	n.a.	n.a.	0.0				
Portugal	1	1	a	none	D,R	12	13.0	13.0	21.7	43.3	86.7	7.2				
Puerto Rico	0	1	n.a.	n.a.	n.a.	n.a.	n.a.	n.a.	n.a.	n.a.	n.a.	0.0				
Qatar	1	0	..	..	R–E	..	0.0	3.0	15.0	30.0	60.0	3.0	12	1.0		
Romania	0	1	..	..	..	..	4.3	4.3	4.3	4.3	4.3	1.9				
Russian Federation	1	..	a	Army, managerial positions	D,R,B	..	8.7	8.7	8.7	8.7	8.7	3.8				
Rwanda	1	..	..	..	R,...	..	0.0	4.3	8.7	13.0	21.7	2.5				
Samoa	0	0	n.a.	n.a.	n.a.	n.a.	n.a.	n.a.	n.a.	n.a.	n.a.	0.0				

(continued)

ANNEX B (Continued)

Economy	Legal base			Coverage	Eligible contingencies	Defined benefits for redundancy							End-of-service pay		Defined contribution	
	Mandatory	Collective agreements	Sectors	Excluded categories	Dismissal/ Redundancy/ Bankruptcy/ Incapacity/ Old-age/ End-of-service	Minimum tenure required (months)	Benefits at 9 months	Benefits at 1 year	Benefits at 5 yrs	Benefits at 10 yrs	Benefits at 20 yrs	Generosity index	Minimum tenure required (months)	Generosity index	Minimum tenure required (months)	Contribution rate (% of salary)
São Tomé and Principe	1	..	..	..	R,...	..	13.0	13.0	21.7	43.3	86.7	7.2				
Saudi Arabia	1	0	a	Expats (own system)	D,E	..	2.2	2.2	10.8	32.5	75.8	2.5	12	0.9		
Senegal	1	1	p	Seafarers	D,R	12	0.0	5.4	9.8	16.3	33.6	3.0				
Serbia	1	..	..	..	R,...	..	0.0	1.4	7.2	14.4	25.3	1.4				
Seychelles	1	..	..	..	R,...	..	1.3	1.7	8.6	17.1	34.3	1.7				
Sierra Leone	1	..	..	..	R,...	..	4.0	4.4	28.0	72.0	180.0	5.7				
Singapore	0	1	n.a.	n.a.	n.a.	n.a.	n.a.	n.a.	n.a.	n.a.	n.a.	0.0				
Slovak Republic	1	..	p	Seafarers	R,I	..	8.7	8.7	13.0	13.0	13.0	4.2				
Slovenia	1	..	p	Firm size less 10, managerial positions	D,R,I	12	0.0	0.9	5.4	10.8	28.9	1.0				
Solomon Islands	1	0	..	..	R,...	..	1.5	2.0	10.0	20.0	40.0	2.0				
South Africa	1	1	a	Army, state security, seafarers	R,B	12	0.0	1.0	5.0	10.0	20.0	1.0				
Spain	1	..	p	none	D,R,B,I	..	2.1	2.9	14.3	28.6	52.0	2.9				

(continued)

ANNEX B (Continued)

Economy	Legal base		Coverage		Eligible contingencies	Defined benefits for redundancy							End-of-service pay		Defined contribution	
	Mandatory	Collective agreements	Sectors	Excluded categories	Dismissal/ Redundancy/ Bankruptcy/ Incapacity/ Old-age/ End-of-service	Minimum tenure required (months)	Benefits at 9 months	Benefits at 1 year	Benefits at 5 yrs	Benefits at 10 yrs	Benefits at 20 yrs	Generosity index	Minimum tenure required (months)	Generosity index	Minimum tenure required (months)	Contribution rate (% of salary)
Sri Lanka	1	0	p	Firm size less 15, members of cooperatives	D–E	60	8.1	10.8	54.2	97.5	169.0	10.5				
St. Kitts and Nevis	0	..	n.a.	n.a.	n.a.	n.a.	n.a.	n.a.	n.a.	n.a.	n.a.	0.0				
St. Lucia	1	..	..	..	R,...	..	0.0	1.0	7.0	20.0	50.0	1.5				
St. Vincent and the Grenadines	1	..	..	..	R,...	..	0.0	0.0	10.0	20.0	50.0	1.3				
Sudan	1	..	..	..	R,...	..	0.0	0.0	21.7	43.3	113.8	2.9				
Suriname	1	..	..	..	R,...	..	4.0	4.0	5.0	17.3	26.0	2.2				
Swaziland	1	..	..	..	R,...	..	0.0	0.0	8.0	18.0	38.0	1.1				
Sweden	0	1	n.a.	n.a.	n.a.	n.a.	n.a.	n.a.	n.a.	n.a.	n.a.	9.0				
Switzerland	1	1	p	Firm size less 20	D,R,E	240	0.0	0.0	0.0	0.0	0.0	0.0				
Syrian Arabic Republic	1	..	p	Domestic workers	D,R,E	..	0.0	0.0	0.0	0.0	0.0	0.0				
Taiwan, China	1	..	..	..	D,R	..	1.6	2.2	10.8	43.3	86.7	2.9				
Tajikistan	1	..	..	..	R,...	..	4.3	4.3	5.4	10.8	21.7	2.2				
Tanzania	1	..	a	Police, army	D,R	12	0.0	1.0	5.0	10.0	10.0	1.0				

(continued)

Economy	Legal base		Coverage		Eligible contingencies	Defined benefits for redundancy							End-of-service pay		Defined contribution	
	Mandatory	Collective agreements	Sectors	Excluded categories	Dismissal/ Redundancy/ Bankruptcy/ Incapacity/ Old-age/ End-of-service	Minimum tenure required (months)	Benefits at 9 months	Benefits at 1 year	Benefits at 5 yrs	Benefits at 10 yrs	Benefits at 20 yrs	Generosity index	Minimum tenure required (months)	Generosity index	Minimum tenure required (months)	Contribution rate (% of salary)
Thailand	1	1	p	Agricultural workers, domestic workers	D,R	4	5.0	15.0	30.0	50.0	50.0	8.7				
Timor-Leste	0	0	n.a.	n.a.	n.a.	n.a.	n.a.	n.a.	n.a.	n.a.	n.a.	0.0				
Togo	1	0	..	..	R,..	..	1.0	1.3	6.5	14.1	31.4	1.3				
Tonga	0	0	n.a.	n.a.	n.a.	n.a.	n.a.	n.a.	n.a.	n.a.	n.a.	0.0				
Trinidad and Tobago	1	..	..	..	R,..	..	2.2	2.2	11.9	28.2	60.7	2.5				
Tunisia	1	1	p	Seafarers, domestic workers	D,R	36	1.3	1.7	8.6	13.0	13.0	1.6				
Turkey	1	1	p	Firm size less 30, agricultural and domestic workers, seafarers, managerial positions, etc.	D,R,I,O	12	0.0	4.3	21.7	43.3	86.7	4.3				
Uganda	1	..	a	Army	I,B	..	0.0	0.0	0.0	0.0	0.0	0.0				
Ukraine	1	..	..	..	D–E	..	4.3	4.3	4.3	4.3	4.3	1.9				
United Arab Emirates	1	0	a	Expats (own system)	D–E	12	2.3	3.0	15.0	36.4	79.3	3.2	12	1.4		
United Kingdom	1	1	a	Police, army, seafarers	R	24	0.0	0.0	2.6	5.1	10.5	0.3				
United States	0	1	n.a.	n.a.	n.a.	n.a.	n.a.	n.a.	n.a.	n.a.	n.a.	0.0				

(continued)

ANNEX B **(Continued)**

| Economy | Legal base | | Sectors | Coverage | Eligible contingencies | Defined benefits for redundancy | | | | | | | End-of-service pay | | Defined contribution | |
	Mandatory	Collective agree-ments		Excluded categories	Dismissal/ Redundancy/ Bankruptcy/ Incapacity/ Old-age/ End-of-service	Minimum tenure required (months)	Benefits at 9 months	Benefits at 1 year	Benefits at 5 yrs	Benefits at 10 yrs	Benefits at 20 yrs	Generosity index	Minimum tenure required (months)	Generosity index	Minimum tenure required (months)	Contribution rate (% of salary)
Uruguay	1	..	a	none	D,R	..	5.2	5.2	26.0	31.2	31.2	4.5				
Uzbekistan	1	..	..	..	D,R	..	13.0	13.0	13.0	13.0	13.0	5.6				
Vanuatu	1	..	..	..	R,...	..	0.0	4.3	21.7	43.3	43.3	4.3				
Venezuela, RB	1	..	p	Firm size less 10,domestic workers	D,R,O	3	..	..	..	..	..	..				
Vietnam	1	..	p	Managerial positions, members of cooperatives, political organizations	D,R,E	12	0.0	4.3	21.7	43.3	86.7	4.3				
West Bank and Gaza	1	0	..	..	R,...	..	4.3	4.3	21.7	43.3	86.7	4.3				
Yemen, Rep.	1	0	p	Agricultural and domestic workers	D,R	..	3.3	4.3	21.7	43.3	86.7	4.3				
Zambia	1	1	a	Domestic workers, police, army, judiciary, managerial positions	D,R,I	..	6.5	8.7	43.3	86.7	173.3	8.7				
Zimbabwe	1	..	p	none	D,R	..	0.0	13.0	65.0	130.0	433.3	13.0				

(continued)

ANNEX B (Continued)

Economy	Funding & taxation				Reforms		Other income support				Employment regulation	Country background variables					
	State contribution	Funding method	Taxation of benefits	Guarantee fund	Type of reform	Year of reform	Type of unemployment benefit system	Unemployment benefit generosity	Type of pension system	Pension benefit generosity	Redundancy notice period (weeks)	Region	Income level	GDP per capita (current US$, 2009)	Unemployment rate, 2000–08 (%)	Trade union density 2008–09	Size of informal economy (%)
Afghanistan	..	I-C	..	..	..	..	none	n.a.	none	n.a.	4.3	Asia	low income	405	..	0.00	..
Albania	..	I-C	fully	..	no reform	n.a.	UI	16	PAYGO	..	11.6	Transition	upper middle income	3,808	..	..	..
Algeria	..	E-F	..	..	Collective Framework Agreement—Introduction of severance pay (nonstatutory)	2006	UI	36	PAYGO	80	4.3	MENA	upper middle income	4,029	18.40	..	..
Angola	..	I-C	..	..	..	..	none	n.a.	Pilot	..	4.3	Africa	lower middle income	4,081	..	..	..
Antigua and Barbuda	..	I-C	..	..	..	..	UA	..	PAYGO	..	3.4	LAC	upper middle income	12,920	..	..	..
Argentina	..	I-C	partially	..	Doubling of severance pay for nonregular employees	2000	UI	10	PAYGO	62	7.2	LAC	upper middle income	7,626	13.50	36.70	25.4
Armenia	..	I-C	fully	..	No reform	n.a.	UI	13	PAYGO	..	8.7	Transition	lower middle income	2,826	28.70	56.20	46.3
Australia	Yes	I-C	partially	..	No reform	n.a.	UA	42	mixed	42	4.0	OECD	high income	42,279	5.50	19.10	15.3
Austria	No	E-A	partially	yes	Move to individual severance savings accounts	2003	dual	61	PAYGO	80	2.0	OECD	high income	45,561	4.30	35.10	10.2

(continued)

ANNEX B **(Continued)**

Economy	State contribution	Funding & taxation			Reforms		Other income support				Employment regulation	Country background variables					
		Funding method	Taxation of benefits	Guarantee fund	Type of reform	Year of reform	Type of unemployment benefit system	Unemployment benefit generosity	Type of pension system	Pension benefit generosity	Redundancy notice period (weeks)	Region	Income level	GDP per capita (current US$, 2009)	Unemployment rate, 2000–08 (%)	Trade union density 2008–09	Size of informal economy (%)
Azerbaijan	..	I-C	fully	..	No reform	n.a.	UI	9	PAYGO	..	8.7	Transition	upper middle income	4,899	7.50	..	..
Bahamas, The	..	I-C	..	..	..	..	UI	..	PAYGO	..	0.0	LAC	high income	..	..	..	..
Bahrain	..	I-C	untaxed	..	..	..	UI	..	PAYGO	79	4.3	MENA	high income	26,021	..	0.00	..
Bangladesh	No	I-C	..	..	Decreased generosity	1985	none	n.a.	PAYGO	..	4.3	Asia	low income	551	4.00	..	..
Belarus	..	I-C	fully	..	No reform	n.a.	UI	8	PAYGO	..	8.7	Transition	upper middle income	5,075	..	79.70	..
Belgium	n.a.	n.a.	n.a.	n.a.	n.a.	n.a.	UI	65	PAYGO	42	6.0	OECD	high income	43,672	7.70	93.20	23.2
Belize	..	I-C	..	..	..	..	none	n.a.	PAYGO	n.a.	3.3	LAC	lower middle income	4,062	..	..	..
Benin	..	I-C	..	..	No reform	n.a.	none	n.a.	PAYGO	..	4.3	Africa	low income	745	..	..	..
Bhutan	n.a.	n.a.	n.a.	n.a.	n.a.	n.a.	none	n.a.	PAYGO	..	8.3	Asia	lower middle income	1,805	..	..	..

(continued)

ANNEX B (Continued)

Economy	State contribution	Funding method	Taxation of benefits	Guarantee fund	Type of reform	Year of reform	Type of unemployment benefit system	Unemployment benefit generosity	Type of pension system	Pension benefit generosity	Redundancy notice period (weeks)	Region	Income level	GDP per capita (current US$, 2009)	Unemployment rate, 2000–08 (%)	Trade union density 2008–09	Size of informal economy (%)
		Funding & taxation			**Reforms**		**Other income support**				**Employment regulation**	**Country background variables**					
Bolivia	..	I-C	..	..	No reform	n.a.	UI	..	mixed	..	..	LAC	lower middle income	1,758	7.80	..	67.1
Bosnia and Herzegovina	..	I-C	fully	..	No reform	n.a.	UI	6	PAYGO	..	2.0	Transition	upper middle income	4,524	27.80	..	..
Botswana	..	I-C	..	..	Introduction of severance pay	1992	none	n.a.	universal	..	4.9	Africa	upper middle income	6,063	19.00	..	..
Brazil	..	E-A	..	..	Contribution to Unemployment Guarantee Fund (FGTS) by employer increased from 8% to 8.5%. The fine for unjustified dismissals increased from 40% to 50% of the FGTS balance, with the extra 10% paid by the firm directly to the government.	2001	UI	9	PAYGO	..	4.3	LAC	upper middle income	8,121	9.00	20.90	39.8
Brunei Darussalam	n.a.	n.a.	n.a.	n.a.	n.a.	n.a.	none	n.a.	mixed	..	3.0	Asia	high income	..	..	..	..
Bulgaria	..	I-C	fully	..	Introduction of severance pay	2001	UI	12	mixed	50	4.3	Transition	upper middle income	6,423	12.30	..	36.9
Burkina Faso	..	I-C	..	..	no reform	n.a.	none	..	PAYGO	..	4.3	Africa	low income	517	..	..	38.4

(continued)

ANNEX B (Continued)

Economy	Funding & taxation				Reforms		Other income support				Employment regulation	Country background variables					
	State contri-bution	Funding method	Taxation of benefits	Guarantee fund	Type of reform	Year of reform	Type of unemploy-ment benefit system	Unem-ployment benefit generosity	Type of pension system	Pension benefit gene-rosity	Redundancy notice period (weeks)	Region	Income level	GDP per capita (current US$, 2009)	Unem-ployment rate, 2000–08 (%)	Trade union density 2008–09	Size of informal economy (%)
Burundi	..	I-C	..	..	..	..	none	n.a.	PAYGO	..	8.7	Africa	low income	160	..	..	..
Cambodia	..	I-C	..	..	..	..	none	n.a.	none	..	7.9	Asia	low income	667	..	..	..
Cameroon	..	I-C	..	..	Establish calculation of employees' severance pay	1993	none	n.a.	PAYGO	..	6.5	Africa	lower middle income	1,136	7.50	..	..
Canada	Yes	I-C	..	..	No reform	n.a.	UI	52	mixed	45	7.0	OECD	high income	39,599	6.90	31.40	16.4
Cape Verde	..	I-C	..	..	..	..	none	n.a.	PAYGO	..	6.4	Africa	lower middle income	3,064	..	..	..
Central African Republic	..	I-C	..	..	..	..	none	n.a.	PAYGO	..	4.3	Africa	low income	454	..	..	..
Chad	..	I-C	..	..	..	..	none	n.a.	PAYGO	..	7.2	Africa	low income	610	..	..	..
Chile	Yes	E-A, E-F	..	yes	Increased access to Solidarity Fund for end-of-service benefits for fixed-term contracts, Increased benefits level and quality	2009	UI	21	mixed	44	4.3	OECD	upper middle income	9,645	7.40	11.50	19.8
China	..	I-C	partially	..	Introduction of statutory severance pay	2008	UI	20	mixed	68	4.3	Transition	lower middle income	3,744	..	..	13.1

(continued)

Economy	Funding & taxation				Reforms		Other income support				Employment regulation	Country background variables					
	State contribution	Funding method	Taxation of benefits	Guarantee fund	Type of reform	Year of reform	Type of unemployment benefit system	Unemployment benefit generosity	Type of pension system	Pension benefit generosity	Redundancy notice period (weeks)	Region	Income level	GDP per capita (current US$, 2009)	Unemployment rate, 2000–08 (%)	Trade union density 2008–09	Size of informal economy (%)
Colombia	No	E-A	partially	yes	Introduction of fully funded severance pay savings accounts	1990	UI	..	mixed	50	0.0	LAC	upper middle income	5,125	13.00	28.70	39.1
Comoros	..	I-C	..	..			none	n.a.	none		13.0	Africa	low income	833			
Congo, Dem. Rep.	..	I-C	..	..			none	n.a.	PAYGO		10.3	Africa	low income	160			
Congo, Rep.	..	I-C	..	..			none	n.a.	PAYGO		4.3	Africa	lower middle income	2,601			
Costa Rica	..	I-C	..	..	No reform	n.a.	UI	..	mixed	89	4.3	LAC	upper middle income	6,385	5.90	..	..
Côte d'Ivoire	..	I-C	..	..	Introduction of severance pay	1996	none	n.a.	PAYGO	..	5.8	Africa	lower middle income	1,105	..	..	..
Croatia	..	I-C	fully	..	No reform	n.a.	dual	11	mixed	38	7.9	Transition	high income	14,222	13.00	..	33.4
Cyprus	n.a.	n.a.	n.a.	yes	..	..	UI	..	PAYGO	..	5.7	OECD	high income	31,410	..	..	..
Czech Republic	Yes	I-C	fully	..	No reform	n.a.	UI	33	PAYGO	50	8.7	OECD	high income	18,139	7.22	20.80	19.1

(continued)

ANNEX B **(Continued)**

Economy	State contri-bution	Funding & taxation			Reforms		Other income support				Employment regulation	Country background variables					
		Funding method	Taxation of benefits	Guarantee fund	Type of reform	Year of reform	Type of unemploy-ment benefit system	Unem-ployment benefit generosity	Type of pension system	Pension benefit gene-rosity	Redundancy notice period (weeks)	Region	Income level	GDP per capita (current US$, 2009)	Unem-ployment rate, 2000–08 (%)	Trade union density 2008–09	Size of informal economy (%)
Denmark	Yes	I-C	..	..	Establish benefits for white collar workers	1996	UI	68	mixed	80	0.0	OECD	high income	55,992	4.63	99.20	18.2
Djibouti	n.a.	n.a.	n.a.	n.a.	..	..	none	n.a.	PAYGO	..	4.3	Africa	lower middle income	1,213	..	..	..
Dominica	..	I-C	..	..	..	..	none	n.a.	PAYGO	..	5.8	LAC	upper middle income	5,132	..	..	..
Dominican Republic	..	I-C	..	..	No reform	n.a.	none	n.a.	mixed	53	4.0	LAC	upper middle income	4,637	16.00	..	32.1
Ecuador	..	I-C	..	..	Increase in severance payments	1991	UI	..	mixed	..	4.3	LAC	lower middle income	4,202	8.70	..	34.4
Egypt, Arab Rep.	..	I-C	untaxed	..	Unfinished years to be considered as full years when calculating tenure	2003	UI	7	PAYGO	..	10.1	MENA	lower middle income	2,270	9.90	26.10	35.1
El Salvador	..	I-C	..	..	..	..	UI	n.a.	PAYGO	..	0.0	LAC	lower middle income	3,424	..	..	..
Equatorial Guinea	..	I-C	..	..	..	..	none	n.a.	none	n.a.	4.3	Africa	high income	15,397	..	..	..
Eritrea	..	I-C	..	..	..	..	none	n.a.	none	n.a.	3.1	Africa	low income	369	..	..	..

(continued)

ANNEX B **(Continued)**

Economy	Funding & taxation				Reforms		Other income support				Employment regulation	Country background variables					
	State contri-bution	Funding method	Taxation of benefits	Guarantee fund	Type of reform	Year of reform	Type of unemploy-ment benefit system	Unem-ployment benefit generosity	Type of pension system	Pension benefit gene-rosity	Redundancy notice period (weeks)	Region	Income level	GDP per capita (current US$, 2009)	Unem-ployment rate, 2000–08 (%)	Trade union density 2008–09	Size of informal economy (%)
Estonia	..	I-C	fully	yes	n.a.	n.a.	dual	..	mixed	52	8.6	OECD	high income	14,238	8.90	7.60	..
Ethiopia	..	I-C	..	..	Introduction of severance pay	2003	none	..	PAYGO	..	10.1	Africa	low income	344	5.00	12.90	..
Fiji	..	I-C	..	..	..	..	none	n.a.	Provident fund	..	4.3	Asia	upper middle income	3,326	..	..	..
Finland	Yes	I-C	..	yes	No reform	n.a.	dual	60	PAYGO	56	10.1	OECD	high income	44,581	8.30	68.00	18.3
France	Yes	I-C	..	..	Statutory min payment and extra benefit for employees with more than 10 years, tenure	2008	dual	67	PAYGO	53	7.2	OECD	high income	41,051	8.30	7.90	15.3
Gabon	..	I-C	..	..	..	..	none	n.a.	PAYGO	..	10.4	Africa	upper middle income	7,502	..	..	..
Gambia, The	n.a.	n.a.	n.a.	n.a.	n.a.	n.a.	none	n.a.	PAYGO	..	26.0	Africa	low income	430	..	..	..
Georgia	..	I-C	fully	..	..	..	UI	6	PAYGO	..	0.0	Transition	lower middle income	2,449	12.80	40.70	67.3
Germany	Yes	I-C	fully	no	No reform	n.a.	dual	64	PAYGO	43	10.0	OECD	high income	40,670	9.20	19.90	16.3

(continued)

ANNEX B **(Continued)**

Economy	Funding & taxation				Reforms		Other income support				Employment regulation	Country background variables					
	State contribution	Funding method	Taxation of benefits	Guarantee fund	Type of reform	Year of reform	Type of unemployment benefit system	Unemployment benefit generosity	Type of pension system	Pension benefit generosity	Redundancy notice period (weeks)	Region	Income level	GDP per capita (current US$, 2009)	Unemployment rate, 2000–08 (%)	Trade union density 2008–09	Size of informal economy (%)
Ghana	..	I-C	..	..	No reform	n.a.	none	n.a.	mixed	..	3.6	Africa	low income	1,098	..	70.00	38.4
Greece	Yes	I-C	partially	..	Increase in severance pay for blue collar workers	2007	UI	33	PAYGO	96	0.0	OECD	high income	29,240	9.50	30.60	28.6
Grenada	..	I-C	..	..	..	..	none	n.a.	PAYGO	..	7.2	LAC	upper middle income	6,029	..	..	..
Guatemala	..	I-C	..	..	No reform	n.a.	UI	..	PAYGO	..	0.0	LAC	lower middle income	2,661	2.40	12.90	..
Guinea	..	I-C	..	..	..	..	none	n.a.	PAYGO	..	2.1	Africa	low income	497	..	..	..
Guinea-Bissau	..	I-C	..	..	..	..	none	n.a.	none	..	0.0	Africa	low income	519	..	..	..
Guyana	..	I-C	..	..	..	..	none	n.a.	PAYGO	..	4.3	LAC	lower middle income	1,518	..	..	..
Haiti	n.a.	n.a.	n.a.	n.a.	n.a.	n.a.	none	n.a.	none	n.a.	10.1	LAC	low income	646	..	..	..
Honduras	..	I-C	..	..	No reform	n.a.	UI	..	PAYGO	..	7.2	LAC	lower middle income	1,918	4.10	..	..

(continued)

ANNEX B (Continued)

Economy	Funding & taxation				Reforms		Other income support				Employment regulation	Country background variables					
	State contribution	Funding method	Taxation of benefits	Guarantee fund	Type of reform	Year of reform	Type of unemployment benefit system	Unemployment benefit generosity	Type of pension system	Pension benefit generosity	Redundancy notice period (weeks)	Region	Income level	GDP per capita (current US$, 2009)	Unemployment rate, 2000–08 (%)	Trade union density 2008–09	Size of informal economy (%)
Hong Kong SAR, China	..	I-C	..	..	No reform	n.a.	UA	32	mixed	38	4.3	Asia	high income	30,863	5.60	21.50	16.6
Hungary	Yes	I-C	fully	yes	Intoduction of wage guatantee fund	1994	UI	48	mixed	77	6.2	OECD	high income	12,868	6.60	19.90	25.1
Iceland	..	n.a.	..	..	..	..	UI	57	mixed	..	10.1	OECD	high income	38,029	..	..	..
India	No	I-C	partially	..	No reform	n.a.	UI	..	mixed	40	4.3	Asia	lower middle income	1,134	4.30	..	23.1
Indonesia	..	I-C	..	..	Pending reform	2000–2007–2011	none	n.a.	mixed	15	0.0	Asia	lower middle income	2,349	9.10	..	19.4
Iran, Islamic Rep	..	I-C	..	..	No reform	n.a.	UI	47	PAYGO	..	0.0	Asia	upper middle income	4,540	10.90	..	..
Iraq	n.a.	n.a.	n.a.	n.a.	..	..	none	n.a.	PAYGO	..	0.0	MENA	lower middle income	2,090	..	..	..
Ireland	Yes	I-C	partially	..	No reform	n.a.	dual	50	mixed	34	4.0	OECD	high income	51,049	4.50	31.50	15.8
Israel	..	I-C	partially	yes	No reform	n.a.	UI	..	PAYGO	..	4.3	OECD	high income	26,256	8.90	..	21.9

(continued)

ANNEX B (Continued)

Economy	State contri-bution	Funding & taxation			Reforms		Other income support				Employment regulation	Region	Income level	Country background variables			
		Funding method	Taxation of benefits	Guarantee fund	Type of reform	Year of reform	Type of unemploy-ment benefit system	Unem-ployment benefit generosity	Type of pension system	Pension benefit gene-rosity	Redundancy notice period (weeks)			GDP per capita (current US$, 2009)	Unem-ployment rate, 2000–08 (%)	Trade union density 2008–09	Size of informal economy (%)
Italy	tax incentives	E-A, E-F	partially	yes	Option to switch to funded occupation pension plan	2007	UI	37	PAYGO	68	8.7	OECD	high income	35,084	8.10	97.10	27
Jamaica	..	I-C	..	..	No reform	n.a.	none	n.a.	PAYGO	..	4.0	LAC	upper middle income	4,471	11.90	..	36.4
Japan	Yes	I-B	..	..	No reform	n.a.	UI	45	PAYGO	34	4.3	OECD	high income	39,738	4.60	18.00	11.3
Jordan	..	I-C	..	..	Change in service period for calculation of severance pay benefits	2010	none	n.a.	PAYGO	68	4.3	MENA	lower middle income	4,216	..	..	19.4
Kazakhstan	..	I-C	fully	..	No reform	n.a.	UI	..	mixed	..	4.3	Transition	upper middle income	7,257	8.30	..	43.2
Kenya	..	I-C	..	..	No reform	n.a.	none	n.a.	Provident fund	..	4.3	Africa	low income	738	..	35.50	34.3
Kiribati	n.a.	n.a.	n.a.	n.a.	n.a.	n.a.	none	n.a.	Provident fund	n.a.	4.3	Asia	lower middle income	1,306	..	..	..
Korea, Rep	No	I-B, E-A	partially	yes	Option to switch to funded occupation pension plan	2005	UI	31	PAYGO	42	4.3	OECD	high income	17,078	3.60	10.00	27.5
Kosovo	..	I-C	..	..	..	..	none	n.a.	funded	..	13.0	Transition	lower middle income	2,985	..	..	..

(continued)

ANNEX B **(Continued)**

Economy	Funding & taxation				Reforms		Other income support				Employment regulation	Country background variables					
	State contribution	Funding method	Taxation of benefits	Guarantee fund	Type of reform	Year of reform	Type of unemployment benefit system	Unemployment benefit generosity	Type of pension system	Pension benefit generosity	Redundancy notice period (weeks)	Region	Income level	GDP per capita (current US$, 2009)	Unemployment rate, 2000–08 (%)	Trade union density 2008–09	Size of informal economy (%)
Kuwait	No	I-C	untaxed	no			none	n.a.	PAYGO	..	13.0	MENA	high income	54,260	..	0.00	..
Kyrgyz Republic	..	I-C	fully	..	Introduction of redundancy payment	2004	UI	6	PAYGO	..	4.3	Transition	low income	860	8.80	..	39.8
Lao PDR	..	I-C	..	..		..	none	n.a.	PAYGO	n.a.	6.4	Asia	low income	940	..	..	..
Latvia	..	I-C	fully	..	No reform	n.a.	UI	12	mixed	58	1.0	Transition	high income	11,616	9.90	13.00	39.9
Lebanon	n.a.	n.a.	n.a.	n.a.	No reform	n.a.	none	n.a.	none	n.a.	8.7	MENA	upper middle income	8,175	8.50	..	34.1
Lesotho	..	I-C	..	..		..	none	n.a.	PAYGO	..	4.3	Africa	lower middle income	764	..	..	..
Liberia	..	I-C	..	..		..	none	n.a.	none	n.a.	4.3	Africa	low income	222	..	..	..
Lithuania	..	I-C	fully	..	No reform	n.a.	UI	6	mixed	53	8.7	Transition	upper middle income	11,141	10.60	10.00	30.3
Luxembourg	..	I-C	..	..	No reform	n.a.	UI	87	PAYGO	88	17.3	OECD	high income	105,044	4.60	43.60	..
Macedonia, FYR	..	I-C	fully	..	Severance pay formula slightly modified	2005	UI	13	mixed	..	4.3	Transition	upper middle income	4,515	34.80	..	..

(continued)

ANNEX B **(Continued)**

Economy	State contri-bution	Funding & taxation			Reforms		Other income support				Employment regulation	Country background variables					
		Funding method	Taxation of benefits	Guarantee fund	Type of reform	Year of reform	Type of unemploy-ment benefit system	Unem-ployment benefit generosity	Type of pension system	Pension benefit gene-rosity	Redundancy notice period (weeks)	Region	Income level	GDP per capita (current US$, 2009)	Unem-ployment rate, 2000–08 (%)	Trade union density 2008–09	Size of informal economy (%)
Madagascar	..	I-C	..	..	No reform	n.a.	none	n.a.	PAYGO	..	3.4	Africa	low income	461	5.60	..	39.6
Malawi	..	I-C	..	..	Right to severance pay not applicable in case of fair dismissal related to employee's conduct	2000	none	n.a.	none	n.a.	4.3	Africa	low income	326	..	20.60	40.3
Malaysia	No	I-C	partially	..	No reform	n.a.	none	n.a.	Provident fund	32	6.7	Asia	upper middle income	7,030	3.40	10.30	31.1
Maldives	n.a.	n.a.	n.a.	n.a.	n.a.	n.a.	none	n.a.	PAYGO	n.a.	5.8	Asia	lower middle income	4,760	..	..	..
Mali	..	I-C	..	..	No reform	n.a.	none	n.a.	PAYGO	n.a.	4.3	Africa	low income	691	8.80	..	41
Marshall Islands	n.a.	n.a.	n.a.	n.a.	n.a.	n.a.	none	n.a.	PAYGO	n.a.	0.0	Asia	lower middle income	2,504	..	..	..
Mauritania	..	I-C	..	..	..	..	none	n.a.	PAYGO	..	4.3	Africa	low income	921	..	..	..
Mauritius	..	I-C	..	..	..	..	none	n.a.	mixed	..	4.3	Africa	upper middle income	6,735	..	..	..
Mexico	..	I-C	partially	..	No reform	n.a.	none	n.a.	funded	36	0.0	OECD	upper middle income	8,144	3.20	17.00	30.1

(continued)

ANNEX B (Continued)

Economy	Funding & taxation				Reforms		Other income support				Employment regulation	Country background variables					
	State contri-bution	Funding method	Taxation of benefits	Guarantee fund	Type of reform	Year of reform	Type of unemploy-ment benefit system	Unem-ployment benefit generosity	Type of pension system	Pension benefit gene-rosity	Redundancy notice period (weeks)	Region	Income level	GDP per capita (current US$, 2009)	Unem-ployment rate, 2000–08 (%)	Trade union density 2008–09	Size of informal economy (%)
Micronesia Fed. Sts.	n.a.	n.a.	n.a.	n.a.	n.a.	n.a.	none	n.a.	PAYGO	n.a.	0.0	Asia	lower middle income	2,476	..	..	..
Moldova	..	I-C	fully	..	Severance pay only for dismissals based on the worker's capacity, state of health, and insufficient qualifications	2003	UI	15	PAYGO	..	8.7	Transition	lower middle income	1,516	6.90	40.00	..
Mongolia	..	I-C	..	..	No reform	n.a.	none	n.a.	PAYGO	..	4.3	Transition	lower middle income	1,573	3.50	..	18.4
Montenegro	..	I-C	..	..	..	..	UI	..	PAYGO	..	2.1	Transition	upper middle income	6,635	..	..	..
Morocco	No	E-F	..	..	Increase in generosity	2003	none	n.a.	PAYGO	70	7.2	MENA	lower middle income	2,911	11.10	..	36.4
Mozambique	..	I-C	..	..	No reform	n.a.	none	n.a.	PAYGO	..	4.3	Africa	low income	428	..	..	40.3
Namibia	..	I-C	..	..	..	..	none	n.a.	PAYGO	..	4.3	Africa	upper middle income	4,267	..	..	..

(continued)

ANNEX B (Continued)

Economy	Funding & taxation				Reforms		Other income support				Employment regulation	Country background variables					
	State contribution	Funding method	Taxation of benefits	Guarantee fund	Type of reform	Year of reform	Type of unemployment benefit system	Unemployment benefit generosity	Type of pension system	Pension benefit generosity	Redundancy notice period (weeks)	Region	Income level	GDP per capita (current US$, 2009)	Unemployment rate, 2000–08 (%)	Trade union density 2008–09	Size of informal economy (%)
Nepal	..	I-C	..	..	Introduction of lump-sum payment in case of redundancy	1991	none	n.a.	Provident fund	..	4.3	Asia	low income	427	..	..	..
Netherlands	n.a.	n.a.	n.a.	n.a.	n.a.	n.a.	dual	71	mixed	88	8.7	OECD	high income	47,917	3.70	20.50	13.0
New Zealand	Yes	I-C	fully	..	No reform	n.a.	UA	38	universal	39	0.0	OECD	high income	29,352	4.60	20.80	12.7
Nicaragua	..	I-C	..	..	No reform	n.a.	none	n.a.	PAYGO	..	0.0	LAC	lower middle income	1,097	6.00	4.10	..
Niger	..	I-C	..	..	No reform	n.a.	none	n.a.	PAYGO	..	4.3	Africa	low income	352	..	..	..
Nigeria	..	I-C	..	..	No reform	n.a.	none	n.a.	funded	..	4.0	Africa	lower middle income	1,118	..	..	57.9
Norway	..	I-C	..	..	No reform	n.a.	UI	72	PAYGO	59	8.7	OECD	high income	79,089	3.70	52.90	19.1
Oman	No	I-C	untaxed	no	..	..	UI	n.a.	PAYGO	..	4.3	MENA	high income	16,207	..	0.00	..
Pakistan	..	I-C	..	..	No reform	n.a.	none	n.a.	PAYGO	..	4.3	Asia	lower middle income	955	7.10	15.70	36.8

(continued)

ANNEX B **(Continued)**

Economy	Funding & taxation				Reforms		Other income support				Employment regulation	Country background variables					
	State contribution	Funding method	Taxation of benefits	Guarantee fund	Type of reform	Year of reform	Type of unemployment benefit system	Unemployment benefit generosity	Type of pension system	Pension benefit generosity	Redundancy notice period (weeks)	Region	Income level	GDP per capita (current US$, 2009)	Unemployment rate, 2000–08 (%)	Trade union density 2008–09	Size of informal economy (%)
Palau	n.a.	n.a.	n.a.	n.a.	n.a.	n.a.	none	n.a.	PAYGO	n.a.	0.0	Asia	upper middle income	8,074	..	..	..
Panama	..	I-C	partially	..	No reform	n.a.	UI	..	mixed	..	0.0	LAC	upper middle income	7,155	11.10	..	64.1
Papua New Guinea	..	I-C	..	..		..	none	n.a.	funded	n.a.	3.3	Asia	lower middle income	1,172	..	..	..
Paraguay	..	I-C	..	..		..	UI	..	PAYGO	..	7.5	LAC	lower middle income	2,242	..	..	..
Peru	..	E-A	..	..	Option to withdraw 50% of account before separation	1991	none	..	mixed	39	0.0	LAC	upper middle income	4,469	7.20	..	59.9
Philippines	No	I-C	untaxed	..	No reform	n.a.	none	n.a.	PAYGO	68	4.3	Asia	lower middle income	1,752	9.70	3.20	43.4
Poland	n.a.	n.a.	n.a.	n.a.	n.a.	n.a.	UI	42	mixed	61	10.1	OECD	high income	11,273	15.70	..	27.6
Portugal	Yes	I-C	..	..	No reform	n.a.	dual	79	PAYGO	54	7.9	OECD	high income	21,903	6.30	19.50	22.6
Puerto Rico	n.a.	n.a.	n.a.	n.a.	n.a.	n.a.	UI	..	PAYGO	..	0.0	LAC	high income	..	..	..	..

(continued)

ANNEX B (Continued)

Economy	Funding & taxation				Reforms		Other income support				Employment regulation	Country background variables					
	State contribution	Funding method	Taxation of benefits	Guarantee fund	Type of reform	Year of reform	Type of unemployment benefit system	Unemployment benefit generosity	Type of pension system	Pension benefit generosity	Redundancy notice period (weeks)	Region	Income level	GDP per capita (current US$, 2009)	Unemployment rate, 2000–08 (%)	Trade union density 2008–09	Size of informal economy (%)
Qatar	..	I-C	..	..	..	..	none	n.a.	PAYGO	..	7.2	MENA	high income	69,754	..	..	..
Romania	..	I-C	fully	yes	Introduction of guarantee fund	2003	UI	16	mixed	..	4.0	Transition	upper middle income	7,500	7.00	32.30	34.4
Russian Federation	..	I-C	fully	..			dual	12	mixed	..	8.7	Transition	upper middle income	8,676	7.70	..	46.1
Rwanda	..	I-C	..	..	..	..	none	n.a.	PAYGO	..	4.3	Africa	low income	506	..	..	..
Samoa	n.a.	n.a.	n.a.	n.a.	n.a.	n.a.	none	n.a.	none	..	5.8	Asia	lower middle income	2,776	..	..	..
São Tomé and Príncipe	..	I-C	..	..	..	..	none	n.a.	PAYGO	..	4.3	Africa	lower middle income	1,184	..	..	..
Saudi Arabia	..	I-C	untaxed	no	Introduction of end-of-service benefit	2005	none	n.a.	PAYGO	..	4.3	MENA	high income	14,540	5.20	0.00	..
Senegal	..	I-C	..	..	No reform	n.a.	none	n.a.	PAYGO	..	3.2	Africa	lower middle income	1,023	11.10	..	43.2
Serbia	..	I-C	..	..	..	..	UI	..	PAYGO	..	0.0	Transition	upper middle income	5,872	..	..	..

(continued)

ANNEX B (Continued)

Economy	State contribution	Funding & taxation			Reforms		Other income support				Employment regulation	Country background variables					
		Funding method	Taxation of benefits	Guarantee fund	Type of reform	Year of reform	Type of unemployment benefit system	Unemployment benefit generosity	Type of pension system	Pension benefit generosity	Redundancy notice period (weeks)	Region	Income level	GDP per capita (current US$, 2009)	Unemployment rate, 2000–08 (%)	Trade union density 2008–09	Size of informal economy (%)
Seychelles	..	I-C	..	..	..	..	none	n.a.	none	..	4.3	Asia	upper middle income	8,688	..	..	..
Sierra Leone	..	I-C	..	..	..	..	none	n.a.	PAYGO	n.a.	8.7	Africa	low income	341	..	..	..
Singapore	n.a.	n.a.	n.a.	n.a.	No reform	n.a.	none	n.a.	Provident fund	13	3.0	Asia	high income	36,537	4.40	31.70	13.1
Slovak Republic	..	I-C	fully	..	No reform	n.a.	UI	32	mixed	56	11.6	OECD	high income	16,176	15.80	12.90	18.9
Slovenia	Yes	I-C	fully	yes	Severance pay for economic reasons or reasons of capacity	2007	UI	27	PAYGO	..	5.7	OECD	high income	23,726	5.90	..	27.1
Solomon Islands	..	I-C	..	..	..	..	none	n.a.	Provident fund	n.a.	4.3	Asia	low income	1,256	..	..	..
South Africa	..	I-C	..	..	Statutory severance pay only in case of redundancy	1997	UI	6	universal	..	4.0	Africa	upper middle income	5,786	26.40	39.80	28.4
Spain	Yes	I-C	fully	..	Introduction of benefit formula, generosity increased	1995	dual	69	PAYGO	81	2.1	OECD	high income	31,774	10.60	14.50	22.6
Sri Lanka	No	I-C	..	..	Introduction of benefit formula	2005	UA	..	Provident fund	..	4.3	Asia	lower middle income	2,068	7.40	6.00	44.6

(continued)

ANNEX B (Continued)

Economy	Funding & taxation				Reforms		Other income support				Employment regulation	Country background variables					
	State contribution	Funding method	Taxation of benefits	Guarantee fund	Type of reform	Year of reform	Type of unemployment benefit system	Unemployment benefit generosity	Type of pension system	Pension benefit generosity	Redundancy notice period (weeks)	Region	Income level	GDP per capita (current US$, 2009)	Unemployment rate, 2000–08 (%)	Trade union density 2008–09	Size of informal economy (%)
St. Kitts and Nevis	n.a.	n.a.	n.a.	n.a.	n.a.	n.a.	none	n.a.	PAYGO	..	8.7	LAC	upper middle income	10,988	..	..	..
St. Lucia	..	I-C	..	..	..	..	none	n.a.	PAYGO	..	3.7	LAC	upper middle income	5,496	..	..	..
St. Vincent and the Grenadines	..	I-C	..	..	..	..	none	n.a.	PAYGO	..	4.0	LAC	upper middle income	5,335	..	..	..
Sudan	..	I-C	..	..	..	..	none	n.a.	PAYGO	n.a.	4.3	Africa	lower middle income	1,294	..	0.00	..
Suriname	..	I-C	..	..	..	..	none	n.a.	none	n.a.	0.0	Asia	upper middle income	5,888	..	..	..
Swaziland	..	I-C	..	..	..	..	none	n.a.	Provident fund	n.a.	5.9	Africa	lower middle income	2,533	..	..	..
Sweden	n.a.	n.a.	n.a.	n.a.	No reform	n.a.	dual	66	mixed	62	14.4	OECD	high income	43,654	5.20	73.60	19.1
Switzerland	Yes	I-C	..	..	No reform	n.a.	UI	80	mixed	58	10.1	OECD	high income	63,629	3.50	23.70	8.8
Syrian Arabic Republic	..	I-C	..	..	No reform	n.a.	none	n.a.	PAYGO	..	8.7	MENA	lower middle income	2,474	11.40	..	..

(continued)

ANNEX B **(Continued)**

Economy	State contri-bution	Funding method	Taxation of benefits	Guarantee fund	Type of reform	Year of reform	Type of unemploy-ment benefit system	Unem-ployment benefit generosity	Type of pension system	Pension benefit gene-rosity	Redundancy notice period (weeks)	Region	Income level	GDP per capita (current US$, 2009)	Unem-ployment rate, 2000–08 (%)	Trade union density 2008–09	Size of informal economy (%)
		Funding & taxation			Reforms		Other income support				Employment regulation	Country background variables					
Taiwan, China	..	I-C	partially	..	Introduction of benefit formula	2005	UI	8	PAYGO	70	4.3	Asia	high income	..	4.20	35.90	19.6
Tajikistan	..	I-C	..	..	..	..	none	n.a.	PAYGO	..	8.7	Transition	low income	716	..	..	..
Tanzania	..	I-C	partially	..	Introduction of severance pay	2004	none	n.a.	PAYGO	..	4.0	Africa	low income	509	5.10	18.70	58.3
Thailand	No	I-C	untaxed	yes	No reform	n.a.	UI	..	PAYGO	50	4.3	Asia	lower middle income	3,894	1.60	2.10	52.6
Timor-Leste	n.a.	n.a.	n.a.	n.a.	n.a.	n.a.	none	n.a.	none	n.a.	4.3	Asia	lower middle income	492	..	..	..
Togo	..	I-C	..	..	..	..	none	n.a.	none	n.a.	4.3	Africa	low income	431	..	..	..
Tonga	n.a.	n.a.	n.a.	n.a.	n.a.	n.a.	none	n.a.	none	n.a.	0.0	Asia	lower middle income	2,991	..	..	..
Trinidad and Tobago	..	I-C	..	..	..	..	none	n.a.	PAYGO	..	6.4	LAC	high income	15,841	..	..	..
Tunisia	..	E-F	..	..	Increase in severance pay	2002	UA	2	PAYGO	64	4.3	MENA	lower middle income	3,792	14.60	..	38.4

(continued)

Economy	State contri-bution	Funding method	Taxation of benefits	Guarantee fund	Type of reform	Year of reform	Type of unemploy-ment benefit system	Unem-ployment benefit generosity	Type of pension system	Pension benefit gene-rosity	Redundancy notice period (weeks)	Region	Income level	GDP per capita (current US$, 2009)	Unem-ployment rate, 2000–08 (%)	Trade union density 2008–09	Size of informal economy (%)
	Funding & taxation				Reforms		Other income support				Employment regulation	Country background variables					
Turkey	Yes	I-C	partially	..	Introduction of severance pay	2003	UI	46	PAYGO	87	6.7	OECD	upper middle income	8,215	9.70	25.10	32.1
Uganda	..	I-C	..	..	Severance pay subject to negotiation between the employer and the workers or the trade union	2006	none	n.a.	Provident fund	..	8.7	Africa	low income	490	3.20	..	43.1
Ukraine	..	I-C	fully	..	No reform	n.a.	UI	15	PAYGO	..	8.7	Transition	lower middle income	2,468	8.50	..	52.2
United Arab Emirates	no	I-C	untaxed	no	..	..	none	n.a.	PAYGO	..	4.3	MENA	high income	50,070	..	0.00	..
United Kingdom	Yes	I-C	partially	..	Statutory severance pay only in case of redundancy	1996	dual	28	mixed	31	5.3	OECD	high income	35,165	5.10	..	12.6
United States	n.a.	n.a.	n.a.	n.a.	No reform	n.a.	UI	28	PAYGO	39	0.0	OECD	high income	45,989	5.10	11.40	8.8
Uruguay	..	I-C	..	..	No reform	n.a.	UA	5	mixed	103	0.0	LAC	upper middle income	9,420	13.50	19.00	51.1
Uzbekistan	..	I-C	fully	..	No reform	n.a.	UI	6	PAYGO	..	8.7	Transition	lower middle income	1,156	..	..	..
Vanuatu	..	I-C	..	..		..	none	n.a.	PAYGO	n.a.	9.3	Asia	lower middle income	2,702	..	..	..
Venezuela, RB	..	I-B, E-A	partially	..	Introduction of severance accounts	1997	UI	6	PAYGO	..	..	LAC	upper middle income	11,490	12.00	..	33.6

(continued)

ANNEX B (Continued)

Economy	Funding & taxation				Reforms		Other income support				Employment regulation	Region	Income level	Country background variables			
	State contri-bution	Funding method	Taxation of benefits	Guarantee fund	Type of reform	Year of reform	Type of unemploy-ment benefit system	Unem-ployment benefit generosity	Type of pension system	Pension benefit gene-rosity	Redundancy notice period (weeks)			GDP per capita (current US$, 2009)	Unem-ployment rate, 2000–08 (%)	Trade union density 2008–09	Size of informal economy (%)
Vietnam	..	I-C	untaxed	..	Introduction of severance pay	2003	UI	..	PAYGO	68	0.0	Transition	lower middle income	1,032	2.30	..	15.6
West Bank and Gaza	..	I-C	..	..	..	..	none	n.a.	PAYGO	..	4.3	MENA	lower middle income	..	..	..	..
Yemen, Rep.	..	I-C	..	..	Introduction of severance pay	1995	none	n.a.	PAYGO	..	4.3	MENA	lower middle income	1,118	15.40	..	..
Zambia	..	I-C	..	..	No reform	n.a.	none	n.a.	PAYGO	..	4.3	Africa	low income	985	..	..	48.9
Zimbabwe	..	I-C	..	..	No reform	n.a.	none	n.a.	PAYGO	..	13.0	Africa	low income	..	..	..	59.4

(continued)

NOTES and SOURCES

Legal base
Statutory = 1 if the country has a legally mandated severance pay system, 0 if not.
Determined by Collective Agreements = 1 if severance payments are determined through collective agreements in a significant manner, 0 if not.

Coverage
Sectors = p if only private sector is covered by severance pay programs in the country, a if both private and public sectors are covered.
Excluded categories refer to the categories of workers to which the legislation under review do not apply.

Eligible contingencies
Type of termination payment refers to the reasons for employment termination that make the worker eligible to receive severance payment (statutory or otherwise); coded as follows:
D = Dismissal/Involuntary separation (Valid reasons other than economic as provided by the employer); R = Redundancy (Economic reasons, Redundancy, Reduction of staff, Retrenchment, Reorganization, Restructuring, Structural changes, Technological change); E = End of service/Voluntary separation (End of contract term, Quits, Voluntary quits, Resignation due to economic condition, Military service, Enters school, Family-related issues); O = Old Age/Retirement ; I = Incapacity/Disability (Worker's incapacity to work due to incompetence or health reasons: illness or permanent disability); B = Bankruptcy/Closure of Organization/Insolvency (Bankruptcy, Business rationalization, Cessation of business, Closure of firm, Organization dissolved/ moved, Liquidation).

Defined benefits for redundancy
Minimum months' employment to qualify refers to the number of months the worker should have worked for the current employer to qualify for severance payment.
9 months refers to severance payment (in weeks of salary) made in case of redundancy dismissal of worker with tenure of 9 months.
1 year refers to severance payment (in weeks of salary) made in case of redundancy dismissal of worker with tenure of 1 year.

ANNEX B (Continued)

5 years refers to severance payment (in weeks of salary) made in case of redundancy dismissal of worker with tenure of 5 years.

10 years refers to severance payment (in weeks of salary) made in case of redundancy dismissal of worker with tenure of 10 years.

20 years refers to severance payment (in weeks of salary) made in case of redundancy dismissal of worker with tenure of 20 years.

Generosity index = average per year of service for employees with 1, 5, and 10 years of service (in weeks of salary)

End-of-service pay

Minimum months' employment to qualify refers to the number of months the worker should have worked for the current employer to qualify for severance payment.

Generosity index = average per year of service for employees with 20 years of service

Defined contribution

Minimum months' employment to qualify refers to the number of months the worker should have worked for the current employer to qualify for severance payment.

Contribution rate refers to the percentage of employee's salary taken as contribution to the severance payment account or fund.

Funding & taxation

State contribution indicates whether firms receive any assistance from the State; coded Yes/No

Funding method indicates how firms finance severance pay; coded as follows: I-C: Internal-Cash Flows; I-B: Internal-Book reserves; E-A: External-Individual Accounts; E-F: External-Centralized Fund

Taxation of benefits indicates the extent to which worker benefits are taxed and employer expenses deductible; coded as follows: a) Workers fully taxed b) Workers partially taxed c) Workers not taxed d) Employer expenses not deductible e) Employer expenses partially deductible.

Guarantee fund: yes, no

Other income support

Type of unemployment insurance system: UI = Unemployment Insurance; UA = Unemployment Benefits

Unemployment benefit generosity: Gross Replacement Rate for Average Income Worker.

Type of pension system: universal; PAYGO = pay-as-you-go system; funded; mixed = both; Provident fund

Pension benefits generosity: Gross replacement rate for average income earner (OECD APEX model)

Employment regulation

Redundancy notice: Average weeks for workers with 1, 5, and 10 years of service (WB, Doing business)

Country background variables

Region:

LAC = Latin America and the Caribbean; MENA = Middle East and North Africa; OECD = Organisation for Economic Co-operation and Development.

Income level is according to World Bank classification system

Unemployment rate is the average unemployment rate in the country over the period 2000–05, except in the following cases: Azerbaijan—rate is for 2003; Ethiopia—rate is for 2005; India—rate is for 2000; the Islamic Republic of Iran—rate is for 2005; Mali—rate is for 2004; Tanzania—rate is for 2001; Zambia—rate is for 2000.

Trade Union Density refers to the ratio of union members earning wages over total wage and salary earners.

Estimated size of informal economy refers to the size of the informal economy as a percentage of GDP (varying time periods).

Share of informal labor refers to the share of the total labor force employed in the informal economy in the capital city of each country as a percent of the official labor force.

Sources

Severance pay and dismissal process:

Angel-Urdinola and Kuddo (2010); Holzmann and Pouget (2011); ILO EPLex (2011); ILO-NATLEX (various years); ILO Termination of Employment Digest (2011b); Kuddo (2009); Mercer (www.mercer.us); OECD Employment Protection Indicators (2008); OECD Employment Outlook (various years); World Bank (2010): Doing Business, Towers Watson Employment Terms and Conditions (2010).

Other income support and country background variables:

Unemployment Insurance: OECD (1999); Social Security Programs throughout the World (2008–10); Pensions: OECD (2010): Pensions at a Glance, OECD (2008): Pensions at a Glance—Asia-Pacific; World Bank (2007); Pension Panorama; Region, Income level, GDP per capita: World Development Indicators, World Bank (2011); Unemployment rate: LABORSTA, ILO (www.laborsta.ilo.org); Trade Union Density: ILO 2008–09; Estimated size of informal economy, Share of Informal Labor: Botero, Djankov, La Porta, Lopez de Silanes, and Shleifer (2004).

.. = not available.

n.a. = not applicable.

Annex C. Note on Econometric Estimation

This annex provides a brief explanation of two key aspects of the econometric explanation in the text: the use of robust regression and a summary of critical factors.

Why Robust Regression?

Robust regression methods are less affected by violations of some of the assumptions underlying ordinary least squares (OLS) estimation. This means they are less influenced by outliers or other influential observations and heteroscedasticity. However, a deviation from independence or normality of error terms (for example, owing to skewness) should be dealt with differently.

In this data set, skewness may be an issue, as several income-related variables are included (GDP per capita and variants, generosity indexes). For GDP per capita, skewness was overcome by using log (per capita GDP) instead. For generosity indexes, a logarithmic transformation is not possible because of the large number of zero generosity values. Experiments with square roots of the dependent variable affected the results of tests of the normality assumption but not the overall results in terms of relevance and statistical significance of explanatory variables.

The function "lmrob" of the R (2010) CRAN package "robustbase" (Rousseeuw and others 2009) is used to analyze the data. It computes fast MM-estimators for linear regression based on Yohai (1987). It uses an S-estimator (Rousseeuw and Yohai 1984) for the errors, which are also computed with a bi-square score function. The S-estimator is computed using the Fast-S algorithm of Salibian-Barrera and Yohai (2006). Standard errors are computed using the formulas of Croux, Dhaene, and Hoorelbeke (2003).

Summary of Critical Aspects

In addition to robust regression, OLS estimation is used. For the latter, the following model assumptions were examined.

Independence of error terms. This assumption is especially relevant for time series (autocorrelation). For cross-section (nontime series) data, it can be checked by means of plotting residuals versus independent variables. For the data analyzed in this chapter, these charts indicate independence of error terms.

Homoscedasticity (variance homogeneity) of error terms. Charts of standardized residuals versus fitted values or the square root of standardized residuals versus fitted values show high residuals for many models, especially those with only one or two explanatory variables, which includes most observations. For some models, the charts indicate the existence of heteroscedasticity with higher variability of residuals for larger fitted values. However, neither the Goldfeld-Quandt test (1965) nor the Breusch-Pagan test (1979) shows significant deviation from the homogeneous variance assumption at the 5 percent level for any model with severance pay generosity as the response variable. For the dichotomous response variable, the Goldfeld-Quandt test indicates significant heteroscedasticity for three models, but this result is not confirmed by the Breusch-Pagan test. Therefore, variance inhomogeneity does not seem to be a problem overall. The Ramsey RESET test (1969) is not significant ($\alpha = 0.05$) for the models analyzed, implying the validity of the results of the two tests for homoscedasticity.

Standard normal distribution of error terms. For hardly any model is this assumption satisfied. Most Q-Q plots indicate higher skewness or heavier tails. The Jarque-Bera tests (1987) confirm this observation. However, linear regression is fairly robust against non-normality in case of reasonable sample sizes based on the central limit theorem. Using log (per capita GDP) is a step toward normality of residuals by reducing the skewness of their distribution. The logarithm or the square root (to avoid issues with zeros) can also be applied to the different generosity index variables used in the model, even to the response variable. However, although the results of the Jarque-Bera test improve, the relevance and significance of explanatory variables hardly change for any model when using the square root of the Severance Pay Generosity Index.

Linearity of relationship between dependent and independent variables. Very few potential explanatory variables show bivariate correlation with the response variables. The only significant ($\alpha = 0.05$) linear correlation coefficients between the Severance Pay Generosity Index and the explanatory variables are those involving log (per capita GDP) and the indicator variables for income level = high and low, respectively. Actually, the correlation between the regressors is stronger (multicollinearity) than between most regressors and the response variables. Although multivariate correlation may exist, the explanatory variables with the weakest pairwise correlation with the response variables in terms of significance and absolute value rarely have significant coefficients in the regression models. In addition, scatterplots indicate that excluding the observations with unemployment benefit generosity, pension benefit generosity, and severance pay generosity equal to 0 might reveal linear relationships between the variables in the remaining countries. This may help overcome the deviation from the linearity assumption.

Goodness of fit. Another way of validating the linearity of the relationship between response and explanatory variables is by evaluating the goodness of fit of a linear regression. In addition to conventional goodness of fit measures—such as adjusted R-squared and various information criteria such as AIC (Akaike 1974) and BIC (Schwarz 1978)—a simple scatterplot of fitted versus observed values of the dependent variable helps assess the goodness of fit of a regression model. In the basic model set, most models have inacceptable levels of the goodness of fit measures; this is also visible in the charts. Only models with multiple explanatory variables show a reasonable goodness of fit, but they have the drawback of a reduced number of observations owing to missing values. Some of the larger models even shrink the number of observations to approximately 20 percent to 25 percent of the original sample size. These models include Organisation for Economic Co-operation and Development (OECD) countries with a rather high GDP per capita. Thus, generalization of results does not seem valid, as income (GDP per capita) and OECD membership are correlated as well as income and the response variable severance pay generosity. Groupwise models based on income level or region are an option here, although splitting the incomplete data set further decreases the number of observations usable by a model. An analysis by region or income level is preferable. The smaller models can be calculated for larger samples but hardly have any explanatory/predictive power and are thus not to be used. The variable log (per capita GDP) is one of the few consistently significant variables.

Absence of multicollinearity of independent variables. A correlation analysis in combination with a scatterplot matrix of the independent variables helps detect pairwise collinearity. Multicollinearity can be determined by generalized variance inflation factors (VIFs) (Fox and Monette 1992). VIFs measure the effect of multicollinearity on the variance of the regression coefficient of an explanatory variable.

Correlation analysis and VIFs show that multicollinearity is present in the analyzed data set. Apart from trade union density and notice period (weeks), all metric variables are pairwise correlated. Including indicator variables of the categorical explanatory variables in the correlation analysis shows that these two variables, as well as the indicator variables for type of unemployment benefit = UA and region = Middle East and North Africa, are not significantly correlated to the other explanatory variables. Still, the majority of the correlation coefficient is smaller than 0.4, which indicates that pairwise collinearity is not as severe. Generalized VIFs indicate that log (per capita GDP), income level, and unemployment benefit generosity are the regressors most heavily affected by multicollinearity. It is advisable to avoid using them all together in one model, especially income level or region in addition to a GDP per capita variable.

References and Other Resources

Abidoye, B., d P.F. Orazem, and M. Vodopivec. 2009. "Firing Cost and Firm Size: A Study of Sri Lanka's Severance Pay System." Social Protection Discussion Paper Series 0916. World Bank, Washington, DC.

Abraham, M., and B. Prosch. 2000. "Long-Term Employment Relationships by Credible Commitments: The Carl Zeiss Foundation." *Rationality and Society* 12 (3): 283–306.

Acevado, G., and P. Eskenazi. 2003. "The Chilean Unemployment Insurance: A New Model of Income Support Available for Unemployed Workers?" Paper prepared for the joint World Bank–IIASA–Boltzmann Institute Workshop on Severance Pay Reform, Laxenburg, Austria, International Institute for Applied System Analysis, November 7–8.

Acevedo, G., P. Eskenazi, and C. Pagés. 2006. "Unemployment Insurance in Chile: A New Model of Income Support for Unemployed Workers." Social Protection Discussion Paper 0612, World Bank, Washington, DC.

Addison, J., and P. Teixeira. 2003. "The Economics of Employment Protection." *Journal of Labor Research* 24 (1): 85–129.

———. 2005. "What Have We Learned About the Employment Effects of Severance Pay? Further Iterations of Lazear et al." *Empirica* 32: 345–68.

Ahsan, A., and C. Pagés. 2009. "Are All Labor Regulations Equal? Evidence from Indian Manufacturing." *Journal of Comparative Economics* 37 (1): 62–75.

Akaike, H. 1974. "A New Look at the Statistical Model Identification." *IEEE Transactions on Automatic Control* 19 (6): 716–23.

Alvarez, F., and M. Veracierto. 2001. "Severance Payments in an Economy with Frictions." *Journal of Monetary Economics* 47 (4): 477–98.

Angel-Urdinola, Diego F., and A. Kuddo. 2010. "Key Characteristics of Employment Regulation in the Middle East and North Africa." Social Protection Discussion Paper 1006, World Bank, Washington, DC.

Asher, M., and P. Mukhopadhaya. 2003. "Severance Pay in Selected Asian Countries: A Survey." Paper prepared for the joint World Bank–IIASA–Boltzmann Institute Workshop on Severance Pay Reform, Laxenburg, Austria, International Institute for Applied System Analysis, November 7–8.

Autor, D. H., W. R. Kerr, and A. D. Kugler. 2007. "Does Employment Protection Reduce Productivity? Evidence from U.S. States." *Economic Journal* 117 (521): 189–217.

Bassanini, A., A. Garnero, P. Marianna, and S. Martin. 2010. "Institutional Determinants of Worker Flows. A Cross-country/Cross-industry Approach." OECD Social, Employment and Migration Working Paper 107, Organisation for Economic Co-operation and Development, Paris.

Bassanini, A., L. Nunziata, and D. Venn. 2009. "Job Protection Legislation and Productivity Growth in OECD Countries." *Economic Policy* 24 (4): 349–402.

Bauer, T., S. Bender, and H. Bonin. 2007. "Dismissal Protection and Worker Flows in Small Establishments." *Economica* 74 (296): 804–21.

Basu, K., H. Horn, J. Shapiro, and L. Roman. 2003. *International Labor Standards—History, Theory and Policy Options.* New York: Blackwell Publishers.

Berstein, S., E. Fajnzylber, and P. Gana. 2011. "The New Chilean Unemployment Insurance System: Combining Individual Accounts and Redistribution in an Emerging Economy." Chapter 9, this volume.

Berstein, S., C. Contreras, and E. Benvin. 2008. "Valoración del Seguro de Cesantía en Chile: Simulación de Beneficios con Datos Individuales." Chilean Pension Supervisor Working Paper 27, Santiago, Chile.

Besley, T., and R. Burgess. 2004. "Can Labor Regulation Hinder Economic Performance? Evidence from India." *Quarterly Journal of Economics* 119 (1): 91–134.

Betcherman, G., A. Luinstra, and M. Ogawa. 2001. "Labor Market Regulation: International Experience in Promoting Employment and Social Protection." Social Protection Discussion Paper 0128, World Bank, Washington, DC.

Boeri, T. 1999. "Enforcement of Employment Security Regulations, On-The-Job Search and Unemployment Duration." *European Economic Review* 43: 65–89.

Boeri, T., and P. Garibaldi. 2009. "Beyond Eurosclerosis." *Economic Policy* 24 (7): 409–61.

Boeri, T., and J. F. Jimeno. 2005. "The Effects of Employment Protection: Learning from Variable Enforcement." *European Economic Review* 49 (8): 2057–77.

Botero, J., S. Djankov, R. La Porta, and F. C. Lopez-de-Silanes. 2004. "The Regulation of Labor." *Quarterly Journal of Economics* 119 (4): 1339–82.

Breusch, T. S., and A. R. Pagan. 1979. "Simple Test for Heteroscedasticity and Random Coefficient Variation." *Econometrica* 47 (5): 1287–94.

Calcagno, R., R. Kraeussl, and C. Monticone. 2007. "An Analysis of the Effects of the Severance Pay Reform on Credit to Italian SMEs." Center for Research on Pensions and Welfare Policies Working Paper 59/07, University of Turin, Turin.

Cesaratto, S. 2008. "The Macroeconomics of the Pension Fund Reforms and the Case of the Severance Pay Reform in Italy." *Quaderni del Dipatimento di Economia Politica* No. 549, University of Siena.

Cesari, R., G. Grande, and F. Panetta. 2008. "Supplementary Pension Schemes in Italy: Features, Development and Opportunities for Workers." MEFOP Working Paper 18, Sviluppo Mercato Fundi Pensione, Rome.

Cingano, F., M. Leonardi, J. Messina, and G. Pica. 2010. "The Effects of Employment Protection Legislation and Financial Market Imperfections on Investment: Evidence from a Firm-Level Panel of EU Countries." *Economic Policy* 25 (1): 117–63.

Corsini, L., P. M. Pacini, and L. Spataro. 2010. "TFR vs. Pension Funds: A Model for the Analysis of the Incentives to Adhere to the Second Pillar in Italy." MEFOP Working Paper 25, Sviluppo Mercato Fundi Pensione, Rome.

Croux, C., G. Dhaene, and D. Hoorelbeke. 2003. "Robust Standard Errors for Robust Estimators." Discussion Paper Series 03.16, K.U. CES, Leuven.

Davis, S., and J. Haltiwanger. 1999. "Gross Job Flows." In *Handbook of Labor Economics*, ed. O. Ashenfelter and D. Card, 2711–805. Amsterdam: North Holland.

De Ferranti, D., G. E. Perry, I. S. Gill, and L. Serven. 2000. *Securing Our Future in a Global Economy*. World Bank Latin and Caribbean Studies. Washington, DC: World Bank.

Fallon, P. R., and R. E. B. Lucas. 1991. "The Impact of Changes in Job Security Regulations in India and Zimbabwe." *World Bank Economic Review* 5 (1): 395–413.

Ferrer, A., and C. Riddell. 2011. "Unemployment Insurance Savings Accounts in Latin America: Overview and Assessment." Chapter 7, this volume.

Fox, J., and G. Monette. 1992. "Generalized Collinearity Diagnostics." *Journal of the American Statistical Association* 87 (417): 178–83.

Fugazza. C., and F. Teppa. 2005. "An Empirical Assessment of the Italian Severance Pay (TFR)." Center for Research on Pensions and Welfare Policies Working Paper 38/05, University of Turin, Turin.

Garibaldi, P., and L. Pacelli. 2003. "Mandatory Severance Payments in Italy: Do They Exist?" Paper prepared for the joint World Bank-IIASA-Boltzmann Institute Workshop on Severance Pay Reform, Laxenburg, Austria, International Institute for Applied System Analysis, November 7–8.

———. 2004. "Firm-Worker Transfers at the End of the Employment Relationship: The Case of Italy." Collegio Carlo Alberto Working Paper, University of Turin, Turin.

Goldfeld, S. M., and R. E. Quandt. 1965. "Some Tests for Homoscedasticity." *Journal of the American Statistical Association* 60 (310): 539–47.

Gomez-Salvador, R., J. Messina, and G. Vallanti. 2004. "Gross Job Flows and Institutions in Europe." *Labour Economics* 11 (4): 469–85.

Grund, C. 2003. *Severance Payments for Dismissed Employees in Germany*. Bonn: Institute for the Study of Labor.

Haffner, R., S. Nickell, G. Nicoletti, S. Scarpetta, and G. Zoega. 2001. "European Integration, Liberalization and Labour Market Performance." In *Welfare and Employment in a United Europe*, ed. G. Bertola, T. Boeri, and G. Nicoletti, 147–250. Boston: MIT Press.

Haltiwanger, J. S., S. Scarpetta, and H. Schweiger. 2008. "Assessing Job Flows Across Countries: The Role of Industry, Firm Size, and Regulations." NBER Working Paper 13920, National Bureau of Economic Research, Cambridge, MA.

———. 2010. "Cross-Country Differences in Job Reallocation: The Role of Industry, Firm Size and Regulations." EBRD Working Paper 116, European Bank for Reconstruction and Development, London.

Haltiwanger, J. S., S. Scarpetta, and M. Vodopivec. 2003. "How Institutions Affect Labor Market Outcomes: Evidence from Transition Countries." Paper presented at the World Bank Economist Forum, Washington, DC.

Hawkins, E. 1940. *Dismissal Compensation. Voluntary and Compulsory Plans Used in the U.S. and Abroad.* Princeton, NJ: Princeton University Press.

———. 1942. *Dismissal Compensation and the War Economy.* Washington, DC: Committee on Social Security of the Social Science Research Council.

Heckman, J. J., and C. Pagés. 2000. "The Cost of Job Security Regulation: Evidence from Latin American Labor Markets." NBER Working Paper 7773, National Bureau of Economic Research, Cambridge, MA.

———. 2004. "Introduction." In *Law and Employment: Lessons from Latin America and the Caribbean*, ed. J. J. Heckman and C. Pagés, 1–107. Chicago: University of Chicago.

Herz, E., 1954. "Protection of Employees on the Termination of Contracts of Employment." *International Labour Review* 69 (4): 295–320.

Hewitt Associates LLC. 2002. "Hewitt International Report." http://was4.hewitt.com/hewitt.

Hofer, H., U. Schuh, and D. Walch. 2011. "Effects of the Austrian Severance Pay Reform." Chapter 5, this volume.

Holzmann, R. 1987. "Integration von Abfertigungszielsetzungen in das soziale Sicherungssystem." In *Abfertigungen im Spannungsfeld der Wirtschaftspolitik—Eine interdisziplinäre Analyse,* ed. B. Genser. Vienna: Manz Verlag.

———. 2005. "Reforming Severance Pay: Toward an Understanding of Program Rationale, Economic Impact and Reform Options." *Empirica* 32: 251–53.

Holzmann, R., K. Iyer, and M. Vodopivec. 2003. "Severance Pay Around The World: Rationale, Status, and Reforms." http://www.ilera-online.org/15thworldcongress/files/papers/Track_4/Poster/CS1W_63_LIMONCUOGLU.pdf

Holzmann, R., and Y. Pouget. 2010. "Social Protection for Temporary Migrant Workers: Conceptual Framework, Country Inventory, Assessment and Guidance." Study prepared for the Global Forum on Migration and Development, World Bank and Marseille Center for Mediterranean Integration, Marseille, October.

Iglesias, A., and R. Palacios. 2001. "Managing Public Pension Reserves: Evidence from the International Experience." In *New Ideas about Old-Age Security*, ed. R. Holzmann and J. Stiglitz, 213–53. Washington, DC: World Bank.

International Labour Organization. 2011a. NATLEX database. http://natlex.ilo.org.

———. 2011b. "Termination of Employment Legislation Digest." http://www.ilo.org/public/english/dialogue/ifpdial/info/termination.

International Monetary Fund. 1998. *Venezuela: Recent Economic Developments (1998)*. IMF Staff Country Report #98/117, Washington, DC.

International Social Security Association. 2003. Social Security Worldwide database. http://www-ssw.issa.int/sswlp2/engl/page1.htm.

Jaramillo, M., and J. Saavedra. 2005. "Severance Payments in Latin America." *Empirica* 32: 275–307.

Jarque, C. M., and A. K. Bera. 1987. "A Test for Normality of Observations and Regression Residuals." *International Statistical Review* 55 (2): 163–72.

Kahn, L. M. 2007. "The Impact of Employment Protection Mandates on Demographic Temporary Employment Patterns: International Microeconomic Evidence." *Economic Journal* 117 (521): 333–56.

Kelegama, S., and R. Salih. 1998. "Labor Retrenchment in a Privatization Programme: The Sri Lankan Experience." *Sri Lanka Journal of Social Sciences* 21 (1 & 2): 1–36.

Koeniger, W. 2005. "Dismissal Costs and Innovation." *Economics Letters* 88 (1): 79–85.

Koman, R., U. Schuh, and A. Weber. 2005. "The Austrian Severance Payments Reform: Toward a Funded Pillar." *Empirica* 32: 255–74. Revision of paper prepared for the joint World Bank–IIASA–Ludwig Boltzmann Institute International Workshop on Severance Pay Reform, Laxenburg, Austria, November 7–8, 2003.

Kuddo, A. 2009. "Labor Laws in Eastern European and Central Asian Countries: Minimum Norms and Practices." World Bank Social Protection Discussion Paper 0920, World Bank, Washington, DC.

Kugler, A. 2002. "From Severance Pay to Self-Insurance: Effects of Severance Payments Savings Accounts in Colombia." Center for Economic Policy Research. http://www.cepr.org.

Kugler, A. D. 1999. "The Impact of Firing Costs on Turnover and Unemployment: Evidence from the Colombian Labor Market Reform." *International Tax and Public Finance Journal* 6 (3): 389–410.

————. 2004. "The Effect of Job Security Regulations on Labor Market Flexibility: Evidence from the Colombian Labor Market Reform." In *Law and Employment: Lessons from Latin America and the Caribbean*, ed. J. J. Heckman and C. Pagés, 183–228. Chicago: University of Chicago Press.

Kugler, A. D., and G. Pica. 2008. "Effects of Employment Protection on Worker and Job Flows: Evidence from the 1990 Italian Reform." *Labour Economics* 15 (1): 78–95.

Kugler, A. D., and G. Saint-Paul. 2004. "How Do Firing Costs Affect Worker Flows in a World with Adverse Selection?" *Journal of Labor Economics* 22 (3): 553–84.

Kugler, A. D., J. F. Jimeno, and V. Hernanz. 2003. "Employment Consequences of Restrictive Permanent Contracts: Evidence from Spanish Labor Market Reforms." CEPR Discussion Paper 3724, Centre for Economic Policy Research, London.

Lazear, E. P. 1990. "Job Security Provisions and Employment." *Quarterly Journal of Economics* 105 (3): 699–726.

Lora, E., and M. Henao. 2000. Colombia: *The Evolution and Reform of the Labor Market*. Washington, DC: Brookings Institution.

MacIsaac, D., and M. Rama. 2001. *Mandatory Severance Pay. Its Coverage and Effects in Peru.* Washington, DC: World Bank.

Malo, M. 2000. "A Simple Model of Severance Pay Determination: The Case of Individual Dismissals in Spain." *Labour: Review of Labour Economics and Industrial Relations* 14 (2): 269–90.

Martins, P. 2009. "Dismissals for Cause: The Difference That Just Eight Paragraphs Can Make." *Journal of Labor Economics* 27 (2): 257–79.

McGill, R., J. Tukey, and A. Wayne. 1978. "Variations of Box Plots." *The American Statistician* 32 (1): 12–16.

Mehmet, O. 1975. "Theoretical Aspects of Severance Pay: A Human Capital Theory Approach." Industrial Relations Centre, Queen's University, Kingston, Canada.

Messina, J., and G. Vallanti. 2007. "Job Flow Dynamics and Firing Restrictions: Evidence from Europe." *Economic Journal* 117 (521): F279–301.

Meyers, Frederic. 1964. *Ownership of Jobs–A Comparative Study.* Los Angeles: Institute of Industrial Relations, University of California.

Micco, A., and C. Pagés. 2006. "The Economic Effects of Employment Protection: Evidence from International Industry-Level Data." IZA Discussion Paper 2433, Institute for the Study of Labor, Bonn.

Miron, J., and D. Weil. 1997. "The Genesis and Evolution of Social Security." NBER Working Paper 5949, National Bureau of Economic Research, Cambridge, MA.

Montenegro, C. E., and C. Pagés. 2004. "Who Benefits from Labor Market Regulations? Chile, 1960–1998." In *Law and Employment: Lessons from Latin America and the Caribbean,* ed. J. J. Heckman and C. Pagés, 401–34. Chicago: University of Chicago Press.

Nickell, S., and R. Layard. 1999. "Labor Market Institutions and Economic Performance." In *Handbook of Labor Economics,* Vol. 3, ed. Orley Ashenfelter and David Card. Amsterdam: North Holland.

OECD (Organisation for Economic Co-operation and Development). 1999. *Benefit Systems and Work Incentives 1999.* Paris: OECD.

———. 2004. *OECD Employment Outlook 2004.* Paris: OECD.

———. 2007. *OECD Employment Outlook 2007.* Paris: OECD.

———. 2010. *OECD Employment Outlook 2010.* Paris: OECD.

OECD (diverse years): *OECD Employment Outlook.* Paris: OECD.

———. *Pensions at a Glance.* Paris: OECD.

Orenstein, M. 2003. "Mapping the Diffusion of Pension Innovations." In *Pension Reform in Europe: Process and Progress,* ed. R. Holzmann, M. Orenstein, and M. Rutkowski, 171–93. Washington, DC: World Bank.

Palacios, R., and M. Pallares-Miralles. 2000. "International Patterns of Pension Provision." Social Protection Discussion Paper No. 0009, World Bank, Washington, DC.

Parsons, D. 2005a. "Benefit Generosity in Voluntary Severance Plans: The U.S. Experience." Draft, George Washington University, Washington, DC. http://ssrn.com/abstract=877903.

———. 2005b. "The Emergence of Private Job Displacement Insurance in the United States: Severance Pay Plans 1930–1954." http://ssrn.com/abstract=872331.

———. 2005c. "Private Job Displacement Insurance in the United States 1954–1979: Expansion and Innovation." http://ssrn.com/abstract=872334.

———. 2005d. "Private Job Displacement Insurance: Information Asymmetries and Separation Pay Design." http://ssrn.com/abstract=878792.

———. 2011a. "Mandated Severance Pay and Firing Cost Distortions: A Critical Review of the Evidence." Chapter 3, this volume.

———. 2011b. "The Firing Cost Implications of Alternative Severance Pay Designs." Chapter 4, this volume.

Pissarides, C. A. 2001. "Employment Protection." *Labour Economics* 8: 131–59.

Rama, M., and R. Artecona. 2002. *A Database for Labor Market Indicators Across Countries.* Washington, DC: World Bank.

Ramsey, J. B. 1969. "Tests for Specification Errors in Classical Linear Least Squares Regression Analysis." *Journal of the Royal Statistical Society* 31 (2): 350–71.

Ranaraja, S. 2005. "Description and Process Analysis of the TEWA System." World Bank, Human Development Network.

R Development Core Team. 2010. "R: A Language and Environment for Statistical Computing." R Foundation for Statistical Computing, Vienna, Austria. http://www.R-project.org.

Reyes, G., J. C. van Ours, and M. Vodopivec. 2010. "Incentive Effects of Unemployment Insurance Savings Accounts: Evidence from Chile." Discussion Paper 5971, Centre for Economic Policy Research, London.

Reyes, G., J. van Ours, and M. Vodopivec. 2011. Reemployment Incentives under the Chilean Hybrid Unemployment Benefit Program Chapter 10, this volume.

Robalino, D. A., and A. Mataoanu. 2005. "Severance Pay in the Middle East and North Africa Region." Middle East and North Africa Region Working Papers, World Bank, Washington, DC.

Rousseeuw, P. J., C. Croux, V. Todorov, A. Ruckstuhl, M. Salibian-Barrera, T. Verbeke, and M. Maechler. 2009. "Robustbase: Basic Robust Statistics. R package version 0.5-0-1." http://CRAN.R-project.org/package=robustbase.

Rousseeuw, P. J., and V. J. Yohai. 1984. "Robust Regression by Means of S-estimators." In *Robust and Nonlinear Time Series, Lecture Notes in Statistics*, ed. J. Franke, W. Härdle, and R. D. Martin, 256–72. New York: Springer Verlag.

Saavedra, J., and M. Torero. 2004. "Labor Market Reforms and Their Impact on Formal Labor Demand and Job Market Turnover: The Case of Peru." In *Law and Employment: Lessons from Latin America and the Caribbean*, ed. J. J. Heckman and C. Pagés, 131–82. Chicago: University of Chicago Press.

Salibian-Barrera, M., and V. J. Yohai. 2006. "A Fast Algorithm for S-regression Estimates." *Journal of Computational and Graphical Statistics* 15 (2): 1–14.

Scarpetta, S., and T. Tressel 2004. "Boosting Productivity via Innovation and Adoption of New Technologies: Any Role for Labor Market Institutions?" Policy Research Working Paper Series, No. 3273, World Bank, Washington, DC.

Scarpetta, S., P. Hemmings, T. Tressel, and J. Woo. 2002. "The Role of Policy and Institutions for Productivity and Firm Dynamics: Evidence from Micro and Industry Data." Economic Department Working Paper 39, Organisation for Economic Co-operation and Development, Paris.

Schivardi, F., and R. Torrini. 2008. "Identifying the Effects of Firing Restrictions Through Size-Contingent Differences in Regulation." *Labour Economics* 15 (3): 482–511.

Schwab, S. 2003. "Mandated-Severance-Pay Laws in Transition Economies." Cornell University, Ithaca, NY.

Schwarz, G. E. 1978. "Estimating the Dimension of a Model." *Annals of Statistics* 6 (2): 461–64.

Suedekum, J., and P. Ruehmann. 2003. "Severance Payments and Firm-Specific Human Capital." *Labour* 17: 47–62.

Sulla, V., S. Scarpetta, and G. Pierre. 2003. Database for Labor Market Regulations and Institutions Across Countries. Washington, DC: World Bank.

Towers Perrin. 2003. Towers Perrin reports. http://www.towers.com/towers.

Tyson, L. A., and D. I. Levine. 1990. "Participation, Productivity, and the Firm's Environment." In *Paying for Productivity: A Look at the Evidence*, ed. A. S. Blinder, 183–244. Washington, DC: Brookings Institution.

U.S. Social Security Administration. 2003. "Social Security Programs throughout the World, 1999, 2002, 2003." http://www.ssa.gov/policy/data_sub50.html.

Visisombat, K. 1968. "Individual Employment Contracts in the New Labour Codes of French-Speaking Africa." *International Labour Review* 98 (2): 121–40.

Vodopivec, M. 2004. *Income Support for the Unemployed: Issues and Options*. Regional and Sectoral Studies. Washington, DC: World Bank.

Vodopivec, M., A. Wörgötter, and D. Raju. 2005. "Unemployment Benefit Systems in Central and Eastern Europe: A Review of the 1990s." *Comparative Economic Studies* 47 (4): 615–51.

Von Below, D., and P. Thoursie. 2010. "Last In, First Out? Estimating the Effect of Seniority Rules in Sweden." *Labour Economics* 17 (6): 987–97.

Watson Wyatt Worldwide. 2011. "Consulting and Beyond—A Look at Towers Watson Research and Publications." http://www.watsonwyatt.com.

Whitehouse, E. 2007. *Pension Panorama: Retirement-Income Systems in 53 Countries*. Washington, DC: World Bank.

World Bank. 2010. Doing Business Indicators (database). 2011. World Bank, Washington, DC. http://data.worldbank.org/data-catalog.

———. 2011. *International Patterns of Pension Provisions: A Worldwide Overview of Facts and Figures*. Social Protection Department. Washington, DC: World Bank.

Yohai, V. J. 1987. "High Breakdown Point and High Efficiency Estimates for Regression." *Annals of Statistics* 15: 642–65.

Yun, Jungyoll, and Jai-Joon Hur. 2011. "Severance Pay Reform in the Republic of Korea." Chapter 6, this volume.

CHAPTER 3

Mandated Severance Pay and Firing Cost Distortions: A Critical Review of the Evidence

Donald O. Parsons

Introduction

Severance pay mandates have a special appeal in developing countries, which have only modest government administrative capacities for direct provision of job displacement insurance. However, economists view such mandates warily, concerned that the implied firing costs might negatively affect the efficient allocation of labor across firms and industries. Robert Holzmann succinctly summarizes some of the major issues:

> Severance pay is quite likely the most widespread benefit program for workers in the world.... These payments at the end of a work contract and, in most cases of an involuntary separation can be found in almost all countries. . . . They are mostly mandated by law but result also from contractual commitments. . . . [They] are often held responsible...[for] poor labor market performance in poor and rich countries alike and are therefore tackled as part of a reform agenda to improve the competitiveness of the national economy. (Holzmann 2005, 251)

Holzmann deplores the fact that "knowledge gaps apply to the effects of severance pay on labor market outcomes such as job creation and unemployment rate, the distributive effects between individuals and over time" (Holzmann 2005, 252). This chapter argues that the empirical literature is, in fact, highly informative on this issue once severance pay effects are separated from other, broader interventions and that the estimated remaining effects are small.

Early work introduced an apparent paradox: Lazear (1990), in his seminal work on the topic, noted that such mandate effects could be avoided by a simple bonding scheme but then interpreted his empirical work as indicating large adverse effects. He conjectured that the paradox could be resolved by an appeal to pervasive worker credit constraints that would make avoidance costly. More recent work has only deepened the paradox, with the recognition that severance mandate effects can be avoided through variants of familiar, widely adopted mechanisms such as private pensions, suggesting that avoidance costs may not be especially onerous (Parsons 2011a, 2011b).

The encouragement of Milan Vodopivec and the financial support of the World Bank were critical in launching this project, and the luxury of a sabbatical year at George Washington University (GWU) enabled its completion. Jacqueline Iwata generously provided research assistance. Robert Holzmann and two anonymous reviewers provided detailed comments. Helpful comments were also received from Bryan Boulier, Robert Goldfarb, Stephen Smith, and participants in the GWU microeconomics seminar and the World Bank's labor economics brown bag lunch.

If avoidance costs are small but avoidance activities are absent, it is natural to conjecture that the original distortions are small. The widespread provision of voluntary severance pay among private firms in the United States would seem to support that argument. Although voluntary severance benefits are often modest, they are equivalent to mandated levels in many OECD countries. Have the firing costs embedded in severance insurance mandates artificially reduced separation rates and perhaps depressed employment rates and increased unemployment levels? This review focuses on what is known about these connections, especially with regard to turnover and equilibrium employment.[1] The chapter also addresses another direct implication—that by protecting the jobs of current employees, severance pay mandates alter the distribution of jobs across demographic groups.

Early work by Emerson (1988) and especially Lazear (1990) stimulated intense interest in the topic and encouraged a variety of estimation efforts.[2] Although a casual review of the evidence might suggest otherwise, severance-induced firing costs do not appear to be a serious problem. To begin, employment protection legislation and even severance pay are complex instruments, with job displacement insurance only one element. Moreover, severance benefit mandates are often a small part of more substantial policy reforms, many of which are themselves distortionary, making identification of the effects of individual elements difficult. The challenge is to isolate severance insurance effects from those of broader interventions.

The next section briefly reviews key design features of severance pay as part of a job displacement insurance plan. Researchers have focused on benefit generosity, but program type—especially whether the plan is an insurance plan, a savings plan, or something in between—is also critically important (Parsons 2011a, 2011b). After all, savings plans have no firing cost implications. The following section provides an informal theoretical discussion of firm avoidance strategies, adopting the standard flow approach (Bertola 1992; Nickell 1978) and focusing on turnover rates and employment levels.[3] Mandate avoidance is not technically difficult.

Separating severance insurance effects from those of other economic market reforms is crucial, and this chapter presents a taxonomy of reform types, with severance pay reform but one element. The review begins with a handful of prominent empirical studies, including Lazear's work, which has strongly influenced subsequent research. Lazear explored severance pay effects on employment and other labor market measures using a cross-national panel drawn from the industrialized (Organisation for Economic Co-operation and Development, OECD) world, admitting few controls and only one additional policy: advance notice. The boldness of the research design perhaps foreshadows the nonrobustness of the results (Addison and Teixeira 2003).

In their analysis, Heckman and Pagés (2004) expand (1) the policy vector, to include severance savings mandates and social security mandates; and (2) the cross-national sample, to include countries in Latin America and the Caribbean (LAC) as well as those in the OECD. The results provide little reason to be concerned about severance insurance mandates.

The logical extension of this approach—introducing a full array of policy characteristics and dimensions—is not feasible.[4] Moreover, policies are often highly correlated in application, making estimation of individual effects imprecise. The OECD took an alternative approach (1999, 2004, 2006), compressing a large number of policy elements into a single employment protection legislation (EPL) index. This overcomes the problem of identifying individual policy effects by assuming that all policy effects are identical. Obviously, this approach does not provide a reliable guide to the impact of any single policy.

The chapter then reviews a handful of other major cross-national and cross-state analyses of labor standards, including severance pay mandates, and their consequences. A prominent study of international labor standards by Botero and others (2004) focused on the origins of such regulations and looked at the gains and losses of alternative regulatory regimes.[5] The authors suggested that the benefits and, more important here, the distortionary costs of such programs are rather small. Studies across Indian states by Besley and Burgess (2004) refined and extended in important ways by Ahsan and Pagés (2008), hinted that other dimensions of labor standards—notably, collective bargaining rules—may be more important than employment protection legislation in molding labor market performance.

The review then turns to quasi-experiments, beginning with whole-scale, economy-wide economic reforms. These studies track the implications of simultaneous changes in capital, labor, and product market regulations as well as the easing or tightening of international trade restrictions. Two paradigm reforms receive special attention: the Colombian reforms circa 1990 (Kugler 1999, 2002, 2004, 2005) and the Peruvian reforms of the same period (Saavedra and Torero 2004). Although interesting in their own right (they provide strong evidence that substantial government interventions in the economy are likely to affect labor market performance adversely), such studies provide little practical guidance on the design of severance plan mandates.

Next, the review focuses on the effect of less comprehensive legislation, especially employment protection legislation, beginning with its impact on job separation rates and redistribution, including recent studies by Micco and Pagés (2006) and Haltiwanger, Scarpetta, and Schweiger (2008). A set of studies designed to estimate EPL effects on jobs (their aggregate number and their distribution across demographic groups) is assessed. The effect of labor market policies on the distribution of jobs across demographic groups emerges as the most robust finding in this literature.

The finding that EPL does appear to reduce job separations and redistribute jobs toward prime-age adults has only the faintest implication for severance pay designers. Once unbundled, is the impact of severance pay mandates similar? This chapter offers evidence of the converse—that large changes in government dismissal policies that leave severance benefit generosity unaltered have large effects on labor market outcomes (Marinescu 2009), while less substantial ones (for example, recent alterations in employment-at-will contracts in the United States) do not. The number of studies that report the effects of variations in severance generosity on labor market performance is surprisingly small; that said, the studies provide little reason for serious concern, at least regarding generosity levels typically observed in the industrialized world. The final section offers conclusions.

Severance as Job Displacement Insurance: An Overview

A variety of severance plan characteristics are important in the discussion, including these:

- Plan type: insurance, savings, or some mixture (eligibility requirements for benefit status)
- Benefit schedules
- Enforcement procedures for regulations

These characteristics are briefly reviewed in the remainder of this section.

BENEFIT ELIGIBILITY

A key element of any severance plan is the conditions under which payouts are made to the worker. Two severance plan types are common: insurance and savings.

> **Severance insurance pay.** Separation payments in excess of accrued wages, vacations, and leave are made if the worker is involuntarily separated from his or her job without worker malfeasance.[6]
> **Severance savings pay.** Accrued benefits are ultimately distributed to the worker, though the timing of disbursement is restricted to job separation of some sort, including retirement.

Severance plans that include the right to borrow under certain contingencies (for example, for education, house purchase, starting a business) imply that the funds will ultimately accrue to the worker and are savings plans. This distinction is fundamental, because severance savings pay ordinarily carries no firing cost implications. Unless the savings accrual formula is seriously at variance with market discount rates, the firm is indifferent between cashing out the worker's savings account now or later.[7] Indeed, the firm may not even hold the worker's savings; savings mandates may specify that financial intermediaries or government agencies hold the funds.

Severance insurance plans and severance savings plans are on opposite ends of a continuum of eligibility requirements, with the traditional severance insurance plan limiting benefit eligibility to involuntary separation and savings plans paying out under all separation circumstances (Parsons 2011a, 2011b). A severance plan that pays out benefits across the universe of job separation reasons, including retirement, is effectively a savings plan.

Holzmann and others (2011, table A1) present information on benefit eligibility requirements for a broad sample of countries that can be used to fashion a sense of the popularity of the insurance and savings forms of severance pay, with their quite different implications for firing costs. The authors systematically canvassed 113 countries and reported that 100 (88 percent) had some form of nationally mandated severance plan. A number of the 13 other countries had severance pay provisions in union contracts, which may be more important in, say, Belgium, than in the United States, with its limited union coverage.

Of the 100 countries, 2 (Italy and Peru) had simple savings plans, while others spanned the range of benefit-eligible separation events. Four countries were sufficiently exotic that they did not cover redundancy (involuntary economic separation) or bankruptcies, and thus defy categorization.[8] The remainder can be divided into three broad groups: (1) redundancy and bankruptcies only (18); (2) redundancies and dismissals or separation with cause (54); and (3) broader eligibility requirements, including redundancies and dismissals, plus voluntary separations or old-age retirement (24).

The third group provided a variety of alternative separation coverage policies. Fourteen covered voluntary separation but not retirement; four covered retirement but not voluntary separation;[9] and six mandated severance plans with sufficiently broad eligibility requirements that they are effectively severance savings plans.[10]

BENEFIT SCHEDULES

The benefit schedule has two key components: individual (the payout to an individual worker) and aggregate (the total expected payout to workers for a given employment reduction). In the voluntary U.S. economy, coverage varies widely by occupation and industry (Bishow and Parsons 2004), but the basic benefit schedule is reasonably uniform (Parsons 2005). For those eligible, benefits are offered at the time of involuntary displacement in proportion to the worker's weekly wage and years of service with the firm, often up to a benefit or years-of-service maximum. Especially for blue collar, service, and clerical workers, the modal plan offers one week of pay per year of service (Parsons 2005).

The one-week-of-pay-per-year-of-service rule is also a feature of many mandated international plans. Figure 3.1 shows mandated benefit levels by occupational group (blue collar, white collar) at 20 years of service for OECD countries. If the U.S. median benefit level of one week per year of service is used as a measure of the level of voluntary plans, many mandates may not be effective in the sense of being binding on the firms.

Firms have considerable leeway in choosing whom to displace and may never have to pay severance benefits to a specific worker. Although large severance liabilities may accumulate among the longest tenured workers, they are canceled when the worker retires under severance insurance plans, though of course not under severance savings plans. As a consequence, the individual benefit schedule is only one factor in the firm's total expenditures and related firing costs. At any point, the firm has a workforce with varying service records and may be free to choose which worker it will lay off.[11] Aggregate severance payouts will be minimized for a given force reduction under the common LIFO (last in, first out) layoff strategy. Severance benefit costs grow at an increasing rate with the depth of the employment cuts, but in ordinary times firms can manage layoffs in a way that limits aggregate severance benefit payouts to modest levels. Indeed, Pagés and Montenegro (2007) argue that severance mandates will induce firms to use LIFO, even if they otherwise would not, to the disadvantage of the young.

ENFORCEMENT

Mandating a specific severance plan that the firm would otherwise not choose to offer requires an enforcement mechanism if it is to be effective. Severance pay mandates differ substantially and importantly in bureaucratic demands. If (as is typical in severance insurance plans) benefit eligibility is restricted to involuntary separations or layoffs, the structure of dispute resolution is important. Which party must prove its case in a dispute? A number of the studies discussed below use enforcement likelihood to identify mandating effects. It appears that no study uses direct measures of compliance with severance legislation.[12] Instead, one is likely to see measures of social insurance compliance or even general measures of the lawfulness of the population.

THE SECOND FACE OF DISMISSAL REGULATIONS

Bureaucratic demands for severance pay administration merge into broader dismissal regulations, including requirements for government or union approval of separations, or even prohibition of dismissal. In an early study, Emerson (1988) cited European employer

FIGURE 3.1 **Mandated Severance Pay for Redundancy by Occupation (weeks' pay at 20 years of service, OECD countries, late 1990s)**

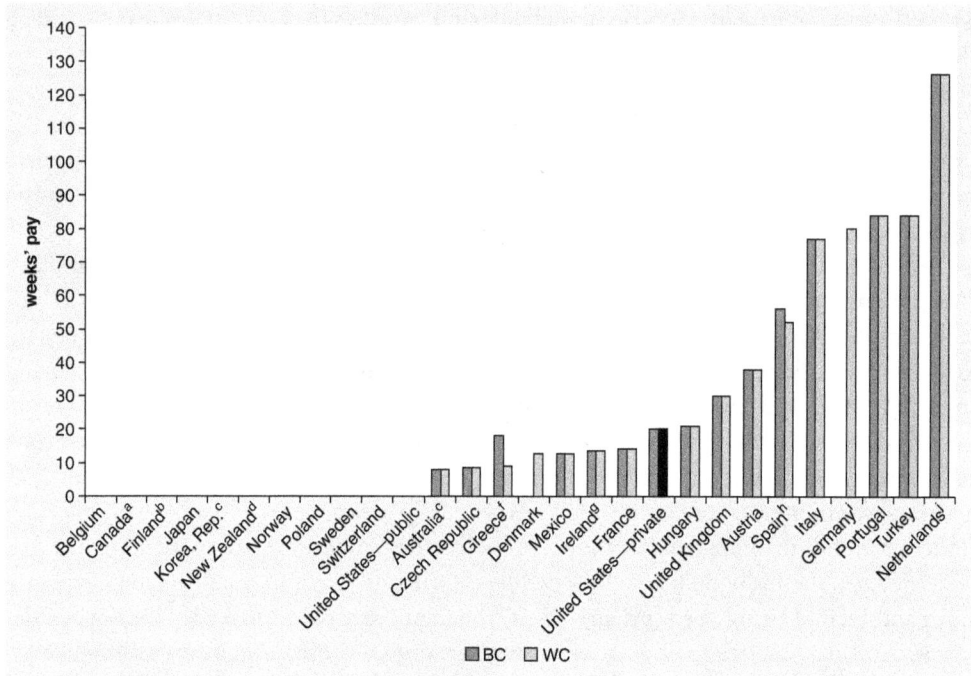

SOURCE: OECD 1999, table 2.A.2.

NOTE: BC = blue collar worker, WC = white collar worker.

a. Ontario, one week per year of service up to 26 weeks' pay if tenure > 5 and in a firm with payroll of Canadian $2.5 million or more.

b. Special exceptions for older workers.

c. Retirement allowance not counted.

d. Higher collectively bargained rates than typical in United States.

e. Eight weeks if more than four years.

f. WC pay doubles if no written notice.

g. Employers partially reimbursed from redundancy fund.

h. Maximum 12 months or 52 weeks.

i. Common in social plans adjudicated by the labor court.

j. If file for permission by a labor court.

surveys that emphasize the importance of these noncash firing costs; employers confronted with unusually high severance benefit mandates were inclined to report serious firing impediments, but the converse was not necessarily true.

Involuntary separations can arise for disciplinary reasons as well as economic ones. Although the focus of this review is on severance as job displacement insurance, dismissal regulations often serve a quite distinct function, reducing the employer's control of workplace discipline.[13] Almost omnipresent in labor union contracts in the United States is the designation of grievance processes: mechanisms designed to regulate the interactions between worker and management, including the resolution of disputes over dismissal for disciplinary reasons, commonly referred to as discharges or fires. Government regulations can and do extend such regulations to the general workplace under the requirement that the employer be penalized for releasing workers without just cause.

It is important to disentangle, if possible, workplace control regulations from consumption-smoothing regulations. There is no reason to assume that regulation of separations for economic reasons—implicit in the insurance perspective—should have the same effect as regulation of disciplinary separations. The regulation of discharge separations, including the total banning of such separations, is not likely to have a large, direct impact on aggregate separations, but it is likely to affect workplace efficiency and therefore separations, accessions, and equilibrium employment if it is not offset by wage adjustments.[14]

Severance Policies and Outcomes: Theoretical Structure

Severance policies can affect a range of economic processes. This review focuses on the following outcomes:

- Job turnover (separations and accessions)
- Employment
- Employment redistribution

Obviously, each of these outcomes must be measured with reasonable accuracy; most countries have developed some capacity for this.

Because severance pay mandates can be viewed as a penalty for job separations, a flow approach is used to organize the analyses to follow. The basic decision mechanism emphasizes worker flows (separations and accessions) with employment stock as an important but indirect outcome.[15] Elegant recent studies have emphasized the dynamics of the process and adjustment costs, but the core principles are sufficient here. Major elements of the flow processes are revealed in the flow model identity:

$$E_t \equiv E_{t-1} + ACC_t - SEP_t, \tag{1}$$

or equivalently:

$$\Delta E_t \equiv E_t - E_{t-1} = ACC_t - SEP_t, \tag{2}$$

where

$E_t \equiv$ employment at the end of period t,
$ACC_t \equiv$ accessions or hires in period t, and
$SEP_t \equiv$ separations in period t.

Firing costs. The direct effect of a severance insurance mandate (firing costs) on separations (SEP_t) is likely to be a negative one, although perhaps smaller than severance benefits alone might suggest (Parsons 2011a, 2011b). For planning purposes, the net cost of a severance benefit payout must be adjusted by any reduction or increase in future liabilities.[16] It is for that reason that severance savings accounts have no firing costs; a future liability is reduced dollar-for-dollar with the payout (assuming some reasonable accrual of interest.)

A reduction in separations will have an immediate but opposite effect on accessions, unless the firm wishes to alter the size of its workforce. If separations and accessions occur at different points in the business cycle, severance pay would presumably limit separations during bad times and accessions during good.[17]

Hiring costs. Mandated severance benefits enter the equilibrium employment decisions through hiring costs, not firing costs. Gross hiring costs—the firm's perception of the expected expenditures under the mandate—will include, in the first instance, the sum of discounted expenditures mandated under the regulation or the cost of avoiding these same regulations, whichever is less. The worker's valuation of the mandated benefit is also important if wages are downwardly flexible. Net hiring costs of a mandate could be zero, or even negative, if the firm is supplying a product the worker values and cannot obtain elsewhere.[18]

The firm has a variety of institutional and contractual means of avoiding a mandate, often with quite different firing and hiring cost implications. The firm can ease into the informal sector, which is rather easily done in the developing world if the firm is not large; it can spin off self-employed workers; or, if law permits, it can hire more temporary workers. Lazear (1990) highlighted the possibility of contractual avoidance behavior. A severance insurance mandate can be "undone" by (1) paying out additional benefits to employed and terminated alike and (2) recapturing the cost through compensating wage differentials. The firing costs can be undone with smaller outlays by promising to pay out benefits only at the time of separation but doing so for separations of all types: involuntary, voluntary, or through retirement (Parsons 2011a, 2011b). This approach converts the insurance plan into a severance savings plan, essentially a defined contribution pension plan. Private pensions are common in many economies, so it seems plausible that the conditions for such an offset are not especially demanding.

The firm can undo a mandated severance insurance plan simply by offering a "cliff-vested" pension plan: a pension plan that pays benefits only if the worker remains with the firm until normal retirement age.[19] Such an integrated severance insurance/cliff-vested pension plan requires a greater outlay by the firm (higher gross hiring costs) than severance insurance alone. Whether net hiring costs are increased depends on the worker's access to capital. If the worker has access to capital at the same interest rate as the firm, the worker might value the pension plan at cost, and net hiring costs might be zero. As with the bonding mechanism of Lazear, pension/savings plans become less attractive as worker discount rates grow.

There is no empirical evidence of contractual avoidance behavior, despite its apparent ease. Indeed, contrary evidence exists for the United States, where firms frequently adopt voluntary severance plans, and these are invariably insurance plans, not savings plans. Moreover, few OECD countries mandate severance savings plans, though presumably they could. The Republic of Korea's severance system is a savings plan, as is the Austrian plan since the 2003 reforms.[20] In Latin America and the Caribbean, severance insurance plans and severance savings plans may be mandated simultaneously (Heckman and Pagés 2004).

The facts that voluntary plans in the United States are typically severance insurance plans and that OECD governments typically mandate severance insurance plans, not severance savings plans, are both consistent with the possibility that firms do not view the mandates as costly. This leads to the working hypothesis of this chapter—that severance insurance mandates at benefit generosity levels normally observed in the OECD are not seriously distortionary.

Government Reforms: A Policy Taxonomy

The severance-induced firing cost literature is critically reviewed below, with special attention to research that appears to uncover substantial severance pay distortions. A problem arises immediately in that reforms that include increasing or decreasing severance generosity often include other, sterner measures. Data from the IFC Cost of Doing Business database (World Bank 2009) illustrate the strong correlation of business and labor market standards imposed by governments worldwide. Figure 3.2, panel a, for example, shows the link between hiring and hours used regulations with termination regulations across selected countries. The prevalence of these three types of labor regulations is presented for the 10 highest ranked and the 10 lowest ranked countries in the sample of 182 countries. Countries with relatively flexible termination rules also have relatively relaxed hiring and hours adjustment rules, and vice versa. The same concern applies to general antibusiness regulations, of which labor regulations are but one (figure 3.2, panel b). It would be difficult to isolate the effect of a single policy; the same firms that face significant labor market rigidities face a wide set of concerns about business startup and closure and operations in between. Moreover, reforms often bundle a variety of these measures.

It is important to separate severance pay effects from those of a wide range of alternative government interventions in product and factor markets. In descending order of policy expansiveness, these initiatives are as follows:

- **Economic regulations (ERs).** This term refers to the full set of economic policies. ERs would include product market, tariff and international trade, and capital market regulations, as well as labor regulations.

- **Labor regulations (LRs).** This term refers to the full range of labor market policies, including **collective bargaining (CB) rules** and **labor standards (LS)** such as hours regulations and minimum wages, as well as employment protection legislation. The OECD (2004) notes that direct legislation of labor standards is only one way to transfer power to workers; collective bargaining rules are quite another.[21] Unions are very much an invention of governments, and the powers governments bestow on them vary greatly. Even when focusing on separation costs, it matters little if the government directly imposes separation regulations or empowers union representatives to do that for them.

- **Employment protection legislation (EPL).** A proper subset of labor standards, EPL refers to regulations for worker separations. A requirement that firms receive government approval for job separations is a dismissal regulation that is not, directly at least, a severance generosity mandate. A pronouncement that job separations are illegal is another, extreme example. The OECD (2004) cites three distinct separation cost elements: (1) the difficulty of dismissal; (2) "procedural inconveniences" that may follow implementation of the dismissal; and (3) any advance notice costs or severance pay that may be required.

- **Severance pay (SP).** Severance pay regulations refer specifically to government rules on the provision of job separation pay. Severance pay is itself multidimensional, with benefit generosity only one dimension of a potentially complex mechanism. If benefits are limited to a class of job separations, say those that cannot be

FIGURE 3.2 **Regulating Employment and Business Practices**

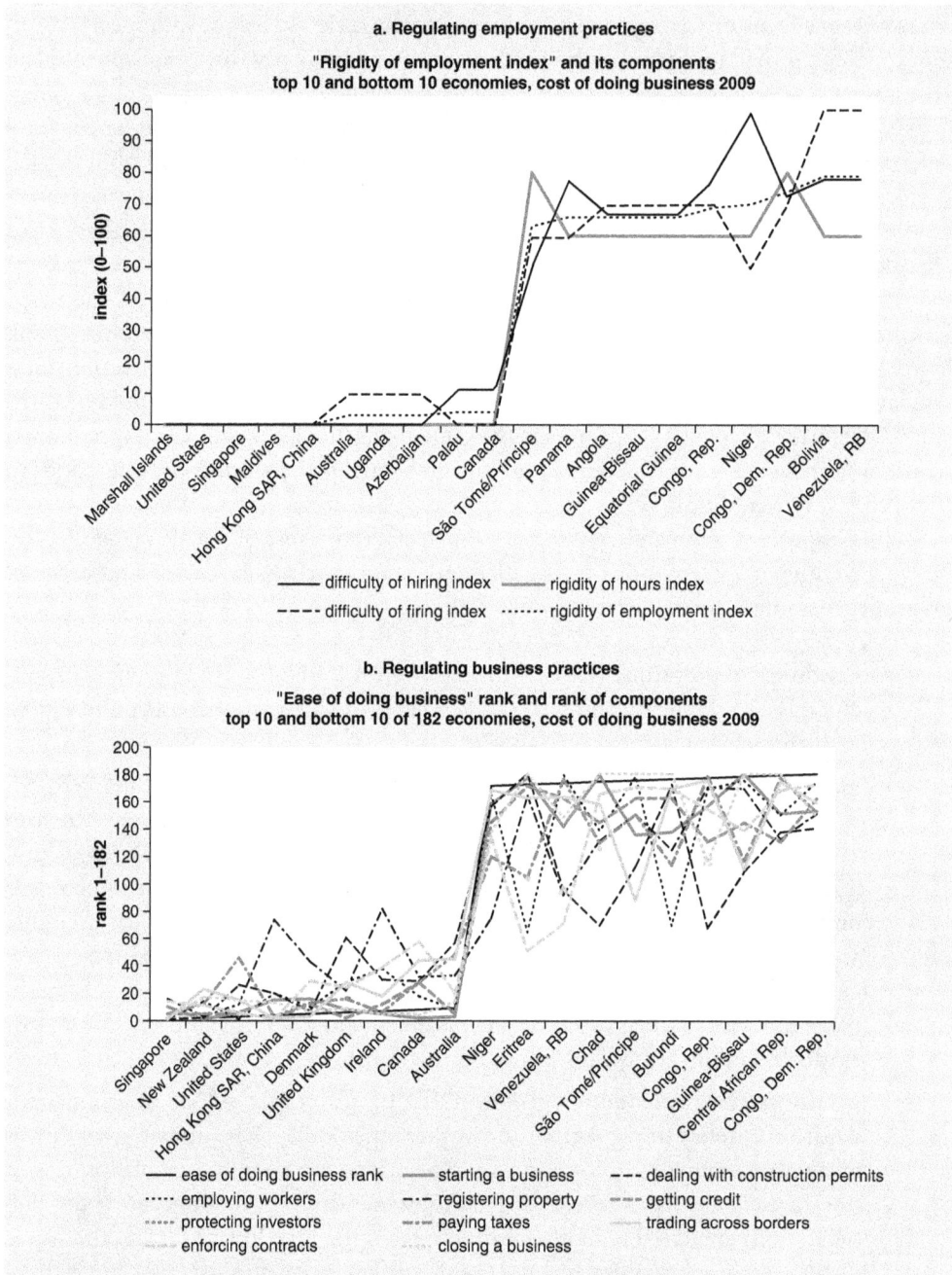

a. Regulating employment practices

"Rigidity of employment index" and its components
top 10 and bottom 10 economies, cost of doing business 2009

b. Regulating business practices

"Ease of doing business" rank and rank of components
top 10 and bottom 10 of 182 economies, cost of doing business 2009

SOURCE: World Bank 2009.

"economically justified," it becomes important to know whether the worker or the employer has the burden of proving the employer's initial classification incorrect.

As a general rule, the more focused the policy reform under review, the more informative the analysis for severance pay design.

An Early Cross-National Study: A Bold Empirical Adventure

Although researchers have long been well aware of the many dimensions of severance pay (for example, Emerson 1988), early research focused on benefit generosity. In his seminal study, Lazear (1990, 707–8) constructed a severance pay measure (*SEV*) as: "the number of months of severance pay or notice a blue collar worker with ten years of service received upon termination without cause." He also experimented with a second dismissal policy measure: advance notice.

Lazear reported estimates from a variety of models but focused his discussion on ordinary least squares (OLS) estimates of a cross-national model of 22 developed countries over 29 years. He proposed to model the employment-to-population (E/P) rate, unemployment rate, labor force participation rate, and average work hours as a function of a severance pay measure and year and year square. For example, suppressing individual subscripts,

$$E/P = \alpha_0 + \alpha_1 SEV + \alpha_2 T + \alpha_3 T^2 + \varepsilon,$$

with T denoting a year index, and ε the random element.

Few economists would use such a model for the aggregate E/P ratio. More astonishing, perhaps even to Lazear: If the country observations are simply pooled, the estimated SEV coefficients in three of the four labor market outcome models are negative and statistically significant, and the unemployment rate effect is also significant, though positive (Lazear 1990, table II, 712). If a second policy variable (notice) is introduced as an explanatory variable, however, all SEV coefficient estimates are sharply less significant, with the estimated impact on unemployment now negative but insignificant.

Given the stability of job dismissal policies within countries across time, it is perhaps not surprising that the results are not robust to the addition of country dummies. In the fixed-effects model with only severance pay as an explanatory variable, the employment and labor force participation coefficients are not significant at customary levels (Lazear 1990, table V, 714). Unfortunately Lazear reported only the OLS version of a model with additional explanatory variables.[22]

Lazear ended his paper with the hope that "these initial estimates provide a departure point for more refined models and data" (1990, 725). And indeed, the study stimulated an explosion of variable measurement, model extensions, and replications. Addison and Teixeira (2003) provide an exceptional review of their own work and that of others that followed Lazear's study, drawing the following conclusions:

1. "Annual rates of job reallocation (i.e., job flows) are often as high in nations with stringent job protection as in countries with weak regulation. This awkward empirical regularity has prompted some ingenious explanations" (121).

2. "Employment is reduced on net" (120), though the effects are not uniform across demographic groups—prime-age males are unaffected, but the young are.
3. "The coefficient estimates for employment protection equations in overall unemployment are of mixed sign" (121).

The need for an explanation of the first result is obvious—it strikes at the core of the firing cost concern.[23] If firing costs do not reduce job separation rates, how important can they be?[24] Fortunately for the simple theory and common sense, this result has been largely overturned in more recent work.

Extending the Dismissal Policy Vector: Heckman-Pagés

As part of an ambitious project that extended the OECD sample to LAC countries, Heckman and Pagés (2004) undertook a cross-national panel study that deepened the Lazear model in a variety of important ways. Their estimates were derived from an unbalanced panel of OECD and LAC countries over the period 1983–99. The broader sample introduced more policy variations and permitted them to estimate the effects of a vector of capitalized termination benefits composed of the following:

*   Indemnity for dismissal (severance insurance pay)
*   Seniority pay (severance savings)
*   Social security payroll taxes
*   Advance notice[25]

Of special note, Heckman and Pagés clearly distinguished between severance insurance mandates and severance savings mandates. Their severance insurance (dismissal indemnity) measure can be viewed as a probabilistic weighting of benefits, namely, "the discounted costs of future indemnities [measured in monthly wages], weighted by the probability of dismissal after i periods at the firm" (Heckman and Pagés 2004, 27).

This is a gross hiring cost measure of the severance mandate (Parsons 2011b).[26] All measures reflect the discounted cost of the programs at the time of hire, unadjusted for equilibrium wage responses. Note that the gross hiring costs of (firing-cost-free) savings plans are always higher than those of insurance plans, given the same benefit generosity. It is therefore important to treat the two mandates separately, which Heckman and Pagés do.

Heckman and Pagés reported average cost figures for the various policies, which provide some perspective on the potential distortions that severance insurance mandates might impose. The gross hiring cost estimates (in multiples of monthly wages) of the four policies are shown in table 3.1. As Heckman and Pagés (2004, 31) note, "In the average Latin American country, social security payments amount to 82 percent of the total costs of labor laws. This percentage is even larger in OECD countries where, on average, they reach 96 percent of the total regulatory costs." It would be unfortunate if a severance insurance pay policy at 2 percent of expected labor law costs in OECD countries and 8 percent in Latin American countries were to have profound negative effects on the performance of the labor market and the economy, although that remains an empirical possibility.

TABLE 3.1 **Expected Cost of Alternative Labor Market Mandates (months of wages, OECD and LAC sample)**

Policy	Full sample	OECD only	LAC only
	(1)	(2)	(3)
Advance notice	0.82	0.87	0.65
	(0.48)	(0.48)	(0.45)
Indemnity for dismissal (severance insurance pay)	1.27	0.86	2.82
	(1.40)	(1.17)	(1.05)
Seniority pay (severance savings pay)	0.65	0.00	3.09
	(2.35)	(0.00)	(4.33)
Social security contribution	35.65	37.12	30.14
	(19.13)	(20.65)	(10.17)

SOURCE: Heckman and Pagés 2004, table 7.
NOTE: Standard deviations in parentheses.

TABLE 3.2 **Estimated Impacts of Alternative Labor Market Mandates on Employment Levels (months of wages, OECD and LAC sample)**

Policy	Full sample	OECD only	LAC only
	(1)	(2)	(3)
Advance notice	13.938	13.775	16.637
	(15.959)	(14.564)	(15.420)
Indemnity for dismissal (severance insurance pay)	1.161	−2.577**	0.330
	(0.897)	(1.196)	(1.637)
Seniority pay (severance savings pay)	3.292***	—	1.887
	(1.195)		(2.197)
Social security contribution	−0.230***	−0.301***	−0.187**
	(0.081)	(0.102)	(0.084)

SOURCE: Heckman and Pagés 2004, table 8.
NOTE: Standard errors in parentheses. — = not available.
*** Significant at 1 percent level. ** Significant at 5 percent level.

The empirical models are reduced-form, fixed-effects models of employment and unemployment regressed on the four labor mandates as well as various GDP and demographic regressors. A sense of the results can be obtained from the policy parameter estimates in the E/P rate model reported in table 3.2, based on results reported in Heckman and Pagés (2004, table 8, 72). The results are not especially intuitive. In the full sample, the severance insurance measure has a positive effect on employment, but neither it nor the advance notice coefficient is significantly different from zero at customary levels. When the model is estimated separately on the OECD sample and the LAC sample, the indemnity (severance insurance) effect in the OECD sample is negative and significant, while that in the LAC sample remains positive and insignificant.

The impact of severance savings mandates is, surprisingly, positive and significant. The circumstances under which a mandated severance savings plan would increase employment rates are not easy to imagine. Perhaps if the economy has no other savings mechanism, the firm may find it profitable to provide the service, though the government need not mandate the practice in that circumstance.

Oddly, the coefficient on the second compulsory savings contribution (to the government social security fund) is negative and significant. The authors provided the following conjecture on this reversal of sign:

> Interestingly, we are able to reject the hypothesis that social security payments exert the same effect on employment as seniority pay [mandated severance savings], despite the fact that both variables imply mandatory contributions defined as a fraction of wages. Perhaps because the

> *contributions to finance seniority pay are capitalized in individual accounts, the link between*
> *contributions and payments is strengthened, and this reduces or eliminates the "tax" effect.*
> *Instead, our results suggest that social security contributions tend to be perceived as taxes on*
> *labor (Heckman and Pagés 2004, 75).*

They summarized their estimates thusly:

> *Unfortunately, few empirical regularities emerge when an honest sensitivity analysis is con-*
> *ducted. Nonetheless, a few robust regularities do appear. Payroll taxes reduce employment and*
> *(less robustly) in OECD countries, job security regulation reduces employment (Heckman and*
> *Pagés 2004, 65).*

Heckman and Pagés do not directly estimate job redistribution effects but summarize the studies, mostly microdata studies: "Regulations act unevenly across different groups in society. Young, uneducated, and rural workers are much less likely to enjoy coverage than older, skilled, and urban workers" (Heckman and Pagés 2004, 70). More on this issue follows.

Employment Protection Legislation: OECD Studies

The four labor policies highlighted by Heckman and Pagés—advance notice, severance insurance, severance saving, and social security contributions—are only a small set of potential policies, each of which has a large number of program parameters. Obviously, multicollinearity concerns emerge as the number of policy instruments expands. Addison and Teixeira (2003) noted one especially important development in the post-Lazear literature—that more detailed measures are accommodated not by expanding the vector of policy parameters in the analysis but by constructing a composite employment protection measure. Grubb and Wells (1993), for example, stressed the multidimensionality of employment protection legislation, picking up on an earlier theme by Emerson (1988). They proposed combining a severance measure with an advance notice measure, weighting a month of mandated advance notice at 0.75 of a month of severance,[27] and provided separate composite indicators for "regular procedural inconveniences" and "difficulty of dismissal" (Grubb and Wells 1993, 12–14). These indices were themselves summed to create a composite strictness measure.

The OECD (2004) extended the indicator approach, creating an elaborate employment protection legislation index involving 18 components (table 3.3). Three of these measures, comprising less than 8 percent of the index weight, were severance generosity at various service levels: severance payouts (in monthly wages) at 9 months' tenure, at 4 years, and at 20 years (OECD 2004, 103). The three elements capture, to some degree, nonlinearities in the benefit schedule, though no attempt was made to estimate their independent impact.

Advance notice mandates are included in the composite index, as are measures that characterize limits on employer control of job discipline discharges (OECD 2004, 103–5). Many OECD countries responded in the 1980s to concerns that mandated severance charges were inducing high unemployment rates by introducing temporary contracts less burdened with job protection regulations. A complete description of the current severance pay environment would necessarily include a vector of permanent contract separation pay characteristics, a similar vector for temporary contracts, and a third vector that connects the two—the conditions under which the firm can choose between the two contracts. Aspects of these are also included in the OECD indicator.

TABLE 3.3 **OECD 18-Point Employment Protection Legislation (EPL) Index**

Policy	Index Weight
1. Notification procedures	0.069444
2. Delay involved before notice can start	0.069444
3. Length of the notice period at:	
a. 9 months's tenure	0.019841
b. 4 years's tenure	0.019841
c. 20 years's tenure	0.019841
4. Severance pay at:	
a. 9 months's tenure	0.026455
b. 4 years's tenure	0.026455
c. 20 years's tenure	0.026455
5. Definition of justified or unfair dismissal	0.034722
6. Length of trial period	0.034722
7. Compensation following unfair dismissal	0.034722
8. Possibility of reinstatement following unfair dismissal	0.034722
9. Valid case for use of fixed-term contract (FTC)	0.104167
10. Maximum number of successive FTCs	0.052083
11. Maximum cumulative duration of successive FTCs	0.052083
12. Types of work for which temporary work agency (TWA) employment is legal	0.104167
13. Restrictions on number of renewals	0.052083
14. Maximum accumulated duration of TWA contracts	0.052083
15. Definition of collective dismissal	0.041667
16. Additional notification requirements	0.041667
17. Additional delays involved before notice can start	0.041667
18. Other special costs to employers	0.041667

SOURCE: OECD 2004, table 2.11.1.

The composite index is not useful in isolating severance pay effects unless the underlying assumptions implied in the index weighting are valid, which is unknown. The resulting studies do, however, provide a broad picture of employment protection legislation and its impact on labor markets in developed economies (OECD 1999, 2004, 2006). The sample is unfortunately fairly homogeneous—few OECD countries mandate extravagantly high severance benefits. Offsetting that weakness, of course, is the likelihood that the underlying unobserved institutional structures are relatively homogeneous and that the laws are likely to be enforced.

The OECD (1999) labor market findings give a sense of the result of this approach. Among the highlighted results, largely derived from simple correlations and random-effects generalized least squares (GLS), are these:

1. "Stricter EPL is associated with lower turnover . . . with both jobs and unemployment spells tending to last longer" (OECD 1999, 50).
2. "The employment-to-population ratio for the working age population tends to be lower in countries with stricter EPL, but this pattern reverses for prime-age men" (OECD 1999, 50).
3. "EPL has little or no effect on overall unemployment, but may affect its demographic composition. In countries where EPL is stricter, unemployment tends to be lower for prime-age men but higher for other groups, especially young workers" (OECD 1999, 50).

Perhaps reflecting the short (five-year) interval between the 1999 and 2004 studies, these three results differed little in 2004. The negative employment effect of EPL (the second result) appears especially robust for prime-age women and youth, and less so for older workers and low-skilled workers (OECD 2004, 85).

The 2004 OECD study, which focused more intensively on temporary contracts, added this result:

4. "Differences in the strictness of EPL for regular and temporary jobs may be an important element in explaining the rise in the incidence of temporary work for youth and the low skilled (this is less the case for other groups, notably prime-age men)" (OECD 1999, 63).

Of interest, the second study noted that the rigor of EPL across contract type (permanent or temporary) is positively and significantly correlated (OECD 2004, 72), which the authors attributed to government concerns that a broad discrepancy in rigor between permanent and temporary contracts would induce a large flow toward the more flexible form.[28]

Labor Standards and Their Consequences

Before leaving the discussion of cross-national studies, two strands of literature provide some interesting speculations on government interventions in the labor markets, including its motivations and consequences. An ambitious study by Botero and others (2004) examined the causes and effects of a broad range of labor market interventions and did so over a wider sample of countries, though one must accept a corresponding reduction in average data quality. For a sample of 85 countries as of 1997, the authors (1) created a broad index of the rigidity of worker protection laws; (2) characterized the forces that make labor markets more rigid; and (3) mapped the resulting indexes into measures of labor market performance.

The labor market performance measures were a little unusual: employment in the unofficial economy, male and female labor force participation, and various unemployment measures. As for the labor standards measures, the one of special interest here is the worker protection index, which included measures of collective bargaining law, social security law, and employment law.

The employment law index is itself an average of indexes for (1) alternative employment contracts; (2) cost of increasing worker hours; (3) cost of firing workers (the monetary cost of dismissal); and (4) dismissal procedures (administrative costs of dismissal). Even the index of the cost of firing workers is a complex construction. Botero and others defined the monetary cost of dismissal as follows:

> *Measures the cost of firing 20 percent of the firm's workers (10 percent for redundancy and 10 percent without cause). The cost of firing a worker is calculated as the sum of the notice period, severance pay, and any mandatory penalties established by law or mandatory collective agreements for a worker with three years of tenure with the firm. If dismissal is illegal, we set the cost of firing equal to the annual wage. The new wage bill incorporates the normal wage of the remaining workers and the cost of firing workers. The cost of firing workers is computed as the ratio of the new wage bill to the old. (Botero and others 2004, table 1, 1348)*

Turning to the analysis, the authors had a special interest in the legal origins of the state interventions in the labor market (economic controls are limited to the log of per capita GDP), and they found, as they thought they would, that legal origins mattered (Botero and others 2004, table 4, 1366). More surprising, perhaps, is the finding that aggregate income did not affect the employment law index or any of its subcomponents.

The outcome models (unofficial employment, unemployment, labor force participation) are as spare as Lazear's, with the employment law index, the collective bargaining
laws index, and the social security law index entered in separate models, and with average
years of schooling as the sole control variable. The four indexes are presumably entered
individually because of multicollinearity problems; theory does not suggest that only one
can affect outcomes.

The various findings are difficult to summarize. The authors themselves reported,
"The strength of results varies across specifications, but in general they show no benefits,
and some costs of labor regulation" (Botero and others 2004, 1376–77). Looking a little
more closely at the results, the employment law index (the index within which firing costs
are embedded) had

(1) an insignificant coefficient in the unofficial employment model;

(2) a negative, significant coefficient in the male labor force participation model;
and

(3) positive, significant coefficients in various unemployment models (Botero and
others 2004, table 7, 1376–77).

The first and third conclusions together suggest that formal employment is depressed by
more vigorous employment laws, though this conclusion is of unknown statistical significance. The collective bargaining index increased activity in the unofficial sector while,
somewhat surprisingly, decreasing the labor force participation of men and increasing that
of women. In contrast to the findings of Heckman and Pagés (2004), the social security
index was insignificant in all outcome models.

Caballero and others (2004) used the same data to shed light on employment security effects on labor market flexibility. For 60 countries over the period 1980–2000, they
merged employment protection data from an earlier version of the Botero and others
paper with rule of law measures from Kaufmann, Kraay, and Zoido-Lobaton (1999) and
employment-by-industry sector data from UNIDO (2002). They estimated the impact of
EPL on employment adjustment speed.

Although dynamic estimates of this sort tend to be highly model-dependent, the
results were intuitive and compelling. They reported, "Moving from the 20th to the 80th
percentile in job security, in countries with strong rule of law [Greece or better], cuts the
annual speed of adjustment to shocks by a third. . . . The same movement has negligible effects in countries with weak rule of law" (Caballero and others 2004, abstract). The
economic security indicator is the sum of zero–1 indexes for four measures: (1) grounds
for dismissal, (2) dismissal procedures, (3) notice and severance pay, and (4) protection of
employment in the constitution (with equal weights). They report similar results using the
Heckman-Pagés job security index. Additional evidence of EPL effects on job mobility are
discussed later in this chapter.

The large variation in labor regulations across states makes India a useful policy laboratory. Besley and Burgess (2004) provided evidence of a substantial negative
effect of a composite pro-worker labor standards index on employment, investment,
output, and productivity in the regulated sector. The composite indicator includes
severance pay mandates but also dismissal appeals processes and collective bargaining
regulations.

Although Bhattacharjea (2006) raised questions about the composite indicator of pro-worker regulation used by Besley and Burgess, Ahsan and Pagés (2008) reproduced the Besley and Burgess findings on a corrected data set and added a refinement. They partitioned the pro-worker labor standards index into two regulatory subcomponents: (1) a labor dispute regulation indicator and (2) an EPL indicator. They found that pro-worker labor dispute resolution regulations had a larger and more systematic negative effect on employment and output than did pro-worker employment protection regulations, suggesting that collective bargaining laws are more critical than employment protection legislation in depressing employment. The labor dispute regulations were especially strong in heavy industry, with EPL disproportionately affecting labor-intensive industries such as textiles.

In another study of broad labor standards, Forteza and Rama (2006) found little evidence of a negative labor standards effect on economic growth in a macro cross-national study. The authors used two measures of labor market rigidity: (1) the number of International Labour Organization (ILO) conventions a country had ratified, and (2) an aggregate indicator of minimum wages, mandated benefits, labor union strength, and size of government employment, as well as each separately. ILO conventions cover a wide range of standards on collective bargaining, minimum wages, and working conditions, in addition to aspects of severance pay. Mandated benefits in Forteza and Rama's aggregate measure did not include dismissal pay because of limited data availability. They added an element, the timing of World Bank–assisted economic reforms, and explored the impact of the various labor market rigidity measures on Bank reform effects on GDP growth rates in 119 countries over the period 1970–96.

On average, the timing of reform (reduced labor standards) had no significant impact on growth. However, the authors found that reform effects were stronger and more efficient (GDP growth-beneficial) when a country already had flexible labor markets in place. Incremental labor reforms may have zero or negative impacts on growth when labor markets are inflexible. This conclusion held more strongly if the policy-aggregate measure of labor market rigidity was used rather than the ILO convention measure. Of special interest, when the four disaggregated policy indicators were separately analyzed, union strength and size of the government (employment) sector appeared to have the most damaging effects on reform, not mandated benefits or minimum wages (again, severance pay was not included in the policy vector).

Summarizing these latter studies, it would appear that (1) vigorous government intervention in the labor market discourages employment; (2) this is especially true of collective bargaining laws; and (3) reforms (reduced intervention) are more likely to have measurable salutary effects if the labor market is already relatively flexible. The last may explain why reforms, when they come, are often broad.

Broad Economic Reforms and Their Consequences

In the sections that follow, a number of micro studies are reviewed. Many exploit natural experiments to estimate policy effects on economic outcomes. It is critical in these studies to be aware of the full set of policies implemented. Serious problems of interpretation arise if a particular reform experiment includes a large number of reforms, not just severance pay reforms. Two Latin American reforms—those of Colombia and Peru—provide concrete examples of this concern.

Colombia. The danger of attributing severance plan effects to a much broader reform package is illustrated in a series of studies of the Colombian Labour Market Reform of 1990 (Kugler 1999, 2002, 2004, 2005). The basic approach in the various studies is quasi-experimental and difference-in-differences, with the change in the dependent variable of interest among covered workers (the formal sector) before and after the reform date compared with the change among uncovered workers. Among the reported impacts of this legislation are these:

- Exit rates out of employment and unemployment and unemployment levels increased (Kugler 1999).
- "Worker flows into and out of unemployment and its implied net effect on unemployment increased" (Kugler 2004, 184).
- Wages of workers in the formal sector fell (Kugler 2002, 2005).

The approach is sound and the estimates of the impact of institutional change on these measures are plausible. The problem is one of interpretation. The claim is that these processes are primarily driven by firing cost reform. The Colombian experiment is prominently described as having "reduced costs for employers as well as distortions to hiring and firing" (Kugler 2005, 499) and to have led to "a reduction in firing costs" (Kugler 1999, abstract).[29] As it happens, the impact of the reform on firing costs was limited and could well have increased. Specifically, the severance insurance component of labor market regulation—unjust dismissals—was made 33 percent more generous, though only for those with 10 or more years of service. For workers with fewer years of service, severance insurance benefits were unchanged. Offsetting that direct increase in severance insurance were other reforms that could have potentially reduced firing costs: (1) workers with 10 years or more of service could no longer sue for back pay and reinstatement; (2) the definition of "just dismissal" was modestly relaxed; and (3) the bounds of temporary contracts were modestly expanded (before the reforms, employers had to offer temporary contracts of at least a year).

In sharp contrast to the ambiguous and possibly perverse reforms of severance insurance plans, changes in severance savings account rules—though having only second-order effects on firing costs—were substantial. Scanning these papers, for example, one finds the following redesign of the severance savings mandate:

- An increase in the formality of a mandated severance savings plan (employers had to deposit the savings into individual third-party accounts rather than pay out the savings account upon job separation).
- The savings account was shifted from a defined benefit plan to a defined contribution plan.
- Borrowing from the savings plan for education and housing was deducted from the worker's final separation payment differently. Before the reform, extant worker

borrowings were deducted as a nominal amount; after the reform, they were deducted as a real amount, discounted for inflation.

Changes in administrative rules for severance savings accounts are unlikely to move economies, but broader reforms might. At almost the same time, serious reforms were undertaken in capital markets and tariff policies:

> In 1990, Law 45 eliminated interest rate ceilings, eliminated investment requirements in government securities and reduced reserve requirements…. In addition, Law 9 of 1991 eliminated exchange controls… reducing restrictions on capital flows." (Eslava and others 2006, 61)

> The gradual decrease in tariffs initiated by the preceding Barco government was accelerated by Gaviria after June 1991. By the end of 1991… effective protection [reached] 26.6 percent… down from 62.5 percent a year earlier. (Eslava and others 2006, 61)

These reforms could have increased turnover and induced a wage decline equivalent to 60–80 percent of the mandated contribution to the worker's severance savings accounts, but these effects are unlikely to have been caused by changes in firing costs.[30]

Peru. For similar reasons, one must interpret cautiously the findings of Saavedra and Torero (2004), who analyzed a large labor reform in Peru in the early 1990s:

> In 1991, labor market regulations were relaxed through a succession of reforms. Firing costs diminished sharply through the progressive elimination of job stability regulations, the reductions in red tape for the use of temporary contracts, and changes in severance pay structure. (Saavedra and Torero 2004, 132)

They employed the Heckman-Pagés hiring cost measure of severance pay: expected lifetime severance payouts, with the severance payout in each period weighted by the likelihood of being laid off in the period and summed.

In Peru, major changes were made to the severance insurance plan. The dismissal pay schedule was reduced sharply, from 12 months' pay for displaced workers with three or more years of service to one month's pay per year of service (Saavedra and Torero 2004, figure 2.1). Saavedra and Torero report that the measure has had a negative and significant impact on employment, as well as the expected effects on various employment hazard functions.

Unfortunately for experimental purposes, many other reforms occurred simultaneously with the reduction in dismissal pay. These included trade liberalization, downsizing of the public sector, the start of a privatization process, the abolition of all state-owned monopolies, tax reform, easing of capital account restrictions, and deregulation of the financial sector (Saavedra and Torero 2004). It would seem impossible to isolate severance pay effects on output, employment, or even turnover in this welter of reforms.

One dramatic outcome that emerges despite the large reduction in mandated severance benefits is a precipitous drop in permanent contracts with the reduction in red tape for temporary contracts; this would appear to signal that firing costs remained high other than through the use of temporary contracts. Saavedra and Torero reported that the share of permanent contracts among private salaried workers in Lima dropped from 80.1 percent in 1991 to 68.6 percent in 1992 (2004, table 2.3).

Apparently, large-scale economic reforms can induce large, positive changes in labor market performance in extremely rigid environments. The implications for severance pay are, however, limited.

Employment Protection Legislation
and Worker Separations

A number of recent studies have, in the spirit of the OECD analyses, estimated EPL effects, usually under the hopeful assumption that other labor market and broader economic reforms were not implemented simultaneously.[31] Several, using cross-national data sets, have focused on the first critical steps in the EPL mechanism—the impact on dismissal rates and job flow rates, and the sum of accession and separation rates. Two recent job flow studies—Micco and Pagés (2006) and Haltiwanger, Scarpetta, and Schweiger (2008)—arrived at remarkably similar conclusions on the basic question of the impact of firing costs on job flows. The studies used somewhat different databases over somewhat different time periods and implemented different strategies for estimating firing cost effects on job flows, which makes the similarity of conclusions reassuring.

Micco and Pagés (2006) estimated the impact of two EPL measures from Botero and others (2004)—the monetary cost of dismissal and the administrative cost of dismissal—on job flow rates.[32] The sample was cross-national, including 11 developed countries and seven Latin American countries (including Mexico) during the 1980s and 1990s. The research design was a difference-in-differences structure in which employment volatility across sectors in the United States was used to identify sectors likely to be especially sensitive to EPL.

Haltiwanger, Scarpetta, and Schweiger (2008) employed a different EPL measure: the Fraser Institute's Economic Freedom of the World (EFW) index of hiring and firing costs. This is a seven-category index, which makes quantitative comparisons impossible.[33] The sample was also somewhat different: 16 countries in the 1990s, consisting of 7 OECD countries, 5 Latin American countries (again including Mexico), and 4 Eastern European countries. The difference-in-differences estimation design also relied on the belief that highly volatile sectors are most likely to be affected by EPL. The researchers implemented this idea through firm size, arguing that small firms are more volatile, with the United States again used as a benchmark. Both studies also included broad indexes for the likelihood of enforcement of regulations.

The two studies arrived at similar conclusions. Micco and Pagés reported, "Our analysis indicates that more stringent legislation slows down job turnover by a significant amount, and that this effect is more pronounced in sectors that are intrinsically more volatile. Employment and output effects are driven by a decline in the net entry of firms" (2006, abstract). Of special note, the impact of EPL effects on the expected sectoral variation in job reallocation (based on U.S. values) is greater the greater the rule of law, leading the authors to conclude that "the effect of EPL on job flows is not statistically significant in countries that score low in the rule of law measure" (Micco and Pagés 2006, 19).[34]

Similarly, Haltiwanger, Scarpetta, and Schweiger (2008, 5) found "support for the general hypothesis that hiring and firing costs reduce turnover, especially in those industries and size classes that require more frequent labor adjustment." They added the refinement that "stringent labor regulations have more of an impact on job flows resulting from the entry and exit of firms than from reallocation among incumbents" (5).

The predicted impact of EPL on job reallocation is roughly comparable in the two studies. Based on a simple model, Micco and Pagés (2006, 8) report that the reallocation rate "in an industry in the 90th percentile of flexibility requirement relative to an industry in the 10th percentile is 6.31 percentage points lower in a country with strict employment protection (that is in the 90th percentile of job security) than in a country with low employment protection (in the 10th percentile)." (The average reallocation rate was 20 percent.) Haltiwanger, Scarpetta, and Schweiger (2008) estimate a 4.4 percentage point decrease on a base of 25 percent.

Conversely, using a natural experiment, Bauer, Bender, and Bonin (2007, 804) reported, "In contrast to the predictions of the theory, our results indicate no statistically significant effects of dismissal protection legislation on worker turnover." Too much can be made of this finding. Experiments may fail to generate reliable estimates of consequences either because the effect was indeed small or because the treatment was modest. The latter appears to be the case in this study.

A careful review of the German quasi-experiment makes the authors' conclusion unsurprising—it was an experiment in which almost nothing happened. In October 1996, the small firm exemption for dismissal regulations was raised from 5 to 10 employees, seemingly freeing employers with fewer than 10 employees from that regulatory burden. But in March 1999, the policy was reversed, and the lower threshold was restored. Without further details, one might imagine this to be an excellent experiment, with the employment behavior of the 5- to 10-employee firms between 1996 and 1999 providing a measure of unconstrained behavior. However, the authors reported,

> The amendment immediately affected only new hires. Those already employed were guaranteed the original level of protection against dismissal for a transition period of three years. Even before the provisions for a gradual transition had expired, in January 1999, dismissal protection legislation was tightened again, by returning to the original threshold value of five employees. (Bauer, Bender, and Bonin 2007, 808)

For the great bulk of the workforce, there apparently was no experiment, only the broken promise of one in the future.

Another recent job flow study considers a more complex effect model. In a cross-national study, Messina and Vallanti (2007) assessed the impact of firing restrictions on job flows—job reallocation as well as its components, job creation and destruction—in a sectoral sample of 14 European countries (roughly the EU 15) from 1992 to 2001. The study relied on a single homogenous database (Amadeus) and used the OECD (2004) index of EPL strictness as the measure of firing costs.[35] The authors concluded, reasonably enough,

> More stringent firing laws dampen the response of job destruction to the cycle, thus making job turnover less counter-cyclical. Moreover, stricter EPL reduces both the creation and destruction of jobs in declining sectors relative to expanding sectors, implying that faster trend growth attenuates the impact of firing costs on firms' hiring and firing decisions. (Messina and Vallanti 2007, F279)

It is plausible to conclude from these studies that more aggressive EPL reduces job separation rates and therefore accession rates, although one cannot rule out the possibility that these effects are the result of simultaneous, unobserved reforms of other sorts. In any case, the implications for severance benefit generosity alone are limited.

EPL: Employment and Its Distribution[36]

If job protection regulations protect the employed by reducing job flows, the impact on those who do not yet hold jobs is likely to be negative; however, the precise impact is likely to vary across economies. In developing countries, the regulations may affect the distribution of jobs between the formal sector and the informal sector. In advanced economies, this might be reflected in redistribution between wage employment and self-employment. Predictions about aggregate employment effects of job security (and certainly their welfare implications) become yet more difficult when low protection employment options (temporary contracts) are introduced, as they were in a number of OECD countries in the 1980s and 1990s.[37]

The OECD studies discussed above suggested that employment rates in aggregate are lower in countries with strict EPL, with only employment rates for prime-age men higher (OECD 1999, 2004). EPL may also explain the high rates of temporary jobs among the young and the less skilled. Additional micro evidence—both natural experiments and cross-national studies—are reviewed in the remainder of this section.

Italy. One reform, in Italy in 1990, has been the subject of intense study. Both before and after the reform, dismissal rules were more stringent for employers with more than 15 workers than for those with 15 or fewer, but the reform sharply narrowed the size advantage of small firms.

For larger firms, the rules were unchanged. Rules were specified for two types of dismissal, individual and collective, from permanent contracts. Although not exclusively, individual dismissals were typically for disciplinary reasons, while collective dismissals were for economic reasons. One additional concept was critical: just cause. Both individual and collective dismissal were allowed only with just cause; severe penalties were imposed for releasing a worker without that designation. A worker found by the courts to have been released without just cause was eligible for lost wages between the dismissal and the court ruling (which could be as long as five years) and given the choice of either reinstatement or a lump-sum payment of another 15 months' wages. The firm had the burden of proof that the dismissal was just, which is notably more difficult for disciplinary dismissals.

Conversely, the treatment of small firms changed significantly in 1990. Before 1990, firms with fewer than 16 workers were exempt from any such rules. After 1990, small firms were also penalized for unjust dismissal, although the firm made the choice between reinstatement and severance pay of 2.5 to 6 months' wages. The change sharply increased firing costs for small firms and sharply reduced disincentives to expansion beyond 15 workers should that be efficient.

Kugler and Pica (2008) used this quasi-experiment to isolate the severance mandate effect on turnover and total employment. They reported, "We find that the increase in dismissal costs decreased accessions and separations for workers in small relative to large firms, especially in sectors with higher employment volatility, with a negligible impact on net employment" (78). The reform effects on turnover were modest, given the generosity of the severance mandate imposed: about a 15 percent reduction in separations and a 13 percent reduction in accessions. At the extensive margin, there appeared to be a significant reduction in entry of small relative to large firms but, oddly, no apparent effect on exit of small firms relative to large ones (Kugler and Pica 2008, table 3).

In a two-part analysis, Boeri and Jimeno (2005) first established (on post-reform data) that the EPL rules remained significantly more stringent for large firms after the 1990 reforms. Using the temporary versus permanent contract distinction in a difference-in-differences framework, they reported that dismissal rates remained sharply lower in large firms: "Workers under permanent contracts in firms with less restrictive EPL are more likely to be dismissed" (Boeri and Jimeno 2005, 2057).

They then considered the reform period. The fact that the extension applied only to workers under permanent contracts set up the possibility of a double difference approach: Is the behavior of workers under permanent contracts in firms of fewer than 15 workers different from that of workers in all other circumstances? The authors used this approach to estimate reform effects on firm employment size. They reported that the reform increased the "persistence" of small firms (mildly, but significantly in a logit model), which seems odd, as the reform leveled the playing field between large and small firms. They found no evidence of an impact on employment growth (change).

Schivardi and Torrini (2008) found modest effects of the EPL threshold of 15 workers on firm growth just above and below the threshold, estimating that the "probability of firms' growth is reduced by around 2 percentage points near the threshold" (482). They also noted the impact of the 1990 reform. "The results . . . show indeed that the threshold effect, equal to around 2 percent before 1990, drops (in absolute value) by between 0.7 and 1.0 percentage point in the second part of the sample" (Schivardi and Torrini 2008, 497).

In sum, the EPL effects on employment appear small and possibly perverse, relative to the simplest severance mandate interpretation.

Spain. Kugler, Jimeno, and Hernanz (2005) explored the distributional consequences of restrictive dismissal policies and payroll taxation of permanent contracts on employment in the Spanish labor market. Reforms introduced in 1997 and extended in 2001 were designed to make permanent contracts more attractive to firms for two demographic groups: younger and older workers. The reforms were substantial, though not limited to dismissal policies:

> Severance payments for unfair dismissals of newly signed contracts of workers in affected groups were reduced from 45 to 33 days per year of seniority and the maximum was reduced from 42 to 24 months. In addition, given the high payroll tax rate in Spain (i.e. 28.3% of the salary), the reform reduced payroll taxes between 40% and 90% for workers in these population groups hired under new permanent contracts. (Kugler, Jimeno, and Hernanz 2005, 7)

Relief from dismissal mandates and from payroll taxes was offered for conversion of temporary contracts to permanent contracts.

As reported by Heckman and Pagés (2004) for a broad sample of OECD and LAC countries, expected dismissal costs are typically quite modest relative to payroll taxes (see table 3.1 above), and that is the case in the Spanish example, both before and after the reforms. The authors estimated "quarterly expected dismissal costs of 17 and 191 Euros for young and older men, respectively, [in 1995]. . . . The payroll tax rate is 28.3%, implying an average quarterly payroll tax cost of 756 and 1,478 Euros for young and older men, respectively" (Kugler, Jimeno, and Hernanz 2005, 20). They also said,

> Our results suggest the Spanish reforms increased permanent employment probabilities for young and older men. . . . In addition we find some evidence that reduced non-wage labor costs for contract conversions increased transitions from temporary to permanent employment for men of all age groups. On the other hand. . . . we find little effect of subsidies and reduced dismissal costs on women. (Kugler, Jimeno, and Hernanz 2005, 2–3)

There is no obvious explanation for the sex difference in the response.[38] The vastly greater magnitude of the payroll tax reduction relative to changes in expected dismissal costs would seem to argue that the behavioral consequences can be attributed largely to the payroll tax.

Chile. Montenegro and Pagés (2004) provided evidence from Chile, which imposed job security mandates of sharply varying severity over the period 1960–98, including an eightfold increase in 1965 and a 50 percent reduction in the early 1970s. The job security measure was a Heckman-Pagés gross hiring cost measure, the probability-weighted sum of advance notice, justified dismissal, and unjustified dismissal payments (Montenegro and Pagés 2004, 408). The timing of major changes was not random, which raises the usual concerns that the authors may be picking up broader labor market and economic changes (they do control explicitly for minimum wage). This study could also belong in the review of economic reforms above.

The authors embedded this policy measure in annual June household survey data and found that the employment of prime-age males rose with greater job security (at the 5–10 percent confidence level, depending on specification) but that the employment of other groups declined: "Job security regulations reduce the employment opportunities of the young and the unskilled—and particularly unskilled youth—while promoting the employment rates of skilled and older workers" (Montenegro and Pagés 2004, 431). They also found "indications that job security regulations may force some workers, particularly women and the unskilled, out of wage employment and into self-employment" (431).

Canada, Finland, Italy, the Netherlands, Switzerland, the United Kingdom, and the United States. Kahn (2007) analyzed the impact of EPL on the demographic patterns of nonemployment and temporary employment for these seven countries. He employed a relatively unused (for these purposes) microsurvey data set, the 1994–98 International Adult Literacy Survey, which contains information on job type, permanent or temporary. Kahn's EPL measure is the OECD permanent employment protection indicator. Kahn found that "greater protection disproportionately lowered the relative probability that youths, immigrants and, possibly, women were employed; in addition, among those with jobs, I generally found that greater employment protection also lowered the relative incidence of permanent work among these groups, as well as those with low cognitive ability" (Kahn 2007, F354).

Kahn included explicit controls for collective bargaining rules, so the EPL effects are not simply a reflection of broader labor market interventions. Collective bargaining rules redistributed jobs in much the same way as EPL.[39] Of special interest, he found that the combination of strong EPL and strong collective bargaining rules compounded the individual policy effects—the combined effect is larger than the sum of the two individual effects. The two sets of rules are not simply alternative means to the same ends.

The evidence seems quite compelling that labor legislation, perhaps even employment protection legislation, does what one might imagine it would do: reduce the separation rate of those with jobs, often prime-age adults, at the expense of new entrants and the more highly mobile—the young and the less skilled.

EPL as Workplace Control

EPL measures are a mixture of severance benefit generosity, access to less protected temporary jobs, and work discipline constraints. One cannot ignore the contribution of work discipline constraints in this mix. Reasonable evidence exists that such constraints have significant and negative effects on employment. The effects are modest if the constraints on workplace control are small, and more substantial if the constraints are severe.

An event of the first type is the much-studied legal shift in the employment-at-will doctrine in the United States (Autor, Donohue, and Schwab 2004, 2006; Dertouzos and Karoly 1993; MacLeod and Nakavachara 2007; and Miles 2000, among others). In a remarkably brief period—the 1980s—U.S. state courts moved away from a narrow interpretation of employment-at-will contracts: in the absence of a written contract to the contrary, employers are free to release workers at will.[40] Courts began systematically overriding employment-at-will for a variety of reasons, many of which might seem unexceptional to an economist. Seemingly narrow exceptions include that a worker can sue for wrongful discharge if released for refusing to break a law (the public policy exception) or if the intent is to deny the delayed compensation due to the worker (the good faith exception). Many state courts embraced a more substantial exception, that of implicit contracts. For example, by 1990, workers in all states could sue for wrongful discharge if they had been released despite having forgone an outside opportunity on a (nonwritten) promise of continued employment with the firm.

The implicit contract exception strikes a contractarian as logical, which makes the change potentially efficiency-augmenting. Much depends on the efficiency of the courts, which become more important players in the employment relationship because judgment is required. If courts function badly, the additional discretion might reduce labor market efficiency. State courts vary in quality, which makes empirical study of the consequences of this change especially interesting.

In the seminal paper on this topic, Dertouzos and Karoly (1993) reported statistically significant but small negative employment effects of the employment-at-will events of the 1980s. Miles (2000) undertook a careful reexamination of the same basic empirical phenomenon and found no significant employment effects, though he did find large temporary employment gains. The speed of the conversion and the localization of its timing—beginning in the high-income states and spreading rapidly to the low-income Southern states—makes empirical assessments of effects somewhat tricky. The low-income states grew more rapidly throughout the period and also adopted temporary contracts later. Autor, Donohue, and Schwab (2004, 2006) generally supported Miles's conclusions, finding that employment effects of the weakening of employment-at-will contracts had little effect on employment, although the estimated coefficient on one policy variation, though small in absolute magnitude, was significantly different from zero (and negative, as expected). Their modifications "restore the conclusion that the implied contract exception caused a small but significant employment reduction" (Autor, Donohue, and Schwab 2004, 445).[41]

MacLeod and Nakavachara (2007), while finding essentially zero aggregate employment effects of the legislated changes, noted an interesting effect once the labor force was disaggregated by skill. Evidence emerged that highly skilled workers experienced positive, though small, employment effects; low-skilled workers, in contrast, experienced small negative effects. The first result is consistent with the argument that the contracting environment for specific human capital had improved. Apparently the U.S. state court systems function sufficiently well that the additional responsibilities of interpreting the employment contract did not have a large negative effect on labor market efficiency.

That does not mean that larger shifts in workplace control would not have more substantial effects. Marinescu (2009) provided evidence from the United Kingdom that larger shifts in job separation regulations could have significant effects on job security independent of severance pay mandates, at least for short-tenured workers, primarily youth. In 1999, the probationary period for permanent employment was lowered from two years to one, while regulations on severance pay and advance notice were unchanged (2009, footnote 7). Marinescu describes the bureaucratic aspect of job protection following the probationary period in the following way:

> If a worker is dismissed (i.e. for cause) or made redundant (laid off) and satisfies the relevant conditions, he can sue his former employer claiming that the dismissal was unfair. The Employment Tribunal decides on the case. If the worker's claim is found to be legitimate, the firm has to pay the worker a compensation that is largely based on the worker's age and seniority. (2009, footnote 4)

One might view this as an administratively determined severance payout of uncertain size. However it is viewed, reducing the exclusion from this process from two years to one had a large negative impact on involuntary worker turnover in the one- to two-year tenure interval. As Marinescu (2009, 465) reported, "The firing hazard for these workers decreased by 26% relative to the hazard for workers with 2–4 years of tenure."

Oddly, the firing rate of those with less than one year of tenure also fell, and by only a slightly smaller amount (19 percent), though one might have expected an increase in separations in the shorter probationary period, Marinescu attributes this apparent anomaly to better recruiting practices induced by the shorter probationary period. Like other curious results that pop up in natural experiments, this explanation might be correct, but it does raise concern that omitted forces are at work.

Severance Pay Generosity

We have at least some evidence, then, of dismissal regulation effects on involuntary turnover independent of severance generosity. What of the converse? Is there similar direct evidence that the severance generosity dimension of EPL alone has significant effects on turnover and employment? The 1990 Lazear study, appropriately reinterpreted by Addison, Teixeira, and Grosso (2000), and the 2004 Heckman and Pagés study both provide severance generosity estimates, though one must be a little concerned about correlated, omitted policy variables in these studies. Taken at face value, the studies yield no statistically significant evidence of severance pay generosity effects on aggregate employment or, for that matter, on unemployment. The OECD studies (1999, 2004) provide estimates of EPL effects, though severance pay implications are limited by the ex ante policy weights.

Additional evidence does exist. Friesen (2005) exploited variations in Canadian severance pay and other employment protection laws to assess the effects on layoff risk. She analyzed survey data from 1988 through1990 to estimate the impact on the layoff hazard of variations in individual and group advance notice and severance pay mandates. Each province, territory, and the federally regulated sector has its own employment protection legislation, and variations across provinces are substantial, particularly for advance notice mandates. Unfortunately, severance pay mandates are found only in Ontario and the federal jurisdiction.

Friesen (2005) found evidence of negative effects on the layoff hazard to employ-ment (shortened job duration) for individual advance notice requirements but not for sev-erance benefit mandates. The absence of measured severance effects may reflect the limited magnitude of variation in severance mandates. Ontario mandated one week of severance for each year of tenure up to 26 weeks, a common level in voluntary plans in larger U.S. firms. Mandates in the federally regulated sectors were smaller.

Sri Lanka. Vodopivec (2004) describes a natural experiment that involved large changes in severance generosity mandates. In 1971, Sri Lanka imposed an unusually generous sev-erance mandate on most large firms, which would seem to offer hope of providing robust estimates of severance effects on labor market activities of various sorts. The objective of the underlying legislation—the Termination of Employment of Workmen Act (TEWA) of 1971—was protection against mass layoffs, not discharge for cause.[42] In 2002, "a Sri Lankan worker with 20 years of service received an average severance package equal to 29 months of wages" (Abidoye, Orazem, and Vodopivec 2009, 6). A laid-off OECD worker with 20 years of experience might expect five or six months' wages.

Abidoye, Orazem, and Vodopivec others (2009) explored the impact of this extraor-dinarily high level of mandated severance pay for larger firms on employment growth by firm size. The study relied on two special features of the legislation and its enforcement: (1) firms with fewer than 15 workers were legally exempt, and (2) firms in export processing zones (EPZs) were not covered owing to the laxity of enforcement.[43] The researchers set up a difference-in-differences approach to employment growth rates (measured as the fraction of firms that expanded employment). As figure 3.3 shows, firms below the legislated threshold were less likely to add workers than were large firms, though somewhat surprisingly (1) the

FIGURE 3.3 **Percentage of Employers with Growth in Employment (by regulation type and size of firm)**

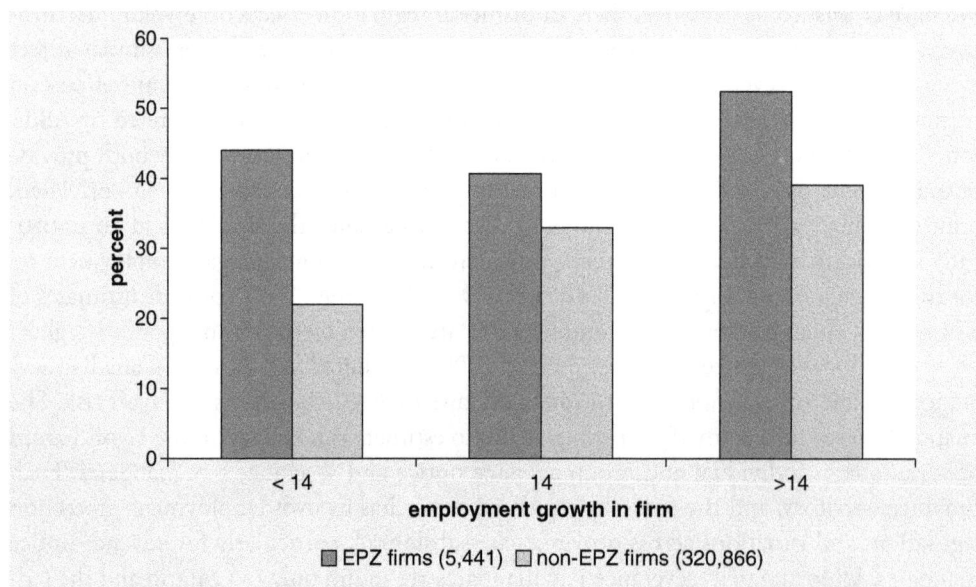

effect is less dramatic among threshold firms (size 14) than smaller ones, and (2) the size effect holds for EPZ firms, in which regulations are not enforced, as well as non-EPZ firms, where they are (which supports the wisdom of using a difference-in-differences approach). As it happens, the threshold effect is even smaller in a difference-in-differences structure—the differential between employment growth in the regulated and unregulated sector for firms with 14 employers was less than for either smaller or larger firms.

The authors developed arguments as to why threshold firms have had less growth than other small firms in response to these extraordinary severance mandates, but the modest, perhaps perverse, threshold growth response argues against serious severance pay concerns.[44] An alternative hypothesis is that policy enforcement was lax throughout the economy, not simply in the EPZs.[45] Unusually large severance mandates may appear only where regulation enforcement is weak. Similar mandates in an OECD country might have quite different results.[46]

So far, it seems that no one has estimated the job distributional effects of a simple variation in severance pay generosity.

Conclusion

The Lazear paradox—that the firing cost consequences of severance pay mandates are easily avoided, yet observed adverse effects are large—appears to be resolved through accumulating evidence that adverse effects of a mandate are small without explicit contract avoidance. The substantial voluntary provision of severance pay in the United States is one clear signal that the distortions are not large. A critical review of the extensive empirical literature on mandate effects supports that interpretation: Severance mandates unaccompanied by other labor regulations have little impact on worker separations (or accessions) or average employment levels, the labor processes considered here.

This conclusion is not always apparent in individual studies. Sufficiently broad interventions in the economy do have substantial negative consequences, and the challenge is to disentangle the effects of these more substantial policies on that of severance pay generosity alone. Employment protection legislation and even severance pay cover a complex of policy instruments, only one of which is job displacement insurance. An even greater impediment for empirical analysis of severance mandate effects is that changes in mandate requirements are typically embedded in broad policy reforms, both positive and negative, making the identification of severance policy consequences difficult.

Evidence of adverse efficiency effects of government interventions is most compelling when the range of interventions is large. In summary:

- Comprehensive government interventions in the economy—heavy tariffs, highly regulated product and factor markets, including capital controls and capital market restrictions as well as those in the labor market—have large negative effects on the labor market. Conversely, broad economic reforms easing these restrictions yield large positive gains.

- Broad labor regulations, especially with regard to collective bargaining and dispute resolution, appear to have large negative effects on the labor force and the economy.

- Employment protection legislation—a combination of severance pay mandates, advance notice mandates, and limits on disciplinary discharges—appears to have substantial negative effects on worker separations and accessions, and therefore aggregate turnover.

- Although there is little compelling evidence of strong EPL effects on employment levels; a best estimate might be that there is a slight negative effect on employment.

- Evidence of EPL distributional consequences is robust. EPL restrictions make permanent contracts more difficult for new workers to secure, which favors prime-age men at the expense, most consistently, of the young and the low-skilled, and, in some circumstances, of women and older workers.

- At least some evidence exists for the importance of more complex processes:

  - The impact of EPL reforms is conditioned on obedience to the law in general and may depend on the regulatory environment in the economy as a whole.
  - There may be important interaction effects between severance mandates and collective bargaining rules.

Identification of the EPL factors responsible for observed distortions remains an important issue for further research. A variety of results point toward workplace control, including the employer's ability to release unsatisfactory workers and collective bargaining rules.

The lesson for job displacement insurance designers is that indirect mandate effects appear to be modest over the range observed in industrialized economies. Benefit generosity can, to a first approximation, be set by the worker's demand for the insurance coverage without concern for moral hazard effects on turnover and equilibrium employment. Larger mandates appear to have only modest indirect effects, although these are observed only in developing economies, and enforcement may be spotty.

Notes

1. Unemployment effects—the policy problem that energizes much of this literature—is a more complex, institutionally specific process (Mincer 1976) and is not dealt with here. For a concise description of the problem, see Blanchard and Portugal (2001). The important work by Layard, Nickell, and associates (for example, Nickell and Layard 1999), which primarily focuses on unemployment processes, is not covered here either.

2. Like any review of a large literature, this one is somewhat idiosyncratic and far from all-inclusive.

3. Blanchard (1998) provides an accessible and oft-cited discussion of this approach.

4. Some of the same difficulties arise in trying to identify individual policy determinants of good governance (Kraay and Tawara 2010).

5. The authors find that "in broad terms, common and civil law traditions utilize different strategies for dealing with market failure: the former rely on contract, the latter on direct supervision of markets by the government" (Botero and others 2004, 1340). Obviously, this observation is incomplete as a theory of labor regulation; it cannot, for example, explain regulatory change, including the many reforms that provide the bulk of the material for the empirical studies to follow. Nonetheless, the finding provides mild support for the idea that the rules, including

severance mandates, are not determined by the impact of the regulations, an idea implicitly embraced in most of the studies reviewed here.

6. These are often called redundancies.

7. Because benefits are typically determined as a fraction of weekly or monthly wages, expected wage inflation is a critical issue if wages are not stable. In that case, neutrality would require both wage inflation and discount factor adjustments.

8. The four countries are Armenia, Israel, the Democratic People's Republic of Korea, and Uganda. Incapacity separation is a simple form of disability insurance and is found in all four of these countries and, in combination with redundancy and other separations, in about 20 percent of the remaining 96 countries.

9. Prereform Austria (2003) provides an example of such a program. Benefits were paid out for involuntary layoffs and retirement but not for voluntary separations (quits).

10. Two of these—Italy and Peru—were simply severance savings plans.

11. For discussions, see Pagés and Montenegro (2007) and Goerke (2006).

12. See, however, the interesting work by Almeida and Carneiro (2009), which exploits variations in labor inspection visits per firm across localities in Brazil to estimate the impact on firm size. All other things being equal, firms in cities with more intense inspection schedules are smaller in a variety of dimensions, presumably to reduce the likelihood of inspection.

13. Holzmann and others (2011) report that severance insurance mandates in the majority of countries (54 of 72, or 75 percent) include dismissal as well as redundancy as benefit-qualifying separation events.

14. See Parsons (1986), Malcomson (1999), and Salanié (2005) for reviews of the contract literature.

15. Nickell (1978) and Bertola (1992) provide clear introductions to the underlying employment dynamics in a world of certainty. Bentolila and Bertola (1990) and Bertola (1990) introduce uncertainty. Bertola (1999) provides a review; Blanchard (1998), an accessible discussion.

16. This argument is developed informally, with a variety of examples, in Parsons (2011a). Parsons (2011b) provides a formal statement of the argument.

17. See Hunt (2000) for an interesting empirical application.

18. Relatively common voluntary severance plans in the United States suggest that this is not wholly fanciful, although voluntary plans in the United States are less generous than many mandated plans elsewhere and more tightly targeted on white collar workers in volatile industries (Parsons 2005 and Bishow and Parsons 2004, respectively).

19. Such plans were once common in the United States but are now illegal under the Employee Retirement Income Security Act of 1974, which mandates rapid vesting of pensions.

20. Before 2003, the Austrian plan could be considered a 90 percent savings plan, with payouts for involuntary job separation and retirement but not for voluntary separations (quits). See Parsons 2011a.

21. Grubb and Wells (1993) give a clear account of the interplay of pro-worker collective bargaining rules and direct severance mandates.

22. In a detailed analysis of the Lazear models, Addison, Teixeira, and Grosso (2000) did report estimates of the fixed-effects model with the additional covariates. They reported that the severance pay index coefficients were insignificant for both the employment rate and the unemployment rate but positive and significant for labor force participation and hours (table 3). Correcting for first order autocorrelation leaves none of the SEV coefficients significant (table 4).

23. This observation is not inconsistent with simple theory if the economy has two sectors, with only one covered by the severance mandate.

24. Hiring costs, of course, remain an issue, even if firing costs are zero.

25. Although the volume editors, Heckman and Pagés, and various authors of the individual chapters clearly stated the importance of distinguishing payroll tax effects, as one might expect for savings mandates, and firing cost effects for severance insurance mandates, some authors were less careful to distinguish between the two.

26. As a practical issue, Heckman and Pagés (2004, 80) report that using the Lazear measure and their own "yields similar results."

27. Advance notice introduces special difficulties for hiring cost measurement. The maximum possible outlay is the corresponding severance payout, which is the typical remedy for noncompliance with a notice period; but the cost could be zero if the firm (1) complies with the regulation and (2) does not experience a reduction in worker productivity during the compliance period.

28. Conversely, Booth, Dolado, and Frank (2002) argued that the fraction of the workforce in temporary contracts depends solely on the EPL of regular contracts, not in any way on the EPL of temporary contracts. If true, this would be theoretically puzzling.

29. See variants of this claim in Kugler (2004).

30. Kugler (2004, 199–200) noted the pervasiveness of the reforms but remained optimistic that her results reflect firing cost effects.

31. Recall, also, the Caballero and others (2004) paper discussed earlier.

32. Unfortunately, the authors did not believe they could reasonably identify the independent impacts of either the monetary or administrative costs of the dismissal measure. They report a simple correlation of 0.71 between the two and estimate only the sum (Micco and Pagés 2006, 14).

33. For completeness: "Hiring and firing regulations: This sub-component is based on the *Global Competitiveness Report*'s question: "The hiring and firing of workers is impeded by regulations (= 1) or flexibly determined by employers (= 7)." The question's wording has varied slightly over the years. Source: World Economic Forum, *Global Competitiveness Report* (various issues)" (Gwartney and Lawson 2009, 198). Haltiwanger, Scarpetta, and Schweiger (2008, 20) report that the measure is highly correlated with the OECD EPL measure—with a correlation of 0.85.

34. The rule of law measure derives from Kaufmann, Kraay, and Mastruzzi (2003).

35. Messina and Vallanti (2007) also conducted a robustness test using a less common EPL measure developed by Blanchard and Wolfers (2000). Here, as elsewhere, the exact form of the EPL measure does not seem of critical importance.

36. See Kugler (2007) for some interesting reflections on this literature.

37. Dolado, Garcia-Serrano, and Jimeno (2002) provide a detailed account of the most dramatic of these developments.

38. The authors argue that "weak effects on women seem to reflect the lack of a good control group as well as pre-existing trends for women" (Kugler, Jimeno, and Hernanz 2005, 22).

39. On collective bargaining effects, see also Bertola, Blau, and Kahn (2007), who found for 17 OECD countries over the 1960–96 period that "time-varying indicators of unionization decrease the employment-population ratio of young and older individuals relative to the prime-aged, and of prime-aged women relative to prime-aged men" (833).

40. Miles (2000) provides an especially clear introduction to the event.

41. Autor (2003) reconfirmed (and expanded upon) Miles's claim of a temporary employment effect.

42. "The TEWA was intended to prevent or discourage mass retrenchment situations in the industrial sector, considered to be likely due to the scarcity of raw materials during a period of inward-looking economic policy in the early 1970s" (Heltberg and Vodopivec 2009, 17).

43. "Firms in export processing zones (EPZs) are said to face lax policy enforcement" (Abidoye, Orazem, and Vodopivec 2009, 3).

44. There is also some question of how closely the program otherwise approximates a severance savings plan.

45. The authors do report the case of one luckless international company, Shell Gas Lanka, that was not spared the full measure of the law (Abidoye, Orazem, and Vodopivec 2009, appendix 1).

46. Recall the findings of Caballero and colleagues (2004) that employment security measures only adversely affect the speed of employment adjustment to a shock if the rule of law is strong.

References

Abidoye, B., P. F. Orazem, and M. Vodopivec. 2009. "Firing Cost and Firm Size: A Study of Sri Lanka's Severance Pay System." Social Protection Discussion Paper 0916, World Bank, Washington, DC.

Addison, J., and P. Teixeira. 2003. "The Economics of Employment Protection." *Journal of Labor Research* 24 (1, Winter): 85–129.

Addison, J. P. Teixeira, and J.-L. Grosso. 2000. "The Effect of Dismissals Protection on Employment: More on a Vexed Theme." *Southern Economic Journal* 67 (1, July): 105–22.

Ahsan, A., and C. Pagés. 2008. "Are All Labor Regulations Equal? Evidence from Indian Manufacturing." IZA Discussion Paper 3394, Institute for the Study of Labor, Bonn.

Almeida, R., and P. Carneiro. 2009. "Enforcement of Labor Regulation and Firm Size." *Journal of Comparative Economics* 37 (1, March): 28–46.

Autor, D. H. 2003. "Outsourcing at Will: The Contribution of Unjust Dismissal Doctrine to the Growth of Employment Outsourcing." *Journal of Labor Economics* 21 (1, January): 1–42.

Autor, D. H., J. J. Donohue III, and S. J. Schwab. 2004. "The Employment Consequences of Wrongful-Discharge Laws, Large, Small, or None at All?" *AEA Papers and Proceedings* 94 (2): 440–46.

———. 2006. "The Costs of Wrongful-Discharge Laws." *Review of Economics and Statistics* 88 (2, May): 211–31.

Bauer, T. K., S. Bender, and H. Bonin. 2007. "Dismissal Protection and Worker Flows in Small Establishments." *Economica* 74: 804–21.

Bentolila, S., and G. Bertola. 1990. "Firing Costs and Labor Demand: How Bad is Eurosclerosis?" *Review of Economic Studies* 57 (3, July): 381–402.

Bertola, G. 1990. "Job Security, Employment, and Wages." *European Economic Review* 34: 851–86.

———. 1992. "Labor Turnover Costs and Average Labor Demand." *Journal of Labor Economics* 10 (October): 389–411.

———. 1999. "Microeconomic Perspectives on Aggregate Labor Markets: Labor Turnover Costs and Average Labor Demand." In *Handbook of Labor Economics* Vol. 3C, ed. O. Ashenfelter and D. Card, 2985–3028. Amsterdam: Elsevier.

Bertola, G., F. D. Blau, and L. M. Kahn. 2007. "Labor Market Institutions and Demographic Employment Patterns." *Journal of Population Economics* 20 (4): 833–67.

Besley, T., and R. Burgess. 2004. "Can Labor Regulation Hinder Economic Performance? Evidence from India." *Quarterly Journal of Economics* 119 (1, February): 91–134.

Bhattacharjea, A. 2006. "Labour Market Regulation and Industrial Performance in India: A Critical Review of the Empirical Evidence." *Indian Journal of Labour Economics* 49 (2): 211–32.

Bishow, J., and D. O. Parsons. 2004. "Trends in Severance Pay Coverage in the United States. 1980–2001" (May). http://ssrn.com/abstract=878144.

Blanchard, O. 1998. "Employment Protection and Unemployment." Draft. Harvard University, Cambridge, MA.

Blanchard, O., and P. Portugal. 2001 "What Hides Behind an Unemployment Rate? Comparing Portuguese and U.S. Labor Markets." *American Economic Review* 91 (March): 187–207.

Blanchard, O., and J. J. Wolfers. 2000. "The Role of Shocks and Institutions in the Rise of European Unemployment: The Aggregate Evidence." *Economic Journal* 110: C1–33.

Boeri, T., and J. F. Jimeno. 2005. "The Effects of Employment Protection: Learning from Variable Enforcement." *European Economic Review* 49 (8): 2057–77.

Booth, A. L., J. J. Dolado, and J. Frank. 2002. "Symposium on Temporary Work: Introduction." *Economic Journal* 112 (480, June): F181–88.

Botero, J. C., S. Djankov, R. La Porta, Fl. Lopez-de-Silanes, and A. Shleifer. 2004. "The Regulation of Labor." *Quarterly Journal of Economics* 119 (4, November): 1339–82.

Caballero, R. J., K. N. Cowan, E. M.R.A. Engel, and A. Micco. 2004. "Effective Labor Regulation and Microeconomic Flexibility," NBER Working Paper 10744, National Bureau of Economic Research, Cambridge, MA.

Dertouzos, J. N., and L. A. Karoly. 1993. "Employment Effects of Worker Protection: Evidence from the United States." In *Employment Security and Labor Market Behavior: Interdisciplinary Approaches and International Evidence*, ed. C. F. Buechtemann, 215–27. Ithaca, NY: ILR Press.

Dolado, J. J., C. Garcia-Serrano, and J. F. Jimeno. 2002 "Drawing Lessons from the Book of Temporary Jobs in Spain." *Economic Journal* 112 (June): F270–95.

Emerson, M. 1988. "Regulation or Deregulation of the Labour Market; Policy Regimes for the Recruitment and Dismissal of Employees in the Industrialized Countries." *European Economic Review* 32: 775–817.

Eslava, M., J. Haltiwanger, A. Kugler, and M. Kugler. 2006. "Plant Turnover and Structural Reforms in Colombia." IMF Staff Papers, Special Issue 53: 58–75, International Monetary Fund, Washington, DC.

Forteza, A., and M. Rama. 2006. "Labor Market 'Rigidity' and the Success of Economic Reforms across More Than 100 Countries." *Journal of Policy Reform* 9 (1, March): 75–105.

Friesen, J. 2005. "Statutory Firing Costs and Lay-offs in Canada." *Labour Economics* 12: 147–68.

Goerke, L. 2006. "Earnings-Related Severance Pay." *Labour* 20 (4, December): 651–72.

Grubb, D., and W. Wells. 1993. "Employment Regulation and Patterns of Work in EC Countries." *OECD Studies* 21: 7–58.

Gwartney, J., and R. Lawson. 2009. *Economic Freedom of the World, 2009 Annual Report. Economic Freedom Network.* Vancouver, BC: Fraser Institute. Data retrieved from www.freetheworld.com.

Haltiwanger, J., S. Scarpetta, and H. Schweiger. 2008. "Assessing Job Flows Across Countries: The Role of Industry, Firm Size, and Regulations." NBER Working Paper 13920, National Bureau of Economic Research, Cambridge, MA.

Heckman, J. J., and C. Pagés. 2004. "Introduction." In *Law and Employment: Lessons from Latin America and the Caribbean,* ed. J. Heckman and C. Pagés, 1–107. Chicago: University of Chicago Press.

Heltberg, R., and M. Vodopivec. 2009. "Sri Lanka, Unemployment Job Security, and Labor Market Reform." Washington, DC, World Bank, Draft, http://ssrn.com/abstract=1208662.

Holzmann, R. 2005. "Editorial." *Empirica* 32 (3-4): 251–53.

Holzmann, R., Y. Pouget, M. Weber, and M. Vodopivec. 2011. "Severance Pay Programs around the World: History, Rationale, Status and Reforms." Chapter 2, this volume.

Hunt, J. 2000. "Firing Costs, Employment Fluctuations and Average Employment: An Examination of Germany." *Economica* 67 (266, May): 177–202.

Kahn, L. M. 2007. "The Impact of Employment Protection Mandates on Demographic Temporary Employment Patterns: International Microeconomic Evidence." *Economic Journal* 117 (June): F333–56.

Kaufmann, D., A. Kraay, and P. Zoido-Lobaton. 1999. "Governance Matters." Policy Research Department Working Paper 2196, World Bank, Washington, DC.

Kaufmann, D., A. Kraay, and M. Mastruzzi. 2003. "Governance Matters III: Governance Indicators for 1996–2002." Policy Research Department Working Papers (May), World Bank, Washington, DC.

Kraay, A., and N. Tawara. 2010. "Can Disaggregate Indicators Identify Governance Reform Priorities?" Policy Research Working Paper 5254, World Bank, Washington, DC.

Kugler, A. D. 1999. "The Impact of Firing Costs on Turnover and Unemployment: Evidence from the Colombian Labour Market Reform." *International Tax and Public Finance* 6 (3, August): 389–410.

———. 2002. "From Severance Pay to Self-Insurance: Effects of Severance Payments Savings Accounts in Colombia." IZA Discussion Paper 434 (February), Institute for the Study of Labor, Bonn.

———. 2004. "The Effect of Job Security Regulations on Labor Market Flexibility: Evidence from the Colombian Labor Market Reform." In *Law and Employment: Lessons from Latin America and the Caribbean,* ed. J. Heckman and C. Pagés, 183–228. Chicago: University of Chicago Press.

———. 2005. "Wage-shifting Effects of Severance Payments Savings Accounts in Colombia." *Journal of Public Economics* 89: 487–500.

———. 2007. "The Effects of Employment Protection in Europe and the USA." *Els Opuscles del CREI* 18 (February).

Kugler, A., J. F. Jimeno, and V. Hernanz. 2003 (2005 Version). "Employment Consequences of Restrictive Permanent Contracts : Evidence from Spanish Labor Market Reforms." CEPR Discussion Paper 3724, Centre for Economic Policy Research, London.

Kugler, A. D., and G. Pica. 2008. "Effects of Employment Protection on Worker and Job Flows: Evidence from the 1990 Italian Reform." *Labour Economics* 15: 78–95.

Lazear, E. P. 1990. "Job Security Provisions and Employment." *Quarterly Journal of Economics* 105 (August): 699–726.

MacLeod, W. B., and V. Nakavachara. 2007. "Can Wrongful Discharge Law Enhance Employment." *Economic Journal* 117 (June): F218–78.

Malcomson, J. 1999. "Individual Employment Contracts." In *Handbook of Labor Economics* IIIB., ed. O. Ashenfelter and D. Card, 2291–372. Amsterdam: Elsevier/North Holland Press.

Marinescu, I. 2009. "Job Security Legislation and Job Duration: Evidence from the United Kingdom." *Journal of Labor Economics* 27 (3): 465–86.

Messina, J., and G. Vallanti. 2007. "Job Flow Dynamics and Firing Restrictions: Evidence from Europe." *Economic Journal* 117 (June): F279–301.

Micco, A., and C. Pagés. 2006. "The Economic Effects of Employment Protection: Evidence from International Industry-Level Data," IZA Discussion Paper 2433, Institute for the Study of Labor, Bonn.

Miles, T. J. 2000. "Common Law Exceptions to Employment at Will and U.S. Labor Markets." *Journal of Law Economics and Organization* 16 (1): 74–101.

Mincer, J. 1976. "Unemployment Effects of Minimum Wages." *Journal of Political Economy* 84 (4, August): S87–104.

Montenegro, C. E., and C. Pagés. 2004. "Who Benefits from Labor Market Regulations? Chile, 1960–1998." In *Law and Employment: Lessons from Latin America and the Caribbean,* ed. J. Heckman and C. Pagés, 401–34. Chicago: University of Chicago Press.

Nickell, S., J. 1978. "Employment and Labour Demand over the Cycle." *Economica* 45 (180, November): 329–45.

Nickell, S., and R. Layard. 1999. "Labor Market Institutions and Economic Performance." In *Handbook of Labor Economics* IIIB., ed. O. Ashenfelter and D. Card, 3029–84. Amsterdam: Elsevier/North Holland Press.

OECD (Organisation for Economic Co-operation and Development). 1999. "Employment Protection and Labour Market Performance." In *OECD Employment Outlook,* chapter 2. Paris: OECD.

———. 2004. "Employment Protection Regulation and Labour Market Performance." In *OECD Employment Outlook,* chapter 2. Paris: OECD.

———. 2006. "Reassessing the Role of Policies and Institutions for Labour Market Performance: A Quantitative Analysis." In *OECD Employment Outlook,* chapter 7. Paris: OECD.

Pagés, C., and C. E. Montenegro. 2007. "Job Security and the Age-Composition of Employment: Evidence from Chile." *Estudios de Economia* 34 (2): 109–39.

Parsons, D. O. 1986. "The Employment Relationship: Job Attachment, Work Effort, and the Nature of Contracts." In *Handbook of Labor Economics* IIIB., ed. O. Ashenfelter and D. Card, 799–949. Amsterdam: Elsevier/North Holland Press.

———. 2005. "Benefit Generosity in Voluntary Severance Plans: The U.S. Experience." George Washington University (December), Washington, DC. Draft. http://ssrn.com/abstract=877903.

———. 2011a. "The Firing Cost Implications of Alternative Severance Pay Designs." Chapter 4, this volume.

———. 2011b. "Severance Pay Mandates: Firing Costs, Hiring Costs, and Firm Avoidance Behaviors." Draft. George Washington University, Washington, DC.

Saavedra, J., and M. Torero. 2004. "Labor Market Reforms and Their Impact over Formal Labor Demand and Job Market Turnover: The Case of Peru." In *Law and Employment: Lessons from Latin America and the Caribbean,* ed. J. Heckman and C. Pagés, 131–82. Chicago: University of Chicago Press.

Salanié, B. 2005. *The Economics of Contracts: A Primer,* 2nd ed. Cambridge, MA: MIT Press.

Schivardi, F., and R. Torrini 2008. "Identifying the Effects of Firing Restrictions Through Size-Contingent Differences in Regulation." *Labour Economics* 15: 482–511.

UNIDO (United Nations Industrial Development Organization). 2002. Industrial Statistics Database: http://www.unido.org.

Vodopivec, M. 2004. "Introducing Unemployment Benefits to Sri Lanka." *HDNSP* (July), World Bank, Washington, DC.

World Bank. 2009. "International Finance Corporation (IFC) Cost of Doing Business." http://www.doingbusiness.org/documents/fullreport/2009/Country_Tables.pdf.

CHAPTER 4

The Firing Cost Implications of Alternative Severance Pay Designs

Donald O. Parsons

Introduction

Job displacement imposes heavy losses on some workers, especially those with long tenure, and many governments mandate service-linked severance benefits as a crude but administratively inexpensive form of consumption smoothing.[1] Economists, however, have long expressed concerns about the firing cost implications of government-mandated severance pay.[2] This chapter focuses on alternative severance payout structures and argues that the firing cost implications of severance pay depend critically on the precise form of the mandate, especially job separation benefit eligibility requirements, and on the underlying turnover probabilities.

The primary objective of this study is to explore the conditions under which mandated savings accounts are superior to mandated severance (insurance) pay as a mechanism for smoothing the consumption of workers permanently separated from their jobs.[3] All other things being equal, insurance is preferred to savings as a method of consumption smoothing in the face of large, low-probability losses such as job displacement, but other things may not be equal. Especially if employers cannot reinsure severance insurance payouts, their job separation decisions may deviate from efficient levels. The implied firing cost distortions have been much discussed in the literature.

Severance savings plans—a simple form of unemployment insurance savings accounts with fixed benefits—have no firing cost consequences. This argument is a simple variant on Lazear's bonding critique of the firing cost effects of severance pay (Lazear 1990). In a multiperiod context, a severance insurance mandate can be undone by converting the insurance plan into a savings plan. Employer savings plans, notably in the form of private pension plans, are common in the United States and worldwide.

Careful consideration of this simple case highlights the crucial importance of plan details, not simply plan type (insurance or savings), in determining the implied firing

An early version of this chapter was prepared for presentation at the World Bank/IIASA/Ludwig Boltzmann Institute International Workshop on Severance Pay Reform: "Toward Unemployment Savings and Retirement Accounts," Laxenburg/Vienna, November 7–8, 2003. It benefited greatly from comments from Robert Holzmann and Milan Vodopivec, as well as from the workshop presentations and discussions. The luxury of a sabbatical year at George Washington University was helpful in the completion of the chapter.

costs, with their implications for worker separations, accessions, and, ultimately, equilibrium employment. The key is that firing costs depend not only on severance benefits paid out but on changes in firm liabilities that accompany the displacement. For example, to the extent that firms are only postponing payout, not avoiding it forever, firing costs diverge from and are less than benefit payouts. Of special importance are the types of turnover that will trigger benefit payout. A savings plan with fair interest accrual carries no firing cost implications. The firing cost implications of severance insurance plans will converge on those of savings plans as the range of job separation coverage expands.[4]

The analysis is theoretical but largely informal and draws a number of illustrative examples from the United States.[5] The U.S. public unemployment insurance system is well known. Voluntary severance pay plans, although less well known, are common and wholly private, provided directly by the employer or through the worker's union (Parsons 2005a, 2005b). Approximately one-fourth of the workforce is covered by severance pay plans, with coverage sharply higher among office workers in large establishments (Bishow and Parsons 2004). A typical plan offers a week's pay for each year of service up to a benefit or service maximum; plans vary greatly in the separations that qualify a worker for benefits (Parsons 2005c).

Both severance insurance and severance savings mandates are common abroad, though labels vary. For example, Heckman and Pagés (2004) label expected severance insurance expenditures as "indemnity costs" and severance savings expenditures as "seniority pay." Parallels for severance savings accounts in the United States can be drawn with employer-provided pension plans.[6] The results provide a primer for the appropriate measurement of firing costs. The difficulty of empirically confirming plausible links between firing costs and employment behaviors in cross-national data sets may arise from inappropriate measurement of the independent variable (Addison and Teixeira 2003; Heckman and Pagés 2004; Parsons 2011a).

Because of the often confusing terminology, especially across countries, the first section includes definitions of key concepts. The following sections offer brief, heuristic discussions of (1) the expected benefits of severance insurance and savings plans, and (2) their firing cost implications. The distinction between severance insurance and severance savings accounts is theoretically important but may be overdrawn. Severance insurance plans and severance savings plans are, in fact, opposite poles on a continuum of severance plan structures, with varying degrees of insurance and firing costs. Examples from U.S. severance plans are used to illustrate the variety of possibilities.

Fringe benefit interdependencies may make it necessary to consider program clusters, not single programs, when assessing firing cost effects of alternative mandates. Again, U.S. severance and pension policies provide examples. The value of the proposed program taxonomy is shown by assessing a rich set of program structures for severance pay and savings accounts discussed in this volume.

Job Separation Benefits: Some Definitions

Job separation insurance comes in a variety of forms, and analysts in different countries may use different terminologies. To avoid confusion, a few key terms are explained here. In carefully defining alternative programs, new programs are suggested, as well as warnings of situations in which the terminology might conflict with common usage. Consider the following program types:

Unemployment insurance. Separation payments that depend on the separated worker's actual unemployment experience. These are typically periodic payments more or less coincident with the unfolding unemployment.

Severance pay (insurance) plan. Separation payments in excess of accrued wages, vacations, and accrued leave that do not depend on the worker's actual loss experience. These may be paid in a lump sum or as periodic payments.

Savings accounts.[7] Contributions to an explicit worker asset account that can be disbursed to the worker under a variety of conditions. Common restrictions include the following four types of funds:

Pensions or retirement savings accounts. These can take a variety of forms, but the focus here is on defined contribution plans, essentially savings accounts with retirement as the obvious permissible disbursal contingency.

Unemployment insurance savings accounts. These are savings plans with a limited set of permissible disbursal contingencies, including unemployment and retirement. Unemployment disbursement could be periodic, more or less coincident with the unfolding unemployment.

Severance savings accounts. These are savings plans with a limited set of disbursal contingencies, including involuntary job separation (not unemployment) and retirement. These may be paid in a lump sum or as periodic payments following separation.

Provident funds. These are savings plans with a relatively large number of permissible disbursal contingencies—job separation/unemployment, disability, retirement—and the possibly of using the funds to purchase a house or finance education.

The lines between these definitions are often blurred, and considerable care must be taken in assessing the individual characteristics of each plan.

For example, a researcher might conjecture that unemployment insurance programs in all but the most highly developed economies are, in fact, severance pay plans with periodic payments. Tracking a separated worker's unemployment experience is difficult in highly developed economies with small informal sectors and probably not possible in economies with a large informal sector and a substantial agricultural sector. Under these conditions, unemployment insurance systems are at best primary sector unemployment insurance; workers released from a primary sector job may find their unemployment benefits stopped if they begin working again in the primary sector.

The distinction between pensions (which theoretically target only retirement needs) and severance savings accounts (which target job separation *and* retirement) is also likely to blur in practice. In the United States, for example, workers can put resources into a tax-deferred retirement savings account, most prominently 401(k) plans. If the worker separates from the employer, he or she may choose to roll the account over into an alternative plan or withdraw the funds for current use.[8] The worker faces substantial economic penalties for withdrawing the funds—the money is taxed as regular income, and the worker is assessed a 10 percent penalty. Still, the penalties are not so severe that withdrawal of funds is uncommon. The introduction of economic penalties for withdrawal essentially generates a continuum of possible combinations of severance savings accounts and pensions, with zero sanctions creating a "pure" severance savings account and prohibitive sanctions a pure pension.

The sections that follow focus on two types of severance programs—insurance and savings—briefly reviewing the consumption-smoothing benefits of each before turning to the impact on firing costs.

Severance Insurance and Severance Savings: Consumption-Smoothing and Firing Cost Consequences

Alternative systems for providing scheduled benefits are not equally good at smoothing consumption over state and time in the face of permanent job displacement, which typically involves a small probability of a large loss. Insurance plans that smooth consumption across "states of nature" have an obvious advantage in this situation; by the definition of "small probability" of loss, the worker has a relatively large number (probability) of good states over which to smooth the potential losses. The ability to smooth consumption across time is naturally limited both early and late in the work life. Late in life, there may be adequate time to build up a reasonable personal reserve, but the impact on retirement income grows as the work life shrinks. In the absence of borrowing, shocks early in the work life are also problematic for savings plans.

Costs are not identical under the two plans. Insurance plans often distort the incentives of the agents who enter into them, and job separation insurance is not likely to be an exception. A key concern is the firing cost distortions generated by mandated severance insurance programs; firing costs are likely to affect separation rates directly and accessions and equilibrium employment indirectly. The direct effect on job separations is the focus of the following firing cost measure.

Firing cost (FC) measurement.[9] The firm will rationally consider both the current outlay—the lump-sum severance payment B—as well as changes in future liabilities. Consider a three-period model (t = 0,1,2) in which the risk-neutral employer is considering the economic costs of laying off a worker. Assume that the three periods involve two potential work periods (t = 0,1) and a retirement period (t = 2). Assume further that there are two reasons for separating from the firm in any period before retirement—involuntary (layoff) and voluntary (quit)—and that the firm is considering an involuntary separation in period zero, perhaps because it is distressed. Looking ahead, the probability of a layoff in period 1 is σ_L and of a quit is σ_Q with $\sigma_L + \sigma_Q < 1$. Any worker retained through the second period is retired, which may or may not induce benefits.

Formally we can denote the worker's expected firing costs at time 0 as $E(FC_0)$, the sum of current severance benefits and the increment to future expected liabilities generated by the decision to release the worker at this time, or

$$E(FC_0) = B + \Delta\Lambda, \tag{1}$$

where B denotes expected separation benefits paid to a worker of tenure by the firm, and $\Delta\Lambda$ denotes the increment (often negative) to expected firm liabilities beyond the cash payout.

The liability change may offset immediate severance payouts if the firm's future liabilities are reduced. If, for example, the employer's program is a savings account, with the employer holding the account on behalf of the worker and crediting the worker with contributions and accrued credit at market rates, the impact of a payout is exactly offset by a reduction in liabilities and firing costs are zero:

$$\Delta\Lambda = -B. \tag{2}$$

The implications of retaining a worker and related liabilities need not be resolved at the time of layoff and, indeed, will be probabilistic if severance payouts are conditioned on stochastic separation events—severance insurance. If the firm retains the worker in the first period, the firm carries a liability equivalent to:

$$\Delta E(\Lambda_0) = \sigma_L B, \qquad \text{if layoffs only are covered;} \tag{3a}$$

$$\Delta E(\Lambda_0) = \sigma_L B + \sigma_Q B, \qquad \text{if layoffs and quits are covered; and} \tag{3b}$$

$$\Delta E(\Lambda_0) = \sigma_L B + \sigma_Q B + (1-\sigma_L-\sigma_Q)B = B, \text{ if layoffs, quits, and eventual}$$
$$\text{retirement are covered.} \tag{3c}$$

Expected firing costs as a result of the severance mandate:

$$\Delta E(FC_0) = (1-\sigma_L)B, \qquad \text{if layoffs only are covered} \tag{4a}$$

$$\Delta E(FC_0) = (1-\sigma_L-\sigma_Q)B, \quad \text{if layoffs and quits are covered;} \tag{4b}$$

$$\Delta E(FC_0) = B - B = 0 \qquad \text{if layoffs, quits, and eventual retirement}$$
$$\text{are covered.} \tag{4c}$$

The last option—(3c) and (4c)—is equivalent to a savings account.

The idea is simple. The firm carries a liability corresponding to the separation insurance benefit into a period based on past service. In deciding whether to evade payment by retaining the worker, the firm must realize that it carries forward a liability that it may have to cover in the future. If it is offering severance insurance and currently faces a layoff situation that it does not expect will recur ($\sigma_L = 0$), firing costs will be equal to current severance payments. Otherwise, the greater the likelihood it will have to cover the severance pay liability in the future (either because the likelihood of layoff is large or because voluntary quits or retirement are covered), the smaller the firing costs.

Diversity of Severance Pay Plans in the United States: Firing Cost Implications

The impact of severance pay plans on hiring and firing costs depends critically on the specific form of the plan, especially on the benefit eligibility rules, which range from pure insurance plans (with benefit payout only for involuntary separation without prejudice to the worker) to pure savings plans (with benefit payout under every type of separation, voluntary or involuntary). Severance plans in the U.S. market illustrate the diversity of possibilities and the care required in attributing hiring or firing costs to severance plans.

Severance pay plans in the United States are privately supplied, largely through the employer but also through labor unions as part of collective bargaining agreements.[10] In a voluntary contract between employers and workers, programs that limit deadweight losses are likely to emerge; indeed, there is little evidence that the modest levels of severance pay embedded in private U.S. severance plans seriously affect employer layoff strategies.[11] Nonetheless, these plans are useful in providing important insights into the design and potential problems of more substantial, government-mandated programs.

As market-determined financial instruments, severance plans take a bewildering variety of forms. Key plan characteristics include the generosity of benefits, the form of payment, qualifying events for benefits, and the nature of benefit funding. Unfortunately the usual government sources—for example, the Bureau of Labor Statistics Employee Benefit Survey (EBS)—provide little information on severance pay structure in the United States, so one is forced to rely on private sources. A series of large-scale surveys conducted by the National Industrial Conference Board (NICB) provides abundant information on severance pay design before 1980 (Parsons 2005a, 2005b), but to explore later developments one must rely on surveys conducted by private consulting firms, which tend to focus on compensation packages for upper level management.

Market-determined severance benefits tend to be modest.[12] For example, Lee Hecht Harrison (a career services company specializing in outplacement) conducted an ambitious survey of 925 organizations in 2001. The firm reported that, in organizations that pay severance strictly based on service—and not, for example, on age or position level—almost three-fourths of all nonexempt workers and two-thirds of exempt workers below the executive level are paid on a scale that offers one week of pay per year of service or less (table 4.1).[13] Only at the level of officer or senior executive would the median displaced worker receive

TABLE 4.1 **Severance Benefit Generosity by Occupation, Organizations with Plan Based on Service Only (percent)**

	Officers	Senior executives	Executives	Exempt	Nonexempt
Weeks of pay per years of service					
< 1 week	5	4	4	6	9
1 week	43	44	47	60	65
2 weeks	28	28	32	30	23
3 weeks	5	5	5	3	2
1 month	12	13	11	5	3
> 1 month	14	11	7	2	1

SOURCE: Lee Hecht Harrison 2001 (4).

NOTE: Column sums exceed 100 percent because some respondents reported multiple formulas.

TABLE 4.2 **Basis of Severance Calculations by Occupation, Organizations with Plan Not Based on Service Only (percent)**

	Officers	Senior executives	Executives	Exempt	Nonexempt
Formula includes years of service	43	45	48	57	60
Formula includes salary/ grade level	34	36	39	45	40
Formula includes title/level	34	34	36	28	20
Formula includes age	8	8	10	11	12
Case by case	35	43	42	38	34
Employment agreement	35	30	17	3	0
Negotiation	23	20	15	5	4
Flat amount	5	5	5	8	8

SOURCE: Lee Hecht Harrison 2001 (4).

NOTE: Column sums exceed 100 percent because some respondents reported multiple formulas.

two weeks of pay per year of service. In plans that involve more complex formulas, the bulk of both nonexempt and exempt employees below the executive level could expect to have such a service-linked plan, perhaps modified by age or title (table 4.2). Pita (1996) reports a similar level of payouts in collectively bargained agreements. Although a week of benefits per year of service is not a large sum, the capital value of benefits in the modal plan exceeds the maximum exhaustion value of benefits in the U.S. public unemployment insurance program (Kodrzycki 1998).[14,15]

The eligibility requirements for benefits—the range of job separation events that will qualify a worker for benefits—vary greatly across plans. Some potentially important attributes of a plan do not affect firing costs. For example, whether the payout is limited to permanent separations or applied equally to temporary and permanent separations does not matter in a service-linear benefit system, assuming that the service "clock" is restarted at each payout.[16] In jobs with frequent temporary turnover, the severance resources would be paid out over time rather than at the time of permanent separation, but the total payouts would be identical, at least in a zero interest world.[17]

Other attributes of a plan, including the range of qualifying events for benefit status, are fundamental. Imagine a severance plan that paid out benefits for all conceivable reasons for job departure; such plans are not unknown in collective bargaining agreements. In this case, the severance plan is essentially a severance savings account, not insurance, and, like payouts in a worker savings account, the expense of current severance payout is offset by a corresponding reduction in the expected future liability. The worker will receive the funds somehow, with payout at the time of layoff only one possibility. The rational employer's layoff decision would be unaffected by the existence of the severance plan. At the opposite pole is a severance plan that strictly limits payouts to involuntary separations without prejudice to the laid-off worker. In the absence of separation effects on other parts of the compensation package (see the next section), the employer would rationally view the severance payment as a simple firing cost and adjust the separation strategy accordingly.

Historically, the qualifying events for severance benefit payments in the United States have varied substantially. The earliest formal plans, introduced on a large scale early in the Depression, were limited in scope (Hawkins 1940). Benefit status normally required that workers be involuntarily and permanently separated from the firm without prejudice to the worker, although small notice plans were often associated with benign inefficiencies:

> *In forty-five of the sixty-six concerns [offering graduated plans] compensation is given only for permanent dismissal, while in the remainder it is granted for extended layoffs as well. . . . Although many plans were originally adopted to facilitate necessary reductions in personnel, their scope has extended in a number of cases to include discharges for inefficiency, in order to eliminate individual misfits who might otherwise remain on the payroll for years. (NICB [Brower] 1937, 6)*

Less commonly, graduated severance plans were used to compensate workers for other reasonable separations; for example, approximately 10 percent of the 66 companies paid severance to those separated for physical incapacity, and some used the plans as a crude form of retirement pension.

An NICB survey conducted in 1953 revealed a substantial expansion in the scope of qualifying events for benefits. Eligibility, as earlier, emphasized involuntary permanent separations initiated by the company:

> *All the plans provide severance pay for causes that might be considered beyond the individual's control. Among such reasons are elimination of the job, consolidation of departments, mergers, abandonment of plants, technological changes, and declining business activity. Thirty-two of the 103 plans analyzed, or about a third, grant severance pay only for such unavoidable layoffs. (NICB [Forde and Brower] 1954, 9)*

However, the ancillary uses of severance pay to insure other involuntary events had expanded. "Forty plans, or nearly 40% of the total, grant severance pay for terminations due to disability. . . . Only about one in ten plans in the 1942 survey included this as a reason" (NICB [Forde and Brower] 1954, 9).[18] Negotiated union plans frequently did not require a specific departure event to make the individual eligible for severance—19 plans, primarily union-negotiated, even covered separation for cause.

A Right Associates survey conducted in 1990 suggests that the range of qualifying events for severance benefits had again narrowed. Respondents with severance plans were asked if benefit eligibility was conditioned on one or more of the following qualifying events: reduction in force, elimination of position, discharge for performance, discharge for cause, discharge for disability, voluntary resignation, retirement with pension, or retirement without pension. The frequency of each response is shown in figure 4.1. The primary qualifying events are reduction in force and elimination of position, each of which is covered in essentially all plans. In approximately 40 percent of the plans, discharge for performance is covered; this separation category includes workers who are making a good faith effort to do a job but not succeeding, which could be viewed as an insurable

FIGURE 4.1 **Eligibility Conditions for Severance Pay, Total and by Organization Size**

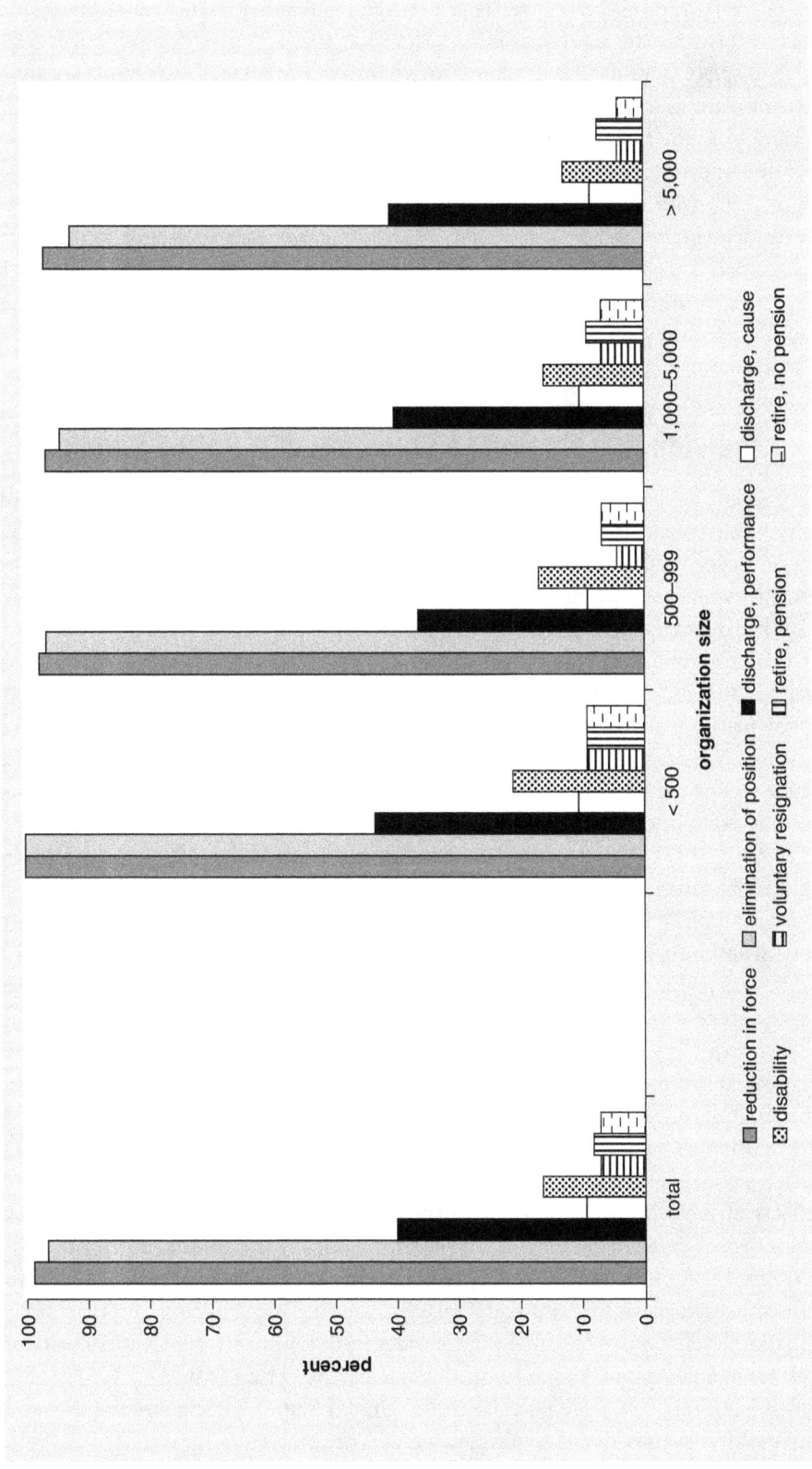

SOURCE: Right Associates 1990.

event, one for which the employer is responsible. Conversely, voluntary separations and discharges for cause are rarely covered.[19] Note the absence of payments to retirees; U.S. plans are displacement insurance plans, not savings or provident funds, but they approach retirement plans as the range of payouts beyond retirement increase and the probability of separating from the firm because of a covered event increases.

The important point is that the mix of insurance and savings in the U.S. severance structure, each with distinct implications for employer and worker behaviors, has varied over time. The inclusion of retirement as a qualifying event for severance payment pushes the instrument mix in the direction of a savings plan. Adding disability and, of greater consequence, voluntary turnover as qualifying events leaves little of the insurance aspect in place. In providing severance pay for job displacement, the employer's liability for other payouts is diminished, perhaps dollar for dollar.

Individual Programs as Elements of a Policy Bundle

The argument of the last section can be generalized: The impact on firing costs of any one program, considered in isolation, may give a misleading predictor of the overall effects on the economic calculations of workers and firms. This is especially clear in U.S. systems, in which a large share of social insurance costs are borne by the employer, at least in the first instance.[20] In the United States, for example, severance pay is most common in large establishments and in workplaces covered by collective bargaining agreements, but these are the same workplaces that disproportionately offer defined benefit company pensions with lengthy vesting requirements.[21]

When considering job separation, worker vesting in a pension plan becomes a key parameter: How are worker pension rights affected by the separation? Maximum vesting periods are established by law in the United States by the Employee Retirement Income Security Act of 1974 (ERISA) and later amendments, but before 1974, firms were free to design vesting rules that were advantageous to them. It was not uncommon for pensions to have, for example, cliff-vesting at 30 years of service. Workers who left the firm's employment with anything less than a lifetime of service could expect no pension. In such firms it would be reasonable for severance pay to be viewed as compensation for forfeited pension rights, and there is occasional evidence of managers who rationalized severance pay on that basis; severance "is granted to compensate older employees in some measure for the loss of their valuable seniority and pension rights and other company privileges which are the concomitant of long service" (NICB [Brower] 1943, 4).

For firing cost measurement, management should rationally calculate firing costs as severance payments net of any future savings to pension plan obligations. In most cases, the effects of job separation on future firm liabilities would be negative.[22] The pension cost offset to severance payments in the United States is not limited to companies with lengthy service requirements for vesting. Economists have long noted that the dependence of defined benefit plans on final years' salary makes the pension cost offset a function of the inflation level. Even moderate inflation rates impose an early departure penalty on the worker. From an employer's viewpoint, this is a negative firing cost.

Although the details are peculiar to the United States, with its unusual dependence on the employer as provider of earnings insurance, the broader point is that the appropriate measurement of firing costs may extend well beyond severance pay, even when considered in detail. Permanent job separation may have consequences for the worker's fringe benefit package that are relevant for the employer's termination calculation.

Firing Costs: Some International Evidence

The variety of mandated separation pay plans internationally provides ample proof of the importance of a careful taxonomy of plans; some plans are likely to have the expected firing costs, while others may not. This argument is illustrated by the programs described in this volume.

Hur (2003) examines the Republic of Korea's severance pay system and finds a savings plan, not an insurance plan. Korea mandates employer participation in a separation benefit plan that seems like a severance pay plan.[23] However, the individual asset accounts accrue linearly with service and are paid out at the time of separation without any restrictions on the reason for departure. Even upon voluntary separation, the worker receives the money. Clearly this is a savings plan, not an insurance plan; the asset does not increase in value with an involuntary job separation; it is only paid out at that time. When a worker is fired, the worker incurs no additional liabilities—barring default, the worker will receive these accrued benefits sometime, although perhaps not today. Of course, the firm may have an economic stake in when it pays its liabilities—now or at retirement—depending on interest accrual practices (Garibaldi and Pacelli 2003).

Recent Korean reforms, which appear to push the current severance pay plan toward retirement pensions, lay bare the need for careful thought about the freedoms workers should have to manage (or consume) their savings. At separation, should workers be required to roll over their accounts and not use the proceeds for current needs? Obviously, conversion into a restricted, retirement-only plan eliminates any consumption smoothing in response to job displacement.

And yet, more recent reforms, in 2005, pushed workers toward converting from a severance savings plan to a pension plan (Yun and Hur 2011). A key distinction between the two is that the pension plan would be fully funded and available at retirement as an annuity. The pension plan also limits worker access to the funds before retirement, specifically for expenditures on housing and long-term care. It is perhaps not surprising that conversion, which requires the approval of both the company and its workers, has been limited (Yun and Hur 2011).

Before the reform in 2003, the Austrian severance pay system provided an interesting example of limited firing costs (Koman, Schuh, and Weber 2005). Employers were required to pay out stipulated benefits upon separation initiated by the employer or by agreement between the employer and the worker. The latter presumably included mutually agreed-upon retirement. Not mandated were payments for voluntary (worker-initiated) separation.[24] Expected firing costs in this case presumably reflect this exclusion. If voluntary turnover is low, the plan is essentially a savings program, and firing costs are approximately zero. If voluntary turnover is high, the firm could anticipate avoiding this charge in time, and firing costs are equivalent to total separation benefits. Again, the relevance of the savings account model to the mandated severance payment is an empirical question. In that respect, it is interesting to note that Koman, Schuh, and Weber (2005,

257) report that, under pre-2003 mandates, "Employers had to make provisions in their accounts for at least half the severance pay entitlements that could fall due."

Since the reforms, the Austrian severance pay system is clearly a savings plan, not an insurance plan: "Entitlement... does not depend on the way of termination of the contract. Employers have to pay a contribution of 1.5377 percent of the payroll into a fund... from the first day on" (Koman, Schuh, and Weber 2005, 258).[25] The plan is perhaps best described as a severance/retirement savings account, because the worker can withdraw the money only upon involuntary separation or retirement. After three years of service,

> [the] employee can choose between receiving her severance payment from the central funds at once, or saving her entitlement towards a future pension. The amount will not be paid out if the employee gives notice herself... [although] the acquired claim... remains. (258)

The employer's payouts at separation are exactly offset by a reduction in future liabilities, so firing costs are now zero.

The effect of the reform on firing costs requires an understanding of prereform (before 2003) payout rules, which were unusual. In the Austrian system, a separated worker qualified for severance benefits if separated involuntarily from the firm or retired, but not if separated voluntarily. This system, which workers found unattractive, provided an obvious disincentive for older workers to quit their jobs. After the reform, job quitters also received the payout. Thus, before 2003 the firing cost measure would be positive for involuntarily separated workers, reflecting the probability that the worker, if retained, would voluntarily quit before retirement.

That is not to say that simple severance insurance plans, with their unavoidable firing cost implications, are unknown internationally. One example of an insurance plan is that of the Philippines:

> Severance pay is mandated for all regular workers. . . .[It] is provided to individuals who are discharged due to redundancy or economic difficulties experienced by the firm; those who are dismissed due to gross misconduct are not entitled to severance benefits. . .the employment protection legislation requires a month of notification and severance pay equal to at least one month pay for every year of service in case of redundancy, and a half-month pay for each year of service in case of retrenchment to prevent losses in cases of closures. (Esguerra 2003, 3-4)

Even in this case, benefit payments from private employers are far from automatic, so the firm's perceived or actual separation liabilities (firing costs) may be much less than the prescribed payouts. Indeed, the conditionality of benefits on the precise reason for the separation itself apparently induces considerable litigation (Esguerra 2003, 5).

Asher and Mukhopadhaya (2003), reviewing severance pay arrangements in six Asian countries, stress the importance of understanding labor law as well as the details of the separation plans in assessing consequences. In India, for example, they report that a permanently displaced worker is potentially eligible for two types of years-of-service-indexed separation benefits: (1) retrenchment benefits, available only if job separation is involuntary, and (2) gratuity benefits, which are paid independent of the reason for job separation. Only the first would seem to generate firing costs; the second is a form of compulsory saving. Asher and Mukhopadhaya assert that neither is relevant in calculating firing costs in India. Labor laws severely restrict involuntary job separations, making a third mechanism, voluntary retirement schemes (VRSs), a more appropriate measure of firing costs. VRSs "are more expensive for the firms and.... the economy as they have higher transaction costs than providing retrenchment benefits.... [and] the flexibility in retaining the more productive staff may be less" (Asher and Mukhopadhaya 2003, 10).

Jaramillo and Saavedra (2005) report somewhat similar dual systems in a number of Latin American countries, with severance payments available to workers who unjustly lose their jobs and seniority payments available to workers who separate from their employer for any reason.[26] "Just causes primarily include serious misdemeanor, dishonest behavior, sabotage, and considerable disrespectful attitudes.... Only during the last decade some countries—namely Argentina, Chile, Colombia, and Peru—have introduced a wider array of reasons, mainly those related to economic conditions of the firm, as just causes for lay-off" (282). They seem to say, however, that severance payments alone are a poor measure of firing costs and that one should look at the sum of severance and seniority payments to assess full costs. República Bolivariana de Venezuela (which mandates approximately 5 weeks of severance pay and 45 weeks of seniority pay for a separated worker with 20 years of tenure) and Colombia (which mandates 25 weeks of severance pay and 25 weeks of seniority pay in the same circumstance) would be equivalent. Although this proposition is certainly amenable to empirical testing, simple economic theory would predict otherwise.

Although most of the examples illustrate how close severance insurance plans are to savings plans in their limited firing cost implications, the converse can also be true. An interesting paper by Garibaldi and Pacelli (2003) illustrates the possibility that savings plans can have positive firing cost implications. The authors first note a recent Bank of Italy study (Brandolini and Torrini 2002) that makes the important point that, contrary to the 1999 Organisation for Economic Co-operation and Development taxonomy, Italy does not have a severance plan, only a savings plan. The program in question, *trattamento di fine rapporto* (TFR, termination pay), involves "deferred wages that accrue to the worker upon separation for any reason." In short, TFR is a savings plan with restrictions on disbursement; it has no immediate firing cost implications. The authors then resurrect the firing cost concern by noting that interest payments in TFR accounts are arbitrarily small and that the firm can reduce future liabilities by postponing payment. The exact magnitude of the interest rate effect is not easily assessed, but the direction of the effect is clear.

Conclusion

Involuntary permanent job separation frequently induces large economic losses in both unemployment spells and lower reemployment wages, and mandated severance payments have emerged worldwide as a public policy response. Concerns about the potentially large deadweight losses of mandated severance pay, however, have led to consideration of alternative job loss "insurance" approaches, including compulsory (severance) savings accounts, which with some regulatory elaboration can be transformed into unemployment insurance savings accounts.

Ideally, insurance is the preferred method of consumption smoothing across risky states, especially in the face of the large, low-probability losses that characterize the permanent job separation of long-tenured workers. However, the choice between insurance and savings depends as well on distortions induced by the alternative programs. The standard scheduled severance insurance plan has a potentially important incentive effect on the employer's layoff decision, discouraging the efficient release of workers. One strong argument for a savings plan is that it would induce zero firing costs; the firm knows that the worker will receive the assets in the account at some point and will not alter its layoff decision as a consequence.[27]

More intriguing, perhaps, is the result that emerges from a careful consideration of these two polar paradigms, that a continuum of policies lies between them. Workers may separate for a variety of reasons that may or may not be covered by the severance plan mandate. The analysis reveals that care must be taken in assessing the impact of a separation plan on behavior. A simple analysis of program types may be misleading, because actual programs are often a probabilistic mixture of types. For example, the greater the variety of separation contingencies covered by a severance plan, the closer it comes to a savings plan. If severance is paid for all separation contingencies, including retirement, it is essentially a savings plan—the worker will receive the benefit in one form or another, and the employer has no incentive to maintain the worker on the payroll inefficiently. Firing costs increase as the range of benefit-eligible separations (and their likelihoods) narrow.

The same calculation applies if the employer is holding a comprehensive set of distinct insurance packages for disability, retirement, and so on, independent of standard severance plans. For example, the traditional 30-year cliff-vested pension plan in the United States presents the employer with a strong incentive to lay off workers before they vest. Severance pay, viewed as part of a benefit bundle, can be seen as an offset, compensating the worker for lost pension rights. Indeed, the complexity of the appropriate measure of firing costs raises serious concerns about broad, cross-national studies of firing cost effects and may explain the difficulties economists have had in reliably estimating a priori plausible negative employment effects in such studies.

Notes

1. For excellent surveys of the U.S. displacement cost literature, see Jacobson, LaLonde, and Sullivan (1993), Fallick (1996), Kletzer (1998), and Farber (2005). For an international perspective, see Kuhn (2002).

2. The empirical firing cost literature is voluminous. Buechtemann (1992) provides an accessible introduction to the debate. See Parsons (2011a) for a recent review.

3. This analysis does not cover a deeper political economy question: whether firing cost distortions are an *intended* consequence of mandated severance plans. Efficiency questions aside, an alternative program that has the same consumption-smoothing properties but less substantial penalties for employer layoffs might not be preferred politically.

4. See Parsons (1977) for an introduction to turnover concepts.

5. A formal presentation and an extension to severance pay–induced hiring costs can be found in Parsons (2011b).

6. The savings account aspect of defined contribution plans makes them an especially apt model to explore, although many large corporations in the United States, as well as the social security system, are defined benefit plans, with benefits unconnected to saving/asset activity.

7. These savings accounts may be notional or fully funded, perhaps even held by the government or financial institutions.

8. For a readable summary of 401(k) plans, go to http://invest-faq.com/articles/ret-plan-401k. html.

9. This discussion is drawn from Parsons (2011b).

10. For a history of the emergence and growth of private severance pay plans in the United States, see Parsons (2005a, 2005b). Freedman (1978) provides some history of collectively bargained severance and SUB contracts. For the genesis of severance pay worldwide, see Holzmann and others (2011).

11. In the United States, employers have considerable flexibility to adjust plan payouts at any time. In an especially serious downturn, they can reduce or even eliminate severance plan benefits. Unless prefunded, the plans are not covered by the regulations in the Employee Retirement Income Security Act (ERISA) of 1974. Although prefunding was unusual even before ERISA, it is unlikely that an employer would decide to do so today unless the firm has its own reasons to invoke ERISA.

12. See Parsons (2005c) for a more comprehensive review of severance generosity in the United States.

13. The terms "exempt" and "nonexempt" refer to categories of workers under the Fair Labor Standards Act of 1938. Various provisions, including government mandates for overtime premium pay, do not apply to all workers. Executives, administrators, and professionals are exempt.

14. In the U.S. public unemployment insurance system, which essentially offers a 50 percent replacement rate for up to 26 weeks, the capital value of severance exceeds that of the maximum (exhaustion-of-benefits) value of public unemployment insurance for workers with more than 13 years of tenure.

15. Adjustments for wage inflation are also critical in the typical fraction-of-final-wage plan.

16. With substantial interest rates, the employer would have to factor in the interest lost on early payouts as an additional cost of a temporary/permanent system.

17. Little is certain in economic life, and even employers who pay out benefits only on permanent separation must from time to time consider the conditions under which a "permanently" separated worker is rehired. Does the worker repay the severance or restart the service clock at zero? Some employers give workers a choice.

18. "About 80% of the cooperating companies with retirement benefit plans do not give severance pay to employees whose services are terminated by retirement, except under certain circumstances" (NICB [Forde and Brower] 1954, 25).

19. "Eligibility rules in union contracts are apparently much more relaxed, with voluntary departures frequently covered" (NICB [Forde and Brower] 1954, 9–10.) Voluntary turnover rates in major unions are, of course, rare.

20. The benefits actually valued by the employee are presumably ultimately borne by the employee.

21. Defined benefit pensions are characterized by retirement benefits linked to previous salary, often in the last years of the employment relationship. Defined contribution plans are simply savings/investment vehicles with the magnitude of benefits a function of the success of plan investments. Vesting in a defined benefit plan refers to the right to receive benefits upon retirement, even if the worker departs the firm before retirement. In a defined contribution plan, vesting refers to the right to retain retirement plan assets.

22. Indeed, one motivation for ERISA 1974, which severely limited long vesting periods, was to regulate the employer's temptation to reduce pension costs by laying off workers just before pension vesting.

23. The original Korean word for this plan apparently does not distinguish severance from retirement, with neither being an especially informative label. This will become clearer later in the discussion.

24. The potential impediment to labor mobility is that workers may pass on attractive job offers rather than forgo accumulated severance benefits. Hofer, Schuh, and Walch (2011) report that the impact of the reform on voluntary mobility has been modest and may be zero, suggesting that this concern is of theoretical but not practical importance.

25. The discussion is silent on the question of payouts upon the death of a worker.

26. For excellent descriptions of the diversity of severance pay designs in Latin America, see Heckman and Pagés (2004) and Ferrer and Riddell (2011).

27. This assumes market rates of asset accrual with postponed withdrawals.

References

Addison, J., and P. Teixeira. 2003. "The Economics of Employment Protection." *Journal of Labor Research* 24 (1, Winter): 85–129.

Asher, M. G., and P. Mukhopadhaya. 2003. "Severance Pay in Selected Asian Countries: A Survey." Paper presented at the World Bank–International Institute for Applied System Analysis–Ludwig Boltzmann Institute International Workshop on Severance Pay Reform: "Toward Unemployment Savings and Retirement Accounts," Laxenburg/Vienna, November 7–8.

Bishow, J., and D. O. Parsons. 2004. "Trends in Severance Pay Coverage in the United States, 1980–2001" (May). Available at http://ssrn.com/abstract=878144.

Brandolini, A., and R. Torrini. 2002. "La Tutela del Rapporto di Lavoro Subordinato Secondo gli Indicatori dell'OCSE." Draft. Bank of Italy.

Buechtemann, C. F., ed. 1992. *Employment Security and Labor Market Behavior: Interdisciplinary Approaches and International Evidence.* Ithaca, NY: ILR Press, Cornell University.

Esguerra, J. 2003. "Toward Unemployment Savings and Retirement Accounts: Philippine Case." Paper presented at the World Bank–International Institute for Applied System Analysis–Ludwig Boltzmann Institute International Workshop on Severance Pay Reform: "Toward Unemployment Savings and Retirement Accounts," Laxenburg and Vienna, November 7–8.

Fallick, B. C. 1996. "A Review of the Recent Empirical Literature on Displaced Workers." *Industrial and Labor Relations Review* 50 (1): 5–16.

Farber, H. S. 2005. "What Do We Know about Job Loss in the United States? Evidence from the Displaced Workers Survey, 1984–2004." *Federal Reserve Bank of Chicago Economic Perspectives* 29 (2): 13–28.

Ferrer, A. M., and W. C. Riddell. 2011. "Unemployment Insurance Savings Accounts in Latin America: Overview and Assessment." Chapter 7, this volume.

Freedman, A. 1978. *Security Bargains Reconsidered: SUB, Severance Pay, Guaranteed Work.* Conference Board Report No. 736. New York: The Conference Board Inc.

Garibaldi, P., and L. Pacelli. 2003. "Mandatory Severance Payments in Italy: Do They Exist?" Paper presented at the World Bank–International Institute for Applied System Analysis–Ludwig Boltzmann Institute International Workshop on Severance Pay Reform: "Toward Unemployment Savings and Retirement Accounts," Laxenburg and Vienna, November 7–8.

Hawkins, E. D. 1940. *Dismissal Compensation*. Princeton, NJ: Princeton University Press.

Heckman, J. J., and C. Pagés. 2004. "Introduction." In *Law and Employment: Lessons from Latin America and the Caribbean*, ed. J. Heckman and C. Pagés, 1–107. Chicago: University of Chicago Press.

Hofer, H., U. Schuh, and D. Walch. 2011. "Effects of the Austrian Severance Pay Reform." Chapter 5, this volume.

Holzmann, R., Y. Pouget, M. Weber, and M. Vodopivec. 2011. "Severance Pay Programs around the World: History, Rationale, Status, and Reforms." Chapter 2, this volume.

Hur, J.-J. 2003. "Korean Severance Pay Reform." Paper presented at the World Bank–International Institute for Applied System Analysis–Ludwig Boltzmann Institute International Workshop on Severance Pay Reform, "Toward Unemployment Savings and Retirement Accounts," Laxenburg and Vienna, November 7–8.

Jacobson, L. S., R. J. LaLonde, and D. G. Sullivan. 1993. *The Costs of Worker Dislocation*. Kalamazoo, MI: W.E. Upjohn Institute for Employment Research.

Jaramillo, M., and J. Saavedra. 2005. "Severance Payment Programs in Latin America." *Empirica* 32 (3–4): 275–307.

Kodrzycki, Y. K. 1998. "The Effects of Employer-Provided Severance Benefits on Reemployment Outcomes." *New England Economic Review*, November/December. Boston Federal Reserve Bank.

Kuhn, P., ed. 2002. *Losing Work, Moving On: International Perspectives on Worker Displacement*. Kalamazoo, MI: W. E. Upjohn Institute for Employment Research.

Kletzer, L. G. 1998. "Job Displacement." *Journal of Economic Perspectives* 12 (1, Winter): 115–36.

Koman, R., U. Schuh, and A. Weber. 2005. "The Austrian Severance Pay Reform: Toward a Funded Pension Pillar." *Empirica* 32 (3–4): 255–74.

Lazear, E. P. 1990. "Job Security Provisions and Employment." *Quarterly Journal of Economics* 105 (August): 699–726.

Lee Hecht Harrison. 2001. *Severance and Separation Benefits: Bridges for Employees in Transition*. Woodcliff Lake, NJ: Lee Hecht Harrison.

NICB (National Industrial Conference Board) [F. B. Brower]. 1937. "Dismissal Compensation." Studies in Personnel Policy 1, NICB, New York.

———. 1943. "Dismissal Compensation." Studies in Personnel Policy 50, NICB, New York.

———[L. E. Forde and F. B. Brower]. 1954. "Severance Pay Plans." Studies in Personnel Policy 141, NICB, New York.

OECD (Organisation for Economic Co-operation and Development). 1999. "Employment Protection and Labour Market Performance." In *Employment Outlook 1999*. Paris: OECD.

Parsons, D. O. 1977. "Models of Labor Turnover: A Theoretical and Empirical Survey." In *Research in Labor Economics, Vol. 1*, ed. R. Ehrenberg, 185–224. New York: JAI Press.

———. 2005a. "The Emergence of Private Job Displacement Insurance in the United States: Severance Pay Plans 1930–1954." http://ssrn.com/abstract=872331.

———. 2005b. "Private Job Displacement Insurance in the United States, 1954–1979: Expansion and Innovation." http://ssrn.com/abstract=872334.

———. 2005c. "Benefit Generosity in Voluntary Severance Plans: The U.S. Experience." http://ssrn.com/abstract=877903.

———. 2011a. "Mandated Severance Pay and Firing Cost Destortions: A Critical Review of the Evidence." Chapter 3, this volume.

———. 2011b. "Severance Pay Mandates: Firing Costs, Hiring Costs, and Firm Avoidance Behaviors." Draft, George Washington University, Washington, DC.

Pita, C. 1996. "Advance Notice and Severance Pay Provisions in Contracts." *Monthly Labor Review* 119 (7): 43–50.

Right Associates. 1990. *Severance: The Corporate Response.* Philadelphia: Right Associates.

Yun, J., and J.-J. Hur. 2011. "Severance Pay Reform in the Republic of Korea." Chapter 6, this volume.

CHAPTER 5

Effects of the Austrian Severance Pay Reform

Helmut Hofer, Ulrich Schuh, and Dominik Walch

Introduction

In 2002, Austria reformed its employment protection legislation (EPL) regulations. The reform replaced a conventional severance payment system with a system of individual savings accounts. This reform of the severance pay law has received international attention as an example of a labor law measure that supports employment transitions (EC 2006a; OECD 2006). Bassanini, Nunziata, and Venn (2009) claim that, based on their estimates of the relationship of EPL and productivity, the reform represents an increase in GDP per capita growth of about 5 percent over 20 years.

A considerable amount of research has been carried out to evaluate the impact of EPL on aggregate labor market variables. EPL reduces the layoff rate and unemployment incidence by making firing more costly to employers and increases unemployment duration because higher labor costs tend to weaken job creation. The overall effect on unemployment is ambiguous and apparently minimal in practice; however, strict EPL tends to compromise employment prospects for young workers, women, and the long-term unemployed (for example, EC 2006b; OECD 2006; Young 2003). Recent literature uses differences in regulations within countries across time or firm size to analyze the effect of EPL on job turnover. The results are mixed. Using Italian firm-level data, Boeri and Jimeno (2005) find a significant effect of EPL on dismissal probabilities. Schivardi and Torrini (2008) report that EPL does influence employment dynamics, but the effects are quantitatively modest. Bauer, Bender, and Bonin (2007) do not find any significant influence of EPL on job turnover in Germany. Martins (2009) examines the impact of dismissal-for-cause requirements on job turnover in Portugal. He does not find robust effects of differentiated change in firing costs on job or worker flows, although some estimates suggest an increase in hiring. Marinescu (2009) uses individual data from the U.K. labor force survey to analyze the impact of job protection legislation on job duration. Her estimates show that tightening job security provisions does not have a negative impact on employment.

The aim of this chapter is to provide an overview of the new severance pay scheme in Austria and investigate its labor market effects. It is not a comprehensive evaluation of the previous and current severance pay laws; rather, it uses available data to provide preliminary evidence on two issues related to severance pay: savings for old-age pensions and labor mobility.

The authors would like to thank two referees and Rudolph Winter-Ebmer for helpful comments.

Data from social security records, covering the universe of Austrian workers, are used to infer the impact of the change in EPL on labor mobility. The introduction of the new severance payment scheme in 2003 forms a quasi-experimental situation. A difference-in-differences strategy is employed to test the hypothesis that the new scheme improves the efficiency of labor reallocation by removing a large incentive for workers to stay in the same jobs and not move to better ones. The results indicate that the impact of EPL on voluntary separations is very limited.

The chapter is organized as follows. It describes the severance payment reform in detail. Because the Austrian government hoped that the reform would contribute to the expansion of the second pension pillar, the potential future development of the system is simulated using the World Bank model PROST. The chapter contains an empirical analysis and presents econometric results of the difference-in-differences approach, as well as conclusions.

Severance Pay Law in Austria

Until 2002, Austria's employment legislation stipulated that severance pay had to be paid to private sector employees in the event of termination of the employment contract (by the employer or by mutual agreement), as long as the employee had worked for the employer for at least the past three years. Starting with two months' wages after three years, payments increased to a maximum value of one year's wages after 25 years.[1] In the accounting system of firms, severance payments were recorded as regular wage payments. Employers had to make provisions in their accounts for at least half of the severance pay entitlements that could fall due.

Reforming the system of severance pay in Austria had been the focus of controversy for a long time (for example, EIRO 2001; Genser 1987; Holzmann 1987; Klec 2007). The previous system was called into question for two main reasons. First, it was criticized for inhibiting mobility in the labor market. For employees, the old system reduced incentives to change employers, because the employee lost the entitlement to severance pay if he or she terminated the employment contract.

The second major problem with the old law was the distribution of the entitlements among employees. The Austrian Trade Union Federation demanded the extension of severance pay entitlement to cover not only dismissals but also voluntary resignations and seasonal employment. According to Kristen, Pinggera, and Schön (2002), only one-third of workers were entitled to severance payments.

The previous system also involved some drawbacks for businesses, especially small and medium-sized enterprises (Kristen, Pinggera, and Schön 2002). Liquidity problems could occur if the firms had to make simultaneous severance payments at some point.

A comprehensive reform of the Austrian system took place in 2002, and the new system was enacted at the beginning of 2003. The reform considerably extends entitlement to severance pay. Entitlement now starts from the first day of employment and does not depend on the mode of termination of the contract. Employers have to contribute 1.53 percent[2] of a worker's pay into a fund, specified by an agreement between employer and work council, from the first day onward. Existing severance pay entitlements under the old scheme remained unchanged.

In the case of dismissal by the employer after three years of job tenure, the employee can choose between receiving the severance payment from the central funds all at once or applying it toward a future pension. The amount will not be paid out if the employee gives notice or job tenure is shorter than three years; however, the employee retains the acquired claim.

The new severance pay system offers advantages for both employers and employees (see, for example, Hofer 2007). For employers, it prevents liquidity problems owing to simultaneous severance payments and uncertainty related to the costs of severance pay at the time of hiring. For workers, it reduces job mobility costs, because they do not lose their entitlement to severance pay by quitting a job.

The government explicitly hoped that the severance payment reform would also contribute to the expansion of the underdeveloped second pension pillar in Austria. To a certain extent, the reform is a first step in this direction. It replaces the former defined-benefit, final-salary severance payment scheme by a contribution-defined, fully funded system. The reform provides tax incentives to use the savings as a retirement income supplement.

Most studies on the impact of the previous Austrian severance pay system are based on theoretical arguments (for example, Walther 1999) or anecdotal evidence. For low-qualified jobs, the system created incentives for employers to terminate employment early to avoid accumulating severance pay claims that were not matched by productivity gains. According to the Organisation for Economic Co-operation and Development (OECD 2001), the propensity of employers to terminate employment early was associated with discretionary hikes in accumulated claims for severance pay. Moreover, the system was biased against labor supply in industries, such as tourism, that have large employment fluctuations owing to structural change or seasonality.

Card, Chetty, and Weber (2007) provide an empirical analysis of the impact of eligibility for severance pay on unemployment duration and subsequent job outcomes. They use a regression discontinuity design, comparing the search behavior of workers who were laid off just before and just after the 36-month cutoff for severance pay eligibility. According to this study, the hazard rate of finding a new job during the first 20 weeks of the unemployment spell is 8–12 percent lower for those eligible for severance pay. And this longer unemployment spell is not compensated by the quality of the subsequent job. Mean wages, job duration, and other measures of job quality are unaffected by entitlement to severance pay. Card and others use a theoretical job search model to derive the welfare consequences of severance pay. According to the model, a pure wealth effect causes the reduced search intensity without any efficiency costs. They find no evidence for selective firing before the 36-month cutoff.

Koman, Schuh, and Weber (2005) provide an ex ante evaluation of the effects of the severance payment reform. Based on retirement income projections and simulations of the pension reform for both the blue and white collar pension systems, they show that the contribution rate of 1.53 percent is too low to generate a significant second pillar retirement income that could help maintain current replacement rates. An increase in the contribution rate to 5 percent could be a major step toward a sufficient second pillar retirement income. Koman and others perform an empirical analysis of a cross-section of employment of different durations, comparing severance pay in the two schemes. According to the simulations, severance payments will be 35 percent lower in the new system in the sample mean, and differences in payments among groups will even be stronger. However, Koman and others do not observe complete individual careers and thus cannot take the accumulation of severance payments during the working life into account.

Capital Accumulation and the New Severance Pay Scheme

This section focuses on the relative importance of the new severance pay scheme to provide savings for old-age pensions in Austria. A brief overview of the most recent developments is followed by a simulation of possible future developments.

Since the introduction of the reform, coverage has increased continuously (figure 5.1). The proportion of covered employees increased from about one-fourth of total dependent employment at the end of 2004 to two-thirds in December 2008. (Civil servants, who account for around 10 percent of total employment, do not participate in the severance pay scheme.) The significant increase in participation in 2008 may be due to the extension of the system that took place in that year, when all apprentices and self-employed persons were included. Freelancers and farmers also may opt into the system. By December 2010, 71.4 percent of non-civil-service employees had accumulated capital under the system.

The volume of contributions also has increased significantly (figure 5.2). In 2003, 60 million euros were directly contributed to the system and an additional 90 million euros were transferred from the old system into the new scheme. The volume of transfers declined to 24 million euros in 2008; however, the volume of contributions increased to 662 million euros. Between 2003 and 2009, the assets held by the *Mitarbeitervorsorgekassen* (employee benefit funds, MVKs) increased from 146 million euros to 2.8 billion euros.

FIGURE 5.1 **Proportion of Employees Covered by the 2003 Severance Pay Law**

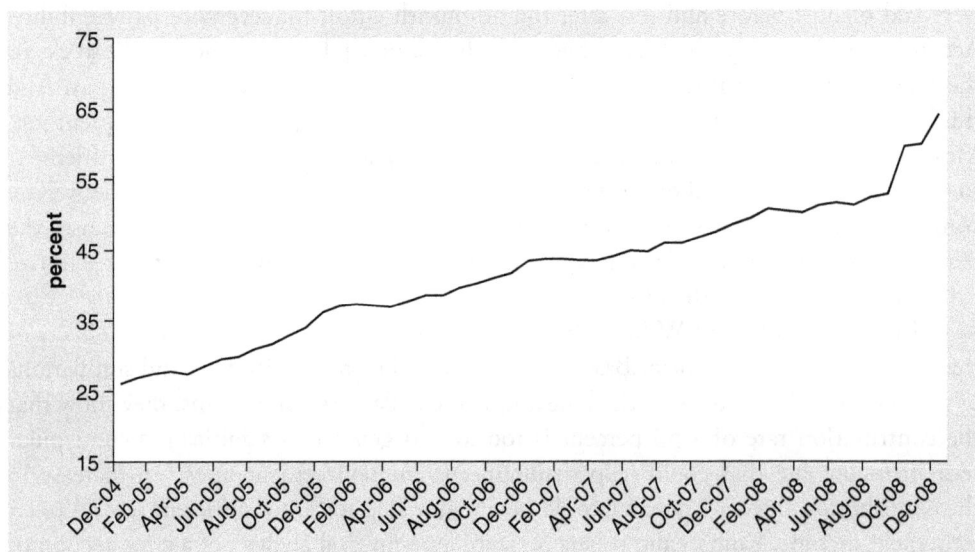

SOURCE: Main Association of Austrian Social Insurance Institutions.

FIGURE 5.2 **Contributions to Austria's Severance Pay Scheme**

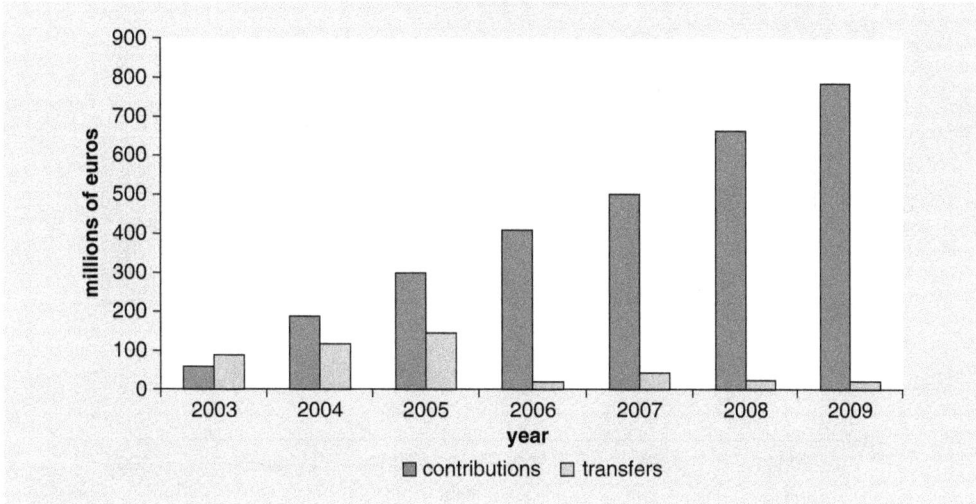

SOURCE: Plattform der Betrieblichen Vorsorgekassen.

One original objective of the Austrian reform was to contribute to the expansion of the underdeveloped second pillar of the Austrian pension system. In 2005, only 11 percent of all Austrian employees had claims to a funded pension scheme on the enterprise level, compared with an average of 27 percent in all European Union (EU) member states. The total savings in the funded pillar amounted to 4.7 percent of GDP in 2005, compared with an average of 87.6 percent for all OECD member states.[3] The structure of savings for old-age benefits in Austria can be explained by the rather generous public pay-as-you-go (PAYG) pension system. However, recent pension reforms imply a significant gradual reduction in replacement rates in the PAYG system—25 percent in the coming decades. The savings from the severance pay system could fill the gap left by the pension reforms. By replacing the former defined-benefit, final-salary severance payment scheme with a contribution-defined, fully funded system, the reform has taken the first step in this direction. The essential condition for establishing an instrument to increase savings for pension benefits is, however, not fulfilled: After 36 months of contributing to the system, employees may withdraw their savings, although the legislature has provided tax incentives to motivate employees to leave their savings in the funds. Benefits from the new severance pay scheme are tax exempt if they are transformed into a pension annuity; otherwise, a reduced income tax rate of 6 percent applies.

An employee's decision regarding whether to withdraw money from the system depends on the rate of return on the funds, which has not been very promising. At the outset of the reform, it was assumed that over the long term the rate of return would be 6 percent per annum.[4] As shown in figure 5.3, this was an overly optimistic target level, as returns declined from 5.5 percent in 2005 to minus 2 percent in 2008. On average, the rate of return was 3 percent for the period 2004–09.

FIGURE 5.3 **Performance of Severance Pay Funds**

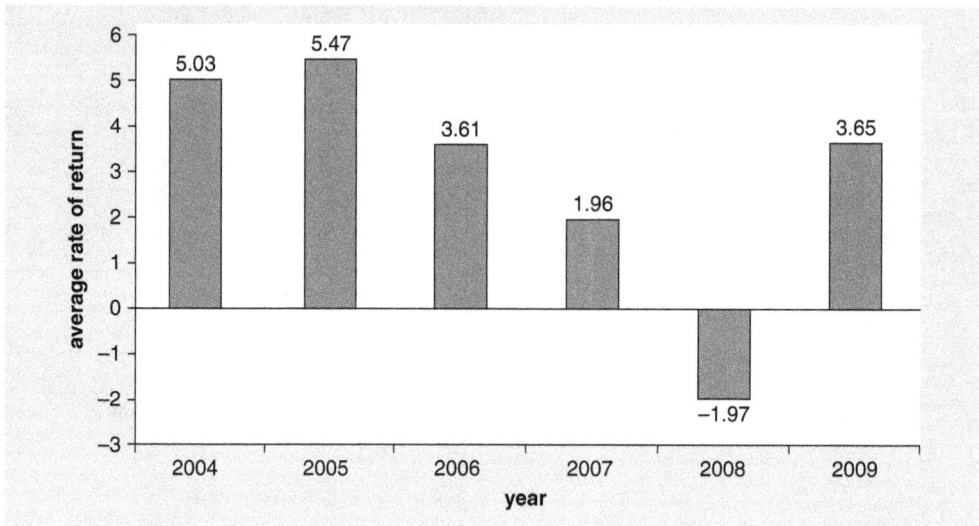

SOURCE: Oesterreichische Kontrollbank.

It thus comes as no surprise that withdrawals from the system have been the rule rather than the exception. In 2006, it became possible for the first time for those who entered the system in 2003 to withdraw money. Withdrawals have increased sharply since then (figure 5.4). The data for 2006 reveal that 88 percent of all participants who had the option of taking their savings out of the system did so. However, given the potential decline in replacement rates in the public PAYG pension system, employees may need to increase their rates of saving for old-age income via the new scheme.

From the perspective of the MVKs, there are two interdependent reasons for the poor performance of the severance pay funds. First, the MVKs are obliged to guarantee the value of the capital corresponding to the contributions; this requires costly insurance of the funds, which reduces the potential rate of return. Second, because participants may withdraw their money after only three years, the MVKs must maintain sufficient liquidity to pay out potential claims. Thus, they are forced to invest large shares of their portfolios in short-term assets, which also reduces the potential rate of return. As these two obligations reduce the rate of return, more employees are motivated to withdraw their savings from the system, which has a further negative impact on the funds' performance.

The MVKs argue for modifications of the legal provisions that will improve fund performance. They propose to allow employees to opt out of the capital guarantee, and they want to raise the minimum contribution period to five years. Another possibility would be to stick to the original intention and restrict withdrawals until the time of retirement.

To assess the potential of the new severance pay system as a prominent part of the development of a second pillar of the Austrian pension system, the future development of the system was simulated using the World Bank's Pension Reform Options Tool-Kit (PROST), which was developed to analyze the long-term structure and financial sustainability of public and private pension systems around the world. It has been applied to Austria to analyze the options for pension reform in recent years.[5]

FIGURE 5.4 **Withdrawals from Employee Benefit Funds**

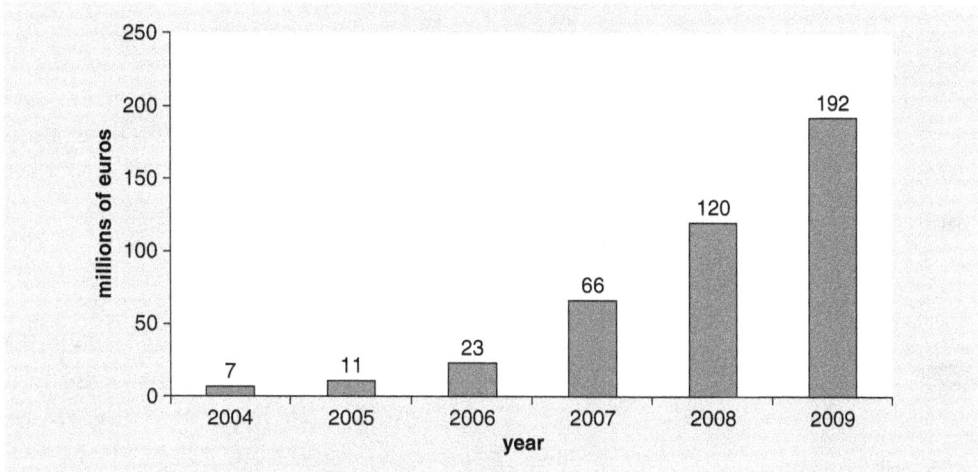

SOURCE: Plattform der Betrieblichen Vorsorgekassen.

PROST contains several modules that depict the main features of pension systems of individual countries. The *demography module* captures the historical and prospective development of the population of a country. For the purpose of this chapter, the current population forecast of the Austrian Statistical Office was used as the input.[6] The *labor market module* describes the labor market participation rates, unemployment rates, and wage rates of age cohorts. Historical data and trend forecasts for the future were used as inputs. The *macroeconomic module* combines the inputs from the demography module and the labor market module with assumptions about the growth rates of labor productivity to produce the evolution of GDP and the wage bill over time. For the period 2010–70, an average growth rate of labor productivity of 1.7 percent per annum was assumed. The *pension module* combines demographic data and labor market parameters to calculate contributions and benefits from different pillars of national pension systems. The pension module was used to simulate the development of contributions, assets, and benefits in the Austrian severance pay scheme.

The simulation begins in 2006, when total assets of the new severance pay scheme amounted to 0.9 percent of GDP and benefits to retirees from this source amounted to 0.01 percent of GDP. The data indicate that, currently, only 12.0 percent of total contributions remain in the system, which implies that only 0.2 percent of the wage bill can be considered potential savings for retirement. Mandatory contributions to the public pension system are currently 22.8 percent of the wage bill, and total expenditures for pension benefits amounted to 10.5 percent of GDP in 2006.

To simulate the future development of the severance pay system as a source of pension income, assumptions are made about the share of contributions that remains in the system. A pessimistic scenario assumes that only 25 percent of contributors will leave their money in the system until they retire. This implies effective contributions of 0.4 percent[7] of the wage bill. An optimistic scenario assumes that half of the contributions will be maintained as savings for retirement income.

TABLE 5.1 **Simulations of the Severance Pay Funds**

	2006	2035	2070
Pessimistic scenario			
Contributions*	0.2	0.4	0.4
Assets**	0.9	3.7	4.4
Benefits**	0.01	0.14	0.24
Optimistic scenario			
Contributions*	0.2	0.8	0.8
Assets**	0.9	7.5	8.8
Benefits**	0.01	0.35	0.49

SOURCE: Authors' estimations.

NOTE: *as a percentage of the wage bill; **as a percentage of GDP.

As can be seen in table 5.1, the relative importance of the severance pay system for the income of retirees may increase over time. In 2070, total assets in the system could increase to 8.8 percent of GDP, and pension benefits from this source could amount to nearly 0.5 percent of GDP in the optimistic scenario. Still, the figures indicate that the relative importance of the severance pay scheme for pension income will be limited.

Mobility in the Labor Market

The previous Austrian severance pay scheme was suspected of distorting the labor market behavior of economic agents (see, for example, OECD 2001). The discrete increase in entitlements led to incentives on the part of employers to dismiss employees just before additional claims could arise. From the perspective of employees, the system reduced the attractiveness of changing jobs with increasing duration of employment. This section investigates the effects of the reforms on job termination probability around three years. The analysis is based on an administrative data set containing all employment episodes in Austria and employs a difference-in-differences approach to estimate the impact of severance payment legislation on job mobility. The effect is identified by calculating the difference in the job termination probability between the third and fourth year of tenure for workers covered or not covered by the former severance pay legislation.

In theory, the reform of the Austrian severance pay law should have increased labor mobility significantly, and the quality of matches between workers and firms should have increased, with beneficial effects on labor productivity.[8] In addition, economic growth may be supported as workers move more quickly to innovative sectors of the economy. Bassanini, Nunziata, and Venn (2009, 394) estimate that the reform would "raise the annual TFP [total factor productivity] growth in EPL [employment protection legislation]-binding industries by about 0.25 percentage points, which translates into an average estimated growth rate of at least 0.1 percentage points for the whole economy." A precondition for these effects is, however, the assumed impact of the reform on labor mobility in Austria.

DATA AND DESCRIPTIVE RESULTS

The empirical part of this study uses an administrative data set that contains all employment tenures relevant for social security in Austria for the period January 2001 to January 2009. For each employment period, personal characteristics (personal identification number, sex, age, wage) and firm data (firm identification number, economic sector, firm size) are recorded.

The data enable a comparison of the durations of job tenure just before and just after the introduction of the new severance pay scheme. The expectation was that job tenure longer than a certain duration would have a positive impact on labor market mobility. The former system reduced the incentive for workers to change employers after three years, because they would lose their entitlement to severance pay. For very short job durations, it is reasonable to assume that the former scheme did not affect the behavior of employers or employees. Thus, the analysis here is restricted to job tenure of at least two years, leaving a sample of 1,167,625 employment periods that started between January 1, 2001, and December 31, 2004. (Employment periods that began later than 2004 were eliminated to ensure sufficiently long observation periods.) A significant proportion of new jobs were recalls to the same employer, which would be relevant for severance pay claims in the old scheme. These matches were eliminated to avoid a bias in the results. Specific legal provisions for firing exist for apprentices (15- to 20-year-old employees) and older workers (above 50 years) in Austria, so the analysis is restricted to employment of persons aged 20 to 45 years. Finally, a separate severance pay regulation existed for employees in the construction sector, so workers in this sector were dropped from the sample. After these adjustments, the sample contained 688,779 employment episodes for empirical analysis.

The treatment group consisted of all workers who started employment in 2003 and 2004; the control group consisted of workers who started in 2001 and 2002. A difference-in-differences approach was applied to study the effects of severance pay legislation on job mobility. Severance payment can be a barrier to efficiency-enhancing labor reallocation by discouraging workers from quitting their current jobs to move to better ones. The reform reduced such mobility obstacles, as workers now retain their entitlement to severance pay if they quit. Therefore, the treatment group should show a relatively higher probability of terminating the job in the fourth year.

Table 5.2 displays the distribution of the duration of employment that lasted for at least two years. The first two columns present the frequencies and corresponding percentages for all employment episodes: 20 percent of those with a duration of two years end in the third year; 14 percent end in the fourth year. (Because the sample continues to January

TABLE 5.2 **Job Tenure**

Duration	All Tenures		Completed Tenures	
	Frequency	**Percentage**	**Frequency**	**Percentage**
2–3 years	136,712	19.8	136,712	40.4
3–4 years	96,567	14.0	96,567	28.5
4–5 years	194,431	28.2	61,364	18.1
More than 5 years	261,069	37.9	43,640	12.9
Total	688,779	100.0	338,283	100.0

SOURCE: Authors' calculations based on social insurance data.

2009, a significant proportion of employment episodes is not included.) Columns three and four present the respective values for all completed episodes. In the sample, 338,283 of all employment episodes with a duration of at least two years had been completed by January 2009. This is roughly half of the sample.

Table 5.3 shows the probability of terminating the job in year 3 and year 4. The calculated probability refers to all employment contracts that still existed at the beginning of the year under consideration (that is, all employment contracts that had a duration of at least two or three years, respectively). Under the old scheme, severance pay entitlement went into effect after three years on the job, so a significant decline in the incentive to change jobs in year 4 was likely.

TABLE 5.3 **Probability of Job Termination in Year 3 and Year 4**

	Aggregate	Prereform	Reform
Year 3	19.9	21.1	18.5
Year 4	17.5	18.8	16.7
Difference	2.4	2.3	1.8
Difference-in-differences			0.5

SOURCE: Authors' calculations.

For the whole sample, the probability of terminating an employment contract in the third year is 19.9 percent; for the fourth year, 17.5 percent. The data set enables a comparison of the probabilities of job changes for the periods immediately before and after the implementation of the severance pay reform. Table 5.3 shows that the probability of leaving a job was significantly higher before the reform. In the third year, 21.1 percent of existing jobs ended in year three, compared with 18.5 percent after the introduction of the new severance pay scheme. The same pattern applies for job terminations in year 4: 18.8 percent were terminated before the reform; 16.7 percent in the postreform sample.

The general decline in job mobility cannot be attributed solely to the introduction of the reform; economic and labor market conditions may have had a significant impact on the turnover. The analysis compares job mobility in 2003–04 with that in 2005–06. In the latter time span, a strong economic recovery took place and employment growth accelerated significantly. These favorable conditions would have supported the stability of employment contracts and may explain the observed patterns of job mobility.

To control for unobserved and time-invariant effects, job mobility in year 4 is compared with that in year 3. The expectation is for a smaller difference in probabilities between years 3 and 4 in the postreform subsample, as the dampening effect on job mobility in year 4 vanishes with introduction of the new severance pay scheme.

As can be seen in rows three and four of table 5.3, the difference in job mobility declined after the reform was implemented. In the prereform subsample, the difference in the probability of job termination was 2.3 percentage points, compared with 1.8 percentage points for the postreform period. The difference-in-differences value indicates that the probability of job mobility increased by 0.5 percentage points after the reform.

Table 5.4 presents the results of the difference-in-differences calculations for females and males. The results confirm the finding of higher job mobility in the prereform time period and support the hypothesis of a positive impact of severance pay reform on job mobility in year 4. This impact is much stronger for females than for males. The difference-in-differences value is 0.9 percentage points for women and only 0.2 for men.

TABLE 5.4 **Probability of Job Termination by Gender in Year 3 and Year 4**

	Females		Males	
	Prereform	**Reform**	**Prereform**	**Reform**
Year 3	21.5	18.0	20.7	19.5
Year 4	18.8	16.2	18.1	17.1
Difference	2.7	1.8	2.6	2.4
Difference-in-differences		0.9		0.2

SOURCE: Authors' calculations.

The analysis surveyed all employment contracts that ended in the third and fourth years. Considerations about higher job mobility in year 4 are based on the financial incentives for employees who quit and consequently lost their entitlement for severance pay under the old system.

TABLE 5.5 **Probability of Direct Job Change in Year 3 and Year 4**

	Aggregate	**Prereform**	**Reform**
Year 3	11.1	11.6	10.7
Year 4	10.1	10.7	9.6
Difference	1.0	0.9	1.1
Difference-in-differences			0.0

SOURCE: Authors' calculations.

Information is not available about the form of the termination, so quits are identified by restricting the analysis to direct job changes, defined as employment contracts that end and are followed immediately by a new job without any unemployment in between. The assumption is that employees who move immediately to a new employer have a much higher probability of a quit compared with the complete set of terminated employment contracts.

In the sample, 194,000 of all employment contracts (28 percent) are followed immediately by a new job contract with a different employer. Eliminating the categories described above (recalls, apprentices, older workers, and construction workers), the number of direct job changes is substantial: more than 57 percent of terminated employment contracts. Table 5.5 shows that 11.1 percent of all employment contracts with a duration of at least two years ended in the third year with a direct job-to-job change. The probability declines to 10.1 percent in year 4. A comparison of the pre- and postreform periods reveals that job mobility declined after the introduction of the reform; however, the analysis finds no support for the hypothesis of increased job mobility in year 4. The difference-in-differences indicator is exactly zero, which implies no relative increase in job-to-job mobility in year 4 for workers under the new regime. This result contradicts expectations and indicates that the impact of the severance pay scheme on job mobility has been limited. One possible explanation for this finding is that financial incentives under the old scheme (at least after three years of job tenure) were not sufficiently large to generate sizable distortions of job mobility behavior.

DIFFERENCE-IN-DIFFERENCES ESTIMATES

The analysis continued, using microeconometric techniques—a difference-in-differences probit model[9]—to control for various factors that might influence the probability of employees' terminating their jobs. The method proposed in Ai and Norton (2003) was used to calculate marginal effects for difference-in-differences estimates in the nonlinear case. These effects are evaluated at the means of the covariates. The dependent variable was the probability of terminating a job. The same sample was used to investigate the probability of terminating a job in year 3 and year 4. The probit equation controls for age (dummies for five-year cohorts), industry (11 industries are used), and firm size (five sizes). The marginal effects of these controls behave according to theoretical considerations: The probability of job termination declines with the age of the employee and increases with the size of the firm. The industry also has a significant impact on job termination. As noted earlier, general labor market conditions may have had a significant impact on job mobility, so yearly employment growth in Austria was included as an additional variable. The model also controls for gender and wage. Table 5.6 shows the marginal effects for selected control variables.

The dummy variable "after reform" takes the value of 1 for workers under the new severance payment scheme. In contrast to the results obtained in the simple analysis above, the marginal effect reveals that the probability of terminating a job is higher for workers under the new scheme. Females generally have a significantly higher job termination probability. The variable "wage" captures the wage level of employees in the original job. The results indicate that employees with higher wages have a significantly higher propensity to move to another job. Because no other variables for human capital are included in the regression, this parameter includes the impact of skills and productivity. As expected, the macroeconomic labor market conditions have a significant effect on the mobility of the workforce. The variable "employment growth" captures the employment growth level in the year under consideration. Better economic and labor market conditions lead to a significant decline in the probability of terminating a job. The variable "year 4" refers to the probability of changing jobs in the fourth year of an employment episode compared with changing in the third year. The marginal effect points to a declining outflow from employment in year 4. The focus of the analysis is on the impact of severance pay reform on job mobility in the fourth year of employment. This impact is modeled

TABLE 5.6 **Probit Difference-in-Differences: Dependent Variable, Job Termination**

	Marginal effect	z-value
After reform	0.3	2.2
Female	1.3	16.4
Wage	2.5	29.4
Employment growth	−1.6	12.0
Year 4	−1.5	12.9
"After reform" times "Year 4"	0.8	6.1
Observations	1,240,514	
Log-likelihood	−583,000	

SOURCE: Authors' calculations.

TABLE 5.7 **Probit Difference-in-Differences: Dependent Variable, Job Termination by Gender**

	Females		Males	
	Marginal effect	z-value	Marginal effect	z-value
After reform	0.3	1.2	0.4	1.9
Wage	1.3	12.7	3.8	26.2
Employment growth	−2.6	13.9	−0.6	3.0
Year 4	−1.0	6.2	−1.9	12.0
"After reform" times "Year 4"	1.2	6.3	0.4	2.5
Observations	611,785		628,729	
Log-likelihood	−284,447		−297,730	

SOURCE: Authors' calculations.

with the interaction term "after reform times year 4" (see also tables 5.7, 5.8, and 5.9). In line with the hypothesis of higher mobility caused by the reform, the analysis finds a positive and significant marginal effect. An increase in the termination probability of 0.8 percentage points amounts to an increase in the overall termination probability of 4.5 percent.

The descriptive analysis showed considerable differences in the results by gender. Table 5.7 presents the probit results for females and males.

According to the direction of the impact of the individual variables on the probability of a direct job change, the results (see table 5.8) correspond to the results reported in table 5.6. Again, the focus is on outcomes for the dummy variable for the reform and the interaction term that measures the influence of severance pay on mobility behavior in the fourth year. Although the marginal effect for the dummy variable is positive, the effect is significantly smaller than in table 5.6, and the statistical significance is definitively lower. The effect of the reform amounts to only 2 percent of the job termination probability, although females have higher job-to-job mobility (table 5.9). Again, the analysis of direct job changes creates doubts about the quantitative effect of the severance pay reform on job mobility.

TABLE 5.8 **Probit Difference-in-Differences: Dependent Variable, Direct Job Change**

	Marginal effect	z-value
After reform	0.7	6.2
Female	1.1	17.3
Wage	3.7	52.5
Employment growth	−1.1	10.3
Year 4	0.3	3.5
"After reform" times "Year 4"	0.2	2.0
Observations	1,240,514	
Log-likelihood	−410,198	

SOURCE: Authors' calculations.

TABLE 5.9 **Probit Difference-in-Differences: Dependent Variable, Direct Job Change by Gender**

	Females		Males	
	Marginal effect	**z-value**	**Marginal effect**	**z-value**
After reform	0.7	4.5	0.7	4.2
Wage	2.2	25.8	5.9	46.2
Employment growth	−1.9	12.8	−0.2	1.4
Year 4	0.1	1.1	−0.8	6.2
"After reform" times "Year 4"	0.5	2.8	0.1	0.4
Observations	611,785		628,729	
Log-likelihood	−284,447		−213,870	

SOURCE: Authors' calculations.

ROBUSTNESS CHECKS

The analysis examines the robustness of the results with respect to the sample period and the selection of workers with at least two years of tenure. A concern exists that business cycle effects drive the mobility decisions of workers; the analysis controls for these effects by including macroeconomic labor demand as one explanatory variable. The business cycle might also affect job duration because of dynamic sorting into unemployment. The analysis considers only workers with job durations of at least two years; this would be misleading if the sample depended on the business cycle.

Figure 5.5 shows the survivor function based on job duration for all workers. The graph shows very similar survivor functions for the 2001 and 2004 cohorts, and the 2002 and 2003 cohorts, respectively. There is no simple correlation between the business cycle and job termination in the second year. Conditions improved in 2005 compared with 2001,[10] so excluding workers with job tenure less than two years does not lead to biased results. However, the possibility of unobserved heterogeneity must be considered in interpreting the results.

Table 5.10 shows the results of comparing only one year before and after the introduction of the new severance pay law. The comparison of the 2002 and 2003 cohorts indicates that the new scheme did not lead to higher job mobility. Some estimates even suggest that voluntary separations declined, at least for females. However, it is not possible to include the business cycle variable in this specification.

Conclusions

In 2003, the Austrian government implemented a comprehensive reform of the severance pay system; this reform has received substantial international attention. It extended the coverage of the system considerably, so that every employee collects entitlements irrespective of the duration of employment. The new system is regarded as a significant improvement, as it removes potential obstacles to job mobility in the Austrian labor market. The reform was

FIGURE 5.5 **Job Duration Estimates, Female and Male**

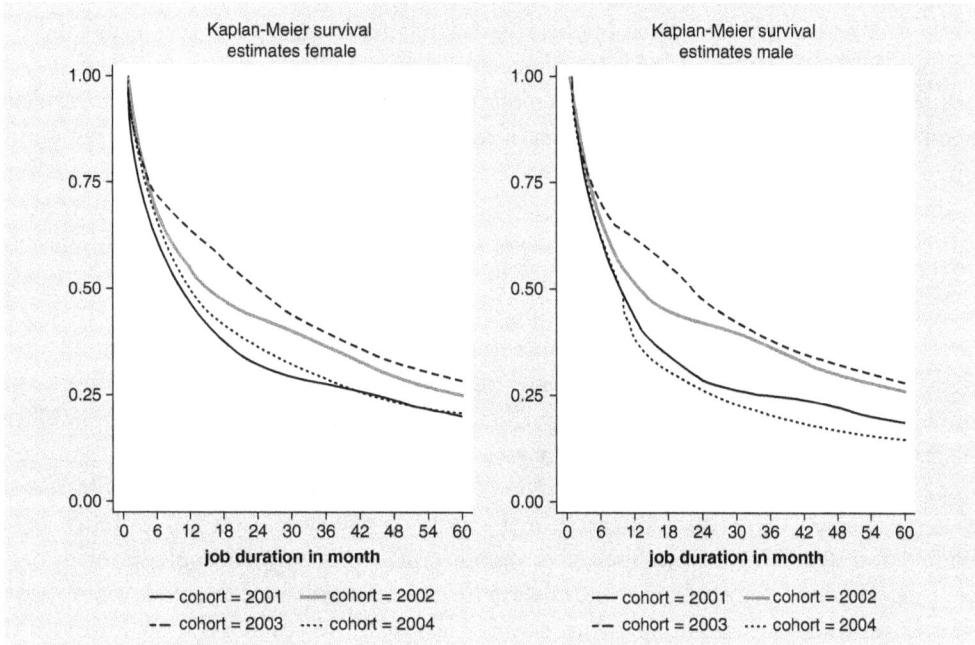

SOURCE: Authors.

TABLE 5.10 **Effect of Reform**

	Marginal effect	z-value
Full sample 2001–02 versus 2003–04		
Job termination	0.80	6.10
Male	0.45	2.49
Female	1.21	6.32
Direct job change	0.21	1.96
Male	0.06	0.42
Female	0.45	2.80
Robustness check 2002–03		
Job termination	0.08	0.43
Male	0.24	0.90
Female	−0.08	0.27
Direct job change	−0.54	3.21
Male	−0.06	0.30
Female	−1.04	4.15

SOURCE: Authors.

also intended to form the nucleus of an improved second pillar for the Austrian pension system.

Since the introduction of the new scheme, coverage has expanded continuously, to the point that two-thirds of all employees are entitled to severance pay. Although contributions to the new scheme have increased significantly, 90 percent of those entitled to withdraw their funds from the system do so. Recent reforms will lead to significant reductions of replacement rates in the Austrian public PAYG pension system in the coming decades. If the new severance pay system is supposed to reduce income losses for old-age pensioners, savings directed to old-age pension benefits should probably be increased.

The main reason for the lack of commitment of Austrian employees to the new system is the modest rates of return generated by the MVKs investing the funds. The performance of the MVKs has been impaired by their legal obligation to guarantee the capital and by the possibility of withdrawal of funds after termination of jobs.

The evidence suggests the need to modify the system. Modifications under consideration include allowing workers to opt out of the capital guarantee and extending the minimum contribution period before workers can withdraw funds. To increase potential returns within the system, individual workers could be given the option of agreeing to longer periods of commitment. To meet the objective of increased savings for retirement, withdrawals could be limited to the time of retirement. The initially assumed rates of return on the funds were far too optimistic; higher contribution rates may be needed in the future.

Using individual employment tenure immediately before and after the introduction of the reform enabled investigation of the potential impact of the severance pay legislation on job mobility in the Austrian labor market. Some evidence suggests that job mobility increased for longer employment tenure as a consequence of the reform. The estimated impact is significantly larger for females than for males. However, the overall results reveal that the quantitative impact of the former severance pay system on job mobility were limited and that other factors, such as economic conditions, seemed to play a much bigger role. The results indicate that the adverse financial incentives of the old severance pay scheme were (at least for employment tenure of less than five years) too small to have had sizable effects on labor mobility in Austria.

Notes

1. Workers receive twice their monthly gross wages for employment durations of at least 3 years, 3 times the monthly wage for at least 5 years, 4 times the monthly wage for at least 10 years, 6 times the monthly wage for at least 15 years, 9 times the monthly wage for at least 20 years, and 12 times the monthly wage for at least 25 years.

2. The contribution rate amounts to 1.5377 of gross salaries. It was set as a result of negotiations among social partners who aimed at moderate costs for employers on the one hand and adequate levels of severance pay for workers on the other hand.

3. See Felderer and others (2008), data sources: Eurostat, OECD.

4. See Koman, Schuh, and Weber (2005).

5. See Koman, Schuh, and Weber (2005).

6. See Hanika (2006).

7. This corresponds to 25 percent of the contribution rate of 1.53 percent.

8. From a theoretical point of view, EPL may increase or decrease productivity (see the discussion in Bassanini, Nunziata, and Venn 2009). It is often mentioned that EPL stimulates firm-specific investment of workers.

9. Schnalzenberger and Winter-Ebmer (2009) also use a difference-in-differences probit model to analyze the impact of layoff taxes on the displacement rate of older workers.

10. The years 2001 to 2005 were characterized by relatively unfavorable labor market conditions. The unemployment rate increased steadily over this period (2001 to 2006: 6.2%, 7.2%, 7.5%, 7.5%, 7.7%, 7.1%). Labor demand was sluggish between 2001 and 2004 (employment growth, 2001 to 2006: 0.4%, -0.5%, 0.2%, 0.3%, 1.0%, 1.7%).

References

Ai, C., and E. C. Norton. 2003. "Interaction Terms in Logit and Probit Models." *Economics Letters* 80: 123–29.

Bassanini, A., D. Nunziata, and D. Venn. 2009. "Job Protection Legislation and Productivity Growth in OECD Countries." *Economic Policy* 58: 351–402.

Bauer, T., S. Bender, and H. Bonin. 2007. "Dismissal Protection and Worker Flows in Small Establishments." *Economica* 74 (296): 804–21.

Boeri, T., and J. Jimeno. 2005. "The Effects of Employment Protection: Learning from Variable Enforcement." *European Economic Review* 49 (8): 2057–77.

Card D., R. Chetty, and A. Weber. 2007. "Cash-on-Hand and Competing Models of Intertemporal Behavior: New Evidence from the Labor Market." *Quarterly Journal of Economics* 122 (4): 1511–60.

EC (European Commission). 2006a. *Green Paper: Modernising Labour Law To Meet the Challenges of the 21st Century.* Brussels: EC.

———. 2006b. *Employment in Europe 2006.* Brussels: EC.

EIRO (European Industrial Relations Observatory). 2001. "Reform of Severance Pay under Discussion." http://www.eiro.eurofound.ie/2001/06/inbrief/at0106220n.html.

Felderer, B., U. Schuh, L. Strohner, and K. Weyerstrass. 2008. *Perspektiven der betrieblichen Altersvorsorge in Österreich.* Research report of the Institute for Advanced Studies on behalf of the Chamber of Commerce, Vienna.

Genser, B., ed. 1987. *Abfertigungen im Spannungsfeld der Wirtschaftspolitik—Eine interdisziplinäre Analyse.* Vienna: Manz.

Hanika, A. 2006. "Zukünftige Bevölkerungsentwicklung Österreichs 2006 bis 2050 (2075)." *Statistische Nachrichten* 10: 868–85.

Hofer, H. 2006. "Reform of Severance Pay Law in Austria." Discussion Paper, Peer Review: Reform of Severance Pay Law in Austria, Vienna.

———. 2007. "Severance Pay Reform in Austria. *CESifo DICE Report* 5 (4): 41–48.

Holzmann, R. 1987. "Integration von Abfertigungszielsetzungen in das soziale Sicherungssystem." In *Abfertigungen im Spannungsfeld der Wirtschaftspolitik—Eine interdisziplinäre Analyse*, ed. B. Genser. Vienna: Manz.

Klec, G. 2007. "Flexicurity and the Reform of the Austrian Severance Pay System." European Economic and Employment Policy Brief 4, European Trade Union Confederation, Institute for Research, Education and Health and Safety (ETUI-REHS), Brussels.

Koman, R., U. Schuh, and A. Weber. 2005. "The Austrian Severance Pay Reform: Toward a Funded Pension Pillar." *Empirica* 32: 255–74.

Kristen, S., W. Pinggera, and R. Schon. 2002. "Abfertigung Neu: Überblick über die Neuregelungen durch das Betriebliche Mitarbeitervorsorgegesetz." *Recht der Wirtschaft* 20 (7): 386–91.

Marinescu, I. 2009. "Job Security Legislation and Job Duration: Evidence from the United Kingdom." *Journal of Labor Economics* 27 (3): 465–86.

Martins, P. 2009. "Dismissals for Cause: The Difference That Just Eight Paragraphs Can Make." *Journal of Labor Economics* 27 (2): 257–79.

OECD (Organisation for Economic Co-operation and Development). 2001. *Economic Survey Austria*. Paris: OECD.

———. 2003. *Economic Survey Austria*. Paris: OECD.

———. 2004. *Employment Outlook 2004*. Paris: OECD.

———. 2006. *Employment Outlook 2006*. Paris: OECD.

Schivardi, F., and R. Torrini. 2008. "Identifying the Effects of Firing Restrictions Through Size-Contingent Differences in Regulation." *Labour Economics* 15 (3): 482–511.

Schnalzenberger, M., and R. Winter-Ebmer. 2009. "Layoff Tax and the Employment of the Elderly." *Labour Economics* 16 (6): 618–24.

Walther, H. 1999. "Ökonomische Funktionen der österreichischen Abfertigungsregel im Lichte von Theorie und Empirie." Institut für Volkswirtschaftslehre, Working Paper Series 2, Wirtschaftsuniversität, Wien.

Young, D. 2003. "Employment Protection Legislation: Its Economic Impact and the Case for Reforms." Economic Paper 186, European Commission, Brussels.

CHAPTER 6

Severance Pay Reform in the Republic of Korea

Jungyoll Yun and Jai-Joon Hur

Introduction

The severance pay system in the Republic of Korea, often called the retirement allowance system, was first introduced in Article 28 of the Labor Standards Act of 1953 as a way of guaranteeing income for the unemployed as well as retirees. The system was voluntary at first; it became mandatory after 1961. Eligibility for the plan has been limited to workers in establishments of a certain size: at first, to companies with at least 30 employees; after 1989, to those with 5 or more employees. Since December 2010, it has applied to all firms with at least one employee, covering around half of the total salaried employees. Severance pay is financed entirely by employers and is given to those who have worked at least one year in the firm, regardless of the reason for separation. The benefit level is one month's salary for each year's service.

In December 2005, the Korean government passed the Workers' Retirement Benefits Guarantee Act, a plan to convert the existing severance pay system into a corporate pension system. The difference between the two systems is that the former is unfunded (even though it is supposed to be funded by employers from their current revenues) and involves lump-sum payments to separated workers, while the latter is funded by employers and involves annuity payments to retired workers.

Korea introduced an Employment Insurance System on July 1, 1995. This system consists of three components: unemployment insurance (UI), job training, and employment maintenance and promotion subsidies. Owing to limited administrative capacity, only workers in firms with 30 or more employees were initially covered. As unemployment increased and low-wage earners in smaller firms became more vulnerable after the financial crisis of 1998, extending the scope of UI was deemed critical to provide adequate social protection to the many workers who had lost their jobs. In 1998, the Korean government extended the scope of UI to all firms with at least one employee.

To be eligible for unemployment benefits, a worker must be involuntarily laid off after paying insurance premiums for more than 180 days out of the previous 12 months. The replacement rate is 90 percent for minimum wage earners and 50 percent in general, with a ceiling of 1.2 million won per month. The payment period varies, depending on the claimant's age and insured employment period, from a minimum of 90 days to a maximum of 240 days. The average benefit period is around four months, which is relatively short compared with that in other Organisation for Economic Co-operation and

Development (OECD) countries. Severance pay frequently supplements the income of the unemployed.

The severance pay or retirement allowance system is expected to play two roles: (1) provide income support to the unemployed and (2) maintain income security for the retired. This is especially important in Korea, where workers tend to be separated from their jobs relatively early in their lifetimes, causing them to remain unemployed for a long time before they are entitled to government pension benefits.[1]

The system is intended to provide consumption smoothing across states and across time for workers who have severe liquidity constraints.[2] However, the market for loans and insurance against unemployment shock are fairly incomplete for various reasons, including asymmetric information.[3] The nonexistence or inefficiency of the private provision of such loans or insurance has led to government intervention to protect the incomes of workers.

However, some believe that the existing government-mandated severance pay system does not serve its purposes effectively. One reason for this belief is that the system is not actually funded—unemployed workers may not be guaranteed severance pay if their employers file for bankruptcy. Another factor that contributes to the insecurity of the existing system as an income-support mechanism for the unemployed is that it cannot provide lifetime annuities for workers. Annuity markets are not well established, and workers who receive lump-sum severance pay may not be well protected for their retirement.[4] Finally, the system may be inefficient because individual workers are not motivated to wisely manage their severance allowances, which are paid in lump sums, over various periods of time. Laid-off workers tend to allocate excessive amounts of money in the early stages of unemployment and may find themselves in need of government help during retirement.

Although the insecurity of the existing system as an income-support program has been frequently noted as a rationale for reform, there has not been much discussion about another point: inefficient intertemporal allocation of allowances under the system. This chapter examines this aspect of the existing system and describes how a corporate pension system could perform better.

The corporate pension system is expected to be an improvement over the old system, but both employers and employees (or unions) may prefer the old system. From the employers' point of view, the new system forces them to provide some funds in each period to their employees as ongoing contributions to the system on behalf of current employees, a requirement that can be burdensome.[5] Employees might also favor the old system because its private benefits are greater than those of the new system, although the social benefits of the new system are greater (this is discussed later in this chapter).

Once they receive their severance allowances, unemployed persons make decisions on intertemporal allocation for consumption or investment; these decisions may not be socially optimal. Individuals may choose to allocate excessive amounts of money for consumption in the early stages of unemployment or may take excessive risks in investments. This chapter examines these behaviors. The focus is on consumption decisions, but the theoretical model is easily applicable to investment decisions as well.

The chapter explains why workers do not currently have the right incentives to allocate their severance allowances over time and how the new system, coupled with appropriate institutional adjustments, could solve this problem efficiently. The popular explanation for the inefficient allocation of consumption over time is that people tend to behave myopically, heavily discounting their future income streams. This chapter proposes an alternative explanation based on rational utility-maximizing behavior.

A critical element of overconsumption during unemployment is the potential government bailout for those who end up with incomes lower than the minimum level for retirement. Knowing that the government will provide retirement subsidies may cause people to overconsume before retirement; that is, moral hazard behavior may occur among unemployed workers who receive severance pay.[6]

The chapter is organized as follows. The next section briefly describes the new corporate pension system. The following section outlines a simple model to capture the inefficiency of intertemporal consumption decisions by individuals. Government options to improve the welfare and some welfare-improving features of the corporate pension system are discussed, and conclusions are offered.

The Corporate Pension System

In the corporate pension system, effective December 2005, employers and employees may, by mutual consent, continue their severance pay system or establish a corporate pension plan, either defined contribution or defined benefit. Conversion to a corporate pension plan is voluntary, as opposed to the severance pay system, which has been mandatory. The new system regards severance pay as the vested right of workers but does not mandate a corporate pension, even for new labor market entrants. It introduces individual retirement accounts (IRAs) for workers who frequently change jobs and workers in firms with 10 or fewer employees; thus the IRAs can be portable and can contribute to old-age income security.

If employers and employees agree to introduce a corporate pension plan, benefits are paid from the age of 55 years. Annuities are also payable from age 55 for workers whose employers have contributed for more than 10 years. Other features of the two systems are summarized in table 6.1.

Simple bookkeeping is not permitted, and financial regulations are imposed to guarantee benefits. Limits on coverage were eliminated beginning in December 2010, so every employee will be entitled to severance pay or a corporate pension as long as his or her tenure exceeds one year.

Theoretical Framework

Once a person receives severance pay at the time of unemployment, he or she is faced with the problem of allocating it over time for personal consumption. If there is no additional unemployment in the person's future career, the consumption decision will be based entirely on intertemporal consumption smoothing. In this case, the private consumption decision would also be the socially desirable one. In reality, however, uncertainty is almost always associated with the possibility of additional unemployment in the future and with an individual's life span. In some countries, the purchase of an annuity insures against these risks, but annuity markets are not well developed in many countries, especially developing countries, because of a variety of informational problems. In this situation, the government, which can effectively resolve adverse selection problems

TABLE 6.1 **Severance Pay System versus Corporate Pension System**

	Severance pay	**Corporate pension**
Main characteristics	- Mandatory - Loss of vesting rights in case of firm bankruptcy, in which only three years' severance pay is guaranteed by the Pay Guarantee Fund	- Conversion to corporate pension, which is managed on an individual account basis, is voluntary
Coverage and eligibility	- Firms with five or more employees - Workers who have served at least one year, regardless of reasons for separation	- All firms[a] - Workers who have served at least one year
Withdrawal of benefit before separation	- Allowed	- Restricted to purchasing a new house or long-term care
Links to loans	- Legally protected from being used as collateral or being transferred to other persons	- Legally protected from being used as collateral or being transferred to other persons
Fund management and administration	- Unfunded but book-kept with tax incentives for reserving	- Entrusted to asset management companies, joint stock companies, insurance companies, and banks
Return accrual	- A month's wages for each year's service, based on the last three months' average wages	- Monthly contribution rate is 8.33 percent of annual wage; returns depend on fund performance
Payment	- Lump sum	- Lump sum or annuity
Portability	- Not portable	- Portable
Legal base	- Labor Standards Act	- Workers' Retirement Benefits Guarantee Act

SOURCE: Authors.

(a) When the Workers' Retirement Benefits Guarantee Act was passed in January 2005, it specified that the new system should be implemented for all firms by the end of 2010.

through the compulsory provision of insurance, should intervene to protect workers against these shocks.

Another factor can lead the private decision on intertemporal consumption to deviate from the socially optimal decision: Government subsidies to those who are unemployed for a long period—while necessary for social protection against long-term unemployment—may provide these unemployed workers with adverse incentives for overconsumption and disincentives to seek work.

The government income guarantee for the long-term-unemployed is financed by taxes, but in making consumption decisions, a typical unemployed person does not care about the effect of these decisions on taxes. If people know that a government bailout will be available, they will tend to allocate more consumption out of their severance pay than the socially optimal level. Thus, the government provision of insurance can reduce precautionary saving or increase consumption out of severance pay during unemployment.

Another important consideration is that overconsumption in the early periods of unemployment may reduce the incentive to go back to work on the part of unemployed persons. This is because the greater amount of consumption in earlier periods and the government guarantee of a minimum consumption would reduce the difference in the amount of consumption in the later periods between when an individual is employed and when he or she is unemployed.

The simple theoretical model used in this chapter captures these points. Consider a three-period model in which a person works for periods 1 and 2 at wage w per period, then retires in period 3.[7] The model assumes no intertemporal wage change or discounting. The worker may be unemployed in period 1 for some exogenous reason with probability q. This worker may also receive unemployment shock with probability p at the beginning of period 2, in which case he will continue to be unemployed in period 2 unless he engages in a certain level of search. Assume that the worker who is not unemployed in period 1 is sure to be employed in period 2.

With unemployment shock at the beginning of period 2, the worker may choose to search or not to search for a job. If he searches, he will incur search costs e but will be immediately reemployed in period 2. If he chooses not to search, he will continue to be unemployed in the period. The search cost e is a random variable with distribution function F. The person will decide to search or not depending on whether the search cost is lower or higher than a certain threshold level (discussed later).

Let $H \equiv \dfrac{f(e)}{1 - F(e)}$ indicate the search elasticity of unemployment—that is, the degree of sensitiveness of unemployment with respect to search activity—and assume that H is constant over e.

The employment or the longevity risk that can make individual consumption inefficient is represented by the risk of unemployment in period 2,[8] which is parameterized by p, the probability that an unemployed worker will be unemployed again in period 2, or the correlation coefficient between the two unemployment shocks in periods 1 and 2. The parameter p would then indicate the size of the unemployment shock (in terms of income lost) or unemployment duration for a person relative to that person's lifetime income, to determine the degree of inefficiency associated with consumption allocation over time.

Severance pay S can be paid to a worker only once in a career: The worker can get S in period 1 if he is unemployed or he can get S at the end of his career (in period 2). Those who are unemployed in period 2 as well as in period 1 may receive some subsidy from the government, which tries to secure a minimum level B of consumption per period for a worker. For analytical simplicity, the amount of severance pay is assumed to be exogenous. It is also assumed that $B < S < 3B$, implying that the severance pay is sufficient to cover minimum consumption for a worker for one period but not enough to cover minimum consumption for a lifetime.

The cost of the severance pay and of securing the minimum level B of consumption for a worker is financed by tax T, which is assumed in this chapter to be imposed in period 1 on an employed worker. Because a worker employed in period 1 finances his severance pay through his own tax payments, the severance pay system would affect his utility only through the tax he has to pay to finance severance pay for workers who are unemployed in period 1. Considering that the tax has to finance the subsidy $(B - (S - C))$ the government provides to those who are unemployed in both periods to secure the minimum consumption B, the government budget constraint will be

$$(1-q)T = q\{S + p(1-F(\bar{e}))2(B-(S-C))\},$$

where $\bar{e}$ indicates the threshold search cost in period 2, so the term $p(1 - F(\bar{e}))$ represents the probability of being unemployed again in period 2. This implies that the tax T that a worker employed in period 1 has to pay will be

$$T = \frac{q}{1-q}\{S + p(1-F(\bar{e}))2(B-(S-C))\}. \tag{1}$$

Note that the subsidy involves a property of insurance against unemployment shock in period 2. In other words, individuals purchase insurance through the subsidy against unemployment in period 2 from the government, which reduces the income difference between the employment and unemployment states in period 2.[9]

A worker employed in period 1 makes savings decisions to smooth out consumption over time. A worker who is unemployed in period 1 and receives severance pay must make two decisions. First, he chooses the amount of consumption C for period 1 out of S. Second, if he is still unemployed in period 2, he decides whether to incur search effort e to find employment in period 2.

In examining these decisions, the expected payoff is characterized for a person in each state at each point in time. Let V_N denote the lifetime expected utility for a worker who is employed in period 1, and let V_U denote the lifetime expected utility for a worker who is unemployed in period 1. Also, let $V_{U,J}(J = N,U)$ indicate the lifetime utility expected at the beginning of period 2 for an unemployed worker who will be employed or unemployed in period 2. The expressions for the expected payoffs are shown in annex A (1).

Next, the search decision that faces an unemployed worker in period 2 can be characterized by the threshold effort level $\bar{e}$ he chooses:

$$\bar{e} = V_{UN} - V_{UU}. \tag{2}$$

Consumption C in period 1 for a worker adversely affects his search incentive in period 2. Specifically,

$$\frac{\partial \bar{e}}{\partial C} = -U'\left(\frac{1+S-C}{2}\right) < 0. \tag{3}$$

In contrast, the choice of consumption level by an unemployed worker who receives lump-sum severance pay will be made as follows:

$$U'(C^*) - U'\left(\frac{1+S-C^*}{2}\right) + \bar{p}\left(U'\left(\frac{1+S-C^*}{2}\right) - U'\left(\frac{2-T}{3}\right)\right) = 0. \tag{4}$$

In setting the amount of consumption C^*, an unemployed worker would not care about the cost of a subsidy he receives in the case of extended unemployment, implying that he might choose to consume an excessive amount in period 1. This is even clearer using the utilitarian social welfare function V and characterizing the socially optimal level of consumption C^o for the unemployed person. The social welfare function can be

$$V = (1 - q)V_N + qV_U. \tag{5}$$

Differentiating V with respect to C, the socially optimal level C^o of consumption for the unemployed individual should satisfy the following condition:

$$\left\{ \left(U'(C^o) - U'\left(\frac{1 + S - C^o}{2} \right) \right) + \bar{p} \left(U'\left(\frac{1 + S - C^o}{2} \right) - U'\left(\frac{2 - T}{3} \right) \right) \right\}$$
$$- \frac{H\bar{p}}{1 - \bar{p}} (B - (S - C^o)) U'\left(\frac{1 + S - C^o}{2} \right) U'\left(\frac{2 - T}{3} \right) = 0, \tag{6}$$

where $\bar{p} \equiv p(1 - F(\bar{e}))$.

It is obvious from (4) and (6) that the annuity payment C depends on risk aversion and p (representing the size of the unemployment shock). In other words, C is increasing in risk aversion, as higher risk aversion implies stronger preference for consumption smoothing, while it is decreasing in p, as larger unemployment shock implies greater incentive costs associated with C.

More important, comparing condition (4) with condition (6), it is clear that the socially optimal consumption takes into account its effect on government expenditure T, which is captured by the last term in (6). The unemployed worker's consumption in period 1 affects tax T in two ways. First, it directly increases T as the remaining severance pay $(S - C)$ decreases. Second, it can further increase T because it reduces the incentive to work in period 2, as shown by (3). Because the worker who is unemployed again in period 2 is guaranteed the minimum consumption B regardless of his consumption in period 1, and consumption C would reduce the difference in income between employment and unemployment states, the person is likely not motivated to seek work.

Conditions (4) and (6) suggest that unemployed workers who receive lump-sum severance pay are likely to consume more than the socially optimal level, which establishes the following proposition.

PROPOSITION 1

Given the social insurance that secures the minimum consumption for retirement, unemployed workers who receive lump-sum severance pay consume more before retirement than what is optimal from the social point of view.

The incentive for excess consumption derives from two factors: unemployment risk in the future and the government guarantee for minimum consumption B. In other words, the government guarantee in the presence of unemployment risk keeps people from choosing the right amount of consumption during unemployment.[10]

One effective way to curb the incentive for excessive consumption on the part of unemployed workers is to directly control their consumption in period 1 through the corporate pension system. That is, the government forces unemployed workers to put their severance pay into their retirement accounts and provides them with an annuity for life (an undetermined period). Thus, the two reasons for the introduction of a corporate pension system are (1) the absence of an annuity market and (2) people's incentive to overconsume in the early periods of unemployment.

The assumption so far has been that there is no other income support program for the unemployed besides severance pay. But suppose there is another program: UI. The presence of UI would obviously alter the need for an annuity payment or a government subsidy for unemployed workers.

Under an unemployment insurance system in addition to the corporate pension, an unemployed worker could get unemployment insurance benefits as well. Unemployment insurance plays a different role than annuity payments from the corporate pension system: UI benefits take care of interstate consumption smoothing, while the annuity takes care of intertemporal smoothing.

To the extent that the UI benefit is provided to an unemployed worker, the government can reduce the amount of the annuity payment from the corporate pension system, so it is possible to determine the optimal combination of UI benefit and annuity payment that the government can set for a worker in this framework. Since the main focus of this chapter is on the government annuity payment, the level of UI benefit will be exogenously given as r^o, for simplicity's sake. As Stiglitz and Yun (2008) show, the level r^o of UI benefit can be determined by a person's risk aversion and incentives to seek work.

Since UI benefit r^o is financed by tax T, which is imposed on the employed workers in period 1, tax T will be

$$T = \frac{q}{1-q}\{r^o + S + p(1 - F(\overline{e}))(B - (S - C))\}.$$

The expressions for the expected payoffs in this case are shown in annex A (2).

Since the social welfare function will be

$$V = Max_{s_1} (1-q)V_N + qV_U,$$

we can determine the optimal amount C^o of annuity payment from the corporate pension system by maximizing V with respect to C. The optimal combination C^o will satisfy the following conditions:

$$\left\{\left(U'(r^o + C^o) - U'\left(\frac{1+S-C^o}{2}\right)\right) + \overline{p}\left(U'\left(\frac{1+S-C^o}{2}\right) - U'\left(\frac{2-T}{3}\right)\right)\right\}$$
$$- \frac{H\overline{p}}{1-\overline{p}}(B - (S-C^o))U'\left(\frac{1+S-C^o}{2}\right)U'\left(\frac{2-T}{3}\right) = 0. \tag{7}$$

This condition suggests that the optimal amount of annuity payment the government provides to unemployed workers under a corporate pension system is determined to balance consumption smoothing across states or periods against the moral hazard costs associated with the benefit.

PROPOSITION 2

As UI increases, the optimal annuity payment from a corporate pension system will decrease.

Differentiating the condition (7) with respect to r^o,

$$A \equiv U''(r^o + C^o) + \frac{\overline{p}}{3}\frac{q}{1-q}U''\left(\frac{2-T}{3}\right)\left(1 + \frac{2H}{1-\overline{p}}(B - (S - C^o))U'\left(\frac{1+S-C^o}{2}\right)\right) < 0.$$

As the second-order condition for C is satisfied, $\dfrac{\partial C^o}{\partial r^o} < 0$. Q.E.D.

The results are intuitive. As an unemployed worker gets a larger amount of unemployment insurance, the expected welfare benefits from annuity payments will decrease, because they would cause limited intertemporal smoothing in the presence of larger UI.

This chapter does not analyze the converse relationship, but it is likely that smaller annuity payments would increase the need for UI. Thus, the conversion of the retirement allowance system into a corporate pension system (which leads to less consumption by the unemployed) may warrant larger amounts of UI.

Policy Implications

These results have certain implications for policy making. The first concerns the government's options for ensuring the optimal allocation of consumption over time on the part of unemployed workers. Instead of forcing people to put their severance pay into corporate pension accounts, the government may choose to provide them with incentives. The model in this chapter can be used to determine the amount of tax incentive or subsidy that would be required to induce unemployed workers to choose a pension account instead of a lump-sum severance payment.

In (4) and (6), unemployed workers would not take the government's budget into account in determining their consumption during unemployment. In other words, the marginal moral hazard effect of their consumption—which can be expressed as $\dfrac{H\overline{p}}{1-\overline{p}}(B - (S - C^o))U'\left(\dfrac{1+S-C^o}{2}\right)U'\left(\dfrac{2-T}{3}\right)$, as in (6)—does not appear in (4), which determines C*, the amount of consumption they would choose. To correct this incentive problem, a subsidy *SS* is required for those who choose a corporate pension account. This subsidy can be expressed as follows:

$$SS = \frac{H\overline{p}}{1-\overline{p}}(B - (S - C^o))U'\left(\frac{1+S-C^o}{2}\right)U'\left(\frac{2-T}{3}\right).$$

However, the model does not address certain factors that make the introduction of a corporate pension system difficult. In Korea, where the individual worker is allowed to choose freely between the current lump-sum severance pay system and the corporate pension system, the government provides tax incentives to those who choose the latter. But the tax incentive is so small that the conversion has not been implemented as much as the government would like. The current system is not accompanied by such incentives under the Income Tax Act. As of November 2010, only 25.7 percent of workers in firms with five or more employees were covered by a corporate pension.[11]

Simulation by Kim and Ahn (2008) shows that, under the present tax rules, the lump-sum payment is more advantageous for high-income earners with long tenure than the 5- or 10-year annuities. Moreover, when national pension benefits and individual private pension benefits are considered together with corporate pension benefits, lump-sum payments are also more advantageous for low-income earners with long tenure.

The generosity of the present Income Tax Act in calculating the tax base of severance pay makes the transition difficult to justify.[12] Forty-five percent of the lump-sum severance pay is deducted, with an additional proportional deduction depending on the length of tenure. The tax incentive for those choosing the new system needs to increase further, or a tax penalty could be imposed on those who stick to the old system.

The second policy implication concerns the government loan program against severance pay, which could be a critical factor in facilitating the transition from the existing system to a corporate pension system. Although the corporate pension system provides insurance against the risk associated with longevity, it does not cover other types of risk, such as disease. This omission could be a major obstacle when workers are deciding whether to move to the corporate pension plan, as the capital market is not perfect. In other words, because the credit constraint is binding in the absence of a perfect capital market, the conversion from severance pay to a corporate pension would be greatly facilitated if the government allowed people to borrow against their individual pension accounts.

In implementing a loan program, the government needs to strictly specify the conditions under which loans are provided; otherwise, people will have excessive incentives to take out loans because of their desire for excess consumption during unemployment (as discussed in the previous section). However, any government effort to prevent this moral hazard is not perfect, as it is impossible for the government to perfectly monitor the health status of an individual.

The problem with the current system in Korea is that it does not explicitly involve a loan program.[13] This problem is especially serious because the current corporate pension system allows annuity payments only after the age of 55 years. Also, with the limited availability of alternatives to severance pay (such as a UI benefit), the absence of a loan program would make the new system unattractive to workers.

The model presented in this chapter is incomplete for two reasons. First, it primarily aims to justify the need for corporate pensions or annuity payments but does not characterize the optimal structure of a severance pay system. The amount of severance pay is fixed in the model; for example, it may be endogenously determined, as the severance pay system plays a role in consumption smoothing across states as well as across time.[14] Also, the amount of severance pay is set in the model to be constant regardless of employment tenure, which is not the case in reality, where severance pay typically increases along with tenure to control for workers' incentives to quit.

Second, in designing the corporate pension system, it would be appropriate to consider it together with other programs of unemployment protection. In other words, the amount of the annuity payment should be part of a package including other unemployment benefits. This chapter analyzes the annuity payment in the presence of fixed unemployment insurance; an analysis is needed in a model in which all types of unemployment protection are endogenously determined. Stiglitz and Yun (2008), for example, examine how the optimal combination of UI benefit and loan-based self-insurance can be determined. However, in their paper, the introduction of a corporate pension system would require the government to provide more UI than would be the case under the old retirement allowance system, because the new system reduces the amount of consumption out of severance pay.

Several specific factors might influence the optimal combination of UI and corporate pension. A certain set of labor market characteristics, for example, might affect the optimal mix. In a labor market where unemployment is high but unemployment duration is relatively short, the optimal package might involve relatively large amounts of UI benefits and smaller amounts of corporate pensions. Individual risk aversion, expected length of unemployment, and seriousness of moral hazard associated with UI benefits might also affect the optimal mix. Greater risk aversion, longer unemployment, and less serious moral hazard would suggest relatively smaller corporate pensions compared with UI benefits.

In setting the size of corporate pensions relative to UI benefits, a distributional factor must also be considered. To the extent that the corporate pension system is managed through IRAs, it would have a negative distributional consequence compared with UI benefits, as it would entail little subsidy across different types of workers. More important, the introduction of a corporate pension system could worsen distributional equity under adverse selection, because other types of private insurance arrangements (which are expected to entail some subsidy across workers) would not be able to attract low-risk workers because they would be attracted to the new system. In other words, the introduction of a corporate pension system would reduce the amount of subsidy across workers in the entire social insurance system.[15]

The corporate pension system has two important welfare-improving features. First, the introduction of the new system could reduce the current ineffective income support by the government. Under the severance pay system, if a firm declares bankruptcy, the Pay Guarantee Fund guarantees only three years of severance pay, regardless of worker tenure.[16] This leads to ineffective income support for the unemployed.

As of November 2010, about 2 million of the 7.7 million eligible workers had joined corporate pension schemes, implying that 25.7 percent of eligible workers have guaranteed corporate pension benefits (table 6.2). When tax incentives are reformed and pension coverage is expanded, the welfare content of the new system will be enhanced.

The second welfare-improving aspect of the new system concerns the pooling of uncertain life expectancies. With the introduction of corporate pensions, the pension market has expanded to 22.4 trillion won (1.9 percent of GDP in 2010) over the past five years. However, pension providers do not offer lifetime annuities. The annuity market sells only fixed-term annuities, which do not cover the risk of uncertain life expectancy. Retired workers will be better protected against the longevity risk after retirement when the financial market starts offering lifetime annuities.

TABLE 6.2 **Number of Workers under Corporate Pension System as of November 2010**
(thousands of persons)

	Total	DB	DC	IRA
Number of workers	1,988	1,292	625	72
Percentage	(100.0)	(65.0)	(31.4)	(3.6)

SOURCE: Korean Ministry of Employment and Labor 2011.

NOTE: DB = defined benefit, DC = defined contribution, IRA = individual retirement account.

Conclusion

This chapter addresses one of the problems with Korea's existing severance pay system—the inefficient intertemporal allocation of consumption on the part of unemployed workers—and makes a case for government intervention. It shows that an unemployed person who receives lump-sum severance pay is not incentivized to efficiently allocate his or her consumption over time because of the redistributive social policy that secures minimum consumption for an individual. Thus, workers do not take into account the adverse effect on the government budget in determining their consumption during unemployment. This situation warrants government intervention in managing intertemporal consumption for unemployed workers through a new system—a corporate pension system.

Other behaviors of unemployed persons—for example, risk taking—can also be problematic. Unemployed persons who receive lump-sum severance pay often make risky investments, which might ruin their economic lives not only during unemployment but during retirement as well. This behavior has frequently been observed in Korea, where it is relatively difficult for unemployed workers to find another job. Those in their late 40s or older, who face a tough job market while receiving a relatively large amount of severance pay, tend to have a strong incentive to engage in risky investments.

Although government intervention is warranted, opposition to the new system on the part of both employers and employees may make the transition difficult. Workers are not attracted to the new retirement insurance system even though it is socially efficient, because the benefits associated with the old severance pay system are greater. Employers are equally reluctant, because under the new system, liquidity-constrained employers are expected to contribute a certain amount of money for their workers in every period; under the existing system, they do not have to make these regular contributions.

With this opposition, it would not be politically feasible for the government to convert the old system into the new one all at once. The Korean government has thus allowed firms to choose between the old and new systems through management-union consultations. Hoping for a smooth transition, the government has also provided some tax incentives for those who choose the new system. However, the tax incentives are small or disadvantageous compared with lump-sum severance pay, so the transition has been slow.

So far, leading firms have been in the forefront of the slow expansion of corporate pensions. However, with 2011 changes in the Corporation Tax Act that permit tax deductions only for funds contributed externally, the transition is likely to be faster. Income tax reform to increase incentives to switch to corporate pensions and increased taxes on lump-sum severance pay will further facilitate the transition.

Annex A

(1)

Normalizing the constant wage to 1 for simplicity,

$$V_N = Max_{s_1,s_2}\{U(1-s_1-T)+U(1-s_2)+U(s_1+s_2+S)\} = 3U\left(\frac{2-T+S}{3}\right)$$

$$V_U = Max_C[U(C)+Max_e\{(1-p(1-F(\overline{e})))V_{UN}+p(1-F(\overline{e}))V_{UU}-\int^{\overline{e}}edF\}]$$

$$V_{UN} = Max_s\, U(1-s)+U(s+S-C) = 2U\left(\frac{1+S-C}{2}\right),$$

$$V_{UU} = 2U(B)$$

where s_1, s_2, s denote savings for an individual, while T is tax for the expenditure for maintaining the minimum consumption B.

(2)

$$V_N = Max_{s_1,s_2}\{U(1-s_1-T)+U(1-s_2)+U(s_1+s_2+S)\} = 3U\left(\frac{2-T+S}{3}\right)$$

$$V_U = Max_C[U(r+C)+Max_e\{(1-\overline{p})V_{UN}+\overline{p}V_{UU}-\int^{\overline{e}}edF\}]$$

$$V_{UN} = Max_s\, U(1-s)+U(s+S-C) = 2U\left(\frac{1+S-C}{2}\right),$$

$$V_{UU} = 2U(B)$$

where $\overline{p} \equiv p(1-F(\overline{e}))$ and $\overline{e}$ is the threshold search cost in period 2.

Notes

1. Workers in the private formal sector in Korea tend to retire in their early 50s, on average, but do not start receiving a pension benefit from the government until age 60. An income-support policy for these middle-aged separated workers is critically important, because this is the age when most of them are apt to be making a large investment in educating their children.

2. If unemployed workers are not severely liquidity-constrained, the need for insurance against unemployment or retirement will not be strong (Stiglitz and Yun 2005). Several studies have shown evidence for the existence of severe liquidity-constraints on the part of workers in developing countries (Deaton 1992; Murdoch 1995; Paxon 1992).

3. This issue has been argued by many authors, such as Gruber (1997) and Browning and Crossley (2001).

4. The annuity market is not well established in developed countries and even less so in developing countries (see Brown 2001; Moore and Mitchell 2000).

5. The requirement to contribute some money in each period would be costly for employers, especially when the capital market is not perfect, which may cause them to be liquidity-constrained during bad times.

6. If the market is complete (that is, free of liquidity constraints and informational asymmetry), individual decisions regarding intertemporal consumption would not be affected by the presence of a severance pay scheme, as the Barro-Ricardian equivalence principle implies. In the framework presented in this chapter, however, the market is not perfect.

7.   Although the wage is fixed in the model, a general equilibrium framework could affect the wage determination. Obviously, the structure of the severance pay system would affect labor demand and supply, and thus the wage level, which would in turn affect the optimal design of the severance pay system. The full analysis of this aspect is beyond the scope of this chapter.

8.   Since the life span is fixed in the model, there is no direct longevity risk. To the extent that the length of employment is variable, however, the model indirectly entails a longevity risk.

9.   In fact, the government subsidy guaranteeing minimum consumption B acts as insurance against unemployment risk in period 2.

10. The critical aspect of this type of moral hazard for unemployed persons is that the government cannot abandon its minimum support for the long-time unemployed.

11. The firms that have adopted corporate pensions show better employment performance than those that have not. According to Hur (2009), with sales and labor costs properly controlled, employment growth was higher in firms that had adopted corporate pension plans, and they spent relatively more on welfare programs for employees. In other words, they were leading firms. These leading firms have initiated the expansion of corporate pensions, which suggests that tax reform will be more important in the coming years to support this trend.

12. Two other types of generosity have also contributed to the slow transition. First, even if a worker has a corporate pension account, if he moves from one firm to another, he is allowed to withdraw from the former firm's corporate pension system and receive a lump-sum payment. Combined with weak incentives to hold an IRA, this regulatory generosity is an important factor in the slow expansion of corporate pensions. Second, until 2010, the Corporation Tax Act allowed tax deductions to internal reserves up to 35 percent of potential severance pay debt. Although the total amount contributed to an external pension fund was regarded as an expenditure, many firms preferred internal reserves. Beginning in 2011, however, corporate tax regulations allow tax deductions only for funds contributed externally.

13. The current system almost prohibits loans or withdrawals by restricting withdrawals or use of pension benefits as collateral to purchase a new house or long-term care.

14. The severance pay system entails cross-subsidies among individuals to a certain extent; that is, one worker's severance pay may be financed partly by other workers.

15. The self-selection effect that self-insurance may entail has been examined in the context of health insurance systems, including medical savings accounts. See Pauly and Herring (2000) and Zabinski and others (1999).

16. Every firm must contribute 0.04 percent of its payroll to the Pay Guarantee Fund to guarantee payment of wages in case of bankruptcy. The payment is limited to three months' wages and three years' severance.

References

Brown, J. R. 2001. "Private Pensions, Mortality Risk, and the Decision to Annuitize." *Journal of Public Economics* 82: 29–62.

Browning, M., and T. Crossley. 2001. "Unemployment Insurance, Benefit Levels, and Consumption Changes." *Journal of Public Economics* 80: 1–23.

Deaton, A. 1992. "Household Savings in LDC's: Credit Markets, Insurance, and Welfare." *Scandinavian Journal of Economics* 94 (2): 53–73.

Gruber, J. 1997. "The Consumption Smoothing Benefits of Unemployment Insurance." *American Economic Review* 87 (1): 192–205.

Hur, Jai-Joon. 2009. "Leading Firms, Corporate Pension and Employment Performance." Draft, Korea Labor Institute.

Kim, Yong-Joo and Jongbum Ahn. 2008. *Tax Reform for Activating Corporate Pension System.* Seoul: Korea Insurance Development Institute.

Korean Ministry of Employment and Labor. 2011. "Statistics on the Corporate Pension." http://pension.moel.go.kr/pension/info/info_02_list.jsp.

Moore, J., and O. Mitchell. 2000. "Projected Retirement Wealth and Savings Adequacy in the Health and Retirement Study." In *Forecasting Retirement Need and Retirement Wealth*, ed. O. Mitchell, P. Hammond, and A. Rappaport, 68–94. Philadelphia: Pension Research Council, University of Pennsylvania Press.

Murdoch, J. 1995. "Income Smoothing and Consumption Smoothing." *Journal of Economic Perspectives* 9 (3): 103–14.

Pauly, M., and B. Herring. 2000. "An Efficient Employer Strategy for Dealing with Adverse Selection in Multiple-Plan Offerings: An MSA Example." *Journal of Health Economics* 19 (4): 513–28.

Paxon, C. 1992. "Using Weather Variability to Estimate the Response of Savings to Transitory Income in Thailand." *American Economic Review* 82 (1): 15–33.

Stiglitz, J., and J. Yun. 2005. "Integration of Unemployment Insurance with Retirement Insurance." *Journal of Public Economics* 89: 2037–67.

———. 2008. "Public Provision of Self-Insurance Against Unemployment." Draft, Columbia University, New York.

Zabinski, D., T. Selden, J. Banthin, and J. Moeller. 1999. "Medical Savings Accounts: Microsimulation Result from a Model with Adverse Selection." *Journal of Health Economics* 18 (2): 195–218.

CHAPTER 7

Unemployment Insurance Savings Accounts in Latin America: Overview and Assessment

Ana M. Ferrer and W. Craig Riddell

Introduction

A variety of economic shocks have hit Latin American countries since the end of the 1990s. The effects of these shocks on the labor market have been severe and have reawakened a long-standing debate about the need for employment stability versus the need for flexible labor markets. For firms, extensive labor regulation implies a costly adjustment to economic changes, loss of competitiveness, and slower economic recoveries.[1] However, without adequate mechanisms of income support, flexible labor markets leave workers to face economic downturns unprotected. Additionally, poor labor stability may have undesirable effects on human capital accumulation and labor productivity.

Many Latin American countries see labor market flexibility as a way to improve economic performance. In these circumstances, providing adequate income support for affected workers is most important. Traditionally, most Latin American countries have protected the unemployed through a combination of high severance payments and low unemployment insurance or subsidies. Both theoretical and empirical research shows that these systems provide low coverage, benefit workers from the formal sector only, impede labor mobility and technological adjustment by firms, and provide incentives for the creation of informal job relations.[2]

The unemployment protection systems that exist in most Latin American economies are generally considered inadequate in terms of providing insurance to workers and tend to generate stratified labor markets. Recent research efforts and policy interest have turned to unemployment insurance savings accounts (UISAs) as an alternative to traditional systems of unemployment insurance. UISAs are schemes of individual mandatory savings that smooth income over a person's lifespan rather than pooling unemployment risk over the total working population at one point in time. Although this form of unemployment insurance diminishes the moral hazards associated with traditional insurance methods, it presents problems of its own. This chapter examines the experience of Latin American countries that use UISAs, highlighting problems and identifying areas for future theoretical and empirical work. The overall effect of UISAs depends on a vast array

An earlier version of this paper appeared as World Bank Social Protection Discussion Paper No. 910 (June 2009). Thanks to Milan Vodopivec and a referee for helpful comments.

of country-specific characteristics and program parameters, including how the system is implemented, existing labor regulations, the size of the informal economy, and the scope for collusive behavior. Understanding the effect of these factors requires a more extensive research effort in the area.

The chapter is organized as follows. The next section discusses the potential advantages of UISAs. The following section describes the UISA systems currently in place in some Latin American countries and analyzes some of the issues that have arisen in these countries. The final section offers conclusions.

Potential Advantages of UISAs

The high levels of unemployment in most Latin American countries call for a review of current and alternative systems of unemployment protection. Recent research efforts and policy interest have turned to UISAs as an alternative to traditional systems of unemployment insurance. UISAs are schemes of mandatory savings, in which workers or firms (or both) are required to make regular deposits to individual accounts. In the event of unemployment, the worker can withdraw funds from his or her account to support the transition to another job. This system has the potential advantage of making workers internalize the cost of unemployment benefits, thus avoiding the traditional moral hazards present in most insurance schemes. In general, this system does not adversely affect the incentive to seek work, as does conventional unemployment insurance. It has, however, potential adverse effects of its own. Theoretical studies by Orszag and others (1999) and Stiglitz and Yun (2006) indicate that unless savings accounts are comprehensive (that is, they become pension funds upon retirement), workers will be motivated to withdraw from the labor force before retirement to claim their accumulated savings. These studies also suggest that as long as the risks a person faces are not perfectly correlated, integration of the various social insurance programs intended to deal with these individual risks will also improve welfare.

UISAs have been assessed against more traditional systems of unemployment insurance (UI).[3] Because UISAs are individual accounts, the moral hazard present in traditional UI programs is expected to vanish. Workers should fully internalize the cost of remaining unemployed and have greater incentives to seek reemployment. This is an important aspect of UISAs, given limited monitoring capacity in developing countries. Because the two systems require different degrees of infrastructure, they are generally suitable for economies at different levels of development. However, most of the debate over UISAs focuses on their advantages over severance pay, the most common form of unemployment protection in Latin America.[4]

UISAs offer some of the same advantages as severance pay.[5] Severance pay is a lump sum—the size of which usually depends on job tenure—collected upon job separation. It should not affect job search effort. It is also unlikely to reduce effort exerted on the job, since dismissal for misconduct often precludes severance pay. Therefore, both UISAs and severance pay may avoid moral hazards for the worker. The main difference between the systems is that severance pay creates additional moral hazards for a firm that UISAs do not. Because severance payments are made at the end of the labor contract and may reach considerable size, firms have incentives to try to avoid payment

(Kugler 2005). Additionally, there is generally no legal requirement for firms to maintain sufficient reserves to support this obligation. This creates liquidity problems when a firm must make substantial labor adjustments. UISAs do not create such incentive problems because smaller payments are made regularly to the individual accounts. Thus, the main advantage of UISAs relative to severance pay is that they avoid the firm's moral hazard and guarantee payments to the worker in the event of unemployment. An additional distinction between the two systems is that a UISA qualifies as a delayed payment rather than a firing cost, which is the case for severance pay. This has important consequences in terms of creating a more flexible labor market without lowering income protection. The same incentives that may induce a firm to avoid making a large severance payment may prevent it from dismissing unproductive workers or (formally) hiring additional workers.

One of the major uncertainties of a UISA system concerns its capacity to provide sufficient coverage and adequacy of benefits against unemployment risk. Because unemployed workers withdraw funds from a personal account rather than from a common pool of resources, benefits may not be adequate for those who experience frequent or long-lasting spells of unemployment. For this reason, UISA systems are usually not conceived as the sole form of unemployment protection. Or they may contain additional features, such as limits on the withdrawal of funds or government contributions to a separate pool, that would alleviate these situations. The most common theoretical proposal includes a combination of self-insurance and public insurance. In these models, workers can borrow from the government in the event that their own unemployment account balance is depleted. Model simulations seem to offer hope that such systems will be viable (Feldstein and Altman 2007; Vodopivec 2010). In line with these models, Chile has implemented a UISA system that also finances, through employer and government contributions, a common unemployment fund, Fondo Solidario (Solidarity Fund). Chilean workers with insufficient balances in their accounts can borrow from Fondo Solidario.

An additional issue regarding the coverage of UISA systems arises in connection with the informal economies in many Latin American countries. In general, any system that significantly increases the burden of labor costs for employers has the potential to promote informal labor contracts (Lozoya 1996). Theoretically, UISAs are less prone than other systems to this effect, since employers' contributions do not usually depend on the length of employment and are not necessarily tied to other labor costs. In practice, however, the effects depend on country-specific issues such as how the UISA system is implemented, its cost relative to the previous program, and how it interacts with other labor regulations. Country-specific case studies are necessary to analyze the effects of UISAs in promoting formal labor contracts.

Another dimension on which UISAs offer a potential advantage relative to more traditional UI and severance payment systems is that they typically have relatively low administrative costs. Because the funds are generally accessible upon any kind of separation, extensive monitoring is not needed. Additionally, the funds are deposited in individual accounts—in most cases in existing financial institutions—which reduces management costs. Again, the extent of this advantage depends on country-specific factors. A system that combines UISAs with social insurance may still have considerable monitoring costs. And if benefits are contingent on the type of dismissal, other costs—such as litigation costs—may have to be considered.[6] On the other hand, because funds in unemployment accounts become pension funds upon retirement, UISAs may provide a foundation for developing individual pension plans. Although this aspect may not be apparent now, given the small balances generally held in these accounts, it may prove important in the face of growing concern about the sustainability of public pension funds. As an alternative to company pension plans, UISAs have the advantage of being fully portable (therefore, not restricting a worker's mobility) and not having high administrative costs.

A final consideration with respect to UISAs involves the capability and credibility of the institutions that manage the funds. If the managing institution does not generate enough real return on the deposits, workers' valuation of the UISA funds will be low. Because of the illiquid nature of the funds, workers with large holdings will have incentives to look for alternative ways to access their accounts. In particular, if the worker's valuation of the fund becomes lower than the employer's cost of payments, incentives will exist for informal agreements that may benefit both parties. Evidence of this behavior has been documented in Brazil, where workers might provoke their own dismissal (and subsequent rehiring) to access the fund (Barros, Corseuil, and Foguel 2001; Gill and others 2002). This type of collusive behavior is difficult to anticipate. It may originate from the lack of credibility of the institutions that are managing the funds or from the severity of liquidity constraints for the covered population. The behavior is also likely to be country-specific, depending on the interaction of the UISA system with existing labor regulations. Other institutional factors may also affect the system. One example is Peru, where the government has authorized withdrawals from individual accounts for purposes other than unemployment protection.[7] As a result, unemployment protection has become limited or even nonexistent for workers who decide to withdraw funds. Although these measures were intended to be temporary, the Peruvian government is finding it difficult to return to the UISA system of mandatory savings, as workers have been enjoying a form of wage increase that is difficult to give up.

Overall, UISAs have the potential to overcome some of the worst features of traditional systems of unemployment protection, reduce moral hazard, lower administrative costs (with respect to unemployment insurance), reduce firing costs, and avoid firms' liquidity issues (with respect to severance payments). Theoretically, they are also likely to promote formal labor markets. However, the system needs to be upgraded with additional features if it is to provide adequate coverage. These upgrades, in turn, may limit the advantages of the accounts. The overall effect of UISAs depends on a vast array of country-specific characteristics and program parameters. Examination of the existing UISA systems is a first step in this direction. A description of the use of UISAs in some Latin American countries may shed light on the common problems of the system and suggest possible directions for future theoretical and empirical work.

UISAs in Latin America

Compiling an overview of UISAs in Latin America presents several challenges. It is often difficult to obtain comparable information on the performance of the institutions under analysis. Some programs have been in place for a relatively short time (Chile, Ecuador), while others have more than 20 years of history (Brazil, Colombia, Peru, Panama). In some countries, all dependent workers are covered by a system of individual accounts, but in Argentina, for example, only construction workers have UISAs. This variation across programs limits the amount of information available to researchers. Accounting methods also vary across countries, making comparisons difficult. For instance, Brazil publishes only the number of active accounts, which may not correspond to the number of workers covered by the system, as accounts are linked to jobs rather than to individuals.

UISAs are mandatory savings schemes in which employers (in the case of Chile, workers as well) contribute a fraction of the monthly wage toward a special individual account. In most cases, a worker can access all these funds upon separation. In all the cases examined here, the funds are available to the worker upon retirement or to the heirs in the case of death. Table 7.1 summarizes the main features of UISAs in Latin America: the year the program was introduced, type of worker covered, amount of contributions, eligibility requirements to access the funds, income protection benefits, other benefits derived from the funds, whether the system provides social insurance, and the type of institution that manages the funds. All the countries except Argentina, Brazil, and Peru cover all dependent workers (employees). Contributions are mostly made by employers and are generally around one month's wages per year, although they may range from one week's wages per year (Panama) to 12 percent of the monthly wage (Argentina). In Chile, the government also contributes to the fund. Most countries allow employees to make voluntary contributions; employee contributions are required in Chile. In terms of the prerequisites to access the money, some countries (Brazil and Ecuador) make payment conditional on the type of separation. This restriction has the potential to increase monitoring and administrative costs (Camargo 2002) and to contribute to collusive behavior between employer and employee regarding how a separation is classified. Such behavior has been extensively documented in Brazil (Barros, Corseuil, and Foguel 2001). In addition, Chile, Ecuador, and República Bolivariana de Venezuela require a minimum in contributions or tenure to access the funds. At job separation, most countries allow access to the entire fund. However, Chile and Ecuador, whose systems are closer to the original unemployment insurance savings account model, limit the benefits that can be collected at one time. This feature reduces the incentive for collusive behavior mentioned above, but increases administrative costs.

Another issue concerning the adequacy of the benefits arises from the severity of liquidity constraints. Because UISAs may be imposing mandatory savings on a potentially credit-constrained population, with perverse effects on family expenditures and investments, most programs (except those in Chile, Ecuador, and Venezuela) allow partial withdrawals to finance human capital investments or pay for housing or health expenses. The effect of these exceptions on the insurance role of the individual funds has yet to be studied. In Peru, for instance, large fund withdrawals are threatening the purpose of the severance fund as a source of income protection against unemployment.

How successful are UISAs in providing income protection in the event of unemployment? One of the main problems of a pure UISA system is that it forgoes the redistributive effects available in a system that pools the unemployment risks of the entire working population. Because of the concentration of unemployment among certain groups, UISAs may not provide adequate benefits for temporary workers or those with low incomes. This creates the problem of providing alternative sources of income for workers with insufficient funds in their accounts. Chile is the only country in this study that offers social protection within the individual account system through the solidarity fund. Ecuador is

TABLE 7.1 **UISA Characteristics**

Country (year of introduction)	Coverage	Contributions	Eligibility requirements	Unemployment benefits	Other benefits	Social insurance	Funds management
Argentina (1975)	Construction workers	Employers: 12% of 1 month's wages for a year, then 8%	Proof of dismissal	Balance on separation	n.a.	No	Banking institutions
Brazil (1989)	Dependent workers not covered elsewhere	Employers: 8% of 1 month's wages	Contingent on type of separation	Balance on separation	Partial withdrawal allowed for housing or health expenses	No/other programs	Government
Chile (2002)	Dependent workers	Employees: 0.6% of 1 month's wages Employers: 2.4% of 1 month's wages Government contributions	Minimum 12 contributions	1 month's wages/ year (up to 5 months) Decreasing benefits with minimum and maximum	n.a.	Minimum benefits guaranteed with the solidarity fund (up to 2 withdrawals every 5 years)	Recognized financial institutions (exclusive dedication)
Colombia (1990)	Dependent workers	Employers: 9.3% of 1 month's wages	Proof of dismissal	Balance on separation	Partial withdrawal allowed; funds can be used to guarantee some house loans	No/other programs	Recognized financial institutions (exclusive dedication)

(continued)

TABLE 7.1 **(Continued)**

Country (year of introduction)	Coverage	Contributions	Eligibility requirements	Unemployment benefits	Other benefits	Social insurance	Funds management
Ecuador (mixed 2001)	Dependent workers	Employer: 1 month's wages/year to individual accounts (monthly contribution)	Involuntary unemployment Minimum 48 deposits + 1 year tenure	Balance on separation up to 3 times the average monthly wage in the previous year	n.a.	No/other programs	Recognized financial institutions (exclusive dedication)
Panama (1972)	Dependent workers	Employer: 1 week's wages/year + 5% compensation Employee: voluntary	Additional compensation contingent on type of separation	Balance on separation	Partial withdrawal allowed for housing, education, or health expenses	No/risk pooling within firms	Collective trust fund with approved financial institution
Peru (1991)	Private workers not covered elsewhere	Employer: 2 deposits of 1/2 of 1 month's wages	Proof of dismissal	Balance on separation	50% withdrawal allowed; additional withdrawal occasionally authorized	No	Banking institutions
Venezuela, R.B. de (1997)	Dependent workers	Employer: 5 days' wages/month Increases with tenure Maximum 30 days' wages/year	3 months' tenure	Balance on separation	n.a.	No/other programs	Recognized financial institutions/ employer

SOURCE: Authors' compilation. For sources, see text.

NOTE: n.a. = not applicable.

moving toward a system based solely on individual accounts, but it is currently a mixed system in which part of the population still withdraws funds from a common pool. In other countries, additional income sources may be available from other programs. Table 7.1 summarizes the main characteristics of UISAs in Latin America.

Another source of difference among countries relates to the administration of the funds. Most programs establish special financial institutions—or create special regulations governing existing institutions—whose sole function is to manage the unemployment/severance funds. Some countries (Argentina and Peru) allow the funds to be deposited in the regular banking system but regulate the type of deposit. In Brazil, the government operates the fund, while Panama gives the employer discretion about the choice of a managing institution. Venezuela has opted for a mixed system for the administration of the severance fund.

The rest of this section offers a detailed review of the features and operation of the UISA systems currently in place in Latin America. It also analyzes some of the issues concerning the performance of UISAs that have arisen in various countries.

ARGENTINA

Argentina has a form of UISA for construction workers. The Collective Bargaining Agreement for Construction Workers in Argentina (Convenio Colectivo de la Construccion 76/75) refers to an unemployment fund for the construction industry. It mandates that employers must make monthly contributions of 12 percent of the monthly wage in the first year and 8 percent in subsequent years. These contributions are deposited in individual accounts in banking institutions and are, presumably, available to the worker upon separation of any kind.

BRAZIL

The Severance Indemnity Fund for Employees (Fundo de Garantia de Tempo do Servicio, FGTS) was established in 1967. The new constitution of 1988 brought major changes to labor regulation and unemployment protection in Brazil. In particular, it mandated that contributions to the FGTS are to be placed in individual accounts rather than into a common pool of resources. It also introduced changes in the penalty a firm must pay if it dismisses a worker without just cause. The two concepts are closely related, because the penalty is set as a percentage of the value accumulated in the worker's account. The 1988 constitution increased the penalty for dismissal without just cause from 10 percent to 40 percent of the amount accumulated in the worker's account during the length of the contract.[8] This amount is paid directly to the worker. In 2001, the government legislated additional social contributions to the fund in the case of dismissal without just cause. These include 10 percent of the deposits accumulated in the FGTS during the contract and 0.5 percent of the last monthly wage. The purpose of these contributions is to cover the deficit generated by a ruling of the Brazilian Supreme Tribunal of Justice that recognized a worker's right to a monetary adjustment on FGTS accounts between 1988 and 1989. Thus, these contributions, although part of the fund, do not increase individual workers' accounts.

The fund is built with contributions from employers of 8 percent of each employee's monthly salary[9]—roughly one month of pay per year of work. Individual accounts are associated with specific labor contracts, so there are as many accounts as there are labor contracts. They can be classified into two main groups:

- Active accounts receive regular deposits and are associated with operating labor contracts.

- Inactive accounts do not receive regular deposits, because the labor contracts under which they were established have been terminated.

The regulatory organ of the system is the Trustee Council (Conselho Curador), which consists of two employer representatives, two employee representatives, and six government officials from various ministries. Its main function is to determine the allocation of the resources. The Ministry of Planning and Budget (Ministerio do Planejamiento e Orcamento, MPO) is the supervisor of the program, and the federal bank (Caixa Economica Federal) operates the fund. The Caixa also keeps a historic registry of accounts to facilitate workers' access to information on their labor history.

Table 7.2 shows the evolution of the number, value, and average balance of accounts with a positive balance. The number of active accounts increased by 63 percent between 1999 and 2009, while the value of these accounts almost quadrupled during the same period. The average balance in 2009 was almost 3,000 Brazilian reais (R$), or approximately US$1,840.

Upon dismissal without just cause, the worker can access 100 percent of the fund, including any portion accumulated from previous jobs. The worker can also access the fund under the following circumstances:

- Indirect dismissal[10]
- Breakdown of contract for reciprocal causes, unavoidable causes, or firm closure
- Termination of the labor contract

TABLE 7.2 **FGTS, Number and Value of Accounts**

	Active Accounts			Inactive Accounts		
	Number of accounts (thousands)	Value (R$, millions)	Average balance (R$)	Number of accounts (thousands)	Value (R$, millions)	Average balance (R$)
1999	48,005	63,286	—	17,858.0	2,623.0	—
2000	54,271	67,121	1,237	9,379.0	1,316.0	140
2001	59,156	73,767	1,247	9,584.0	1,338.0	140
2002	63,632	80,799	1,270	4,976.0	757.0	152
2004	55,184	99,277	1,799	646.8	350.0	541
2006	55,043	125,765	2,285	15,088.0	3,854.0	255
2009	78,700	235,000	2,986	7,200.0	1,600.0	222

SOURCES: FGTS Prestacâo de Contas Exercicio 2001, 2000; Relatorio de Gestão 2002, 2004, 2006.
NOTE: R$1 = US$0.6133; — = not available.

- Retirement (persons older than 70 years have automatic access to the fund), death, disability, and specific health issues
- Inactive account for more than three years (unemployed or out of the labor force)
- House acquisition or financing of mortgage payments

Withdrawals for dismissal constitute around two-thirds of all fund withdrawals; those for housing are approximately 15 percent. The composition of withdrawals remained stable between 1999 and 2002, with a slight increase in the value of withdrawals associated with dismissals and a decline in the value of those to finance the purchase of a house. The fund itself has been very active in financing housing and home improvements.

Between 1997 and 1999, the fund experienced liquidity issues (see figure 7.1), which could be partially attributed to rising unemployment at the end of the decade. The year 2000 saw the beginning of a recovery that continued through the decade, led by a decline in the unemployment rate and efforts of the Caixa to recover past credits and increase the number of accounts.

CHILE

Traditionally, unemployment protection in Chile included an unemployment subsidy and severance pay. The first instrument covered workers dismissed for unjust cause who had 12 months of contributions to any insurance system. This instrument had low benefits (12–25 percent of the minimum wage over a maximum period of 12 months) and low coverage (30 percent of potential beneficiaries). The second instrument covered workers in the event of dismissal for economic reasons. The benefits were one month of wages per year of tenure, with an alternative severance payment that could be negotiated after six years. This form of severance pay was closer in spirit to a UISA system, but it covered only a small fraction of unemployed workers. It did not cover dismissal for reasons other than

FIGURE 7.1 **Liquidity of FGTS**

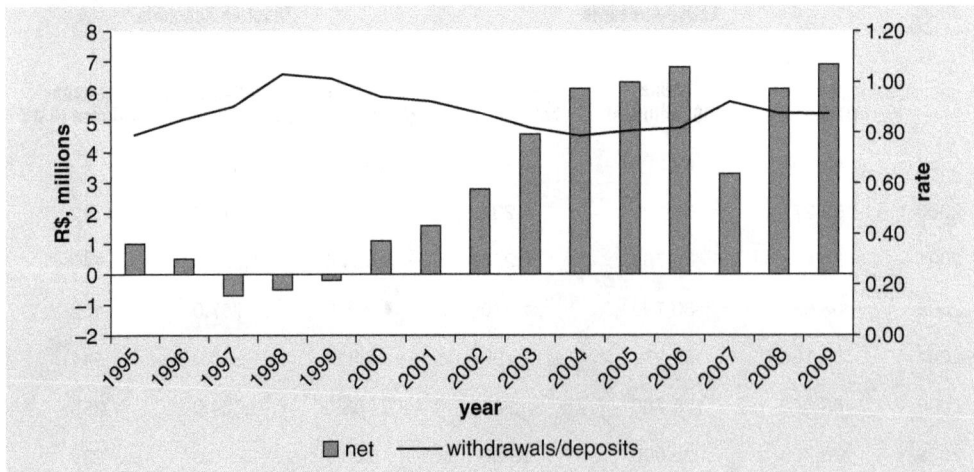

SOURCE: Authors' calculations based on Relatórios de Gestão do FGTS, http://www.caixa.gov.br/fgts/relatorios_balancos_fgts.asp#.

economic, including retirement, death, and voluntary quitting. Since 1991, a system of individual accounts has also been in place for domestic workers (Chilean Labour Code, art. 163–165). Dismissal for any reason entitles domestic workers to a severance payment for the value of the accumulated fund. Employers contributed 4.11 percent of the person's monthly wage to the domestic worker fund for a maximum of 11 years.

Since 2002, Chile has had a new system of unemployment protection. The law regulating the current Chilean unemployment protection system was approved in 2001. The new system is based on a mix of individual and public funds and funded by contributions from the employer, the employee, and the government (see figure 7.2). The system covers all paid workers except public employees, domestic workers, apprentices, retirees, and minors. The funding comes from contributions from employees (0.6 percent of the average monthly remuneration over the past 12 months, with a ceiling around US$2,000 monthly) and employers (2.4 percent of the average monthly remuneration over the past 12 months, with a ceiling around US$2,000 monthly). Employee contributions are limited to 132 months in each employment period.[11] The employer contributions can be deducted from payment of compensation for unjust or economic dismissal. The employer deducts and deposits the employee's contributions plus part of its own contribution (1.6 percent of monthly remuneration) in an individual unemployment account. There are penalties for failure to comply. The rest of the employer contribution (0.8 percent) is deposited in a solidarity or common unemployment fund. The government contributes an annual fixed amount of around US$8.8 million to the solidarity fund. In case of unemployment, the worker will receive unemployment insurance from his or her individual account. Any reason for unemployment is valid, including dismissal for economic reasons, retirement, disability, or voluntary quitting. The worker may also be entitled to other compensation, such as severance payments. The main characteristics of the individual account payments are as follows:

- Limited payments
- Decreasing benefits with ceilings and minimum benefits

FIGURE 7.2 **Financing the Chilean Unemployment System**

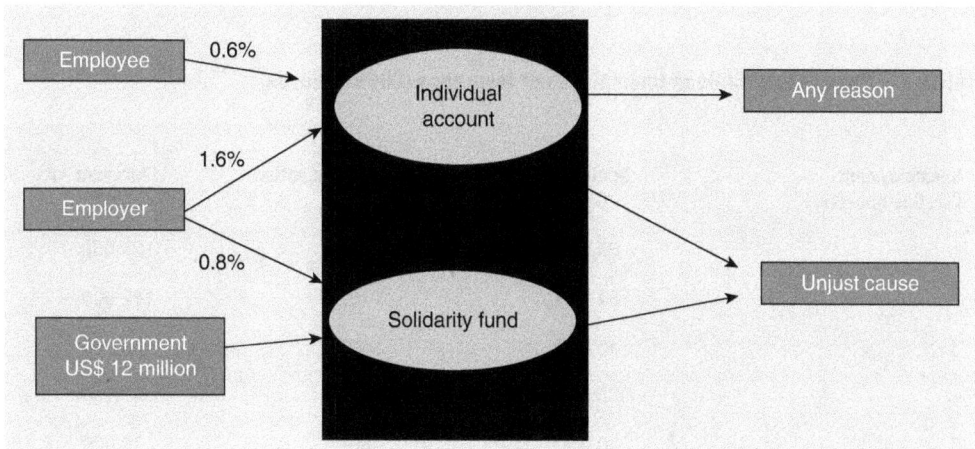

SOURCE: Authors.

- Requirement of at least 12 contributions before accessing any benefits
- Benefits indexed annually

The length of the benefits depends on the worker's contributions—workers may receive one month of benefits for every year of contributions up to a maximum of five months. In the case of voluntary or involuntary unemployment, withdrawals occur for up to five months, with the amount of benefits decreasing over time and the initial amount depending on the number of years of previous contributions. The payments stop if the person initiates a new contract. The final withdrawal is for the balance in the individual's account. In the event of death, disability, or retirement, withdrawals are for the balance. This system is in place for new contracts (after October 2001), but workers with previous contracts also have the option to participate.

An important feature of the new system is that it guarantees a minimum amount of unemployment insurance (defined in table 7.3) for low-income workers who have not accumulated enough resources in their individual accounts. To fund this safety net, 0.8 percent of employer contributions are deposited in the solidarity fund. Unemployed workers who satisfy the requirements (minimum contributions and involuntary unemployment) and have insufficient funds in their own accounts can withdraw from the solidarity fund. Payments stop if the worker is not actively looking for employment or rejects (without justified cause) employment with a wage that is 50 percent or more of his or her last wage. Payments from the common fund are a decreasing percentage of the average wage in the previous 12 months, with a minimum and maximum amount that both decrease as unemployment persists. Individual withdrawals from this fund are limited to two every five years. Total withdrawals from the solidarity fund are limited to 80 percent of the last monthly balance.

Administradora de Fondos de Cesantia de Chile (AFC) won the right in a 2002 public auction to manage the unemployment funds for 10 years. The seven existing pension fund administrators in Chile own AFC. They are monitored by the superintendence of pension fund administrators. AFC is responsible for collecting and assigning contributions to the individual accounts and the common fund, paying benefits, investing resources, and providing customer service. The investment structure is regulated according to the

TABLE 7.3 **Payments of Chilean Unemployment Insurance (Chilean pesos)**

Unemployment duration (months)	Minimum (Ch$)	Benefits (% average 12 months' wages)	Maximum (Ch$)
1	65,000	50	125,000
2	54,000	45	112,500
3	46,000	40	100,000
4	38,500	35	87,500
5	30,000	30	75,000

SOURCE: Seguro de Cesantia 2002.

NOTE: Ch$ = Chilean pesos.

norms that rule investments for pension funds. AFC charges an annual commission of 0.6 percent of the funds' balances (Acevedo, Eskenazi, and Pagés 2006).[12]

The new Chilean unemployment protection system combines various features of individual account programs with more traditional ones. First, it facilitates worker mobility and job matching because it offers protection from all forms of unemployment, including voluntary unemployment, retirement, disability, and death. This way, the worker does not renounce better employment opportunities because of fear of losing accumulated benefits. Second, the system may reduce the moral hazards typically associated with the existence of unemployment insurance, because workers must deplete their own resources before they can access the common fund. Moreover, important restrictions limit access to this fund, and there are requirements regarding cause of unemployment and availability to work. At the same time, the system offers some social insurance to low-income workers who may not have accumulated sufficient resources. Sehnbruch (2004) suggests that although the new system offers better coverage than the previous system, it does not particularly benefit those who hold irregular, short-term jobs and are in more need of income protection.

However, the fund has been very successful. By the end of 2010, almost 7 million Chilean workers had joined the new insurance system (see table 7.4). Of these, 40 percent are young workers (18–30 years of age), 48 percent are prime-age workers (31–50 years of age), and 12 percent are mature workers (over 50 years of age). The value of the fund as of December 2010 was estimated at over US$3.8 billion, of which the solidarity fund accounts for

TABLE 7.4 **Chilean Unemployment Fund**

	Participants (millions)	Value (Ch$, thousands)	% value of Solidarity Fund
(1) Participants and value			
2003	2.2	71,481	11
2004	3.2	181,533	16
2005	4.0	333,911	19
2006	4.7	548,914	21
2007	5.3	837,581	22
2008	5.8	1,182,221	24
2009	6.3	1,526,712	26
2010	6.7	1,974,140	27
(2) Real return on investments (%, annual average in November)			
	2010	**2008–10**	**2002–10**
Unemployment fund	4.11	3.25	2.79
Solidarity fund	7.07	4.20	3.14

SOURCES: (1) Estados Financieros Fondo de Cesantia, AFC. http://www.safp.cl/safpstats/stats.
(2) "Investments and Rentability of the Unemployment Fund 2010," report. http://www.spensiones.cl/573/article-7572.html.

NOTE: Ch$ = Chilean pesos. Ch$1 = US$0.00192448.

27 percent, more than doubling its participation since 2003. The average (deflated) return on the unemployment fund since its inception (2002–10) has been 2.8 percent (3.1 percent for the common fund), and the short-term returns (2008–10) are even higher at 3.25 percent and 4.2 percent, respectively, over the past three years. Since the average (deflated) interest rate on deposits in that period has been 2.4 percent, the fund seems to be a safe investment for workers. In terms of the stability of contributions, around 60 percent of the affiliates hold indefinite work contracts; therefore, the evolution of the fund so far strengthens its role as a source of social insurance.

COLOMBIA

Law 50 of 1990 introduced several reforms to the Colombian labor code. One of these involved switching from a traditional system of severance payments to one that required the creation of individual reserve funds. The traditional system had several disadvantages. The employer handled the severance fund, on which it was required to offer an annual interest rate of 12 percent. However, the employer was not required to generate or maintain sufficient reserves to cover group dismissals; in those cases, funds often were insufficient to make severance payments to all laid-off workers. Under the new system, the employer deposits into the individual reserve fund an amount equivalent to one month's wages per year of work (9.3 percent of the annual salary). Accounts are balanced annually, and the fine for employers who fail to comply with the regulation is equivalent to 12 percent of the severance payment. Workers with contracts under the previous legislation were permitted to switch to the new system.

Upon retirement or termination of the labor contract, the worker may withdraw the total amount in his or her account. Partial withdrawals are allowed under the following circumstances:

- To finance education for the worker or a family member (In this case, the Sociedades Administradoras de los Fondos de Cesantia [Society of Fund Administrators, SAFC] administrator deposits the necessary amount directly with the educational institution.)
- To acquire, improve, or release the mortgage of a house
- To pay the worker's property tax

The money may also be used as collateral for house purchase loans granted by workers' funds and cooperatives.

The workers may choose any of the existing SAFC administrators as the depositary for their funds. These are financial institutions, supervised by the banking superintendency, whose exclusive purpose is the administration and handling of severance pay. The SAFCs charge a 4 percent commission and are required to maintain a solvency margin and guarantee at least the average return on three-month Colombian treasury bonds. The SAFCs are monitored by a board of directors that includes representatives of both workers and employers. Investments must be made in accordance with the conditions and limits established by the banking superintendency concerning the risk of the assets. Currently, 86 percent of the fund is held in fixed-term securities (see figure 7.3).

FIGURE 7.3 **Colombian Severance Pay Fund Portfolio**

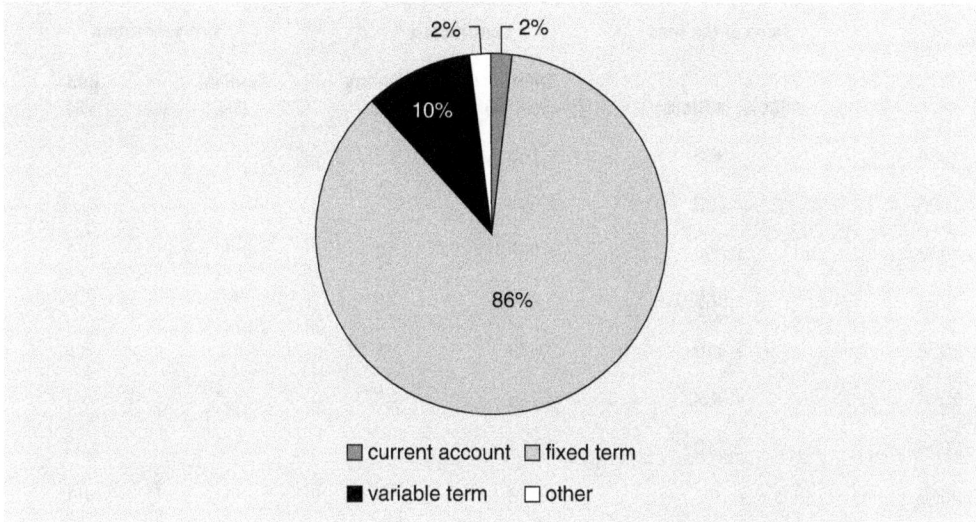

SOURCE: Informes de Coyuntura, Boletin Mensual Superintendencia Bancaria, Colombia.

By the end of 2007, almost 4 million workers belonged to the fund. Most of the participants (70 percent) earn less than twice the minimum wage. The value of the severance pay fund has been increasing over the past several years. Contributions rose considerably during 2002, which was interpreted as a sign of the recovery of the labor market in Colombia, particularly the formal sector. In general, withdrawals are greater than new deposits. However, the liquidity of the fund has not been compromised, thanks to healthy returns. So far, the sum of new deposits plus returns has always exceeded total withdrawals. These returns have encouraged voluntary participation. In 2008, the returns dropped sharply; however, they are always above the minimum set by the banking superintendency.

ECUADOR

Since November 2001, Ecuador has a new social security law that regulates a comprehensive social insurance program, Seguro General Obligatorio (SGO). The SGO includes health, disability, retirement, and death benefits, with special provisions for rural or agricultural communities. Contributions to the SGO vary by economic sector, but for most workers amount to 20.5 percent of the monthly wage (11.15 percent from the employer and 9.35 percent from the employee).

The regulatory organ is the Instituto Ecuatoriano de Seguridad Social (IESS), which collects the contributions and controls compliance with the law in matters of social security. The SGO includes two unemployment insurance programs: The new individual account system covers new workers and those 40 years old or younger, as well as those between

TABLE 7.5 **Evolution of the Colombian Fund**

	Value of the fund	Contributors		Two-year return	
	(Col$, millions)	Total (thousands)	Voluntary (%)	Nominal (%)	Real (%)
1994	352	1,165		—	
1996	703	1,689		—	
1998	1,250	1,968	12	25	6.5
2000	1,865	2,274	28	17	6.2
2002	2,410	2,679	61	13	5.5
2004	4,287	2,996	48	13	6.4
2006	3,740	3,711	—	16	11
2008	4,013	4,478	—	—	4.4
2010	5,598	5,430	—	—	18

SOURCE: Informes de Coyuntura, Banking Superintendency of Colombia.
NOTE: Col$ = Colombian pesos. Col$1 = US$0.000526039; — = not available.

40 and 49 who choose to register; other workers are covered under the old system of intergenerational insurance. The employer contributes the equivalent of one month's wages per year to an individual account or reserve fund. Workers with more than one year of tenure are entitled to income protection if they are involuntarily unemployed. The worker must have a balance equivalent to 48 monthly contributions in his or her individual account, and the amount available for withdrawal is three times the regular monthly wage averaged over the previous year. In case of retirement, disability, or death, the total balance in the account is available to the worker or the heirs. Workers who are not covered under this program can draw UI benefits under the previous law.[13]

Mandatory savings funds are administered by the Entidades Depositarias del Ahorro Previsional (EDAPs) under the supervision of the banking superintendency. The EDAPs also administer the individual reserve accounts and can offer loans against the balances. In 2003, around 1.2 million workers participated in the system; half were under 50 years of age. The most recent report from the banking superintendency (February 2009) valued the unemployment fund at US$1.4 billion, with a 7.8 percent rate of return on investments.

PANAMA

Workers in Panama are entitled to a severance payment of one week's wages per year worked, payable at the end of the labor contract. The employer also must offer compensation in the case of dismissal without just cause, if the worker leaves the job for justified causes (including economic reasons), or if the labor contract ends by mutual consent. This compensation varies according to the worker's tenure (see table 7.6).

TABLE 7.6 **Severance Payments in Panama (wages/tenure)**

| | Old contracts | | |
Tenure	Work before 1972	Work after 1972	New contracts
Less than 1 year	1 week/3 months	1 week/3 months	3.4 weeks/year
1–2 years	1 week/2 months	1 week/2 months	
2–5 years	3 months	3 additional weeks/year	
5–10 years	4 months		
10–15 years	5 months		
15–20 years	6 months	1 additional week/year	1 week/year
More than 20 years	7 months		

SOURCE: Panama Labor Code 1972.

Before 1972, the labor code established that these payments were a liability of the firm, but it left the management to the employer. This created a moral hazard for firms and led to bankruptcy and liquidity problems in the case of substantial dismissals. The new labor code, effective in 1972, requires the employer to deposit each trimester the corresponding fraction of the worker's severance payment, plus 5 percent of the amount he or she would collect if the contract terminated, in a trust fund with a private financial institution (this amounts to slightly over 80 percent of the unemployment fund; the other 20 percent comes from voluntary contributions by the employee). This part of the fund constitutes a system of individual unemployment accounts—the funds are locked in for the workers and cannot be used by the employer. Workers may make individual contributions to their accounts, but these have not been substantial (see table 7.7). The account can be used as a guarantee for loans for the purchase of a house.

No particular institution is in charge of managing the severance pay funds. The employer establishes a trust fund with an approved financial institution. Banks, insurance companies, law firms, and other types of firms can apply to become a depositary of these unemployment funds and trusts; mostly banking institutions (around 60 percent). The financial institutions in charge of the unemployment trusts offer the market rate of return—figure 7.4 shows the rate of return on funds held by each type of management firm.

PERU

In Peru, significant labor reforms were implemented in 1991. Before that, the Peruvian labor code had established a very rigid labor market. What used to be a tenure bonus has become the Compensación por Tiempo de Servicio (CTS). The law establishes the CTS as an individual account, financed by the employer with a deposit equivalent to 0.5 percent of the monthly salary, payable every six months (in May and December). The system covers only private employees who are not covered by other special regimes. Workers may choose the financial institution where they want their funds deposited. Employers and

TABLE 7.7 **Composition of Panama's Unemployment Fund**

Accounts (balboas, thousands)	2001	2003	2005	2007
Tenure fund	81,041	111,435	124,476	144,438
Unjust cause compensation	11,356	10,846	17,425	21,779
Voluntary contributions	544	322	316	146
Subtotal	**92,941**	**122,603**	**142,218**	**166,363**
Available to employer [a]	21,553	17,932	30,283	55,634
Total	**114,494**	**140,535**	**172,501**	**221,997**
Agents (number)				
Employers	3,321	2,833	2,725	2,704
Employees	194,602	179,438	213,297	248,433
Managing institutions	20	17	14	11

SOURCE: Banking Superintendency of Panama.

NOTE: B1 = US$1.00000.

(a) The employer may access interest on the fund that is in excess of labor obligations toward workers.

FIGURE 7.4 **Rate of Return for Panama's Unemployment Funds**

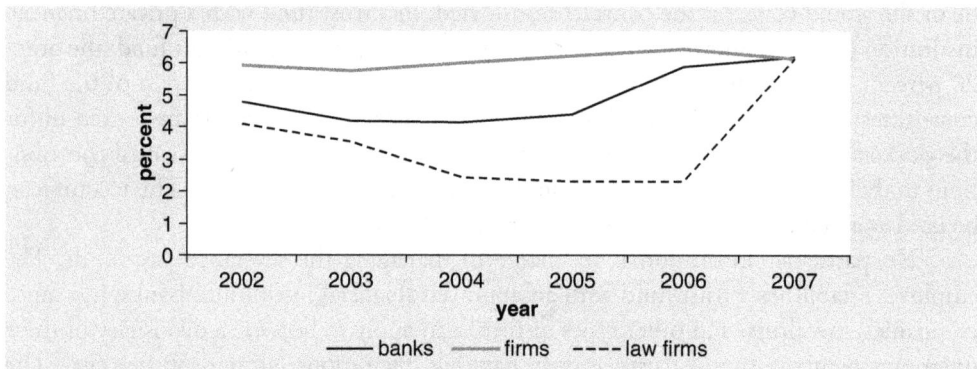

SOURCE: Authors' calculations based on figures from the Banking Superintendency of Panama.

employees can make private arrangements under which the employer becomes responsible for managing the account.

Generally, withdrawal of funds requires proof of dismissal. Originally, workers could withdraw 50 percent of their funds for an emergency and could use up to 50 percent as a guarantee for loans from the employer or from credit unions or savings cooperatives. The government has authorized additional withdrawals on occasion. For instance, in December 2002, through Decreto de Urgencia 67-2002, the government authorized the withdrawal of 100 percent of the funds to cancel loans and debts incurred with financial institutions. Earlier that year, Decreto de Urgencia 19-2002 allowed workers to withdraw the full amount of deposits made between May and October 2002, to stimulate domestic demand. These allowances continued through 2003 and 2004 and ended in January 2005.

According to the banking superintendency, on December 2007, more than 2 million CTS deposits were valued at 4.769 million nuevos soles (around US$1.615 million). The majority of these accounts hold small amounts—less than S/.20,000—representing 54 percent of the value of the fund. Most deposits are held in the banking system (93 percent), while the rest are deposited in savings cooperatives. However, deposits into savings cooperatives have grown at a much faster rate than deposits into the banking system, owing to higher interest rates.[14,15]

URUGUAY

Although Uruguay does not have a system of individual accounts for unemployment insurance purposes, the country does have the necessary infrastructure (individual accounts) to implement such a system with relative ease. As in Ecuador, the Banco de Prevision Social administers a comprehensive social insurance program that includes medical, life, retirement, disability, and unemployment. Approximately half (7.47 percent) of the total employee contributions (15 percent) are deposited in private accounts. Employers contribute an additional 12.5 percent of payroll, and the government finances any deficit from tax revenue. This individual account can be accessed only in the event of retirement, disability, or death. However, the current unemployment protection system in Uruguay does not rely on this comprehensive insurance scheme, but on a traditional UI system.[16]

REPÚBLICA BOLIVARIANA DE VENEZUELA

República Bolivariana de Venezuela's labor code dates from 1997. After three months of service, workers are entitled to a severance package equivalent to five days of pay per month worked, with an additional two days of pay per year after the first year, up to a maximum of 30 days. The worker may choose to accumulate funds in one of three ways: (1) in an individual account, (2) in an individual trust fund, or (3) in an individual account registered in the firm's accounting records. The employer makes monthly deposits into the selected account. The return on trust funds and individual accounts deposited with financial institutions is the market rate. For funds deposited with the firm, the employer must pay the average rate established by the central bank. If the employer fails to make these deposits, it must pay a penalty on the amount owed (that is, not deposited as requested) determined by the central bank.

The fund is available to the worker upon termination of the contract, although workers have access to the annual returns yielded by the deposits. The worker also has the right to advance notification of dismissal, ranging from one week (after one month's tenure) to one month (after one year's tenure). If the employer does not supply advance notification, it must pay the corresponding amount of salary at the time of dismissal.

Like UISA systems in other countries, the Venezuelan system allows partial withdrawals to finance certain investments. An employee can obtain a loan of up to 75 percent of his or her severance fund to purchase a home or pay educational or health expenses for himself or herself or a family member.

Outcomes of UISAs

Table 7.8 provides a summary of the performance of funds in different countries. Some programs have limited or almost no information available (Ecuador, Uruguay). Other programs are small (Argentina), and no information could be found on their operation. In some cases (Brazil), information on the number of beneficiaries is not available.

UISAs in Latin America are typically small, except for those in Chile (3.2 million contributors at the end of 2009, approximately 50 percent of the employed population) and Brazil. In other countries, low coverage reflects, in part, the extent of the informal economy. Average balances held in the individual accounts usually exceed minimum monthly wages; however, this may be a poor indicator of the performance of the funds in terms of income protection because, with the exception of Chile, no program guarantees minimum payments.

Although the programs offer some protection against unemployment risk, they are heavily concentrated among those at lower risk of unemployment (workers who are formally employed, educated, and older). Berstein, Fajnzyber, and Gana (2011) show that, in Chile, the estimated median benefit for older and more educated workers is three to five times that for younger, uneducated workers. A similar situation exists in Brazil, where the majority of FGTS beneficiaries are above the 50th percentile of the income distribution

TABLE 7.8 **Analysis of Funds**

	Brazil[a] (End 2009)	Chile (Dec 2010)	Colombia (Sept 2010)	Peru (March 2007)	Panama (2007)
Number of accounts (thousands)	78,700 (active)	6,673	5,430	2,000	248
Number of accounts/employed[b]	3.58	0.50[c]	0.29	0.13	0.32
Fund balance (millions, US$)[d]	77,094	3,800	2,967	—	222
Average balance (US$)	1,840	1,640	542	—	894
Minimum monthly wage (US$)	277.00[e]	24.70	208.00[f]	117.90	142.00[g]
Net deposits (thousands, US$)	33,547,510	358,264	(−10,872)	1,615	—
Withdrawals/deposits	87.4%	39.0%	242.0%	—	—
Average withdrawal (US$)	339.00	21.00	5.87	—	—
Rate of return	3.00% (fixed)	3.20%	12.00% (minimum guaranteed)	4.38%	Market rate[h]
Costs/commissions	—	0.6%	4%	—	—

SOURCE: Authors.

— = not available. (a) Accounts represent jobs rather than individuals. (b) Employment figures obtained from the official statistics agency in each country. (c) Active accounts only (3,200 thousands). (d) Nominal dollars. (e) Average wage, 2006 information. (f) Average monthly income. (g) Average median income is US$121. (h) Minimum wage ranges from US$142 to US$273 in the Panama/San Miguelito region for a 40-hour week. (i) Average interest rate on domestic deposits is 6 percent.

(Barros, Courseil, and Foguel 2001; Carneiro 2003). In Brazil, this could be a consequence of poor past performance of the funds, which has forced low-income workers in particular to access their accounts often to avoid losses in the purchasing power of their savings. However, the FGTS has an important redistributive role in the way it is managed: A substantial part of the fund is devoted to alleviating the housing deficit in Brazil and to sanitation and urbanization projects, which mainly benefit the low-income population. A complementary credit system linked to savings overwhelmingly benefits low-income workers. In 2006, 89 percent of the beneficiaries of the credit system were workers with less than five times the minimum wage in their accounts.[17]

The performance of the funds has been volatile, reflecting the instability of Latin American financial markets. This problem has been particularly acute in Brazil, where the FGTS has been poorly managed by the government. Initially, the government guaranteed interest rates on the accumulated funds to maintain the real value of the fund. These interest rates were dependent on the length of the labor relationship and varied from 3 percent for employees with fewer than 2 years of tenure to 6 percent for employees with more than 10 years of tenure. During the 1970s, various regulations influenced these rates, which were finally reduced to 3 percent for all deposits initiated after 1970. These changes greatly complicate the calculation of the return on individual deposits, as deposits made at different times and for workers with different tenures will have different associated interest rates. A review of the returns finds two main issues. First, hyperinflation has made it difficult to maintain the real value of the funds. The biggest losses occurred between 1968 and 1979, when deposits initiated with a nominal interest rate of 3 percent depreciated by more than 40 percent. Only during the first half of the 1990s were the returns on FGTS accounts high enough to compensate for inflation for all account types. Second, the rate of return on the fund compares poorly with the return on other assets. Because the deposits to the fund constitute a form of forced savings, the returns should be compared with those of other savings instruments, namely savings accounts. In other countries, such as Colombia, the performance of the severance fund steadily improved over the 1990s. However, with the exception of Brazil, no studies compare the returns on UISAs with those of other financial assets.

An additional problem arising from poor fund management and low rates of return is that liquidity constraints create strong incentives for workers to try to access the fund. Barros, Corseuil, and Foguel (2001) provide some evidence of collusive behavior between workers and firms to label voluntary quitting as dismissals.[18] In general, these incentives create higher rates of turnover in the labor market than would otherwise be observed. It is difficult to determine the extent to which this problem arises from the particular characteristics of the Brazilian fund or the general performance of the economy, or a combination of both. One factor could be that Brazil is the only country among those that offer an individual savings account system that makes payment contingent on the type of dismissal, thus creating incentives for collusive behavior. The penalty for unjust dismissal in Brazil may reinforce these incentives. Another possibility is that Brazilian workers may have faced particularly severe credit constraints and therefore had particularly powerful incentives to engage in collusive behavior. Yet another explanation involves the poor management of the fund, which earned negative real returns over long periods. Most likely, a combination of these factors shaped this particular effect of UI individual savings accounts in Brazil. Therefore, it may be incorrect to assume that this type of collusion would disappear if, for instance, the fund were made accessible to the worker upon any type of separation. Moreover, some of these problems might have different effects in different countries; for instance, credit constraints may generate sufficient political pressure to induce the government to allow additional withdrawals for reasons other than unemployment, as happened in Peru.

Transitioning from a system of severance pay to a system of individual accounts is relatively easy in terms of the administrative infrastructure, as the Panama case shows. However, such a transition can create an issue that has received some attention in the literature on UISAs; namely, the effect on wages. In particular, it creates the possibility that workers and firms will negotiate lower wages to compensate for the distortionary effects of severance pay regulation. (This was not possible under the traditional system, because of the firm's moral hazard problem.) Kugler (2005) finds evidence of this phenomenon. At the same time, her results suggest that the insurance role of the new severance payment system is very limited and that the individual account system has important effects in increasing turnover rates.

The UISA systems that exist in Latin America may increase the flexibility of the labor market without imposing the high administrative costs and creating the moral hazard problems of traditional unemployment insurance systems. However, individual case studies show that these systems can pose problems of their own. One of the most serious problems is that they do not seem to be a good source of unemployment protection in the presence of severe liquidity constraints or deficient financial management.

Conclusion

This chapter provides an overview and assessment of the basic features of UISAs in Latin America. Unemployment insurance savings accounts offer an alternative to traditional systems of unemployment insurance—one that seems particularly suitable for developing countries. Their main potential advantages are as follows:

- UISAs might reduce the moral hazard problems associated with the traditional systems, both on the part of the worker and on the part of the firm. If the systems are well designed, they can provide adequate incentives for workers to return to work and for firms to comply with payments for dismissal.

- UISAs have the potential to promote flexibility in the labor market by facilitating worker mobility and job matching.

- A system of individual accounts is, in principle, less expensive to implement than unemployment insurance. In addition, the transitions from most of the actual systems of severance payment seem relatively easy in terms of infrastructure.

A major caveat is that it is not yet well understood whether these programs will provide adequate income protection. Evidence suggests that this form of income protection for the unemployed should be complemented with other forms of insurance.

The main conclusion from this study is that UISAs seem particularly well suited for developing economies and economies in transition, but assessment of their effects will require country-specific studies. A key lesson learned from this examination of UISAs in Latin America is that any assessment requires country-specific analysis. Even though the model implemented in most countries is basically the same—namely, unemployment insurance premiums regularly deposited into individual accounts—it is difficult to extract general conclusions regarding the consequences for labor markets. This difficulty may be due to small differences in implementation, but it may also be due to the idiosyncrasies of individual countries.

Future country-specific research should take note of the particular political and institutional environment of each country studied. The goal is to understand whether differences in the outcomes of UISAs across countries are due to differences in program design and implementation or differences in the economies and institutions of these countries. Individual country studies may enable us to identify general patterns. In addition, despite researchers' efforts, data are not very comparable across countries, which makes country-specific research more effective than cross-country studies.

One of the most pressing matters for research is the ability of UISAs to provide adequate income protection. For countries in which the informal or "underground" economy is abnormally large, particular attention should be paid to the effects of UISAs on the creation of formal employment and to the potential for the fund administrators to extract rents from employers or employees. Other matters—such as ascertaining whether UISAs are contributing to increasing inequality by eliminating the role of social insurance in protecting against unemployment risk—might be more relevant for other countries. In any of these cases, researchers should consider the alternative income protection programs that are available in each country.

Additionally, the labor market effects of implementing UISAs should be more thoroughly examined. Particularly important, although by its nature a difficult task, is understanding the effects of UISAs on the informal economy. The problem of collusive behavior between firms and workers to reduce wages should also be considered.

One of the objectives of this chapter is to summarize the basic features of UISA systems and examine evidence related to the performance of these arrangements. This type of assessment can help identify desirable directions for reform, but political constraints often make it difficult to move in the desired directions, even when there is general agreement on the problems associated with the current system.

Overall, UISAs have the potential to overcome some of the worst features of traditional systems of unemployment protection—reducing moral hazard, lowering administrative costs (with respect to unemployment insurance), reducing firing costs, and avoiding firms' liquidity issues with respect to severance payments. Theoretically, they are also likely to promote formal labor markets. However, the system needs to be upgraded with additional features if it is to provide adequate coverage, and this may limit its advantages. The overall effect of UISAs depends on a vast array of country-specific characteristics and program parameters, and assessing or evaluating the performance of UISAs will require individualized studies in the context of each country.

Notes

1. The effects of labor market regulation on various aspects of employment and unemployment in Latin America have been studied by Barros and Corseuil (2004), MacIsaac and Rama (2000), Marquez and Pagés (1998), Mondino and Montoya (2000), and Saavedra and Torero (2004).

2. See Blanchard and Tirole (2008), Blondal and Pearson (1995), and Heckman and Pagés (2000).

3. See Vodopivec (2004).

4. See Parsons (2011a, 2011b) for a discussion of the differences between UISAs and severance pay income protection systems for workers who are permanently separated from their jobs.

5. For an overview of severance pay systems around the world and in Latin America, see Holzmann and others (2011) and Jaramillo and Saavedra (2005).

6. This is the case in Brazil—see Camargo (2002).

7. Peru, Decreto de Urgencia 67-2002 (to repay loans guaranteed with CTS) and Decreto de Urgencia 19-2002 (to increase domestic demand).

8. See Barros, Corseuil, and Bahia (1999) for a complete account of these constitutional changes to labor regulations.

9. Temporary workers get a contribution of 2 percent. The severance penalty for dismissal for unjust cause is waived for temporary employees.

10. Indirect dismissal refers to a court request initiated by the employee to be dismissed from his or her job because of breach of the labor contract.

11. Term or temporary workers do not have to make personal contributions. The employer will cover 3 percent of the remuneration. These workers will withdraw all funds at the end of the contract.

12. In August 2008, a new law modified the unemployment fund to increase coverage and introduce more flexibility in requisites to access the funds. The new law also allows more flexibility in the administration of the funds, with a view to increasing return on investments (see Berstein, Fajnzylber, and Gana 2011).

13. After a waiting period of 90 days, these workers can access a common unemployment fund if they have made a minimum of 60 nonconsecutive contributions to the SGO.

14. CTS deposits to the banking system rose by 3 percent over 2007, while deposits to municipal savings cooperatives rose by 80 percent (Association Peruana de Consumidores y Usuarios, Boletin de Noticias, August 29, 2008, http://www.aspec.org.pe).

15. Banks pay, on average, 4.5 percent (on accounts held in soles) and 2.29 percent (on accounts held in U.S. dollars), whereas savings cooperatives pay 11 percent and 4.5 percent, respectively (*La Republica*, August 29, 2008, http://www.larepublica.com.pe/content/view/220336/484).

16. Unemployment insurance in Uruguay covers employees from the private sector who have been formally employed for at least 6 months during the 12 months before becoming unemployed. For workers who receive daily or hourly wages, the formula is 150 percent of these wages or six months' minimum wages during the period. Qualified unemployed workers receive 50 percent of the average monthly wages over the previous six months for a maximum period of six months. Refusal of available work without legitimate cause ends unemployment assistance.

17. One should be careful when discussing the welfare effects of unemployment insurance programs in general, as they can have distortive effects on the distribution of employment (Montenegro and Pagés 2007).

18. The firm dismisses the worker, granting him or her access to the funds, and the worker renounces the penalty. This type of collusive behavior has become more difficult to engage in with the creation of additional penalties for firms in the case of dismissal without just cause, because the penalties must be paid into a common pool and thus cannot be "returned" by the employee.

References and Other Resources

Acevedo, G., P. Eskenazi, and C. Pagés. 2006. "Unemployment Insurance in Chile: A New Model of Income Support for Unemployed Workers." Social Protection Discussion Paper No. 612, World Bank, Washington, DC.

Amadeo, E. J, and J. M. Camargo. 1993. "Labor Legislation and Institutional Aspects of the Brazilian Labor Market." *Labour* 7 (1, Spring): 157–80.

Argentina, Decreto Ley 17.258/67.

Asociacion Colombiana de Administradoras de fondos de Pensiones y Cesantia. 2001/2002. Boletin Asofondos num. 28. http://www.asofondos.org.co.

Barros, R., and C. Corseuil. 2004. "The Impact of Regulations on Brazilian Labor Market Performance." In *Law and Employment: Lessons from Latin American and the Caribbean*, ed. James Heckman and Carmen Pagés, 273–350. Chicago: University of Chicago Press.

Barros, R., C. Corseuil, and M. Bahia. 1999. "Labor Market Regulations and the Duration of Employment in Brazil." Texto para Discussão n 676, Instiduto de Pesquisa Economica Aplicada, Rio de Janeiro.

Barros, R., C. Corseuil, and M. N. Foguel. 2001. "Os Incentivos Adversos e a Focalização dos Progamas de Proteção ao Trabalhador no Brasil." Texto para Discussão n 784, Instiduto de Pesquisa Economica Aplicada, Rio de Janeiro.

Barros, R., C. Corseuil, and G. Gonzaga. 1999. "Labor Market Regulation and the Demand for Labour in Brazil." Texto para Discussão n 656, Instiduto de Pesquisa Economica Aplicada, Rio de Janeiro.

Berstein, S., E. Fajnzylber, and P. Gana. 2011. "The New Chilean Unemployment Insurance System: Combining Individual Accounts and Redistribution in an Emerging Economy." Chapter 9, this volume.

Blanchard, O. J., and Tirole, J. 2008. "The Joint Design of Unemployment Insurance and Employment Protection: A First Pass." *Journal of the European Economic Association* 6 (1): 45–77

Blondal, G., and M. Pearson. 1995. "Unemployment and Other Non-employment Benefits." *Oxford Economic Review of Economic Policy* 11 (1): 136–69.

Brazil, Lei n5.107 de 13/09/66.

Camargo, J. M. 2002. "Fake Contracts: Justice and Labour Contracts in Brazil." In *Making Brazil's Labour Market Work for Everyone*, ed. F. G. Carneiro, I. Gill, R. P. Barros, and A. Blom. World Bank/IPEA.

Carneiro, F. G. 2003. "A Poverty Profile and Functional Aspects of the Brazilian Labor Market." Draft. Economic Commission for Latin America and the Caribbean, UK Department for International Development.

Colombia, Ley 50 de 1990.

Cortazar, R. 2001. "Unemployment Insurance Systems for Latin America." In *Labor Market Policies in Canada and Latin America: Challenges of the New Millennium*, ed. Albert Berry, 97–107. Boston/Dordrecht/London: Kluwer Academic Publishers.

DeMarco, G., and Rofman, R. 1998. "Supervising Mandatory Funded Pension Systems: Issues and Challenges." Social Protection Discussion Paper 9817, World Bank, Washington, DC.

Ecuador, Ley del Seguro Social Obligatorio 2001-55, Noviembre 2001.

Feldstein, M., and D. Altman. 2007. "Unemployment Insurance Savings Accounts." *Tax Policy and the Economy* 21: 35–63.

Gill, I. S., E. Haindl, C. E. Montenegro, and C. N. Sapelli. 2002. "Dealing with Employment Instability in Chile." In *Crafting Labor Policy: Techniques and Lessons from Latin America*, ed. I. S. Gill, C. E. Montenegro, and D. Domeland, 191–214. Washington, DC: World Bank; New York: Oxford University Press.

Grosh, M. E., and P. Glewwe. 1995. "A Guide to Living Standards Measurement Study Surveys and Their Data Sets." Living Standards Measurement Survey Working Paper 120, World Bank, Washington, DC.

Heckman, J., and C. Pagés. 2000. "The Cost of Job Security Regulation: Evidence from Latin American Labor Markets." NBER Working Paper 7773, National Bureau of Economic Research, Cambridge, MA.

Holzmann Robert, Yann Pouget, Milan Vodopivec, and Michael Weber. 2011. "Severance Pay Programs around the World: History, Rationale, Status, and Reforms." Chapter 2, this volume.

Hopenhayn, H. 2001. "Labor Market Policies and Employment Duration: The Effects of Labor Market Reform in Argentina." Research Network Working Paper R-407, Inter-American Development Bank, Washington, DC.

IDB (Inter-American Development Bank). 1996. *Economic and Social Progress in Latin America. 1996 Report*. Special Section: Making Social Services Work. Washington, DC: IDB.

Jaramillo, M., and J. Saavedra. 2005. "Severance Payment Program in Latin America." *Empirica* 32 (3–4): 275–307.

Kugler, Adriana D. 2005. "Wage-Shifting Effects of Severance Payments Savings Accounts in Columbia." *Journal of Public Economics* 89: 487–500.

Lipsett, B. 1999. "Supporting Workers in Transition: Income Support Programs for the Unemployed in Brazil and Argentina." Paper prepared for Gordon Betcherman, Social Protection Group, World Bank, Washington, DC.

Lozoya, N. 1996. "The Economics of the Informal Sector: A Simple Model and Some Empirical Evidence from Latin America." *Carnegie-Rochester Conference Series on Public Policy* 45: 129–62.

MacIsaac, D., and M. Rama. 1997. "Determinants of Hourly Earnings in Ecuador: The Role of Labor Market Regulation." *Journal of Labor Economics* 15 (3): 136–65.

———. 2000. "Mandatory Severance Payment in Peru: An Assessment of Its Coverage and Effects Using Panel Data." Draft paper for the World Bank, Washington, DC.

Marquez, G., and C. Pagés. 1998. "Ties That Bind: Employment Protection and Labor Market Outcomes in Latin America." Working Paper 373, Inter-American Development Bank, Washington, DC.

Mazza, J. 1999. "Unemployment Insurance: Case Studies and Lessons for Latin America and the Caribbean." RE2/S02 Technical Study, Inter-American Development Bank, Washington, DC.

Mondino, G., and S. Montoya. 2000. "The Effects of Labor Market Regulations on Employment Decisions by Firms: Empirical Evidence for Argentina." Research Network Working Paper R-391, Inter-American Development Bank, Washington, DC.

Montenegro, Claudio E., and Carmen Pagés. 2007. "Job Security and the Age-Composition of Employment: Evidence from Chile." *Estudios de Economia* 34 (2): 109–39.

Oliveira, F., K. Beltrão, M. T. Pasinato, and M. Ferreira. 1999. "A Rentabilidade do FGTS." Texto para Discussão n 637, Instituto de Pesquisa Economica Aplicada, Rio de Janeiro.

Orszag J. M., P. R. Orszag, D. J. Snower, and J. E. Stiglitz. 1999. "The Impact of Individual Accounts: Piecemeal vs. Comprehensive Approaches." Paper presented at the Annual Bank Conference on Development Economics, World Bank, Washington, DC, April 29.

Panama, Codigo del Trabajo.

Parsons, Donald O. 2011a. "Severance Pay Mandates: Firing Costs, Hiring Costs, and Firm Avoidance Behaviors." Draft, George Washington University, Washington, DC.

———. 2011b. "The Firing Cost Implications of Alternative Severance Pay Designs." Chapter 4, this volume.

Peru, Decreto de Urgencia n. 019-2002.

Peru, Decreto de Urgencia n. 026-2002.

Peru, Decreto Supremo n 001-97-TR Texto Unico Ordenado de la Ley de Compensacion por Tiempo de Servicios. (01/03/97).

Programa de Estadisticas y Estudios Laborales. 2002. "La Duracion de las Relaciones de Trabajo: la Permanencia en los Empleos y la Rotacion Laboral." *Boletin de Economia Laboral* 21: 3–28.

Reyes Hartley, G., J. C. van Ours, and M. Vodopivec. Forthcoming. "Incentive Effects of Unemployment Insurance Savings Accounts: Evidence from Chile." *Labour Economics*.

Saavedra, J., and M. Torero. 2004. "Labor Market Reforms and Their Impact over Formal Labor Demand and Job Market Turnover: The Case of Peru." In *Law and Employment: Lessons from Latin American and the Caribbean*, ed. James Heckman and Carmen Pagés (131–82). Chicago: University of Chicago Press.

Seguro de Cesantia Chileno. 2002. "Informe Tecnico." Superintendencia de Administradora Fondos de Pensiones, Santiago de Chile.

Sehnbruch, K. 2004. "Privatised Unemployment Insurance: Can Chile's New Unemployment Insurance Scheme Serve as a Model for other Developing Countries?" Working Paper Series 12, Center for Latin American Studies, University of California at Berkeley.

Stiglitz, J., and J. Yun. 2006. "Integration of Unemployment Insurance with Pension through an Individual Account." *Journal of Public Economics* 89 (11–12): 2037–67.

Venezuela, Ley Organica del Trabajo. 1997. Caracas.

Vodopivec, M. 2010. "How Viable Are Unemployment Insurance Savings Accounts: Simulation Results for Slovenia." *Comparative Economic Studies* 52: 225–47.

———. 2004. *Income Support Systems for the Unemployed: Issues and Options.* World Bank Regional and Sectoral Studies Series, Washington, DC: World Bank.

Vroman, W. 2002. "Unemployment Protection in Chile: Draft Report." Report for the World Bank, Washington, DC.

CHAPTER 8

The Welfare Consequences of Alternative Designs of Unemployment Insurance Savings Accounts

Hugo Hopenhayn and Juan Carlos Hatchondo

Introduction

The purpose of this chapter is to examine the performance of alternative designs for the provision of unemployment insurance. As in the case of many other programs of social insurance, there has been growing concern about the adverse incentives that might be generated. Recent proposals for replacing standard forms of unemployment insurance with a system of savings accounts have received considerable attention, and they are being implemented in several countries. This chapter evaluates the performance of alternative implementations of a system of unemployment insurance savings accounts (UISAs).

In a system of UISAs, workers have individual accounts to which they contribute in periods of employment and from which they withdraw funds when they are unemployed. Interest payments are credited or debited to this account, depending on its balance. If a balance exists at retirement age, it is available to the worker; if the worker dies, the balance goes to the heirs. If the balance is negative at retirement or death, most systems forgive the debt. A typical design specifies the following features: rates of contribution to the system, limits and rules for withdrawing funds, limits on total liability, and the interest rate applied to balances.

The advantage of UISAs is that incentives are considerably improved when the cost of becoming or remaining unemployed is internalized. This is particularly true for workers with lower unemployment risk who are more likely to retire with positive balances. The more likely this system results in positive final balances, the higher are the incentives for keeping a job or searching for employment.

Feldstein and Altman (1998) consider the introduction of UISAs in the U.S. economy as a replacement for the current system. In their proposal, rates of contribution are roughly 4 percent of wages (with some variation depending on income level), the limits and rules for withdrawing funds are identical to those in the current system (roughly, a replacement rate of 0.5 during the unemployment spell, with a time limit of six months) and rates of interest are market rates for alternative funds.[1] Negative balances are forgiven at retirement age. Using a panel study of income dynamics, Feldstein and Altman simulate this system over a 25-year historic period. Most workers' accounts still have positive

---

Thanks to Jan van Ours and Milan Vodopivec for comments and suggestions.

balances at the end of their unemployment period. About half the benefit dollars go to persons whose accounts are negative at the end of their working life; less than a third go to persons who also have negative account balances when they are unemployed. Because these simulations take as given the behavior of workers under the current system, the relative importance of negative balances is exaggerated. So this proposal seems to go far in terms of providing better incentives.

Vodopivec and Rejec (2001) apply and extend this accounting procedure to the Estonian labor market. Assuming a 3 percent contribution rate and a 0.6 replacement rate, their calculations show that only 9–17 percent of workers end their working life with negative cumulative balances in their UISA accounts, although 30–45 percent experience a negative balance at least once during their working life. These accounting exercises are very interesting, but they show only one side of the story. To evaluate the UISA system and its alternative designs, the accounting analysis needs to be viewed side-by-side with the welfare implications. This chapter complements Vodopivec and Rejec by providing welfare calculations of alternative UISA designs for the Estonian labor market. In contrast to the accounting analysis, this requires a structural approach and extensive modeling.

A simple life-cycle model captures in a stylized way some of the key trade-offs faced by workers. In their working lives, people transit between unemployment and employment according to an exogenously given Markov process, which is calibrated to the Estonian data. When they are employed, workers receive a fixed salary and incur a cost of effort. Moral hazard arises because a worker may decide to quit a job or not accept a job offer. This is what workers would choose to do if they were perfectly insured. The model assumes that workers can save at the market rate but cannot borrow. Savings occur in the model for precautionary motives and for life-cycle considerations, to complement retirement benefits.

The first part of the chapter compares three systems. The baseline system is one of full insurance with no moral hazard, in which the government can monitor job offers and enforce employment. This system provides workers with constant consumption independent of their employment state. The transfers are financed by a wage tax that equates the expected discounted revenues to transfers on a worker-by-worker basis. This system provides the worker with perfect consumption smoothing without a change in wealth; it represents an increase in utility equivalent to raising the worker's wage by 2–16 percent, depending on the degree of risk aversion. The utility provided to the worker under this full-insurance scheme is used as a benchmark to evaluate the performance of the two alternative designs.

The first alternative design is a liquidity provision system that gives the worker an initial lump-sum payment to be used for self-insurance. Holding the utility of the worker at the benchmark level, the cost of this system is equivalent to a 1.2–6 percent wage subsidy. The cost decreases considerably with the initial wealth of workers. The second alternative design is an optimal unemployment insurance (OUI) system that extends the method described in Hopenhayn and Nicolini (1997) to the case of repeated unemployment spells. (This extension is discussed in annex A.) The OUI system is the lowest-cost alternative that gives the worker the utility of full insurance while providing incentives for employment in all periods of the working life. The cost of this system is extremely low—in most cases, equivalent to less than a 1 percent wage subsidy. These results suggest the limited value of monitoring and enforcement, which is required for a full-insurance scheme.

The second part of the chapter considers the performance of alternative designs of UISAs. These designs involve different tax rates and replacement rates, a lower limit on balances, and a maximum contribution level (upper limit on balances). A set of parameter values corresponds to the ones analyzed in Vodopivec and Rejec (2001). The baseline case involves a 3 percent tax rate, 0.6 replacement rate, and lower and upper limits on the account equivalent to six months' wages. The alternatives consider variations in tax rates (1 percent and 5 percent) and replacement rates (0.3 and 0.9), and the extension of benefits to 12 months' wages. To analyze the alternatives, it is necessary to find the corresponding points in cost and utility space. There is obviously a trade-off between the cost savings for the government and the welfare of the worker. The analysis suggests that a moderate amount of insurance can be cost-effective.

The analysis also considers an alternative set of parameters involving considerably higher tax rates (10 percent and 20 percent) and a higher contribution limit (18 months). The designs with the lowest replacement rate (0.3) and the highest tax rates appear to be the most cost-effective. Moreover, for moderate degrees of relative risk aversion, the performance of the corresponding UISAs is remarkably close to the full-insurance benchmark and OUI. A comparison of the baseline design with the two alternatives shows that, in the environment considered, UISAs should be financed with fairly high tax rates if a balanced budget is an important consideration.

The chapter is organized as follows. The next section describes the economic environment used in the analysis. The life-cycle model and the method used for assigning parameter values are discussed. Then the full-insurance benchmark, lump-sum scheme, and OUI system are analyzed, as are alternative UISA designs.

Economic Environment

The worker can be either active or retired. All workers are assumed to be active until compulsory retirement, which occurs at the exogenously given age T. After retirement, workers live for an extra D years and receive security benefits b_r, which are independent of their work history. Active workers can be employed (E) or unemployed (U). For simplicity, the model assumes that all jobs are identical, with constant wage w and disutility e. While unemployed, the worker receives an offer each period with probability p. Jobs can terminate exogenously (through a layoff) or because the worker quits. Layoffs occur each period with probability λ, which is assumed to be independent of the length of employment. Moral hazard arises for two reasons: (1) quits cannot be distinguished from layoffs, and (2) job offers are not observed unless the unemployed worker takes the job. In each period, the worker's utility depends on consumption c and the corresponding effort level e, according to the utility function $u(c) - e$. Lifetime utility is given by:

$$E\left(\sum_{t=0}^{\infty} \beta^t \left(u(c_t) - e_t\right)\right),$$

where β is the discount factor. An employed worker gets wage w_i, which depends only on the characteristics of the worker and not on the job.

The Life-Cycle Model

This section describes the consumption/savings/employment decisions of a representative worker. Assume that workers can save at the market rate r but cannot borrow, so assets must be nonnegative at all times. The gross interest rate $R = 1+r$. Employed workers choose whether to keep their jobs or quit. Unemployed workers decide whether to accept a job offer or not. The optimal decisions of the worker are derived by first considering the situation of a retired worker and then considering that of an active worker.

RETIRED WORKER

In every period, a retired worker chooses consumption as a function of his wealth (k) and the social security benefit received (b_r). If $W_t(k)$ represents the expected discounted utility of a retired worker with capital k in period t of his lifetime, the corresponding decision problem is given by

$$W_t(k) = \underset{k'}{Max}\left\{u(c) + \beta W_{t+1}(k')\right\} \quad \text{for } t = T, T+1,\dots,T+D$$

$$s.t. \quad c + k' = Rk + b_r \text{ and}$$

$$k' \ge 0,$$

where k_0 are the assets carried into the following period, which cannot be less than a lower bound $k = 0$, representing a borrowing limit; R is the gross interest rate; and β is the subjective discount factor. Since the worker dies $D+1$ periods after retirement and there is no bequest motive, $W_{T+D+1}(k) = 0$. Obviously, a worker will not leave any assets at the end of his life. Given the specification of preferences, the optimal decision rule followed by the retired worker is quite simple. Letting k_T denote the assets at the time of retirement, the worker will exhaust these savings by consuming a constant amount per period, including benefits received.

ACTIVE WORKERS

The decision problems of employed and unemployed workers are defined value functions $V_t^e(k)$ and $V_t^u(k)$, which correspond to the lifetime expected discounted utilities of a worker who starts the period with a job offer and a worker who starts the period with no job offer, respectively. In both cases, the worker has assets k. A worker with a job offer first decides whether to quit or stay in the job and next, contingent on the employment decision, how much to consume and how much to save. If the worker remains employed, the consumption/savings decision is given by

$$V_t^e(k,w) = \underset{k'}{Max}\left\{u(c) - e + \beta\left[\lambda V_{t+1}^e(k',w) + (1-\lambda)V_{t+1}^u(k',w)\right]\right\}$$

$$s.t. \quad c + k' = (Rk + w)(1 - \tau)$$

$$k' \ge 0$$

$$\text{for } t = 1, 2, \dots T-1,$$

where $V_T^e(k,w) = W_T(k)$, given compulsory retirement at age T. If the worker chooses to quit, the consumption/savings decision is given by

$$V_t^e(k,w) = \underset{k'}{Max}\left\{u(c) + \beta\left[\rho V_{t+1}^e(k',w) + (1-\rho)V_{t+1}^u(k',w)\right]\right\}$$

$$s.t. \quad c + k' = Rk(1-\tau)$$

$$k' \geq 0$$

for $t = 1,2,...T-1$.

Notice that the only differences between the two are the deduction of the disutility of effort in the first case and the corresponding probabilities of employment for the following period. The worker picks the alternative with a higher value. Intuitively, one might expect this decision to depend on the level of wealth: A sufficiently rich worker will choose not to work, while a poor worker will always stay or take a job.

A worker with no job offer simply chooses how much to consume and how much to save, according to the following problem:

$$V_t^u(k,w) = \underset{k'}{Max}\left\{u(c) + \beta\left[\rho V_{t+1}^e(k',w) + (1-\rho)V_{t+1}^u(k',w)\right]\right\}$$

$$s.t. \quad c + k' = Rk(1-\tau)$$

$$k' \geq 0$$

for $t = 1,2,...T-1$.

In this simplified model, there is only one source of risk: unemployment risk. As usual, consumption will be an increasing function of asset holdings. Workers save for precautionary purposes and, if retirement benefits are low relative to employment income, they also save for retirement.

Calibration

The procedure used to assign parameter values to the model was as follows:
1. The utility function follows the standard formulation used in the literature: a time-separable utility function with period utility given by

$$u(c) = -\frac{exp(-\alpha c)}{\alpha},$$

where α is the (constant) coefficient of absolute risk aversion.
2. The time period is six months. The discount factor is set at $\beta = 0.98$, reflecting an annual discount rate of 4 percent. This is also the value assigned to the interest rate.
3. The rate of job termination λ is assigned using the 1997–99 employment surveys discussed below. The mean value is 15 percent. The rate of arrival of job offers for unemployed workers was set at 60 percent, according to the estimates given below.
4. Results are provided for workers at three different wage levels: low, medium, and high: high salary = 2.5 times medium salary = 2.85 times low salary. The difference in wages turns out to be important for two reasons:

(a) A constant absolute risk-aversion utility function in consumption is assumed. The employment and unemployment process implies a lottery with values of zero if unemployed and equal to the wage if employed. Higher wages mean higher risk, so the risk premiums for higher salaried workers are higher.

(b) Total utility is $u(c)-e$, which is separable in consumption and effort. Because of the concavity of the utility function, it is harder to provide incentives to workers with higher salaries, because they can choose to work for a while and then enjoy leisure.

The coefficient of absolute risk aversion α was chosen so that the high-wage worker has a coefficient of relative risk aversion equal to 4. This is actually quite high relative to the typical values used in the macro literature. The implied coefficients of relative risk aversion for the other types of workers are considerably smaller: 1.6 for a medium-wage worker and 0.5 for a low-wage worker.

Transition estimates measure the probability of transition from employment to unemployment and vice versa, using pooled information from the 1997–99 employment surveys conducted in Estonia (Vodopevic and Rejec 2001). The surveys included questions on current employment status, past employment and unemployment, wages, schooling, and demographic characteristics. Information is provided for each employment and unemployment period. The following method was used to estimate transition probabilities from employment to unemployment; a similar procedure was used to estimate the flow from unemployment to employment.

For given initial dates $t \in$ jan 97, oct 97, jan 98, and oct 98, all workers were considered who were employed at time t and unemployed for at least a month during the following six months. This defines a transition to unemployment. These employment periods are pooled to estimate a logistic regression for the probability of transition to unemployment. The following covariates were used in this regression: months of elapsed duration in the job at time t (durat_e); dummies for high school studies (SEC), for specialized high school education (SSEC), and for university education (UNIVER); and dummies for the dates of employment considered (d97o, d98j, and d98o.)

Table 8.1 provides some basic statistics for the covariates and dependent variable. Of all employed workers, approximately 11.5 percent transition to unemployment in the six-month period. Estimates of the logistic model are given in table 8.2. The significant explanatory variables are duration and dummies for university and jan 98. According to the mean estimates, duration of one month decreases the probability of job termination by 0.3 percent. For example, a worker with 2 years of experience has a 7 percent lower probability of termination; a worker with 5 years of experience, 16.5 percent lower; and a worker with 10 years of experience, 30 percent lower. The probability for the baseline case (d97j, duration = 0, and elementary education) is 22 percent, almost twice the unconditional mean. Based on these estimates, an intermediate value of 15 percent was used for the calibration.

Tables 8.1 and 8.2 also show the corresponding results for estimates of transition from unemployment to employment. The mean transition probability is around 46 percent (monthly rate of approximately 6.5 percent), while average duration of unemployment is 19 months (which would correspond to an average monthly rate of only 5 percent). Turning to the estimates of logistic regression, the significant explanatory variables

TABLE 8.1 **Mean of Variables for Transitions from Employment to Unemployment and Vice Versa**

Variable label	E to U	U to E
d97j	0.83	0.59
d97o	0.79	0.57
d98j	0.75	0.62
d98o	0.40	0.20
SEC	0.43	0.44
SSEC	0.24	0.22
UNIVER	0.12	0.08
NO JOB LOSS	0.89	n.a.
Durat_u	n.a.	19.30
Continue employed	n.a.	0.54

SOURCE: Authors' calculations using Estonia Household employment surveys, 1997–99.

NOTE: There are 1,657 observations of transitions from employment to unemployment and 360 observations of transitions from unemployment to employment. The variable Durat_u (measured in months) takes a minimum value of 1 and a maximum value of 94, and has a standard deviation of 20.
E = employment; U = unemployment; n.a. = not applicable.

TABLE 8.2 **Maximum Likelihood Estimates of Logistic Regressions**

	Transitions from E to U		Transitions from U to E	
	Estimate	S.D.	Estimate	S.D.
Intercept	−1.272 (***)	0.201	0.641 (**)	0.273
Durat_E	−0.003 (***)	0.001	n.a.	n.a.
d97o	−0.202	0.231	0.258	0.281
d98j	−0.666 (***)	0.237	−1.036 (***)	0.267
d98o	0.278	0.176	−0.936 (***)	0.327
SEC	0.063	0.188	0.374	0.267
SSEC	−0.096	0.221	0.424	0.317
UNIVER	−0.662 (**)	0.323	1.399 (***)	0.497
Durat_u	n.a.	n.a.	−0.028 (***)	0.008

SOURCE: Authors' calculations using Estonia Household employment surveys, 1997–99.

NOTE: S.D. = standard deviation; E = employment; U = unemployment; ** coefficient is significantly different from 0 with probability up to 5%; *** coefficient is significantly different from 0 with probability up to 1%; n.a. = not applicable.

are unemployment duration, dummy 8 for university education, and dummies for jan 98 and october 98 (both negative, implying a rate of exit that is less than half the rate of jan 97). Exit rates are four times higher for the highly educated. As usual in unemployment duration studies, there is considerable negative duration dependence. A worker who has been unemployed for a year has a 30 percent lower probability of getting a job compared with a worker who has just become unemployed. The probability of exit from unemployment for the baseline case (d97j, duration = 0, and elementary education) is 65 percent. Given the considerably higher risk of unemployment found for later periods, the probability of exit was set slightly lower, at 60 percent.

Benchmark and Other Mechanisms

This section develops a full-insurance benchmark and compares two alternative designs: pure liquidity provision and optimal unemployment insurance. The benchmark is used later to evaluate the performance of alternative designs of UISAs.

FULL-INSURANCE BENCHMARK

This benchmark abstracts from incentive considerations. Workers are provided with full insurance, obtaining the same level of consumption whether employed or not, until retirement. After that, they receive the constant benefit b_r. Transfers received while unemployed are financed with a wage tax that in expected term matches the present value of these transfers for each type of worker. For any positive value of effort e while employed, full insurance is not incentive-compatible—the consequences of such a scheme would be disastrous, as no worker would choose to be employed. Only in the extreme case where effort cost is zero do incentive problems disappear and does full insurance becomes incentive-compatible. However, it is a useful benchmark in gauging the costs of alternative unemployment insurance designs. The full-insurance case can also be interpreted as a situation in which job offers can be monitored and the unemployment insurance authority enforces the policy of no quitting and always accepting jobs when unemployed.

LIQUIDITY PROVISION

By definition, this full-insurance scheme has zero cost. Table 8.3 shows the cost of two alternative mechanisms. In all cases, these costs are calculated keeping the utility of workers at the same level as that provided by the full-insurance scheme. The costs are expressed as the equivalent percentage increase in wages for a given type of worker. The first alternative mechanism is a lump-sum transfer scheme. The idea is simple. At the beginning of the working life, a worker is given a lump-sum transfer. This increases the worker's initial wealth, which is then used to self-insure against unemployment risk. Formally, the lump-sum transfer is the compensating variation in initial wealth that the worker needs if full insurance is not offered. Calculations are shown for low-, medium-, and high-wage workers, and workers are considered with different initial wealth measured in years-of-wage-equivalence (0, 4, 10, and 20). As an example, for a low-wage worker with no initial wealth, the cost of the lump-sum scheme is equivalent to giving this worker a 1.19 percent wage subsidy in each period of employment.

TABLE 8.3 **Cost of Insurance Mechanisms for Different Transfer Schemes and Different Costs of Exerting Effort (e)** (per period % increase in wages)

Initial wealth	Lump-sum transfer	Optimal unemployment insurance									
		$e=10$	$e=20$	$e=30$	$e=40$	$e=50$	$e=60$	$e=70$	$e=80$	$e=90$	$e=100$
Low-wage worker											
0	1.19	−0.03	−0.03	−0.01	0.02	0.05	0.10	0.16	0.20	0.22	0.15
4	0.52	−0.03	−0.03	−0.01	0.03	0.07	0.12	0.18	0.25	0.30	0.32
10	0.31	−0.03	−0.02	0.00	0.04	0.09	0.16	0.23	0.31	0.40	0.48
20	0.25	−0.02	−0.01	0.02	0.07	0.14	0.22	0.32	0.43	0.55	0.68
Medium-wage worker											
0	3.14	0.00	0.01	0.04	0.08	0.14	0.20	0.28	0.37	0.45	0.53
4	1.85	0.00	0.02	0.06	0.11	0.18	0.27	0.37	0.47	0.56	0.64
10	1.33	0.00	0.03	0.09	0.18	0.29	0.41	0.53	0.63	0.71	0.78
20	1.16	0.01	0.08	0.21	0.38	0.56	0.70	0.77	0.80	0.80	0.81
High-wage worker											
0	5.97	0.07	0.31	0.55	0.68	1.01	n.a.	n.a.	n.a.	n.a.	n.a.
4	3.64	0.17	0.69	1.36	n.a.	n.a.	n.a.	n.a.	n.a.	n.a.	n.a.
10	2.39	0.78	n.a.	n.a.	n.a.	n.a.	n.a.	n.a.	n.a.	n.a.	n.a.
20	2.07%	n.a.	n.a.	n.a.	n.a.	n.a.	n.a.	n.a.	n.a.	n.a.	n.a.

SOURCE: Authors' calculations.

NOTE: Initial wealth is measured in terms of years of wages; n.a. = not applicable.

The cost of the lump-sum scheme decreases with the level of wealth of the worker and increases with the wage. Both of these qualitative features have intuitive explanations. Workers with higher wealth value the full-insurance scheme less, because they are in a better position to self-insure against unemployment risk. Thus, the compensating variation in initial wealth is smaller. With regard to the effect of higher wages, if one assumes that all workers have the same utility function of constant absolute risk aversion, the process of unemployment and employment implies a lottery on income, with values either equal to zero (unemployment) or to the wage (employment). The risk in this lottery increases with the worker's wage. Thus, workers with higher wages value full insurance most, which explains the higher compensating variations.

The cost of this lump-sum transfer scheme is actually not that high, ranging from an equivalent 0.25 percent increase in salary for a low-wage worker with the highest wealth to 6 percent for a high-wage worker with zero wealth.

OPTIMAL UNEMPLOYMENT INSURANCE

The remaining columns in table 8.3 give the cost of the OUI described in annex A. Transfers (and taxes) to workers are calculated to provide the highest level of insurance compatible with giving incentives to the workers to keep their jobs or to accept job offers. This may not be feasible in some cases, particularly for workers with high wealth if the cost of effort is high. Incentives are more costly to provide the higher cost of effort. Though this is a key parameter, there is no straightforward way to set its value. For that reason, this model varies the value from $e = 0$ to $e = 100$ and computes the OUI for each case. How high are these costs of effort? Table 8.4 expresses the cost in terms of an equivalent percentage wage reduction: The percentage values given in the three columns can be interpreted as the wage reduction a worker is willing to accept to avoid the corresponding cost of effort. For example, an effort cost $e = 10$ represents an equivalent 12 percent reduction in the wage of a low-wage worker; an effort cost $e = 50$, an equivalent 52 percent reduction; and an effort cost $e = 100$, an equivalent 93 percent reduction. The range of effort costs chosen is quite comprehensive.

For each level of effort, the cost is calculated for an OUI that provides the worker with an initial utility (net of effort costs) equal to the utility he or she would get under the full-insurance scheme with perfect monitoring and enforcement. As shown in table 8.3, the cost of the OUI is very small in virtually all cases.[2] The largest cost is 1.36 percent for a high-wage worker with initial wealth equivalent to four years of wages and effort cost $e = 30$. (The blank spaces for the high-wage worker correspond to situations in which providing incentives to accept jobs in every period is not feasible.) As expected, the cost of the OUI rises with effort cost, the worker's initial wealth, and the worker's wage. The low cost of the OUI suggests that if incentives are properly designed, the gains from monitoring and enforcement can be quite small.

Unemployment Insurance Savings Accounts

This section compares the performance of alternative specifications for UISAs. The results complement those of Vodopivec and Rejec (2001), who calculated the cash flow performance of UISAs with different parameter values. Welfare calculations are also provided here that can be useful in cost-benefit analysis of UISAs. A UISA is defined by the following parameters:

1. Tax rate applied to monthly wages until the savings account reaches a certain limit
2. Replacement rate with an upper bound (replacement rate x wage) that the worker can extract per period
3. Lower limit on account (a negative value expressed in months of benefits)
4. Contribution limit expressed in months of salary—when the account is at this limit, taxes are zero

The assumption is that interest accrues on the balance of the account (if positive) or is charged at the market rate r (if negative). Once the negative balance reaches its lower limit, no interest is charged. The cost of effort $e = 50$, which is equivalent to a 40–60 percent reduction in wages (table 8.4).

OPTIMAL DECISIONS

The inclusion of a UISA introduces some changes in the life-cycle model described in this chapter. An unemployed worker will draw as much as possible from the UISA; that is, up to the replacement value of the wage, unless the lower limit on balances is reached. The reason for this is quite simple: When the balance reaches its lower bound, no further interest is charged. In contrast, if the worker moves funds from the UISA to personal savings, interest accrues continuously. This leads to an obvious arbitrage opportunity

TABLE 8.4 **Cost of Effort**

	Equivalent wage reduction (%)		
Effort	Low-wage worker	Medium-wage worker	High-wage worker
10	12	10	27
20	22	19	40
30	33	26	49
40	42	33	55
50	52	40	60
60	61	45	64
70	69	51	68
80	77	56	71
90	85	60	74
100	93	65	76

SOURCE: Authors' calculations.

NOTE: Each cell represents the wage reduction (in %) a worker is willing to accept to avoid the corresponding cost of effort.

and justifies the need for a limit on extractions. Thus, the decision rule concerning UISA funds is trivial. The existence of a positive balance in the UISA displaces some private savings and thus modifies the optimal private savings rule. The higher the tax rate, the larger this displacement. Finally, employment is somewhat discouraged if the worker has a negative balance in the UISA account. In particular, a worker with a high level of personal savings and a negative account balance may choose to quit his or her job and not accept new job offers.

RESULTS

The first set of results corresponds to the parameter values considered by Vodopivec and Rejec (2001). The alternatives considered are shown in table 8.5. Figures 8.1–8.3 and table 8.5 give the results of the analysis. The figures describe Pareto sets on the space of utility to the agent and cost savings to the government. In all cases, workers start the first period of their working life unemployed and with zero wealth. The origin corresponds to autarky, which obviously represents zero cost for the government. The x-axis is normalized in the following way. For each of the above scenarios, the certainty equivalent (per period) consumption is calculated, that is, the constant level of consumption that gives the worker the same expected discounted utility as obtained in the scenario considered. The certainty equivalent under autarky is subtracted from this value. Since workers are always better off under a UISA than in autarky, the numbers are always positive. On the y-axis, the cost to the government is normalized to a per period basis. There is no need to subtract the corresponding value for autarky, as it is zero by definition. With this normalization, the value to consumers and cost savings to the government are expressed in comparable units. A 45 degree line is included, which represents constant total utility (additional certainty equivalent consumption minus cost to the government), as in autarky. This line is drawn for comparison purposes only. Two special points correspond to full insurance with budget balance and optimal unemployment insurance. In the case of low and medium salary, these two points are so close that they completely overlap in the graphic. The remaining

TABLE 8.5 **Marginal Cost of Effort in the Baseline Case**

		Policy				
Tax rate (%)	Replacement ratio	Months of benefits	Maximum months' contributions	Low wage	Medium wage	High wage
3	0.6	6	6	0.68	0.58	0.41
1	0.6	6	6	0.72	0.65	0.48
5	0.6	6	6	0.60	0.50	0.33
3	0.3	6	6	0.42	0.33	0.26
3	0.9	6	6	0.76	0.68	0.43
3	0.6	12	6	0.68	0.59	0.41

SOURCE: Authors' calculations.

NOTE: Marginal cost is measured as the cost of each program divided by the increase in equivalent consumption. The most cost-effective program is highlighted.

FIGURE 8.1 **Pareto Set, low salary, baseline case**

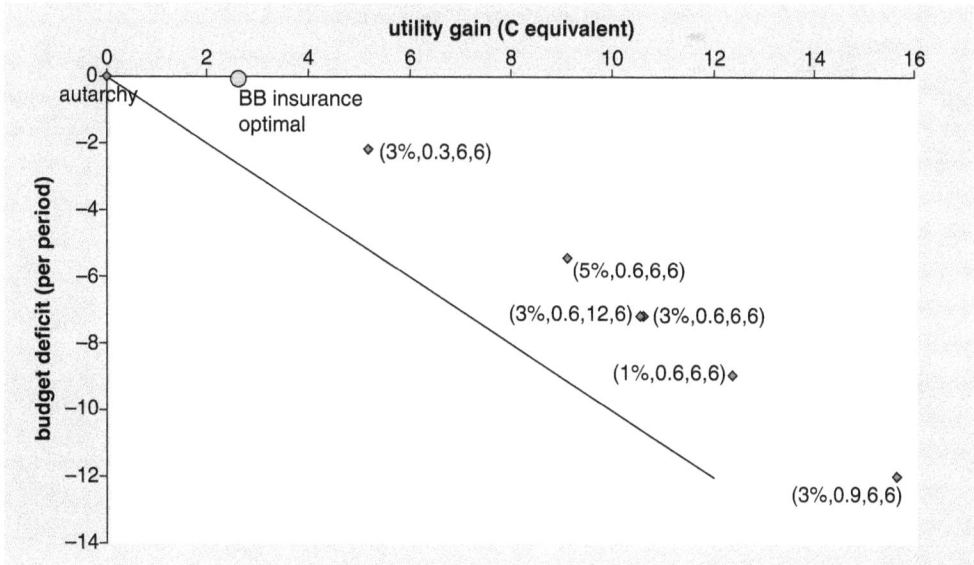

SOURCE: Authors' calculations.

FIGURE 8.2 **Pareto Set, medium salary, baseline case**

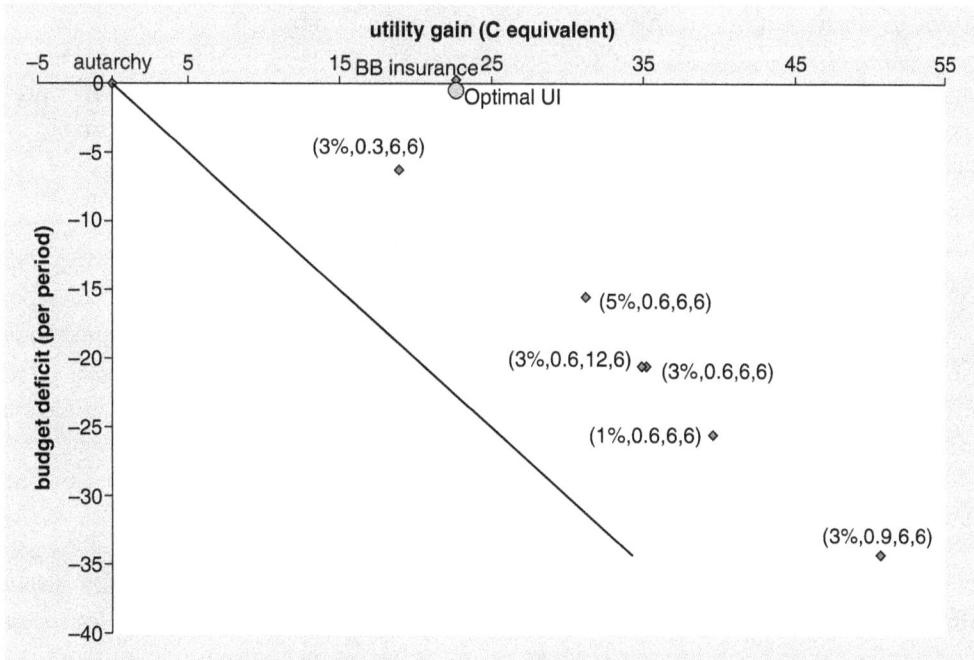

SOURCE: Authors' calculations.

FIGURE 8.3 **Pareto Set, high salary, baseline case**

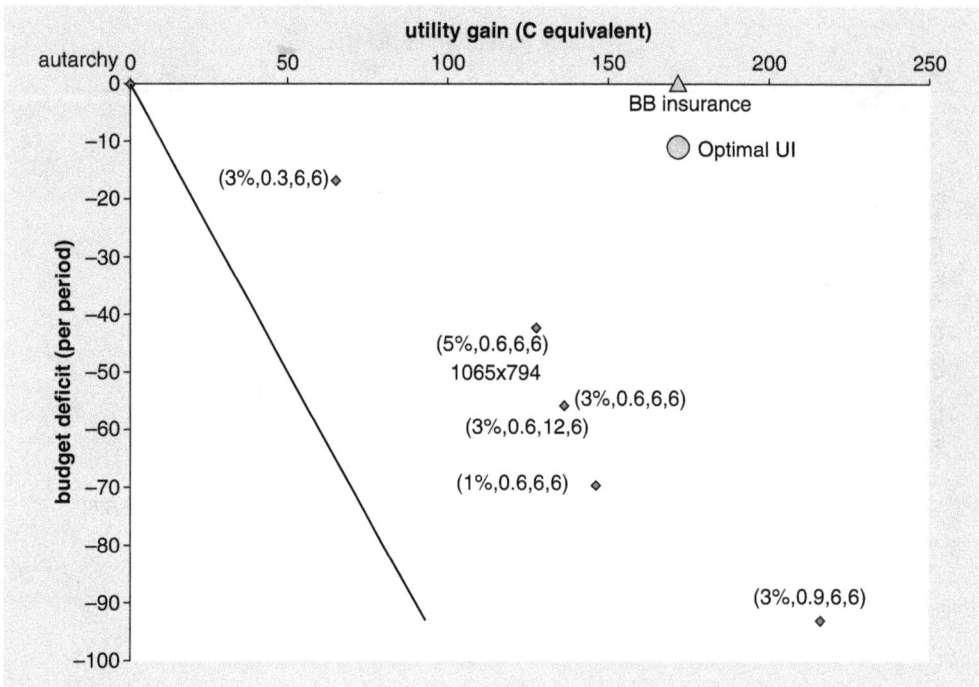

SOURCE: Authors' calculations.

points correspond to alternative UISA formulations. The numbers in brackets correspond to the parameters of the UISA design in the order given in table 8.5.

Most of the UISA designs lie close to the 45 degree line, and none is Pareto-dominated by others. Compared with autarky, the full-insurance and OUI schemes provide moderate increases in welfare for low- and medium-wage workers and a substantially larger gain for high-wage workers.

The points in the graph can be ordered according to their corresponding slopes, measured in absolute values from the origin. These slopes give the per unit cost of providing extra utility with the corresponding design (marginal cost). Slopes that are lower in absolute value correspond to a larger sum c equivalent utility + government cost savings, a particular measure of total welfare. The results are shown in table 8.5. The marginal costs of the alternative designs are not that different, although the lowest marginal cost in all cases corresponds to the case with a low replacement rate. This suggests that a moderate amount of insurance can be cost-effective.

A second set of parameter values is evaluated in figures 8.4–8.6 and table 8.6. The alternatives considered are shown in table 8.6.

The results differ somewhat according to the worker's wage. For low-wage workers, all points except those corresponding to the lowest replacement rate lie below the 45 degree line. Given the constant absolute risk-aversion utility function, low-wage workers have the lowest degree of relative risk aversion. So these results suggest that high

FIGURE 8.4 **Pareto Set, low salary**

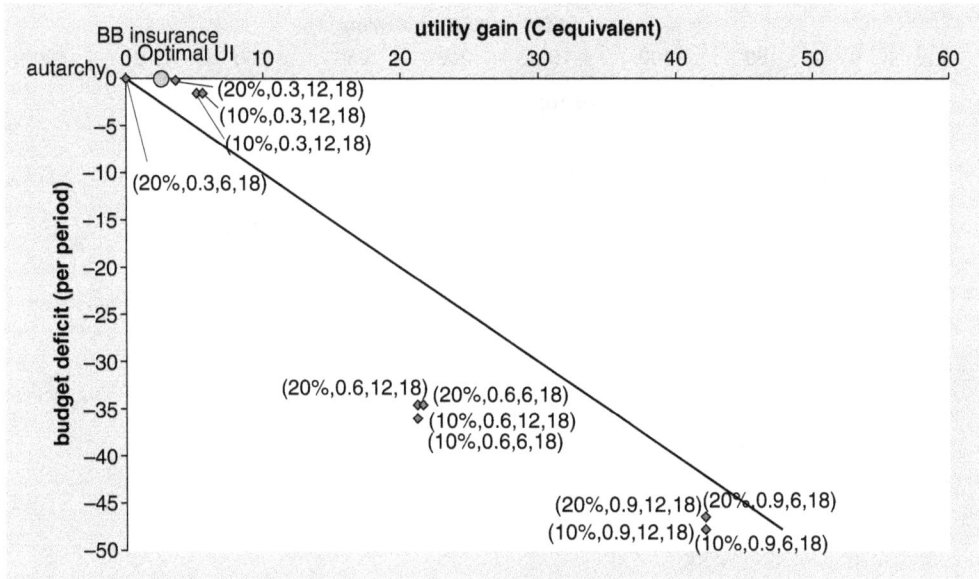

SOURCE: Authors' calculations.

FIGURE 8.5 **Pareto Set, medium salary**

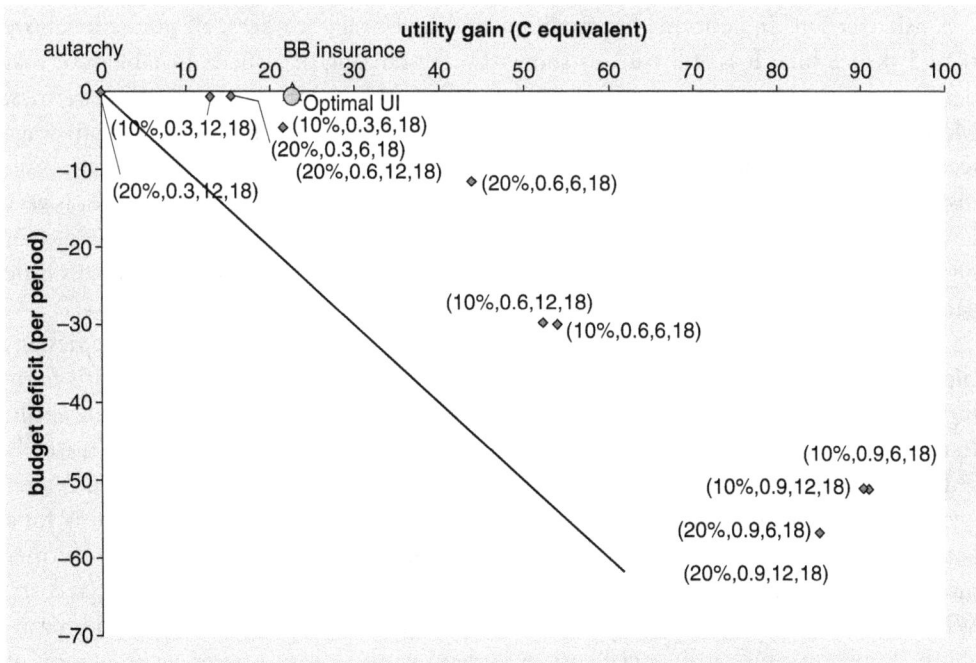

SOURCE: Authors' calculations.

FIGURE 8.6 **Pareto Set, high salary**

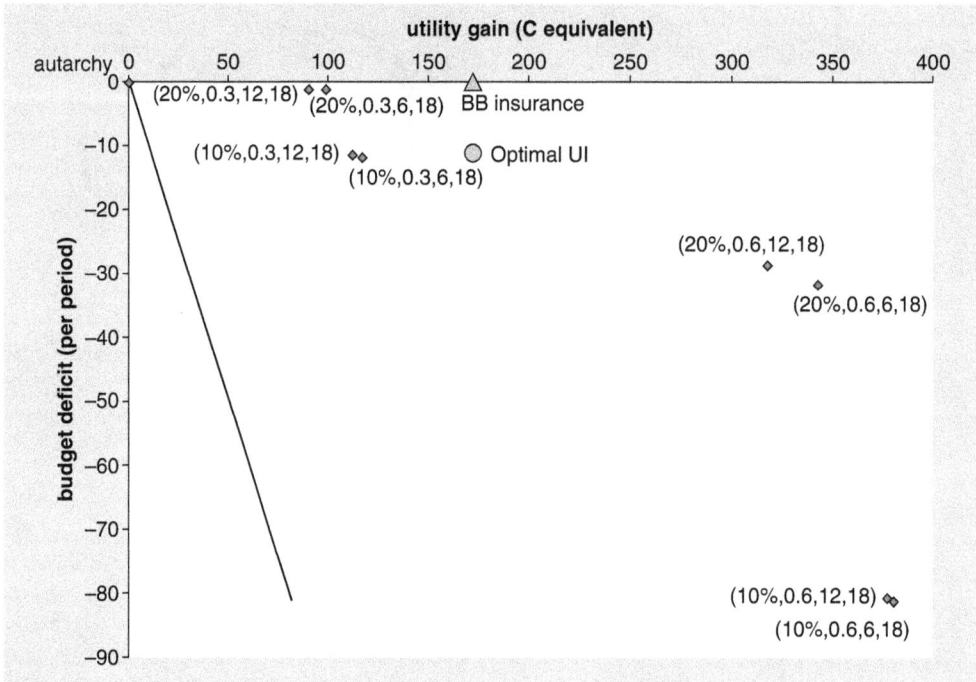

SOURCE: Authors' calculations.

replacement rates may not be very cost-effective for workers with a low degree of relative risk aversion. In contrast, for medium- and high-wage workers, all points lie above the 45 degree line. It is still true, as shown by the ranking of policies in table 8.6, that designs with the lowest replacement rates have the lowest marginal cost for all categories. Moreover, an examination of figures 8.4 and 8.5 indicates that for low- and medium-wage workers, the performance of the corresponding UISAs is remarkably close to the full-insurance benchmark and the OUI. In the case of high-wage workers, marginal cost is very low for all alternatives, suggesting that higher replacement rates may be worthwhile for higher degrees of relative risk aversion. A close examination of the figures also reveals little gain from extending the duration of benefits from 6 to 12 months.

A comparison of the baseline designs (figures 8.1–8.3) with the alternative designs (figures 8.4–8.6) shows that in this environment UISAs should be financed with fairly high tax rates if budget balance is a consideration. Several factors contribute to this result. In this chapter's analysis, workers start out unemployed and with no wealth, so in the early stages of the working life the balance of the individual accounts is always negative. Moreover, unemployment duration is high, so the lower bound on the accounts is binding for a large number of young workers. Recall that when the lower bound is reached, no further interest is charged on the account and the government bears all the ensuing financial costs. With higher replacement rates, this lower bound is reached faster and with higher probability, implying a higher financial cost. A higher tax rate leads to faster accumulation of positive balances, thus reducing the probability of reaching this lower bound. Again, this explains the better performance of the high-tax alternatives. These observations suggest an alternative design not considered in this chapter, in which two lower bounds could

TABLE 8.6 **Marginal Cost of Effort for Alternative Designs**

Tax rate (%)	Replacement ratio	Months of benefits	Maximum months' contributions	Low wage	Medium wage	High wage
		Policy				
10	0.3	6	18	0.28	0.21	0.10
10	0.3	12	18	0.29	0.22	0.10
10	0.6	6	18	1.70	0.55	0.21
10	0.6	12	18	1.70	0.57	0.21
10	0.9	6	18	1.13	0.56	—
10	0.9	12	18	1.13	0.57	—
20	0.3	6	18	0.05	0.03	0.01
20	0.3	12	18	0.06	0.04	0.02
20	0.6	6	18	1.59	0.26	0.09
20	0.6	12	18	1.62	0.27	0.09
20	0.9	6	18	1.10	0.67	—
20	0.9	12	18	1.10	0.74	—

SOURCE: Authors' calculations.

NOTE: The most cost-effective program designs are highlighted; — = not available.

be defined. When the first lower bound is reached, the worker may not withdraw any more funds from the account, but interest continues accumulating until the second lower bound is reached.

Conclusions

The design of better institutions for social insurance is a great challenge. One of the most critical considerations is the trade-off between insurance and incentives. In the case of a UISA, the costs and benefits depend on the specified rules and the behavioral response of the workers involved. The methodology in this chapter can be used to eliminate some specifications that may be Pareto-dominated and to provide the policy maker with a better picture of the trade-offs between government costs and worker welfare.

The analysis suggests some preliminary conclusions in this regard. First, the model shows that a properly designed system can be a good substitute for full insurance, which requires very costly monitoring and enforcement. Second, for moderate degrees of risk aversion, a cost-effective system can be created with moderate replacement rates and relatively high levels of worker contributions to their accounts. The analysis suggests some additional features that could be considered in the design of UISAs. In particular, some special treatment might be worthwhile in the early stages of a worker's life, when unemployment risk is higher and the worker is more likely to reach the lower limits of the account. The associated high financial costs to the government can be mitigated by accumulating interest even beyond the point at which the worker is not allowed to withdraw more funds from the account. This should be balanced against the incentives that non-participants in the labor market may have to enter the labor market, withdraw funds from their accounts, and exit the labor market once the lower limit is reached.

Annex A

This annex develops a simple model of employment and unemployment choice to derive some general properties of optimal unemployment insurance design.

An employment match is defined by a pair $x = (w,e)$, where w is the wage paid to the worker and e is the effort or disutility of work. For unemployed workers, $x = (0,0)$ is normalized. For simplicity, the assumption is that all jobs are identical, with constant wage w and disutility e. While unemployed, the worker receives an offer each period with probability p. Jobs can terminate, either exogenously (a layoff) or because the worker quits. Layoffs occur each period with probability λ, which for simplicity is assumed to be independent of the length of employment. Moral hazard arises for two reasons: (1) quits cannot be distinguished from layoffs, and (2) job offers are not observed unless the unemployed worker takes the job.

In each period, the worker's utility depends on consumption c and the corresponding effort level e, according to the utility function $u(c,e)$. Lifetime utility is given by

$$E\left(\sum_{t=0}^{\infty}\beta^t u(c_t,e_t)\right),$$

where β is the discount factor. A recursive representation of the optimal unemployment insurance design is considered. Let $C(V)$ denote the expected discounted cost (budget) of providing a level of discounted utility V to an unemployed worker and $W(V)$ the same for an employed worker. The dynamic program that defines these functions are given by

$$C(V) = \underset{c,V^u,V^e}{Min}\left\{c - w + \beta\rho W(V^e) + \beta(1-\rho)C(V^u)\right\}$$

$$s.t. \quad V = u(c) + \beta\rho V^e + \beta(1-\rho)V^u$$

$$V^e \geq V^u.$$

$$W(V) = \underset{c,V^u,V^e}{Min}\left\{c + \beta\lambda W(V^e) + \beta(1-\lambda)C(V^u)\right\}$$

$$s.t. \quad V = u(c) + \beta\lambda V^e + \beta(1-\lambda)V^u$$

$$V^e \geq V^u.$$

Notice the similarity between the two problems. The only difference is in the arrival probabilities and the disutility of effort at work.

The first-order conditions for the above problems are given by

$$C'(V) = u'(c)^{-1} = \gamma$$

$$W'(V^e) = \gamma + \mu$$

$$C'(V^u) = \gamma - \frac{\mu}{1-\rho}$$

for the case of unemployment, where γ is the multiplier of the value evolution equation and μ is the multiplier of the incentive compatibility constraint. It follows that

$$V^e = V^u < V.$$

For an employed worker, the equations are very similar:

$$W'(V) = u'(c)^{-1} = \gamma$$

$$W'(V^e) = \gamma + \mu$$

$$C'(V^u) = \gamma - \frac{\mu}{1 - \rho}$$

and it follows that

$$V < V^e = V^u.$$

Letting c, c^e, c^u correspond to consumption in the current period and in the following periods, if employed or unemployed, respectively:

$$\frac{1}{u'(c_t)} = \theta \frac{1}{u'(c_{t+1}^e)} + (1 - \theta)\theta \frac{1}{u'(c_{t+1}^u)},$$

where $\theta = p$ if the worker is currently unemployed and $\theta = \lambda$ otherwise. For all initial states, consumption falls if the worker is unemployed in the following period and increases if he or she is employed.

Notes

1. Replacement rates are expressed as numbers in this chapter (for example, 0.5 stands for the replacement rate of 50 percent).

2. Negative costs result from numerical errors. These are cases where the cost of the OUI is virtually zero.

References

Feldstein, M., and Daniel Altman. 1998. "Unemployment Insurance Savings Accounts." NBER Working Paper 6860, National Bureau of Economic Research, Cambridge, MA.

Hopenhayn, H., and Juan Pablo Nicolini. 1997. "Optimal Unemployment Insurance." *Journal of Political Economy* 105 (2): 412–38.

Vodopivec, M., and Thomas Rejec. 2001. "How Viable Is the System of Unemployment Insurance Savings Accounts? Simulation Results for Estonia." Unpublished manuscript, World Bank Human Development Network, World Bank, Washington, DC.

CHAPTER 9

The New Chilean Unemployment Insurance System: Combining Individual Accounts and Redistribution in an Emerging Economy

Solange Berstein, Eduardo Fajnzylber, and Pamela Gana

Introduction

Developing countries are often faced with the necessity of protecting their workers in times of unemployment, but they face challenges in designing unemployment insurance schemes because of the extent of their informal labor markets and their limited capacity to monitor labor market regulations.

The standard risk-pooling arrangements often present in developed economies are similar to regular insurance contracts, in which all workers pay a similar premium in exchange for a certain schedule of unemployment benefits. Resources are transferred across individuals and time from good to bad states. When sustainable, this type of arrangement provides an effective form of protection for most workers. However, when risk is heterogeneous, inefficient redistribution can occur from stable workers or economic sectors to high-turnover workers or industries. In addition, the pooled nature of resources can introduce moral hazard by reducing workers' incentives to keep their current jobs or look for new ones.

Another common protection scheme—severance payment regulations—implies an additional level of job protection by providing benefits and raising firing costs, but at the cost of potentially affecting labor reallocation, as employers' incentives to hire and fire workers are affected by the relative firing costs for workers with different tenures. In addition, coverage is often limited to certain types of firms or contractual arrangements and to specific causes of separation.

Pure unemployment insurance savings account programs (UISAs), on the other hand, are relatively neutral in terms of employers' hiring and firing decisions (Parsons 2010). Furthermore, the absence of redistribution makes the individual fully internalize the cost of his or her job search decisions, reducing the potential for moral hazard.[1] The direct link between benefits and the length of the contribution period, however, reduces the effectiveness of UISAs in providing appropriate protection against income loss associated

Eduardo Fajnzylber is currently assistant professor at the Universidad Adolfo Ibáñez. The chapter was written while he worked at the Chilean Pensions Supervisor.

with unemployment: Workers with short contribution periods receive insufficient benefits, while those with long contribution periods tend to be overcovered.[2]

In 2002, Chile introduced an innovative scheme that combines the effectiveness of risk pooling with the incentive neutrality of individual accounts. Under this scheme, dependent workers contribute to two funds: a fund formed by individual accounts (IAs) and a solidarity fund (SF). In case of unemployment, they can access their own savings and, under some circumstances, complement them with resources provided by the SF to finance five monthly payments, defined as a percentage of their previous wage. In this context, the initial use of one's own funds can be seen as a deductible for accessing the SF, thus providing a self-policing mechanism.

The experience during the first eight years of the Chilean scheme was very positive in terms of coverage and sustainability, and the accumulated knowledge allowed the government to introduce a set of reforms in May 2009 that improved benefits by facilitating access to the pooled component. Current welfare evaluations (Berstein, Contreras, and Benvin 2008) suggest that, in general, most workers value the program, even if the extent of their valuation depends on their level of risk aversion and their labor history: Risk-averse, older, and more educated workers will benefit more from the consumption-smoothing properties, whereas Chilean women are less likely to benefit from the program, because their labor histories are more interrupted than those of men. Evaluations of the system in terms of labor incentives are under way.

This chapter provides a brief discussion of the literature relating to unemployment insurance (UI) design considerations; a description of the system; an evaluation of its recent performance (in terms of coverage, adequacy, and sustainability); and a description of the 2009 reform and offers some suggestions for countries that are considering introducing similar schemes.

Description of the System

An unemployment insurance program was introduced in Chile in 2002 in response to the high level of unemployment after the Asian crisis, when the unemployment rate was near 10 percent in winter 2009.[3] The system was designed to provide private employees with a source of income in case of unemployment and requires them to make contributions to both an IA and an SF. Benefits are defined according to the type of labor contract and certain eligibility conditions. Management of the system for a period of 10 years was assigned to a private firm, AFC (Administradora de Fondos de Cesantia de Chile), which was selected through a public auction.[4] The investment performance of this manager is measured against a benchmark. The government, through the Chilean Pension Supervisor, is responsible for regulating and supervising the system, which ensures that private companies comply with standards for the provision of this insurance.

An interesting feature of the Chilean scheme is the existence of the Users Committee. The committee is made up of three workers' representatives and three employers' representatives; it is headed by a president who must be an academic from a Chilean university. The main responsibilities of this committee are to be familiar with the criteria implemented by the private administrator in managing the fund and to compile an annual report on the performance of the unemployment insurance system. These reports have been an important source of ideas for improving the system and designing the reforms implemented in 2009 and 2010.

To assess the system, it is important to understand some general characteristics of the Chilean labor market. By 2009, Chile had a population of around 17 million people, with around 13 million aged 15 years or older. In this group, 55.9 percent participate in the labor force, either working or actively searching for a job—6.5 million are actually working. Labor force participation shows a gap between men and women: 70.1 percent and 41.9 percent, respectively. The unemployment rate for the decade ending in 2009 ranged 7–9 percent, reaching its highest level (10.8 percent) in mid-2009 as a result of the global economic crisis.

This section describes the main characteristics of the system before the 2009 reform.[5] The reform is covered later in the chapter.

TARGET AND COVERED POPULATION

The target group for the UI program is employees over 18 years of age whose contracts are governed by the labor code, with the exception of workers with apprenticeship contracts, workers in domestic service, and pensioners (except for those receiving partial disability pensions).[6] Self-employed workers and those employed in the public sector are excluded from the program. Workers in the informal sector are neither targeted nor covered by the system because they are not enrolled for unemployment insurance.

Workers with contracts before October 2, 2002, have been incorporated into the system gradually, either when they start a new employment relationship or via voluntary enrollment. All parties to labor contracts that started after the law went into effect must enroll in the program. Figure 9.1 shows the breakdown of these groups for the 6.5 million Chilean workers. The target population (57.2 percent of all workers) is employees of private firms. Despite the gradual introduction of the system, by 2009 it had already reached 78.6 percent of the target population.

CONTRIBUTIONS, ELIGIBILITY, AND BENEFIT STRUCTURE

The unemployment insurance law stipulates different forms of funding, depending on the type of labor contract (figures 9.2, 9.3). For workers with an open-ended contract, the contribution into the UISA consists of 0.6 percent of covered wages paid by the worker and 1.6 percent paid by the employer, with a covered wage ceiling of 97.1 Unidades de Fomento (UF).[7] The employer must also pay a contribution of 0.8 percent of the worker's taxable income to the solidarity fund. The total contribution rate is therefore 3.0 percent of covered wages. In addition, the government contributes an annual amount equivalent to approximately US$15.7 million to the solidarity fund.

The employer's contribution to the worker's individual account—plus the accumulated yield and minus the commissions paid to the administrator—is deductible from the amount payable as severance payment, to which the worker is entitled if the termination of the employment relationship falls under article 161 of the labor code. In practice, this means that the employer annually prefunds in the individual unemployment account about 20 percent of the compensation it would have to pay the worker if the contract were terminated.

FIGURE 9.1 **Unemployment Insurance Coverage**
(second quarter 2009)

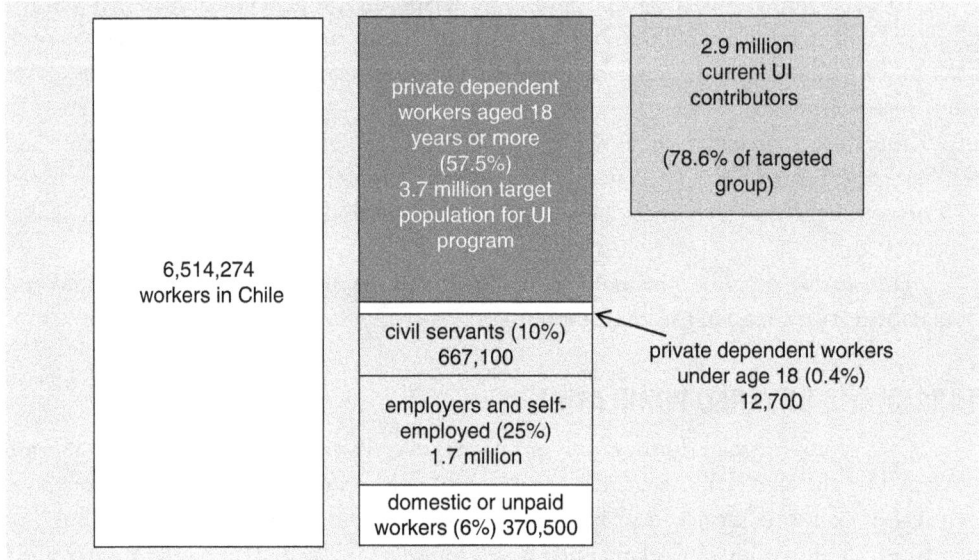

SOURCE: Authors.

The obligation to contribute into the UISA ceases for both worker and employer after 11 years of an employment relationship. The employer's obligation to contribute to the SF continues until the termination of the employment relationship.

In the case of workers with fixed-term contracts, the contribution is paid by the employer at a rate of 3 percent of taxable income with a ceiling of 97.1 UF; it is paid entirely into the worker's individual unemployment account. The worker can access these funds in case of unemployment, regardless of the cause of termination.

Monetary benefits from the program, as in the case of funding, depend on the type of contract.

Access to the Individual Account: Workers with Open-Ended Contracts

Workers with open-ended contracts can opt for benefits funded by the IA and may also have access to the SF if they meet the requirements. If the employment relationship is terminated, the worker can access the funds accumulated in his or her IA, provided at least 12 monthly contributions have been made, either continuously or noncontinuously. Benefits charged exclusively to the IA are not controlled by the reason for termination; they constitute an unconditional benefit.

The number of monthly payments is determined by the number of years and the fraction over six months that the worker has contributed, with a maximum of five payments. If the worker contributed between 12 and 18 months, the benefit is delivered in a single withdrawal, equivalent to the balance accumulated in the IA. The number of payments increases by one for every 12 months in excess of 18 (for example, two payments for 19–30 monthly contributions, and so on). In the case of workers who are entitled to more

FIGURE 9.2 **Unemployment Insurance Program: Workers with Open-Ended Contracts**

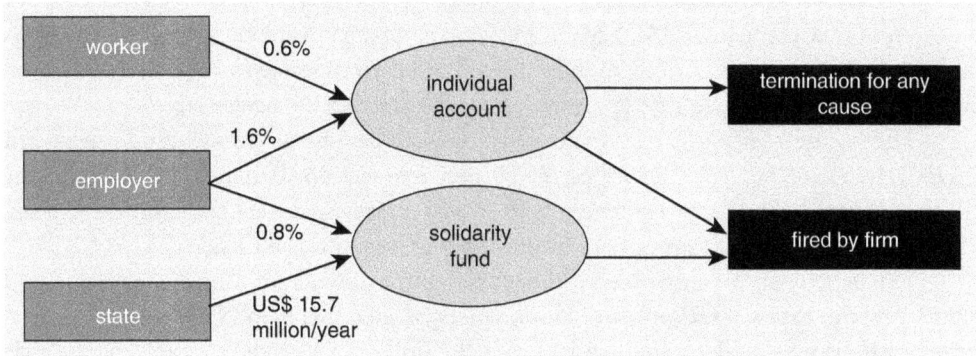

SOURCE: Authors.

FIGURE 9.3 **Unemployment Insurance Program: Workers with Fixed-Term Contracts**

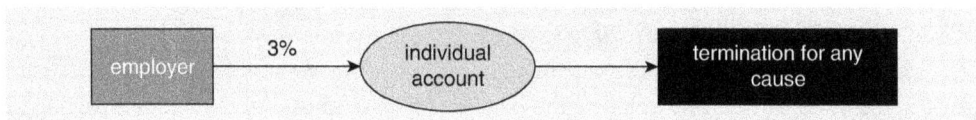

SOURCE: Authors.

than one payment, the amount of the first payment is determined by dividing the balance in the individual account by a factor.[8]

The amounts of the second, third, and fourth withdrawals will correspond to 90 percent, 80 percent, and 70 percent of the amount of the first payment. The amount of the fifth withdrawal will correspond to the balance remaining in the IA. In this way, the worker can withdraw all the funds accumulated in the IA in each unemployment event, as long as he or she remains unemployed.

Access to the Individual Account: Workers with Fixed-Term Contracts

For workers with fixed-term contracts, the benefit consists of a one-time withdrawal of all the funds accumulated in the IA, provided they represent at least six monthly contributions (either continuous or discontinuous) since enrollment in the program or since the last benefit was paid out. The benefit is independent of the cause of termination, but the person must be unemployed to apply for it.

Access to the Solidarity Fund

The program includes a solidarity fund to help pay benefits to workers with open-ended contracts who, while fulfilling the conditions listed below, do not have sufficient resources in their IAs to fund the level of benefits established in the law.

Workers with open-ended contracts who meet the following requirements can opt to complement their savings with resources from the SF: (1) they must have registered 12 continuous monthly contributions to the SF in the period immediately before the dismissal from the time of enrollment or from the last benefit paid on their behalf; (2) the employment relationship must have ended for "unforeseeable circumstances or force majeure" or "the needs of the company";[9] (3) they must have accumulated insufficient resources in the IA to fund the SF benefit, according to the amounts and periods stated in the law; and (4) they must be unemployed when they apply and while they receive the benefit.

The worker may reject access to the SF, in which case he or she will fund the benefit exclusively out of the IA as described in the previous section. If the worker opts for the SF, the amount of the monthly benefit is fixed as a replacement rate based on the average earnings of the past 12 months, with minimum and maximum limits.[10]

The benefit can be suspended if the worker turns down a training grant offered and funded by the national training and employment service (Servicio Nacional de Capacitación y Empleo, SENCE) or unjustifiably rejects a job offer received through the municipal employment agency (Oficinas Municipales de Inserción Laboral, OMIL) in his or her neighborhood that would have provided a wage equal to or higher than 50 percent of the last wage received. To certify these requirements, beneficiaries must report to the OMIL of their choice each month. On the other hand, AFC, the unemployment fund management company, in making benefit payments, must certify that the recipients are still unemployed, as this benefit is incompatible with any paid activity.

The current law establishes a mechanism for adjusting the solidarity fund benefits in exceptional cases: If the total value of the benefits to be paid out by the SF in a particular month exceeds 20 percent of the balance accumulated in the fund, benefits are adjusted so that the total payments do not exceed that percentage.

Besides the benefits provided by the unemployment insurance system, the Chilean labor code mandates severance pay for open-ended contract workers who have been with the same employer for 12 months or longer and whose cause of dismissal is "the needs of the company." Severance pay in Chile is equal to one month's salary for each year worked with the employer, to a maximum of 11 years. The only connection between severance pay and the UI system is that the employer's contribution to the individual account is considered a way of prefunding the severance payment.

Administrative data are not available in Chile regarding the coverage of severance pay. According to information from the UI administrative database, around 17 percent of the open-contract employment relationships that ended by 2009 would have been eligible for severance pay (that is, they met the requirements for cause of dismissal and duration of employment).

Design Considerations and Reemployment Incentives

Unemployment protection is one of the most important social protection policies in any country. The main objective is consumption smoothing, which might not be accomplished by individuals themselves because of myopic behavior or the impossibility of saving in the face of liquidity constraints.

Unemployment insurance can also improve welfare, not only through risk sharing but also by increasing output in the face of risk aversion (Acemoglu and Shimer 1999). However, in the absence of government intervention, the development of an unemployment insurance market faces serious problems. Strong moral hazard and adverse selection problems, as well as difficulties dealing with correlated risks, can preclude private market provision of insurance and impose a challenge on the design of public provision. Conversely, compulsory self-insurance through saving and borrowing can have important limitations. In fact, to be effectively protected, a worker might need more savings than it is possible to accumulate given the family income. And, in the end, the worker might not become unemployed and hence might have unnecessarily reduced his family consumption. These drawbacks on private sector provision of insurance, which would add to redistribution considerations in developing countries, mean that the government has an important role to play in providing unemployment benefits.

Unemployment protection in Chile combines saving and risk pooling. In principle, risk-pooling arrangements are effective; however, where risk is heterogeneous, potentially inefficient redistribution could occur from stable workers or economic sectors to high-turnover workers or industries. In addition, the pooled nature of resources can introduce moral hazard by affecting workers' incentive to remain in their current jobs or look for new ones. The empirical evidence supports this statement.[11]

Compulsory unemployment savings accounts might substantially mitigate this moral hazard, as the absence of redistribution forces workers to fully internalize the cost of their job search decisions. However, the direct link between benefits and length of the contribution period reduces the effectiveness of UISAs in providing appropriate protection.

While it seems reasonable to assume that a combination of saving and risk pooling would create a middle ground between the two extremes, no formal theoretical model or empirical evidence supports this statement. The closest model considers individual savings accounts for unemployment from which borrowing is allowed.[12] This borrowing can be from the government or from the person's future income. If money is borrowed from the government and the debt is forgiven at retirement, this constitutes redistribution. Moreover, it can be a mechanism for intragenerational risk pooling if workers with excess savings are taxed and those with debt are not required to pay it back. However, with this type of design, moral hazard is reduced, because workers use their own savings or borrow against future income and therefore internalize the cost of unemployment. The consumption-smoothing purpose of unemployment insurance is achieved and the negative efficiency impact is minimized.

Feldstein and Altman (1998) present a model that considers mandatory savings accounts for unemployment; if the resources are not sufficient and job loss occurs, the worker can borrow from the government. If the balance is negative at retirement, the government covers the debt; a positive balance can be applied to retirement income, so redistribution is limited and there is no pooling.

However, it needs to be determined whether these types of systems (with borrowing) are viable, as they eliminate pooling.[13] Vodopivec (2008) says they are not viable if many workers lack sufficient savings to support periods of unemployment. He shows that the system in Slovenia would become unviable if the benefits were high enough, although it would be viable with moderate benefits. He analyzes the distributional effects, which are significantly smaller than those in traditional unemployment insurance. Feldstein and Altman (1998) also show that, in the United States, these effects are small.

Stiglitz and Yun (2002) develop a model in which individual savings accounts are integrated with mandatory savings accounts for retirement benefits. In this design there is no redistribution; among heterogeneous workers, a portion would experience frequent unemployment periods that would deplete their pension benefits. As in Vodopivec (2008), this arrangement might not be viable under certain circumstances, especially in economies with significant labor heterogeneity. Moreover, if workers have hyperbolic discounting, or there is large discounting, the incentives against borrowing up to the limit might be low.

In Chile, the SF provides resources for workers who meet certain requirements and have depleted their savings. This fund plays the role of an insurance component, allowing some degree of risk pooling across individuals and making the system viable. Moreover, there is some integration with the pension system, as workers can use positive IA balances at retirement to increase their pensions (although this option is voluntary). The prospect of having these funds available as a lump sum at retirement strengthens the incentive for careful use of the unemployment scheme, if we assume a low degree of discounting. Borrowing from individual pension savings to finance unemployment benefits is not allowed in Chile, because it has been shown that pension savings are relatively small to allow for the risk of reaching retirement with a negative balance in the UI account.

In the Chilean system, unemployed workers first use the savings in their IAs and then, if necessary, access the SF so individual savings can be considered a deductible for the pooled component. In the insurance literature, moral hazard is traditionally addressed through the use of deductibles. In this system, the individual internalizes at least part of the unemployment cost and therefore has less incentive to abuse the system. Additionally, the requirement to use savings first creates a waiting period. Mortensen (1977) said that the use of private savings can be seen as a substitute for a waiting period, discouraging temporary layoffs and forcing unemployed workers to use their own wealth first, which motivates them to seek reemployment.

According to the literature, a time limit is a desirable feature for an unemployment insurance scheme. Mortensen (1977) states that a time limit implies that the reservation wage declines as the worker gets closer to the benefit expiration date. He suggests that an "entitlement effect" emerges as benefits are increased; that is, an increase in UI benefits motivates unemployed workers who do not qualify for the benefit to search for a job so they will be entitled to UI benefits in the future. Additionally, a newly unemployed worker would have a higher reservation wage, while a worker who is close to the expiration date would have a lower reservation wage. In Chile, the benefit is paid for a shorter period than in many other countries: five months under normal circumstances, which can be increased to seven if the national unemployment rate is sufficiently high. A time limit also applies to use of the solidarity fund: A person may access the fund only twice in any five-year period. This limits the moral hazard by giving workers who expect to be reemployed an incentive to postpone use of the SF in case they need it in the future.

With respect to how the benefit should be paid, Shavell and Weiss (1979) support the idea of decreasing payments. Unemployment insurance can have a negative impact on job search behavior—increasing the duration of unemployment—and monitoring job search efforts is costly, so unemployment insurance should be designed to minimize the efficiency cost. Shavell and Weiss present a theoretical model that supports the hypothesis that this can be achieved through decreasing benefit payments. If there is no saving or borrowing and moral hazard exists because workers' decisions affect the probability of finding a job, the optimal benefit pattern is a decreasing one. If saving or borrowing is part of the scheme, the optimal benefit pattern is increasing, then decreasing, so that savings are spend first. The hypothesis is that workers should spend their wealth before getting the benefit; then the benefit should decrease to provide an incentive for job search.

Werning (2002) extends this model and assumes that the government has no information about workers' savings and that it can lend to unemployed workers. In this case, the optimal benefit profile might be increasing, which is consistent with Mortensen (1977), because it assumes that workers would use their savings during the first periods. In fact, Werning argues that what should be decreasing is consumption rather than the benefit provided by the system and that this might be achieved with an increasing benefit in the presence of savings. In Chile, the benefit profile might be described as zero (while the worker is accessing savings) to increasing (when the savings are depleted and the worker accesses the solidarity fund) to decreasing (because the benefit starts at 50 percent replacement rate and gradually decreases to a fifth payment of 30 percent of replacement rate).

Finally, even if monitoring is costly, it might be useful for the efficient provision of unemployment benefits. Boone and others (2007) say that the worker should be available for work and actively seeking employment, and they show that monitoring and imposing sanctions result in welfare improvements at a reasonable cost. However, other studies (for example, Van den Berg and van der Klaauw 2006), show limited or no effect from monitoring. The Chilean system includes monitoring, as well as sanctions if the person improperly rejects a job or training offer. Monitoring is handled by OMIL and entails a relatively low administrative cost.

Even though no formal model has been developed to test the Chilean design, features such as the relative integration with the pension system, the use of one's own savings as a deductible for the pooled component, the existence of time limits and decreasing benefits, and monitoring by the OMIL seem consistent with the relevant theoretical literature on insurance and social protection.

Evaluation

COVERAGE

The number of workers enrolled in the program has increased more quickly than expected, amounting to more than 6 million by June 2009.[14] This rapid growth was the result of an unexpectedly high turnover rate experienced by a large proportion of the Chilean labor force: Private workers who initiated a new contract after October 2002 were required to enroll in the program, so a high turnover rate implies a high affiliation rate.[15]

The number of contributors has followed a similar path, amounting to almost 3 million in June 2009. This means that the system covers approximately 78.6 percent of the target population, measured as the ratio between the number of contributors and the number of private wage earners over 18 years of age reported by the national statistical agency. Although the number of wage earners is also increasing over time, it is hoped that the gap between the two groups will disappear (see figure 9.4).

Fixed-term contract workers have a higher turnover rate, so they initially dominated the program in terms of participants, contributors, and beneficiaries. Over time, however,

FIGURE 9.4 **Contributors by Type of Contract and Wage Earners in the Private Sector, 2002–09** (number of contributors and number of workers)

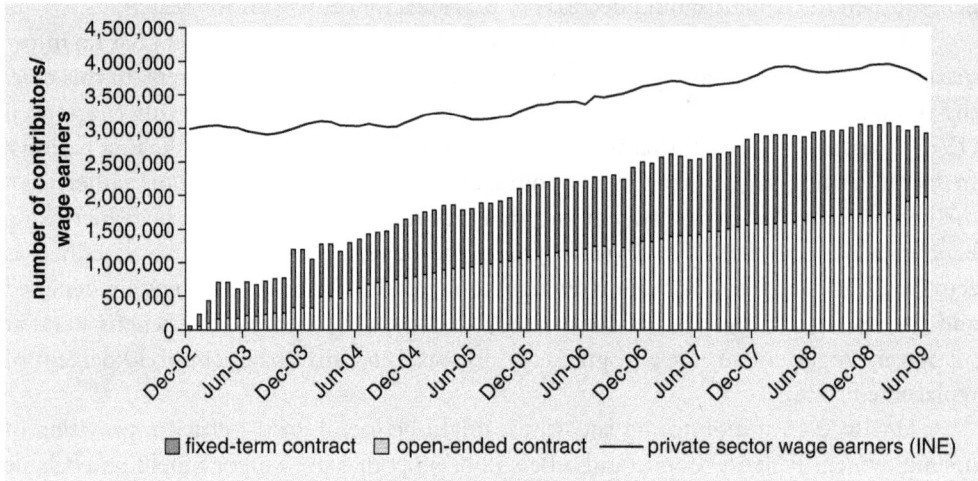

SOURCES: Chilean Pension Supervisor and National Statistical Institute (Instituto Nacional de Estadística, INE).

open-ended contract workers have been naturally selected into the program. Currently, they represent over half of all contributors: 67.6 percent as of June 2009, compared with 57.2 percent in June 2008 and 29.9 percent in June 2003. Fixed-term contract workers will continue to have a high degree of participation in the future, probably representing about a third of all private wage earners.

Most members and contributors to the unemployment insurance program are young, primarily in the 25- to 34-year age bracket. This is to be expected; many of these workers are entering the labor market for the first time and they may exhibit a high degree of job mobility, because they have not yet acquired job-specific skills. With regard to gender composition, in June 2003 women represented about 26.4 percent of all contributors; by June 2009, the percentage of women had increased to 33.6 percent, approaching the gender composition of the national labor force. The geographical distribution of contributors shows centralization in the large cities, a clear reflection of the formal payroll in the Chilean labor market.

With regard to distribution by economic sector, in June 2009 the contributors most widely represented were those working in high-turnover sectors: retail (20.1 percent); financial, real estate, business, and rental activities (18.0 percent); community, social, and personal services (15.9 percent); and construction (11.1 percent). These groups account for almost 65 percent of contributors, which is not surprising. Finally, with regard to distribution of covered wages, over 60 percent of contributors are in the low- and middle-income range, with monthly wages between US$154 and US$614.

ADEQUACY

As of June 2009, the total number of benefits granted by the unemployment insurance program was over 4.4 million, most of them paid to fixed-term contract workers. Of all benefits granted, only 148,000 were partially funded by the SF.[16]

During 2009, the average number of monthly beneficiaries was around 146,000. The number of unemployed in the same period was around 600,000; obviously, the UI system does not cover all unemployed workers. Average benefits paid depend on the source of funding (IA or SF) and on the type of contract. In absolute terms, average payments financed by the SF have consistently exceeded those from individual accounts. Among the latter group, workers with fixed-term contracts receive lower benefits than those with open-ended contracts, probably because open-ended contract workers have jobs that are more stable and long-lasting and may therefore accumulate more funds in their individual accounts. Furthermore, eligibility for withdrawing IA funds is higher for open-ended contracts (12 months) than for fixed-term contracts (6 months).

Observed replacement rates have also shown that IA payments have consistently provided a lower level of income substitution than SF-financed benefits (see figure 9.5).[17] The replacement rates corresponding to the first transfer for members who received benefits funded only by IAs were 35.8 percent and 37.8 percent for open-ended and fixed-term contract workers, respectively. When they are averaged over the unemployment periods, these rates fall to 24.0 percent and 25.2 percent. In contrast, benefits funded by the SF have replacement rates that are very close to those that were legally established.[18]

SUSTAINABILITY

The net worth of the unemployment funds (IA and SF) has shown persistent growth since the creation of the system in 2002, reaching US$2.578 million in June 2009[19] (see figure 9.6); 73 percent of the accumulated total is in the IAs, 24.8 percent is in the SF, and 2.2 percent is in unassigned contributions.

FIGURE 9.5 **Beneficiaries' Replacement Rates, 2002–June 2009**

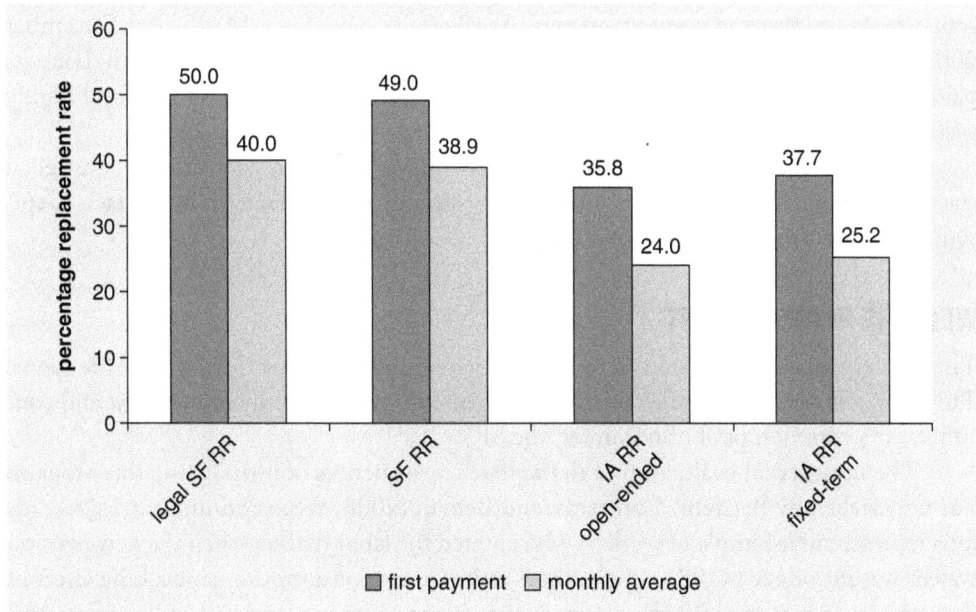

SOURCE: Chilean Pension Supervisor.
NOTE: RR = replacement rate.

FIGURE 9.6 **Unemployment Funds, Net Worth, 2002–June 2009**

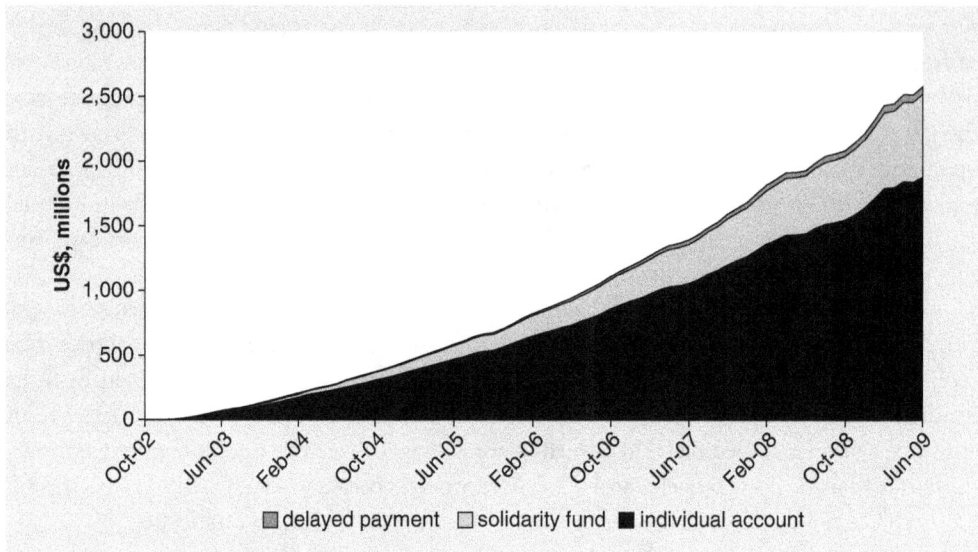

SOURCE: Chilean Pension Supervisor.

The flow of contributions to the unemployment funds since they were established in 2002 is due to the increasing coverage of the program, the inclusion of members with higher taxable income, and the low level of SF use. Most withdrawals from the system (practically all corresponding to unemployment payments and a few to death transfers or retirement) come from the IAs. Benefits paid from IAs during December 2008 were equivalent to 43.3 percent of contributions during the same month; benefits paid from the SF were only 9.2 percent of contributions, which makes the fund highly sustainable.

Actuarial studies performed on the system have all shown that under the original rules, the solidarity fund will continue to grow steadily over time, even in the face of episodes of high unemployment.[20]

WELFARE IMPROVEMENT

The primary goal of the system is to help workers smooth income during their life spans. This protection requires workers to save for their own periods of unemployment and contribute to a common pool of resources, the SF.

The most recent evaluation of the welfare consequences of introducing this program was undertaken by Berstein, Contreras, and Benvin (2008). Using administrative records for a representative sample of workers who entered the labor market when the new pension system was introduced (1981), the authors estimate the consumption-smoothing effect of the introduction of the UI program by comparing the lifetime expected utility of workers as if the system had started in 1980 and without the UI system.

The results suggest that, in general, most workers value the program.[21] Its value depends, however, on the individual's labor history and level of risk aversion. More risk-averse workers will benefit more from the consumption-smoothing properties. Similarly, the welfare of older and more educated individuals increases under the program, as they are more likely to benefit from the solidarity fund (access to which depends on having a minimum level of labor continuity). For a similar reason, Chilean women are less likely to benefit from the program, as their labor histories are more likely to be interrupted than those of men. These effects are summarized in figure 9.7 and table 9.1.

INCENTIVE EFFECTS

Even though the literature suggests that the existence of unemployment insurance could create incentives for beneficiaries to reduce job search efforts and increase unemployment periods while receiving benefits, no formal evaluation of the Chilean system has been published. One reason for this lack of results is the extent of unobserved selection among those who receive benefits: Only a fraction of the workforce participates in the UI system (in general, those with high labor turnover); only a fraction of those who stop making contributions claim benefits; and only a fraction of those who claim benefits and are eligible to access the solidarity fund actually do so (most choose to receive benefits only from their own savings accounts). Even if part of this selection process can be explained by observable characteristics (for example, workers with higher expectations of finding another job

FIGURE 9.7 **Estimated Median Benefit from the UI System, by Education and Age**

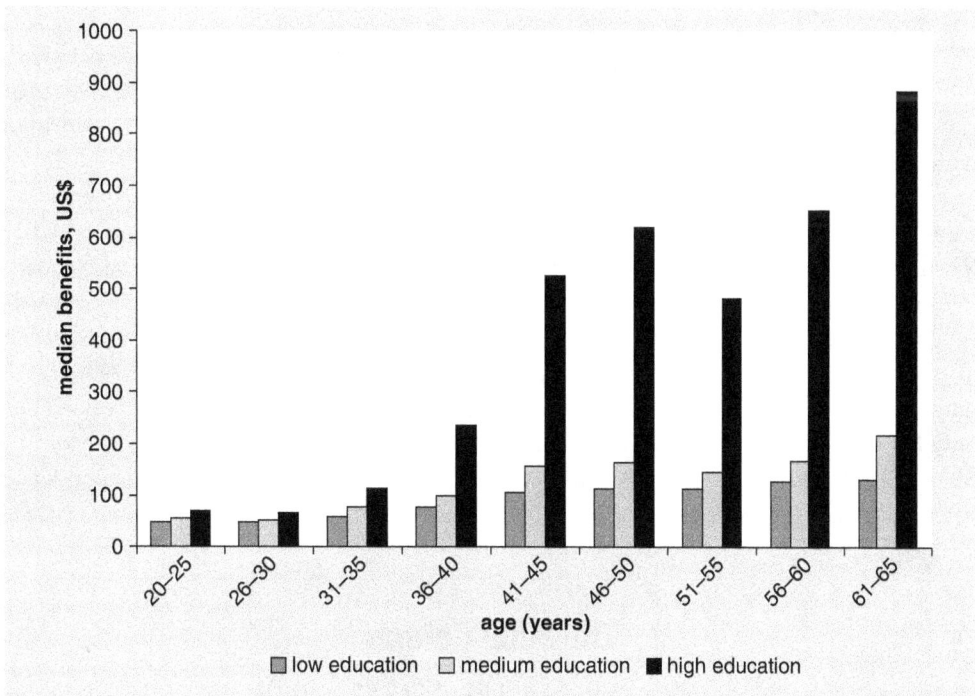

SOURCE: Based on Berstein, Contreras, and Benvin (2008).

TABLE 9.1 **Valuation of Unemployment Insurance by Education Level (percent)**

Risk aversion (γ)	Primary education	High school education	Graduate education	Total
1	3.6	3.7	6.5	4.4
1.5	5.2	6.1	13.0	7.5
2	7.2	9.1	20.1	11.3
2.5	9.6	12.2	25.4	14.7

SOURCE: Berstein, Conteras, and Benvin 2008, table 5.1.

NOTE: γ is the risk-aversion coefficient of the CARA (constant absolute risk aversion) utility function, and the valuation is measured as a percentage of salary, where the contribution to unemployment insurance is 3 percent in total, so valuation over that percentage would imply more value than the cost at an individual level.

tend not to take advantage of the SF), it has been difficult to come up with a strategy to identify the impact of the system on job search effort, length of unemployment period, or reentry wages. However, some evaluations are under way.

Figure 9.8 shows the empirical hazard rates for the duration of unemployment periods among beneficiaries of the UI system.[22] It shows that workers who chose to receive benefits of the SF type (that is, benefits defined as a function of wages, financed first by one's own savings and then by the SF) exhibit quite different hazard rates during the first four months than workers who chose to withdraw funds only from their individual accounts. Only 34 percent of beneficiaries who chose the SF option started making contributions during the first four months, compared with 62 percent of those who chose the IA option.

This finding could be interpreted as evidence of significant moral hazard behavior, but this interpretation must be made with caution, because of the strong self-selection process among persons who make different choices. Also, a comparison should be performed with comparable workers who do not participate in the UI system.

Using the difference in the accumulated UI balances of different workers entering a period of unemployment, Reyes, van Ours, and Vodopivec (2010) investigate whether job-finding rates are affected by SF eligibility and use. Their results support the theory that including a savings account in the UI program, and thus forcing workers to internalize part of the cost of unemployment benefits, tends to mitigate the moral hazard effect of traditional UI schemes. They find a positive association between the hazard rate from unemployment and the amount of savings at the start of the unemployment period, but only for workers who take the SF option. Also (and consistent with the pattern shown in figure 9.8), they find a significant difference in the unemployment duration dependence pattern between SF users and workers who rely only on their own savings to finance their UI benefits.

The 2009 Reform

In August 2008, the administration of President Michelle Bachelet sent the Chilean congress a bill reforming the UI system. The bill attempted to address the main challenges

FIGURE 9.8 **Hazard Rates from Not Contributing, by Type of Benefit Received (beneficiaries with open-ended contracts, Oct. 2002–Sept. 2007)**

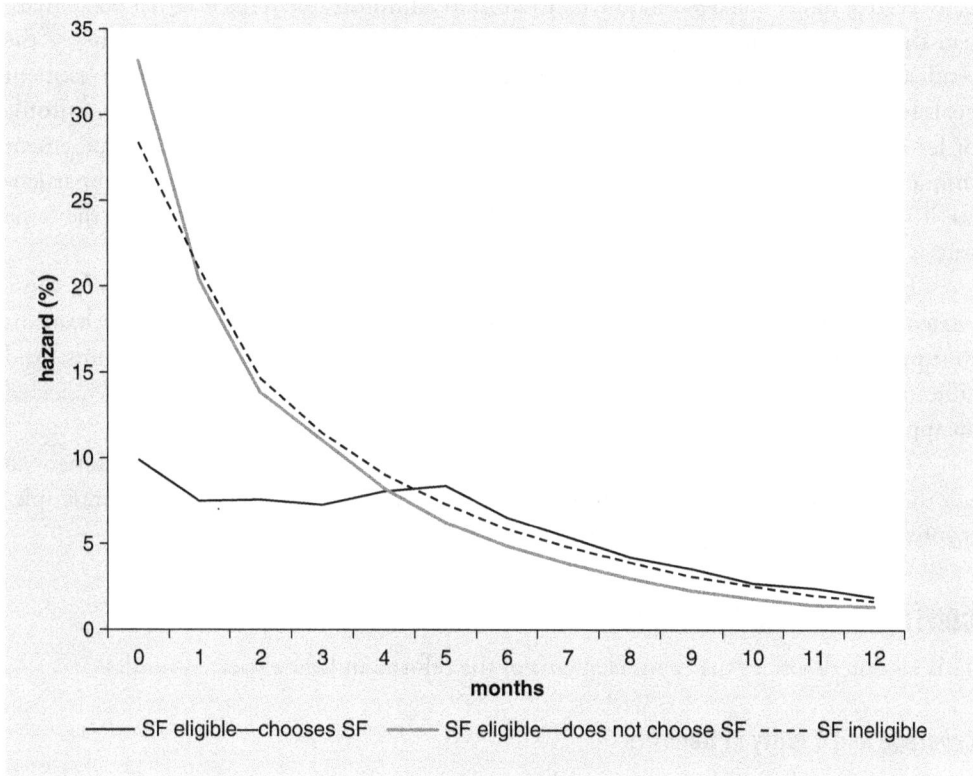

SOURCE: Administrative data from the Chilean Pension Supervisor.

in the effort to provide reasonable income protection for unemployed workers. The reform focused on four aspects of the system.

First, there was a need to increase the limited coverage of the SF. Results of the first evaluations of the system showed that the eligibility requirements to qualify for SF benefits were too stringent, even for open-ended contract workers, who were most likely to have registered 12 monthly contributions to the SF before applying. Only 4.1 percent of workers received SF benefits during 2008. Fixed-term contract workers, who usually have shorter periods of employment, were not allowed to apply for SF benefits (which are higher and cover a longer period).

Second, the relatively low quality of benefits needed improvement. The replacement rates observed in the system were relatively low, especially considering the monthly average for the unemployment period and especially for those not eligible to access the SF. Some workers who received SF benefits saw their benefits capped by the maximum limit established for the monthly payment. Additionally, the duration of the SF benefit did not take into account how difficult it might be to find a new job: The maximum was five months of benefits, regardless of the national unemployment rate.

Third, a more suitable investment regime was needed for unemployment funds. Unemployment funds could be invested in the same financial instruments as the more conservative funds managed by the pension fund administrator. This external benchmark had the advantage of being relatively safe, and it was externally determined, being the result of market competition among pension fund managers. However, the investment goals for pension funds (designed for workers who prefer a conservative investment profile or for those nearing retirement age) were not necessarily appropriate for unemployment insurance benefits, which have different liquidity and maturity requirements. In particular, it was not clear that the funds in individual accounts should be invested in the same way as the solidarity fund.

Fourth, the coverage of nonmonetary benefits was too limited, especially those related to promoting reemployment among beneficiaries.[23] The system lacked mechanisms to support workers in finding a new job through training or job-seeking programs. And although the UI law stated that SF payments would be suspended if a beneficiary rejected an appropriate job or training offer, it was not being enforced.

The emergence of the global economic crisis motivated the Chilean government to put the bill on a fast track. It was approved in January 2009, and the changes were implemented beginning in May of that year.

CONTENTS OF THE REFORMS

This section describes the main elements of the reform and the expected results.

Coverage and Quality of Benefits

- *Allow fixed-term workers to access the SF*

  Since May 2009, fixed-term contract workers and those employed for a specific project or task have been allowed to access the SF.[24] Eligible workers will receive benefits from the SF equivalent to a replacement rate of 35 percent for the first month and 30 percent for the second month.[25]

- *Relaxation of the prerequisites to qualify for SF benefits*

  The reform relaxed the eligibility requirements to qualify for SF benefits by transforming the continuous contribution requirement into a minimum density requirement. Before the reform, workers had to make 12 continuous monthly contributions to the SF before they could apply for the benefit; now workers must have made at least 12 contributions (continuous or not) over the previous 24 months, regardless of the type of contract. The last three contributions must be continuous and with the same employer.[26]

- *Increase in minimum and maximum SF benefits*

  As of May 2009, the minimum payments increased between 14 percent and 35 percent (14 percent for the first payment, 35 percent for the fifth payment), and a 28 percent increase in maximum benefits financed by the SF was established. This increase will allow the system to guarantee a reasonable defined benefit, in terms of replacement rate, to workers opting for the SF with covered wages up to US$718.20 (almost 80 percent of all contributors).[27]

- *Change in the payment structure of IA benefits*

  Funds available in individual accounts will be paid following a path similar to the one defined for the SF (50 percent of the average wage for the first payment, 45 percent for the second, and so on) until the funds are exhausted. If the funds exceed the amount necessary to finance five SF payments, the person will receive 25 percent of covered wages for as long as he or she remains unemployed and has funds in the IA.[28] Before the reform, IA benefits were paid according to the number of years of contribution, so the replacement rate varied according to the last employment period. For instance, under the old law, a worker who had contributed for three years received IA benefits in three monthly payments with replacement rates equal to 30 percent, 27 percent, and 24 percent. Under the new law, this person would receive benefits in two payments with replacement rates around 50 percent and 32 percent.

- *Additional payments during periods of high unemployment*

  Because a UI system should provide social protection for a longer period of unemployment, when it is harder to find a new job, the reform introduces the flexibility to increase the SF benefits to two additional months if the national unemployment rate is at least 1 percentage point higher than the four-year moving average. The additional benefits will be paid to those who received their last payment from the SF and will be equivalent to 25 percent of the worker's covered wage, regardless of the type of contract.

Investment Regime

The investment regime will no longer be established by law but by the Chilean Pension Supervisor, through a special Technical Investment Council created for this purpose. The law established only general minimum and maximum limits by classes of assets. The new approach is more flexible, allowing changes in the investment regime in response to variations in economic conditions or any other important variable. The council will propose a new benchmark to the Chilean Pension Supervisor, implying higher commissions for good performance and lower commissions for underperformance by fund managers. The commissions will be charged to contributors to the UI system. Before the reform, the benchmark was the most conservative funds offered to members of the national pension system. Special benchmarks for the IA and SF funds will create incentives for private administrators to make better investment decisions.

Nonmonetary Benefits

- The SF will finance (up to 2 percent of its accumulated balance) programs aimed at improving the employability of UI/SF beneficiaries, especially those who are having difficulty finding a new job. The program was budgeted for 2011 but had not yet started as of mid-2011.

- A labor information system was developed to improve the available information on the evolution of key labor market variables, such as job creation by wage level, geographic area, or economic sector. The goal of this system is to inform workers about the kinds of jobs that are being created in the economy.

- A national job search system will improve the matching process between labor demand and supply, thereby reducing unemployment, especially for workers with frictional unemployment. Through a public auction, the administration of this system was awarded for three years to a national firm with long experience in the area of web-based labor intermediation. The national job search system commenced operation in June 2011.[29]

EXPECTED RESULTS OF THE REFORM

The architects of the reform are optimistic about the expected results: (1) greater access to the solidarity fund, regardless of the type of labor contract; (2) a higher level of benefits and replacement rates, mainly because of the higher coverage of the SF; (3) a higher level of social protection when it is harder to find a job; (4) a more coordinated and better informed job search system available to employers and workers; and (5) a solidarity fund that will, according to current assessments, remain sustainable even in the event of an unemployment crisis with intensive use of benefits.

According to the analysis by the Chilean Pension Supervisor, the impact of the UI reform on the number of beneficiaries from the SF will be quite important. Since the implementation of the reform in May 2009, the number of SF beneficiaries has increased from 10,000 a month by the end of 2008 to around 30,000 a month by the end of 2010. In addition, the quality of benefits (measured as the replacement rate) is expected to increase, especially for workers under fixed-term contracts. Fixed-term workers who accessed the SF would have an average replacement rate of around 32.5 percent.[30] In the base scenario, this group would not have had access to this benefit.

Finally, regarding the sustainability of the solidarity fund, in spite of the increase in beneficiaries, it is expected that even in the event of a high unemployment scenario, the SF will be highly sustainable. The estimations suggest that under a crisis scenario, the SF would reach an accumulated balance of around US$1.4 million by 2015; in a noncrisis scenario, the balance would be 35 percent more, or around US$1.9 million.

Lessons for Other Countries

The performance of the Chilean UI program depends, in many respects, on country-specific characteristics: the composition and habits of its workforce (for example, labor force participation of men and women); the institutional arrangements in the labor market (type of contract, level of turnover in the private sector, and size of the self-employed and informal sectors); and previous experience with individual accounts under the privately managed pension system established in 1980.

However, some conclusions could be useful for countries that are considering implementing a similar program. The following issues arose in the original implementation of the program and in the recent reform discussions:

- How much risk pooling should be included in the system?
- How should the system be introduced—gradually or all at once?
- What is the best way to monitor compliance?

- What is the relationship between the introduction of UISAs and reform of the severance payment scheme?
- What other nonmonetary benefits should be considered along with UISAs?
- What alternative designs should be considered? Limited borrowing from the solidarity fund against future contributions?

OPTIMAL RISK POOLING

The Chilean design is a mix of individual accounts and risk pooling. Workers with open-ended contracts contribute 2.2 percent of their wages to their individual accounts and 0.8 percent to the SF in exchange for potential coverage for up to five months.

The scheme could have been designed to make all contributions go into individual accounts.[31] This would mitigate moral hazard considerations (as benefits would be entirely financed by individual savings) and would avoid overaccumulation in the solidarity fund. However, this approach would mean renouncing any form of risk pooling or redistribution within the system, as well as small benefits for workers with interrupted careers. As shown earlier, the average Chilean participant accumulates a small balance in the IA, allowing him or her to finance a small replacement rate from this account. At a 3 percent contribution rate, it would take a worker almost five years to accumulate sufficient resources to finance an entire SF benefit schedule (five payments of 50 percent, 45 percent, 40 percent, 35 percent, and 30 percent of wages).

On the other hand, if the entire contribution went into the SF, the system would be the equivalent of a traditional UI scheme, with full risk pooling. With a strong monitoring capacity to effectively enforce adequate job search efforts and avoid fraud (or with a small or nonexistent informal sector), this system would provide an optimal degree of consumption smoothing at a very reasonable cost. At a 3 percent contribution rate, it would be able to finance the same benefits (an average 40 percent of wages, paid for five months), as long as no more than 2 percent of the participants claimed benefits in any given month. However, these conditions are unlikely in developing economies, where a large informal sector typically coexists with the covered economy and where the administrative capacity to enforce job search efforts or help people find adequate jobs is usually limited. In such an environment, the system could easily become unsustainable as workers learned to manipulate it—working in the formal sector the minimum number of months required to be eligible for benefits, then working in the informal sector while receiving payments.

In conclusion, the appropriate combination of savings and risk pooling should depend on the importance of moral hazard considerations and the effectiveness of controls—even if it is difficult to determine the optimal level of risk pooling, it might be beneficial to at least consider the trade-offs when design decisions are being made. These issues are relatively difficult to assess in advance, but the Chilean approach seems reasonable. Start conservatively on the moral hazard front by imposing strong eligibility requirements for access to the pooled component and relax these requirements gradually in response to the behavior of workers and beneficiaries. The use of limited benefits (50 percent maximum replacement rate), a small number of payments (five), a requirement to use individual savings before accessing the SF, a limited number of withdrawals from the SF over a five-year period, and the administrative requirement to check in with an OMIL once a month while receiving benefits are all mitigating factors for the moral hazard risk. The exclusion from the SF of fixed-term contract workers (who turned out to be the main group of participants during the first few years of the program) was an additional factor explaining the sustained growth of the SF over this period. Other countries might start by restricting access to the SF by other moral hazard risk groups.

The 2009 reform essentially relaxed the eligibility conditions and allowed access to the SF for a previously excluded group: fixed-term contract workers. This was possible because a strong body of data was gathered and projection models were developed to assess the sustainability implications of the reform.

HOW TO INTRODUCE A NEW SYSTEM

When Chile's new UI system was implemented in 2002, workers with labor contracts created after October 2002 were required to participate.[32] In retrospect, policy makers did not anticipate two effects of this choice on the evolution of the system: the rapid incorporation of a large proportion of the target population in a short period and the particular worker mix (strongly biased toward fixed-term contract workers) that has prevailed. This pattern illustrates the highly dynamic nature of the Chilean labor market, in which many employment relationships are created and terminated every month.

Initially, the system composition was strongly biased toward certain types of workers and economic sectors (for example, construction, services, and seasonal agriculture); it had relatively large administrative costs associated with the high number of benefits being paid each month; and it had a relatively small solidarity fund, owing to the underrepresentation of workers with open-ended contracts.

Another option would be to make the system compulsory for all private dependent workers from the beginning. This would effect a massive change in the labor market, raising the cost of formal employment across the board. It would modify previous contractual arrangements and trigger a more complex political discussion, as current workers would be directly affected, especially if the changes included a reduction in severance pay benefits. Gradual introduction does not affect current employment contracts and allows the system to slowly evolve. Conversely, the system could benefit from the radical approach because it would immediately start receiving contributions from the more stable group of workers, which would enable it to finance more risk pooling or redistribution.

An intermediate alternative would be to impose the system immediately on certain groups of workers (for instance, those in large firms or more stable economic sectors) and gradually on the rest.

In conclusion, the introduction decision involves trading off the smoothness of a gradual approach against the resulting worker mix that naturally arises from it.

ADMINISTRATIVE DETAILS

The system is intended to provide workers with the necessary resources to smooth consumption during periods of unemployment. The main proxy for unemployment verification is the UI administrative system itself. Contributions made on behalf of a worker are prima facie evidence of noncompliance.[33] This method is quite transparent and comes at practically no additional marginal cost for the employer or the institution in charge of managing the system. The main problem is that it comes with a lag: Employers are given up to 43 days to make contributions on behalf of their workers.[34] Thus, if a worker stops working for an employer, claims UI benefits, and start working immediately for a new employer (or the same one), the system will not detect this at least until the second payment is made.

To avoid this situation, firms are required to inform the AFC of all new employment relations, with a small fine for noncompliance. Compliance with this regulation has been extremely low, and enforcement is restricted by the limited capacity of the labor supervisory authority to prosecute. The result has been extensive withdrawal of funds when workers (especially fixed-term contract workers) switch jobs, even without an interruption in contributions.[35] This severely limits the capacity of the system to provide reasonable benefits when workers are faced with periods of real unemployment.

Unless other sources of verification are readily available (such as matching with tax records), alternative regulations could be considered; for example, delaying payment or making a small or no payment during the first month or until unemployment can be verified.[36]

REFORMING SEVERANCE PAYMENTS WHILE INTRODUCING UISAs

Some countries might consider their current severance pay (SP) structures to be inefficient (limiting productivity and increasing labor reallocation); too costly for the development of the formal sector; or prone to generate excessive use of fixed-term contracts (or other forms of avoidance behavior), which ultimately affects the level of protection of workers during labor crises. However, reducing or eliminating the SP system can face strong political opposition from current workers, who consider it a labor right, acquired after a long period of struggle.

In this context, the introduction of UISAs could be seen as a more efficient (and in some cases, effective) form of protection for the worker. The pure savings component provides prefunded protection for workers and can be available under any type of employment separation (voluntary or involuntary). The prefunded nature ensures that workers will receive the benefit even if the firm faces financial hardship. This system also eliminates the need for costly negotiation or judiciary conflict between the worker and the employer over the nature of the labor separation. In some circumstances, the introduction of a UI system is the ideal moment to negotiate a reduction in severance payments (assured payment in exchange for eventual and possibly reduced severance payment).

The solidarity fund could be interpreted as a prefunded substitute for traditional SP schemes, in the sense that it is only available for involuntary separations, although differences exist between SF and SP benefits. The prefunded nature of the SF is associated with lower disincentives for firing workers on the part of the employer but, at the same time, a higher likelihood that the benefit will be paid according to the rules of the program. The benefit structure is also different: SPs are usually proportional to the duration of employment, whereas SF benefits are fixed proportions of covered wages. This benefits workers with shorter periods of employment but negatively affects workers dismissed after long contract periods. In addition, the SF scheme allows for broad-based risk pooling and redistribution (from workers in low-risk firms or industries to workers in temporarily or persistently affected firms or industries), while SPs pool risk at the firm level, leaving workers partially unprotected against significant firm- or industry-level shocks.

In Chile, severance payments were only partially replaced by the introduction of the UI scheme, as employers' contributions can be deducted from severance payments in case of dismissal.

PROTECTION IS NOT JUST INCOME REPLACEMENT

The long experience with traditional unemployment insurance schemes in developed countries suggests that UI benefits should be complemented by other forms of protection, particularly if the latter are less prone to moral hazard considerations. They might include other forms of income replacement (family allowance, health insurance, education subsidies) or interventions specifically designed to facilitate reemployment (training, job search assistance, transportation subsidies). These interventions can also serve as effective unemployment verification tools.

The original Chilean law did not give enough emphasis to these issues. The 2009 reforms take a number of steps toward strengthening the protective role of these complementary measures.

Conclusions

The design of an unemployment protection system must consider the impact on the labor market. On the one hand, the provision of unemployment insurance is desirable as an effective way of pooling risk and smoothing consumption. On the other hand, UI might result in important efficiency costs because of moral hazard and the difficulty of controlling compliance. The Chilean system addresses these two problems by combining insurance and savings. So far, the system has provided a reasonable level of protection with limited distortions, making it highly sustainable.

Distortions are limited mainly because the system started conservatively, imposing strong eligibility requirements for access to the insurance component. Also, the benefits are relatively low—limited to a 50 percent maximum replacement rate and only five payments. Participants may make only two withdrawals from the solidarity fund over a five-year period, and beneficiaries are required to check in with an OMIL once a month while they are receiving SF payments.

On top of these mitigating factors for the moral hazard risk in the insurance component, the system includes a savings component, which must be used before the SF is accessed. This compulsory savings account provides additional protection, as well as incentives for the proper use of unemployment insurance.

The exclusion of fixed-term contract workers from the original UI scheme prevented excessive use of the solidarity fund. These workers make up a large part of the labor market in Chile and are responsible for significant labor turnover.

All of these elements in the original design ensured the sustainability of the solidarity fund and provided a solid starting point for the reforms implemented in May 2009. These reforms considered the labor market information gathered during six years of operation of the Chilean system and used this information to construct a model that allowed policy makers to project replacement rates and sustainability of the SF under various conditions.

Essentially, the 2009 reform relaxed the eligibility conditions and gave access to the insurance component to a previously exempt group (fixed-term contract workers). Other important components of the reform were an increase in SF benefits and the possibility of two additional payments in case of a significant increase in the national unemployment rate.

Other countries interested in introducing a similar system would have to decide how much risk pooling to allow. The appropriate combination of savings and insurance should depend on the importance of moral hazard and the effectiveness of controls; these two elements are specific to each country and depend on how the labor market and institutions operate in the country. For instance, other countries might choose to start by restricting access to the solidarity fund on the part of other high moral hazard risk groups.

An important element to consider in deciding to implement a UI system is the existence of severance payments. In Chile, the system allowed for partial substitution of the severance payment by unemployment insurance: the employer's contribution to the worker's individual account is deductible from the amount payable as severance payment. This element must be carefully analyzed in the context of the country's labor market with special attention to the effects of replacement on firms of different sizes and levels of formality.

Finally, the design of the UI system should align with the country's existing social protection policy to allow the country to take full advantage of the different components and of synergies among them. For example, unemployment insurance could be integrated with pension savings. In Chile, excess savings in the unemployment account can be transferred to the pension account at retirement; however, a worker cannot borrow against his or her pension wealth. In Chile, pension wealth is relatively low for a large proportion of the population, and there is significant heterogeneity in the labor market. Under other circumstances, integration between the two accounts could be considered as an alternative design.

Notes

1. However, if the scheme is poorly designed (for example, with an excessively high contribution rate or a low return on investments), it might affect the job search behavior of participants, increasing or reducing their "normal" turnover rate.

2. For example, with a 3 percent contribution rate and a 4 percent real interest rate, a person would need 74 months of contributions to finance a benefit equivalent to 50 percent of his or her salary for five months.

3. Before the introduction of the UI program, a special scheme for domestic helpers was created in 1991. This was pure unemployment insurance: savings accounts from which workers can withdraw, upon termination for any cause, the result of a 4.11 percent monthly contribution. With this program in mind, a more extended scheme for unemployed workers was proposed during the 1990s but never approved. The forerunner program, Proteccion al Trabajador Cesante (PROTRAC), was similar in concept to the current UI program, except that it was only for permanent workers, and benefits for laid-off workers with more than 12 months of contributions were financed out of government transfers (as opposed to the solidarity fund in the current design). For more details on the PROTRAC and how it evolved into the current UI scheme, see Acevedo, Eskenazi, and Pagés (2006).

4. The choice of private administration was a natural one, given the long previous experience (since 1980) of a strongly regulated pension system managed by private firms. In this case, however, a different competition ground was chosen. The strong competition *in* the field of the pension system was replaced by competition *for* the field in the case of the UI system.

5. For more details on the system and its performance after five years of operation, see Berstein and others (2007) and Berstein (2010).

6. Domestic service workers have their own unemployment insurance scheme, which corresponds to a pure individual savings account administered as a separate account by pension fund managers, to which employers contribute 4.11 percent of covered wages. Workers may withdraw all their funds upon termination of the labor relationship for any cause.

7. The Unidad de Fomento is an inflation-indexed unit of account equivalent, in June 2009, to 20,933.02 Chilean pesos, approximately US$40 (exchange rate of Ch$529.07 per US$1).

8. The factors are equal to 1.9, 2.7, 3.4, and 4 if the worker is entitled to two, three, four, or five payments, respectively.

9. The exact causes are specified in paragraph 6 of article 159 and article 161 of the labor code.

10. When the initial law was passed, the minimum amount for the first payment was approximately equivalent to the first replacement rate applied to the minimum wage. The maximum amount for the first payment approximately corresponded to twice the minimum wage. Until the 2009 reform, adjustments to minimum and maximum benefits were lower than the increases in the official minimum wage.

11. See chapter 4 in Vodopivec (2004) for a review of the empirical literature on efficiency effects of unemployment insurance programs.

12. Borrowing is not permitted in the Chilean system.

13. "Not viable" means that a large proportion of workers would reach retirement with a negative balance.

14. In this chapter, "enrolled workers" refers to those who, at some point in their lives, joined the program by making at least one monthly contribution. "Contributors" are workers who are making contributions during a particular month.

15. Workers can voluntarily join the program, but most of the participation (97.8 percent) is the result of mandatory enrollment.

16. The number of benefits provided is not equivalent to the number of people benefiting, because the same person may apply for various benefits at different times.

17. The replacement rate for the first payment is calculated as the ratio of the amount paid in the first month of the benefit and the average wage during the previous contribution period. The replacement rate for the monthly average is calculated as the ratio of the total amount of monthly payments (as many months as the worker receives benefits while unemployed) and the average wage during the previous contribution period; this ratio is divided by the number of months the person was unemployed (not making contributions), with a maximum of five.

18. Actual replacement rates may differ from those legally established, as high-income workers can be affected by maximum benefits and workers with low wages (or part-time workers) might benefit from minimum benefits.

19. Ch$529.07 per US$1 (June 30, 2009).

20. See Bravo Ruiz-Tagle, and Castillo (2007); Cerda and Coloma (2009); Fajnzylber and Poblete (2010); and Johnson, Zurita, and Muñoz (2004). See the next section for more details on the projected sustainability of the solidarity fund.

21. The authors note that the results should be considered as an upper bound on the welfare effect of the program, as they assume that individuals are liquidity constrained and no other savings vehicle is allowed. Additionally, the study does not consider the existence of severance payments or other benefits that employees might have besides the UI scheme.

22. To be more precise, the results correspond to periods in which a worker did not make contributions to the UI system, from the moment he or she stopped making contributions and requested the benefit.

23. Many important aspects of the changes introduced by the system reform were originally recommended by the Users Committee in its annual reports.

24. The contribution rate for fixed-term contract workers is still 3 percent of covered wages paid by the employer, but 0.2 percent now goes to the SF.

25. It was decided to give these workers a shorter benefit period and lower replacement rates, to maintain the incentives for reemployment efforts.

26. This last requirement was introduced to avoid moral hazard behavior, especially among fixed-term workers, given the lack of knowledge about their behavior once they are allowed to access the SF.

27. This amount is calculated using the exchange rate of Ch$529.07 per US$1 (June 30, 2009).

28. A worker with about seven years of contributions could finance a five-month benefit at the targeted replacement rate.

29. To access the system, go to http://www.bne.cl.

30. Fixed-term workers are allowed to receive two monthly payments, equivalent to 35 percent and 30 percent.

31. This is the case of the Chilean contributory pension system, which is based entirely on individual savings. There is no explicit risk pooling, and the redistributive role is played by a new solidarity pillar introduced in 2008—a noncontributory program financed by general revenues.

32. As mentioned earlier, firms could voluntarily participate in the program; in practice, few did.

33. This method is not robust in terms of avoiding SF fraud through self-employment or work in the informal sector. The use of individual savings and high eligibility requirements are the mitigating factors in this area.

34. The employer must pay the contribution for the earnings received during a given month until the 13th of the following month. In addition, there is a delay between when the contribution is paid and when it is credited to the individual's account.

35. Between 2002 and 2007, almost 41 percent of fixed-term contract workers who claimed benefits from their UI accounts made a contribution in the same month they received the benefit.

36. This requirement could be imposed on workers who have repeatedly exhibited this conduct in the past.

References

Acemoglu, Daron, and Robert Shimer. 1999. "Efficient Unemployment Insurance." *Journal of Political Economy* 107 (5, Oct.): 893–928.

Acevedo, Germán, Patricio Eskenazi, and Carmen Pagés. 2006. "Unemployment Insurance in Chile: A New Model of Income Support for Unemployed Workers." Social Protection Discussion Paper No. 0612, World Bank, Washington, DC.

Berstein, Solange, ed. 2010. "Seguro de Cesantía en Chile." Chilean Pension Supervisor, Santiago, Chile. www.spensiones.cl/573/article-7513.html.

Berstein, Solange, Carmen Contreras, and Evelyn Benvin. 2008. "Valoración del Seguro de Cesantía en Chile: Simulación de Beneficios con Datos Individuales." Chilean Pension Supervisor Working Paper 27, Santiago, Chile.

Berstein, Solange, Eduardo Fajnzylber, Pamela Gana, and Isabel Poblete. 2007. "Five Years of Unemployment Insurance in Chile: Diagnosis and Challenges for Improvement." Chilean Pension Supervisor Working Paper 23, Santiago, Chile.

Boone, Jan, Peter Fredriksson, Bertil Holmlund, and Jan C. van Ours. 2007. "Optimal Unemployment Insurance with Monitoring and Sanctions." *Economic Journal* 117 (518, March): 399–421. http://ssrn.com/abstract=978573 or DOI: 10.1111/j.1468-0297.2007.02023.x.

Bravo, David, Jaime Ruiz-Tagle, and José Luis Castillo. 2007. "Estudio Actuarial de los Fondos de Cesantía 2005." Chilean Pension Supervisor Working Paper 22, Santiago, Chile.

Cerda, Rodrigo, and Fernando Coloma. 2009. "Estudio Actuarial de los Fondos de Cesantía 2008—Informe Final." Chilean Pension Supervisor Working Paper 33, Santiago, Chile.

Fajnzylber, Eduardo, and Isabel Poblete. 2010. "Un modelo de proyección para el Seguro de Cesantía." Chilean Pension Supervisor Working Paper 41, Santiago, Chile.

Feldstein, Martin S., and Daniel Altman. 1998. "Unemployment Insurance Savings Accounts." NBER Working Paper W6860, National Bureau of Economic Research, Cambridge, MA. http://ssrn.com/abstract=144933.

Johnson, C., S. Zurita, and A. Muñoz. 2004. "Informe Parte I: Evaluación de la Sustentabilidad del Seguro de Cesantía." Actuarial study contracted by the Administradora de Fondos de Cesantía, Santiago, Chile.

Mortensen, Dale T. 1977. "Unemployment Insurance and Job Search Decisions." *Industrial and Labor Relations Review* 30 (4, July): 505–17.

Parsons, Donald O. 2010. "The Firing Cost Implications of Alternative Severance Pay Designs." Draft. George Washington University, Washington, DC. http://ftp.iza.org/dp4967.pdf.

Reyes, Gonzalo, Jan C. van Ours, and Milan Vodopivec. 2010. "Incentive Effects of Unemployment Insurance Savings Accounts: Evidence from Chile." Chilean Pension Supervisor Working Paper 40, Santiago, Chile.

Shavell, Steven, and Laurence Weiss. 1979. "The Optimal Payment of Unemployment Insurance Benefits over Time." *Journal of Political Economy* 87 (6, December): 1347–62.

Stiglitz, Joseph E., and Jungyoll Yun. 2002. "Integration of Unemployment Insurance with Retirement Insurance." NBER Working Paper No. W9199, National Bureau of Economic Research, Cambridge, MA. http://ssrn.com/abstract=330338.

Vodopivec, Milan. 2004. *Income Support Systems for the Unemployed: Issues and Options.* World Bank Regional and Sectoral Studies Series, Washington, DC: World Bank.

———. 2008. "How Viable Are Unemployment Insurance Savings Accounts? Simulation Results for Slovenia." IZA Discussion Paper 3438, Institute for the Study of Labor, Bonn.

Werning, Iván. 2002. "Optimal Unemployment Insurance with Unobservable Savings." Unpublished manuscript.

CHAPTER 10

Reemployment Incentives under the Chilean Hybrid Unemployment Benefit Program

Gonzalo Reyes, Jan C. van Ours, and Milan Vodopivec

One approach to improve reemployment incentives under unemployment insurance (UI) programs is to introduce an individual savings component to complement the traditional risk-pooling compontent of the program. The pioneer in this approach was Chile, which introduced its innovative hybrid program in 2002. (See chapter 9 for a description of the Chilean program and an evaluation of its performance.) This chapter summarizes a recent paper by Reyes, van Ours, and Vodopivec (2011)—the first paper to provide an econometric analysis of the incentive effects of the Chilean program. The empirical findings are largely consistent with the argument for internalizing the unemployment cost and suggest improved reemployment incentives, although other mechanisms may be at work that could account for the observed correlations.

The Quest to Reduce Work Disincentives in UI Programs

Unemployment insurance offers financial compensation to workers who lose their jobs. While such programs usually provide protection against the hardship of job loss, the evidence shows that this protection typically reduces incentives to seek other work—the so-called moral hazard problem, which has been extensively documented (see reviews by Holmlund 1998 and Vodopivec 2004). The question is how to minimize adverse incentives created under a UI program while still providing suitable income protection.

Several mechanisms can help reduce work disincentives in UI benefit programs: monitoring and benefit sanctions, work requirements, and financial incentives.[1] First, recipients' job search activities and labor market status can be monitored; if they do not meet certain performance criteria, sanctions may be imposed, such as benefit reductions. Second, work or other requirements can be imposed on benefit recipients; for example, requiring them to participate in training or public works if they want to keep receiving benefits. Third, financial incentives can be introduced to make reemployment more attractive. Options include reducing benefit levels over time, introducing bonuses for speedy reemployment, lowering income tax rates, and introducing employment subsidies (such as earned income tax credits) and unemployment insurance savings accounts (UISAs).

Among the new approaches used to reduce work disincentives, UISAs may be the most radical and promising. Under the UISA system, each worker is required to save a fraction of earnings in his or her account, and then to draw unemployment benefits from this account. At retirement, the worker can access any remaining balance in the account. By internalizing the costs of unemployment benefits, the UISA system reinforces the incentive to seek reemployment (and thus avoids or reduces the moral hazard inherent in traditional UI programs) while, under some variants of the program, providing the same protection as the traditional UI system. The USIA system has the potential to substantially decrease overall unemployment and, by lowering payroll taxes, increase wages.

In contrast to other mechanisms used to address work disincentives in UI programs and other cash benefit systems, UISAs have not yet been analyzed or evaluated to any great extent. Most research is limited to theory or simulations. So far, no empirical evidence has been put forth on whether UISAs can reduce the moral hazard problems plaguing traditional UI schemes, mainly because only Austria, Mauritius, and a few countries in Latin America have introduced these systems. The scarcity of experimental approaches and the heavy informational requirements have hampered or prevented such studies (for an overview of UISAs in Latin America, see chapter 7 in this volume).

The Chilean program has been in existence long enough to offer a rare opportunity to provide an empirical answer to an important and so far unanswered question: Is a savings account system an effective tool to combat the moral hazard plaguing traditional UI programs? That is, by forcing unemployed workers to draw on UISAs (in combination with solidarity funding), does the program improve job search incentives or reduce reservation wages, and thus increase the exit rate from insured unemployment, as theoretical models predict? After all, people can be myopic and may heavily discount resources to which access can be gained only after a long time, often a decade or more. Moreover, if people distrust the government, they may also distrust a scheme that postpones their access to resources into the distant future, as they have no reason to believe that present rules will still be in effect at a later time.

By analyzing transitions to work on the part of benefit recipients in the Chilean program, the forthcoming paper by Reyes, van Ours, and Vodopivec is the first to empirically examine the question. The authors find that beneficiaries who use solidarity funding are less likely to exit unemployment in the early months than those who rely on UISAs only. Moreover, job-finding rates are positively correlated with preseparation UISA balances among those who use the solidarity fund but uncorrelated with balances for other groups. While these findings are consistent with the effects expected from internalizing unemployment costs and thus support the idea of UISAs, the evidence stops short of confirming a definitive causal link. As discussed below, other mechanisms—primarily, selection of beneficiaries into groups that receive different types of benefits—may provide an alternative explanation for the correlations.

This chapter describes the data and the empirical strategy employed to identify incentive effects of the Chilean program. It analyzes the determinants of opting to use the solidarity fund (SF) by those who are entitled to do so. To identify work incentives under the program, the authors graphically and econometrically analyze job-finding rates, comparing various groups and estimating proportional hazard models. The chapter concludes with reflections on the findings and suggestions for further research.

Data and Methodology

The study relies on administrative records of the contribution histories of and benefits paid to workers participating in the Chilean UI program. These records are maintained by the Pension Supervisor, the agency in charge of regulating and supervising the program. Samples were selected of males and females born between 1958 and 1981 who lost a permanent job before 2007—49,702 men and 26,276 women. The focus was on the duration of their first unemployment period. For these prime-age workers, in addition to their records of contributions and benefits, information was available on UISA account balance, educational attainment, region of residence, and labor sector of their previous employer.

While certain differences appear between the men and women in the sample (for example, in duration of unemployment), they have similar rates of access to the solidarity fund: 68 percent of men and 63 percent of women have no right to access the fund. The average number of potential withdrawals from UISAs ranges from 1.7 to 1.9. For men not entitled to use the SF, the average unemployment duration is 8.1 months including incomplete spells and 5.6 months excluding them. Men who are entitled but do not use the SF have a shorter unemployment duration; on average, 7.5 months; 5.2 months for completed spells only. Men who use the SF have a longer unemployment duration: 11.1 months; 8.0 months for completed spells only. Women stay unemployed longer: The average duration is about 13 months; the average for completed spells only is 7.5–9.5 months (for details, see Reyes, van Ours, and Vodopivec, forthcoming).

Theoretical modeling by Orszag and Snower (2002) shows that workers who rely on UISAs internalize the costs of their unemployment and thus are motivated to search harder for jobs than workers who do not rely on UISAs.[2] Applying this logic to the Chilean program (and taking its hybrid nature into account) leads to the following predictions. For workers only eligible to use their UISAs, the account balance will not affect their job-finding rate. For workers who may use the SF, their job-finding rate will increase in proportion to the share of potential benefits that can be financed by their own accounts. Moreover, as the benefit expiration date approaches, one can expect that workers who use the SF will increase the intensity of their job search or reduce their reservation wage, thereby increasing the rate of job finding (see Mortensen 1977), while no such effect will be detected for workers who are not using the SF.

The empirical strategy is to estimate models of job-finding rates for various groups of beneficiaries and infer the effects of UISAs though the comparison of parameters of different groups. The focus is on three groups: (1) those who use the SF, (2) those who are entitled to use it but opt not to, and (3) those who are not entitled to use it. All workers in the sample have access to UISAs, but while workers in the first group finance their UI benefits via both the USIA and the SF, those in the other two groups use UISAs only (for details of financing under the Chilean system, see chapter 9). Moreover, beneficiaries differ in their account balances, as measured by the number of potential withdrawals—a feature that is taken advantage of in the empirical analysis.

Two approaches were used to identify the incentive effects of UISAs. The first was to exploit the leverage provided by variations in preseparation UISA accumulation. Even if they are subject to a common withdrawal schedule (the same replacement rate and potential benefit duration), beneficiaries differ in the amount of savings accumulated in their UISAs, so researchers can determine whether job-finding rates are positively correlated with UISA balances for workers who use the SF and uncorrelated with UISA balances for those who rely on UISAs only, as the logic of internalization of unemployment costs would suggest. These balances are determined by the length of covered employment (the period during which contributions were made), as well as by any withdrawals from the account during previous episodes of unemployment.

The second approach focuses on the time pattern of job finding. Workers who use the SF can draw benefits for a maximum of five months, which introduces nonstationarity in their job search behavior. As the date approaches when benefits expire, unemployed workers may increase the intensity of their job search or reduce their reservation wage, thereby increasing the rate of job finding (Mortensen 1977). Workers who do not use the SF do not face such incentives. Moreover, one could expect that over the initial period of benefit receipt, the job-finding rates for those drawing on the SF would be lower than the rates for those relying on UISAs only. This study compares job-finding rates and survival functions among different groups and estimates hazard rate models to net out the effects of observable (and, to the extent possible, unobservable) characteristics of workers.

The proposed analysis will document correlations, but will it enable the inference of causal links? In particular, does this approach allow one to attribute higher job-finding rates to the change of behavior caused by the internalization of the unemployment cost under UISAs? While the study establishes important relationships, it cannot claim to firmly determine the causality link, because other mechanisms may influence selection into various groups and because questions may exist regarding the validity of the econometric tests used.

Selection into the use of the SF (that is, whether to use it or not) may produce endogeneity in the duration of unemployment. Workers who expect their unemployment period to be short may choose to rely on their UISAs so as not to exhaust future eligibility for the SF, while those who expect to be unemployed for a long time would probably opt to receive funds from both their UISA and the SF. If this is true, workers who select the UISA-only option will have shorter unemployment periods. Similarly, systematic selection into unemployment may render the variable "number of potential withdrawals from UISAs" endogenous. If the least productive workers are more likely to be laid off, the preseparation account balances may systematically vary among workers, with more productive workers accumulating more, both because of longer employment periods and because of lower incidence of unemployment, if the latter is related to the use of UISA balances. This mechanism implies that workers with larger balances leave unemployment sooner. Without further tests, it is not possible to determine causality.

The study addresses selectivity and causality issues by (1) comparing groups along various observable characteristics to see if they differ in their preseparation outcomes (age, education, and industry); (2) modeling the probability of the use of the solidarity fund; and (3) formally testing whether unobserved heterogeneity varies across the three groups in the analysis. The empirical analysis begins by investigating the determinants of SF use and proceeds to an analysis of the job-finding rate.

Eligibility and Use of the Solidarity Fund

The richness of the design of the Chilean program allows the empirical investigation of incentive effects of the program along several dimensions, and this chapter focuses on two of them. The central issue is the impact of the program on reemployment incentives; specifically, on the job-finding rate. The second issue is the driving force influencing the decision to use the SF. While access to the SF leads to obvious gains (higher replacement rate and longer potential benefit period; see chapter 9), only about half of the eligible workers access the fund—a puzzling fact that deserves consideration.[3] This section examines the factors that influence this decision, focusing on the number of potential UISA withdrawals (an indication of the size of the account balance) as a possible determinant.

Eligibility to use the SF is not a matter of choice, but the actual use of it is. Eligibility is determined by technical rules (above all, sufficient employment history; see chapter 9). In practice, a clear monotonic relationship is revealed between use of the SF and the number of potential withdrawals from UISAs: The higher the number of potential withdrawals, the lower the use of the SF. This finding applies to both men and women (table 10.1). For example, among men who are entitled to use the SF and have just one potential withdrawal from their UISA, 61 percent use the SF; among men who have four potential withdrawals from their UISA, only 27 percent use the SF.

Among workers entitled to the SF, a logit model was used to investigate how personal characteristics and the number of potential withdrawals from the UISA affect the use of the SF. Conditional on observed characteristics, parameter estimates show that the higher the number of potential withdrawals (that is, the larger the individual accumulation and thus the lower the potential gain from using the solidarity fund), the lower the probability of using the SF (Reyes, van Ours, and Vodopivec, forthcoming). This has a simple, intuitive interpretation: The more unemployed workers can rely on their own funds, the less likely they are to access the SF, because the use of the SF is associated with certain costs. These costs include the transaction costs of contacting the employment office and satisfying continuing eligibility requirements (which include accepting suitable

TABLE 10.1 **Eligibility and Use of the Solidarity Fund by Number of Potential Withdrawals from the Individual Account**

| Potential withdrawals | Males | | | Females | | |
	Entitled (% of total)	Used SF (% of entitled)	Total (%)	Entitled (% of total)	Used SF (% of entitled)	Total (%)
1	23	61	45	30	76	46
2	40	57	38	44	70	38
3	36	43	15	39	52	14
4	35	27	2	40	38	2
Total	32	55	100	37	69	100

SOURCE: Reyes, van Ours, and Vodopivec, forthcoming.

job offers) and the possible stigmatization of persons who use employment office services. Other results show significant effects related to industry, region, educational attainment, and birth cohort.

Empirical Analysis of Job-Finding Rates

Figure 10.1 shows the job-finding rates and survival rates for prime-age men in the three groups: workers who are not entitled to access the SF, those who are entitled but do not use it, and those who use it. The main differences occur at the beginning of the unemployment period, when the job-finding rate for workers who are not using the SF exceeds

FIGURE 10.1 **Exit Rates and Survival Rates, Prime-Age Males**

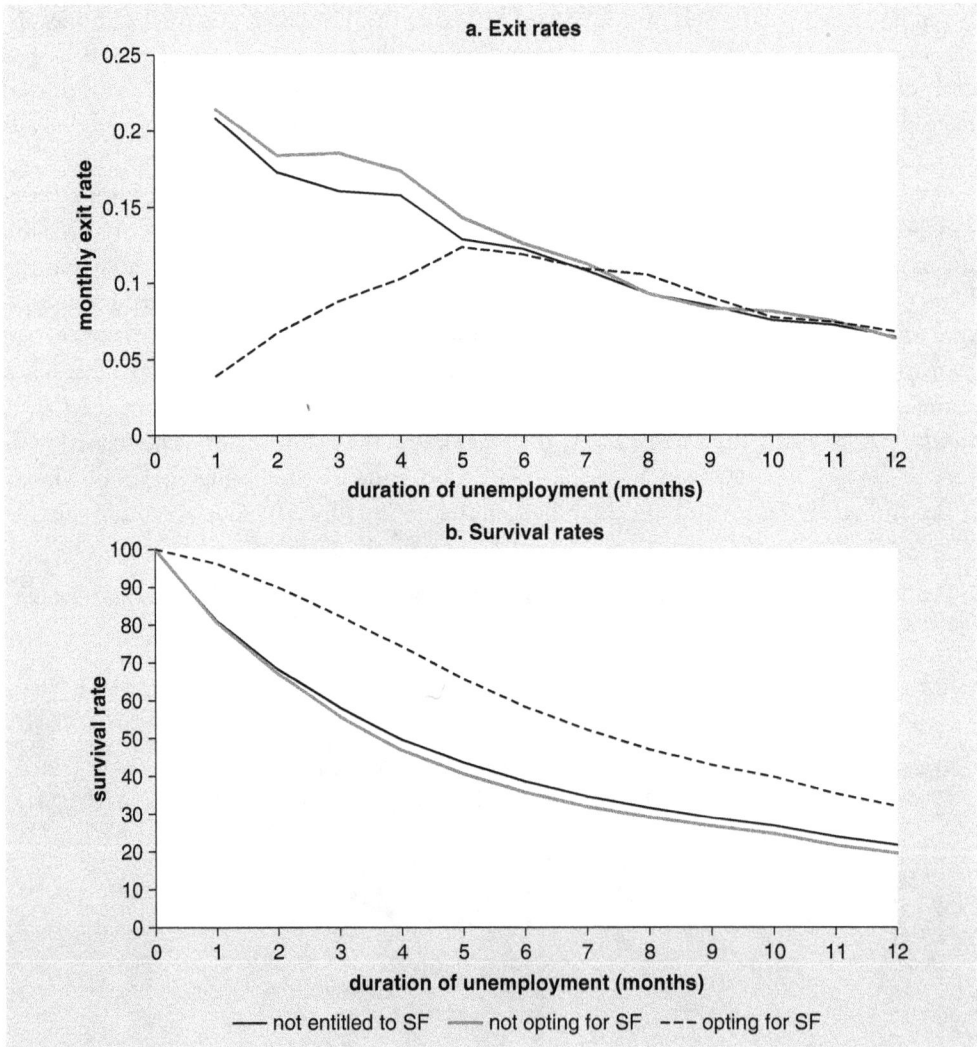

SOURCE: Reyes, van Ours, and Vodopivec, forthcoming.

the rate for workers who do use the fund. In fact, the job-finding rate of the latter group increases over the first five months of unemployment, but from the sixth month on, the differences in job-finding rates among the three groups are small (figure 10.1, panel a). Consistent with this, the survival function shows that workers who use the SF are unemployed longer than those who do not use the fund (figure 10.1, panel b).

Figure 10.2 provides a similar overview for prime-age women. The exit rates are lower, but the patterns are very similar to those of men. Women who use the SF have a low and increasing exit rate in the earlier months of unemployment. Women who do not use the SF initially have a higher unemployment exit rate but, after about five months, their exit rates are similar to those of women who use the fund.

FIGURE 10.2 **Exit Rates and Survival Rates, Prime-Age Females**

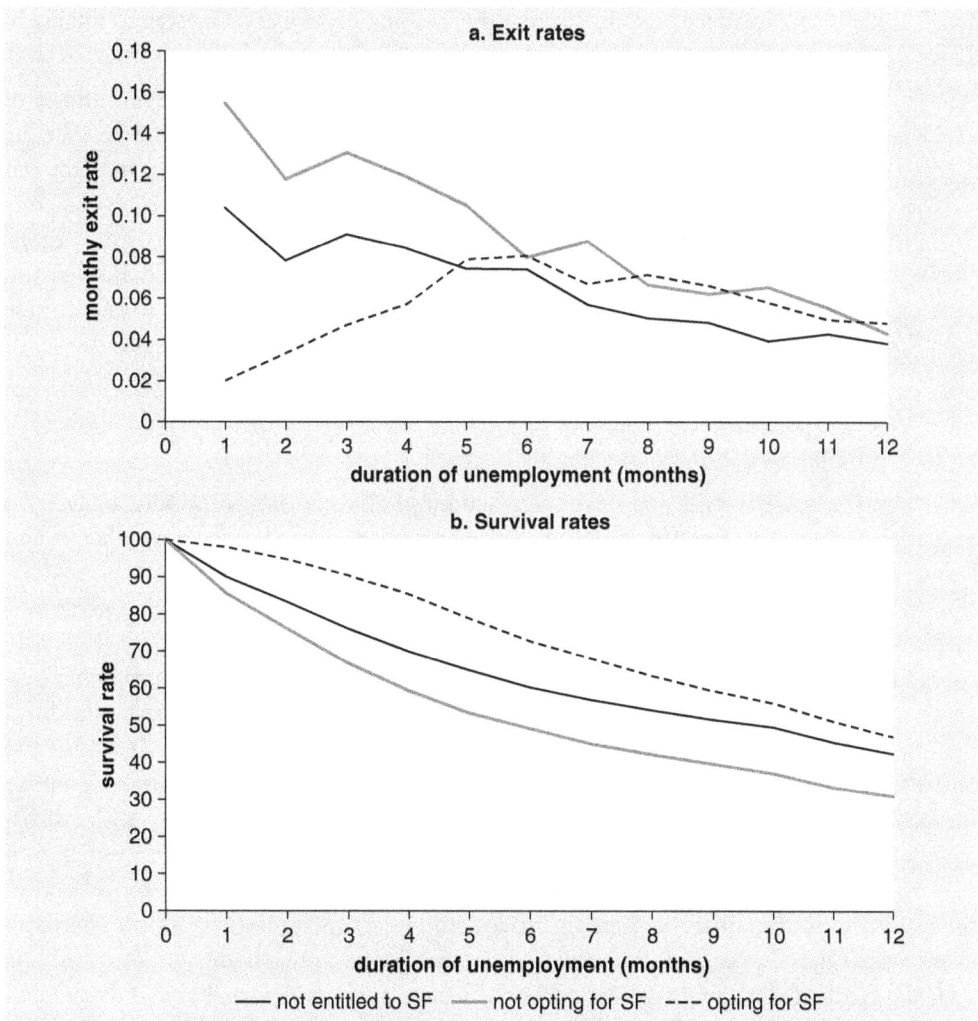

SOURCE: Reyes, van Ours, and Vodopivec, forthcoming.

Reyes, van Ours, and Vodopivec (forthcoming) also provide econometric modeling of the job-finding rate, analyzing transitions from unemployment using mixed proportional hazard rate models. The parameters are estimated separately for men and women, for the same three groups of benefit recipients studied above. The key results are as follows:

- For beneficiaries who opted to use the SF, the higher the balance in the UISA, the higher the job-finding rate, as evident from the positive coefficients of the dummy variables for the number of potential withdrawals for both men and women (Reyes, van Ours, and Vodopivec, forthcoming table 5). This is consistent with the cost-internalization argument. The only deviation from the pattern is the point estimate for "4 potential withdrawals," which is small and statistically insignificant. Moreover, the coefficients of monthly dummies reflecting the time pattern of the job-finding rate show a monotonic increase in the rate in the first five months and a steady reduction thereafter for both men and women. This pattern is consistent with disincentives related to the receipt of benefits, with the smaller job-finding rate at the beginning of the unemployment period reflecting the "waiting behavior" connected to the use of the SF over the period of potential benefit receipt (five months in this case).

- For both men and women who are not entitled to use the SF, the number of potential withdrawals has no effect on the job-finding rate. This means that the UISA balances among beneficiaries who rely solely on UISAs do not affect exit rates, as expected under the cost-internalization argument. Moreover, the time pattern of the job-finding rate as determined by the coefficients of monthly dummies shows no correspondence to payment of unemployment benefits—again, consistent with the internalization argument. For both men and women, these coefficients show strong and monotonic negative duration dependence.

- Equally telling, for the group of beneficiaries who could use the SF but choose not to, the parameter estimates are very similar to those of workers who do not use the fund because they are not eligible.

Reyes, van Ours, and Vodopivec (forthcoming) also perform sensitivity analysis on potential selectivity in the use of the SF. Namely, workers who decide to use the SF and workers who decide not to may differ in terms of their labor market position. If the decision to use the SF is not exogenous to the job-finding rate, econometric parameter estimates may be biased.

The sensitivity analysis consists of two approaches: checking for unobserved heterogeneity between different groups of workers and applying a matching method to form treatment and control groups as an alternative way of accounting for selectivity in the use of the SF. Overall, the sensitivity results confirm the previous results, but they do point to the possibility of selectivity issues in women's use of the SF. First, in checking the distribution of unobserved heterogeneity among different groups of workers, the suspicion of selectivity is found to be stronger among women: In contrast to men, the comparison of the distribution of unobserved heterogeneity could reject the hypothesis of no selectivity in the use of the SF.[4] Second, the results of the matching approach are very much in line with the results from the mixed proportional hazard analysis reported above. For males, selectivity in the use of the SF does not seem to be important; for females, selectivity may be an issue (for details, see Reyes, van Ours, and Vodopivec, forthcoming).

Conclusions

This chapter examined work incentives generated under the Chilean unemployment benefit program. This is a unique, innovative program that combines social insurance with self-insurance in the form of savings accumulated in UISAs. It was designed in part to mitigate the moral hazard problem present in traditional UI programs. The study estimated the determinants of the job-finding rate of unemployment benefit recipients, taking advantage of the design features of the program to identify incentive effects. The findings show that beneficiaries who use solidarity funding are less likely than those who rely solely on UISAs to exit unemployment in the early months. Moreover, job-finding rates are found to be positively correlated with preseparation UISA balances among workers who use solidarity funding but uncorrelated with account balances for the other groups.

While key empirical findings are largely consistent with the argument of internalization of unemployment cost, it is not clear whether these results can be attributed, in the causal sense, to the UISA system.[5] The evidence does not provide a definite answer, as other mechanisms may be at work that could account for the observed correlations. In particular, the higher job-finding rate for workers who choose not to use the SF compared with those who use it may be a result of selection into those two groups; that is, those who expect speedier reemployment may choose not to access the SF. The sensitivity analysis of unobserved heterogeneity suggests that selection is likely not an issue for men but that it matters for women. Similarly, the positive correlation between the job-finding rate and the potential number of withdrawals from the UISA may be a consequence of the fact that less productive workers with less stable employment histories accumulate smaller UISA balances. Of course, these explanations rely on assumptions of their own, and thus cannot be taken to disprove the internalization-of-costs explanation.

Although not conclusive, the evidence suggests the potential for UISAs to cause internalization of UI benefit costs. With some exceptions, the findings are consistent with this theory. The results on the use of the solidarity fund are also very much in line with the stylized facts about the employment disincentives produced by standard UI programs, lending further credibility to the analysis.

Clearly, more empirical research is needed to obtain further insights into the effects of UISAs. In addition to probing into the causality and incentive effects of the program, other promising areas include examining the consumption-smoothing effects of adding a UISA component to the standard Organisation for Economic Co-operation and Development–style UI program and studying the effects of such a change on the quality of postunemployment jobs—above all, on wages and stability of employment.

Notes

1. Compare Fredriksson and Holmlund (2006a, 2006b). For an evaluation of various mechanisms that help reduce work disincentives in UI programs, see, for example, Abbring, Van den Berg, and van Ours (2005); Lalive, van Ours, and Zweimuller (2006); and van Ours and Vodopivec (2006).

2. To compare incentives under unemployment accounts (UAs) and regular unemployment benefits (UBs), Orszag and Snower (2002) created a two-period model based on discounted lifetime

utility maximization. Under the UA, they assume that workers are required to make ongoing contributions to their unemployment accounts and that the balances in these accounts are available to them during periods of unemployment. Under the UB, each unemployed worker receives an exogenously given unemployment benefit that is financed through a payroll tax.

3. Some insights come from the literature on take-up of UI programs. According to Anderson and Meyer (1997), the decision to claim benefits depends on the level of those benefits. This finding would imply that the decision to use solidarity funding depends on the perceived costs of maintaining continuing benefit eligibility (requirements include visits to employment offices and, possibly, participation in training).

4. The analysis checked whether the distribution of unobserved heterogeneity is the same for workers who were entitled to use the SF and opt to use it compared with those who were entitled to use the fund but chose not to use it.

5. The internalization-of-costs argument is also weakened by the fact that the econometric results are not completely consistent—some parameters in the estimations of job-finding rate deviate from those expected under the internalization argument.

References

Abbring, J. H., G. J. Van den Berg, and J. C. van Ours. 2005. "The Effect of Unemployment Insurance Sanctions on the Transition Rate from Unemployment to Employment." *Economic Journal* 115: 602–30.

Anderson, P. M., and B. D. Meyer. 1997. "Unemployment Insurance Take-up Rates and the After-Tax Value of Benefits." *Quarterly Journal of Economics* 112: 913–37.

Fredriksson, P., and B. Holmlund. 2006a. "Improving Incentives in Unemployment Insurance: A Review of Recent Research." *Journal of Economic Surveys* 20 (3): 357–86.

———. 2006b. "Optimal Unemployment Insurance Design: Time Limits, Monitoring, or Workfare?" *International Tax and Public Finance* 13 (5): 565–85.

Holmlund, B. 1998. "Unemployment Insurance in Theory and Practice." *Scandinavian Journal of Economics* 100: 113–41.

Mortensen, D. T. 1977. "Unemployment Insurance and Job Search Decisions." *Industrial and Labor Relations Review* 30: 505–17.

Lalive, R., J. C. van Ours, and J. Zweimuller. 2006. "How Changes in Financial Incentives Affect the Duration of Unemployment." *Review of Economic Studies* 73 (4): 1009–38.

Orszag, M., and D. Snower. 2002. "From Unemployment Benefits to Unemployment Accounts." IZA Discussion Paper 532, Institute for the Study of Labor, Bonn.

Reyes, G., J. C. van Ours, and M. Vodopivec. Forthcoming. "Incentive Effects of Unemployment Insurance Savings Accounts: Evidence from Chile." *Labour Economics.* (A previous version of this paper was published in 2010 as Center for Economic and Policy Research Discussion Paper 5971.)

van Ours, J. C., and M. Vodopivec. 2006. "How Shortening the Potential Duration of Unemployment Benefits Affects the Duration of Unemployment: Evidence from a Natural Experiment." *Journal of Labor Economics* 24 (2): 351–78.

Vodopivec, M. 2004. *Income Support for the Unemployed: Issues and Options.* Regional and Sectoral Studies Series, World Bank, Washington, DC.

Contributors

Solange Berstein graduated from the Universidad de Santiago de Chile as an economist and received a master's degree in economics from the Latin American Institute of Doctrine and Social Studies (ILADES), Georgetown University. After receiving her PhD from Boston University, she worked as a senior economist at the Central Bank of Chile. Between 1994 and 1997, she worked in the Studies Division of the Chilean Pension Supervisor; she led this division from 2003 until February 2006. She is currently superintendent of pensions in Chile and chair of the International Organisation of Pension Supervisors (IOPS) Technical Committee. As head of the institution that regulates and supervises the pension and unemployment systems in Chile, She has led reforms in these areas, including a major change to the pension system in 2008. She has written articles related to investment of pension funds, competition in the pension fund industry, and coverage issues and has been a consultant for the World Bank on pension matters.

Eduardo Fajnzylber has a PhD in economics from the University of California at Los Angeles and a degree in industrial engineering from the University of Chile. He joined the School of Government of the Universidad Adolfo Ibáñez in March 2009 as a full-time professor. Before that, he was head of the Research Department at the Studies Division of the Chilean Pension Supervisor, where his team participated in the technical discussion of the 2008 pension reform and the 2009 unemployment insurance reform. His research focuses on applying impact evaluation techniques to questions regarding social security, financial education, and program participation. He is a director of the Chilean Economic Society.

Ana M. Ferrer is a professor at the University of Calgary and an associate researcher at the Canadian Labour and Skills Research Network. She graduated from Boston University. Her research career developed in Canada, where she focused on labor markets, education, and family economics. Her work has been published in journals such as *Economica* and the *Journal of Human Resources*. She is currently priority leader of the Canadian Metropolis Network, where she coordinates labor market research on immigrant integration. She is an active member of the Princeton Global Network on Child Migration at Princeton University.

Pamela Gana is an economist with a master's degree in public affairs and 10 years of experience in the area of social protection. She has focused mainly on designing policies in the areas of unemployment, old age, gender, and poverty. Since 2006 she has worked at the Chilean Pension Supervisor. She was in charge of the assessment, design, congressional discussion, and implementation of the 2009 reform to Chile's unemployment insurance system. Her current work focuses on follow-up on the pension and unemployment insurance system, primarily the assessment and design of proposals aimed at improving these systems. She has also worked as a consultant for the International Labour Office and the International Development Bank.

Juan Carlos Hatchondo is an economist in the Research Department of the Federal Reserve Bank of Richmond. He holds a PhD from the University of Rochester. His work has been published in the *International Economic Review, the Journal of International Economics,* and the *Review of Economic Dynamics.*

Helmut Hofer is senior economist at the Institute for Advanced Studies in Vienna. In 1996, he earned his PhD from the University of Economics and Business Administration in Vienna. His main research areas are the analysis of the labor market and macroeconomic forecasting. He has worked on topics such as interindustry wage differentials, evaluating active labor market policy, microsimulation, severance payments, and aging. He has published his work in journals such as *Regional Economics, Applied Economics, Labour Economics, Empirica, Journal of Manpower, Fiscal Studies, Population and Development Review, and Journal of Economics and Statistics.*

Robert Holzmann, professor of economics, returned to Austria in March 2011, after a distinguished career in international organizations and academia. Before his return he was the research director at the Marseille Center for Mediterranean Integration. From 1997 to 2009, he was sector director and head of the World Bank's Social Protection and Labor Department, where he led strategic and conceptual work on pensions and labor. Before joining the Bank, he was professor of economics and director of the European Institute at the University of Saarland, Germany; professor of economics at the University of Vienna; and senior economist at the International Monetary Fund and Organisation for Economic Co-operation and Development (OECD). His research and operational involvement extend to all regions of the world, and he has published 28 books and more than 150 articles on social, fiscal, and financial policy issues in journals such as *Economica, Empirica, Finanzarchiv, International Tax and Public Finance, IMF Staff Papers, Journal of Economics, Journal of Emerging Market Finance, Journal of Pension Management, Journal of Public Policy, Journal of International Development, and Schweizer Zeitschrift fuer Aussenwirtschaft.*

Hugo Hopenhayn is a professor of economics at the University of California at Los Angeles. He received his PhD in economics from the University of Minnesota in 1989. He has published papers in economic journals, including *Econometrica, American Economic Review, Journal of Political Economy, Quarterly Journal of Economics, and Review of Economic Studies.* He is a Fellow of the Econometric Society and has received numerous awards from the National Science Foundation and the Guggenheim Foundation. His research spans industrial organization, macroeconomics, public finance, and economic theory.

Jai-Joon Hur is director-general of the Social Policy Division of the Korean Labor Institute (KLI). He received his PhD in economics from the University of Paris X-Nanterre and joined the KLI in 1995. He has led many studies to improve the Korean employment insurance system and has published papers diagnosing the Korean labor market vis-à-vis changes in the international economic environment and technological changes. He has been a senior economist at the World Bank and a consultant for the International Labour Organization. He is currently serving on the Minister of Labor's Advisory Committee and the Labor Policy Evaluation Committee.

Donald O. Parsons is a professor of economics at George Washington University, emeritus professor of economics at Ohio State University, and research fellow at the Institute for the Study of Labor (IZA) Bonn. He served as economics department chair at the George Washington University from 2003 to 2006. He has also held appointments as Fulbright professor at the University of Siena, Italy, in 1991; visiting scholar at the Centre for Socio-legal Studies (Wolfson College, Oxford University, 1993); visiting professor at Copenhagen Business School (1998); and distinguished foreign scholar, Brain Korea 21 Project, at Soong Sil University (2001). His primary professional interests are in the area of labor economics and social insurance design, including the economics of public disability insurance systems. His current work centers on the foundations of unemployment insurance systems, including private severance pay plans. His research has appeared in leading journals such as *American Economic Review, Journal of Political Economy, Quarterly Journal of Economics*, and *Economica*.

Yann Pouget is a migration economist at the World Bank, Middle East and North Africa Human Development Department, and a member of the labor mobility team at the Marseille Center for Mediterranean Integration. Before joining the World Bank, he worked in the microfinance sector in Argentina and Peru and has conducted several field surveys on migration and local development in Morocco and among diverse migrant communities in Europe. He has also served as junior researcher at the French Development Agency. He holds an MA in economics of international development from the Paris Institute of Political Sciences and an MSc in local economic development from the London School of Economics.

Gonzalo Reyes is a senior economist at the World Bank. He received a PhD in economics from Harvard University and an undergraduate degree in economics and business from the Catholic University of Chile. He currently works in the Social Protection Unit at the Latin American Region of the World Bank. Before joining the World Bank in 2009, he was head of the Research Department and the Studies Division of the Chilean Pension Supervisor, where he conducted technical analysis of the pension reform process of 2008 and the modifications to the unemployment insurance system in 2009, as well as the process of incorporation of Chile into the OECD in the area of private pensions. He has published research articles and book chapters focusing on social insurance, pension provision, and unemployment insurance.

Jan van Ours is professor of labor economics at the Department of Economics, Tilburg University, the Netherlands. He is also a professorial fellow at the Department of

Economics, University of Melbourne, and a fellow of CentER, CEPR, CESifo, and IZA. He studied mining engineering at the Technical University in Delft and economics at Erasmus University Rotterdam, where he also earned his PhD. In 1996, he received the Hicks-Tinbergen medal from the European Economic Association. His research concerns unemployment and employment dynamics, labor market institutions, and labor market policy and the microeconomics of drug use. In 2008, he and Tito Boeri published a text-book entitled *The Economics of Imperfect Labor Markets* (Princeton: Princeton University Press, 2008). His papers have appeared in international journals including *American Economic Review, Journal of Political Economy, Review of Economic Studies, Economic Journal, Journal of Labor Economics, Journal of Public Economics*, and *Journal of Health Economics*. In 2009, he served as president of the European Society of Population Economics; in 2011, he was elected president of the European Association of Labour Economists. Currently, he is associate editor of *Labour Economics*, managing editor of *De Economist*, and one of the managing editors of *Economic Policy*.

W. Craig Riddell is Royal Bank Faculty Research Professor in the Department of Economics at the University of British Columbia (UBC) and academic director of the Canadian Labour Market and Skills Research Network. His teaching and research interests are in labor economics, labor relations, and public policy. His current research is focused on skill formation, education and training, unemployment and labor market adjustment, unemployment insurance, program evaluation, immigration, and unionization. He has published numerous articles in academic journals, including the *American Economic Review, Canadian Journal of Economics, Economic Journal, Econometrica, Journal of Labor Economics, Journal of Human Resources*, and *Review of Economics and Statistics*. Professor Riddell is the former head of the Department of Economics at UBC, past president of the Canadian Economics Association, and former academic co-chair of the Canadian Employment Research Forum. He currently serves on Statistics Canada's Advisory Committee on Labour and Income Statistics and on the board of directors of the Centre for the Study of Living Standards. In 2007–08, he was a member of the Expert Panel on Older Workers established by the government of Canada.

Milan Vodopivec is a lead economist with the World Bank. He received his PhD in economics from the University of Maryland, College Park. In 1989, he joined the World Bank, where he has worked in the Research Department and in the Human Development Network. He also served as a state undersecretary at the Ministry of Labor of Slovenia, and was a teacher and dean of the first private university college in Slovenia. His research interests focus on labor market and cash benefit systems. He has published widely in these areas, including in the *Journal of Public Economics, Journal of Labor Economics, European Economic Review, Labour Economics*, and *Economics of Transition*. He is the author of the book *Income Support for the Unemployed: Issues and Options*, published by the World Bank in 2004.

Michael Weber is an economist with the World Bank, where his work on the Labor Markets (LM) team covers income protection for the unemployed, youth employment, and LM intermediation. In addition to the supply side of labor markets, his research also addresses labor demand. He holds master's degrees in economics and business administration, and received his PhD in economic and social sciences from Vienna University of Economics and Business. Before joining the World Bank, he worked in an interdisciplinary research organization and co-authored several conference and journal contributions dealing with innovative methods of data collection, analysis, and recommendation systems. He published a book on innovation networks in 2004 and one on recommender systems for private sector development in 2010.

Jungyoll Yun, professor of economics at Ewha University, Seoul, Korea, received his PhD in economics at Princeton University in 1986. He has worked as a visiting research fellow at the World Bank (2000) and at Columbia University (2008). His research interests include labor contract theory, unemployment, and social insurance. Recently, he has been working on the role of self-insurance in the efficient provision of social insurance and on the reform of mandatory public pension systems. He has served as president of the Korean Econometric Society (2005) and of the Korean Labor Economic Association (2011), as well as on several government advisory committees, including the Minimum Wage Committee.